NATURE'S ACTION GUIDE

How to Support Biodiversity and Your Local Ecosystem

SARAH F. JAYNE

Foreword by Douglas W. Tallamy

OLD GARDEN | OXFORD, PENNSYLVANIA

The author and publisher of this book deeply respect original authorship in all media and every effort has been made to accurately credit references, photographs, and other media. The author was granted permission to use images of web pages of the following organizations or individuals for illustrative purposes and all copyrights related to these images and quoted text from these websites remain with these organizations or individuals and may not be reused without their express permission: Beyond Pesticides, Biota of North America Program, Butterflies and Moths of North America, DarkSky International, Ecological Landscaping Association, Jarrod Fowler, Homegrown National Park, Annie Martin and Mountain Mosses, National Wildlife Federation, Reforestation Nurseries, & Genetic Resources, U.S. Environmental Protection Agency, University of Georgia Center for Invasive Species and Ecosystem Health (Early Detection & Distribution Mapping System [EDDMapS] and Invasive Plant Atlas), Wild Ones, Wild Seed Project, and the Xerces Society of Invertebrate Conservation. For additional information about these organizations, please refer to the Appendix (pages VI - XI). Credits for photographs not taken by the author are listed in the Appendix (pages XII - XIII). All image copyrights remain with the original copyright holder and may not be used without their express permission. Please email publisher@oldgarden.com to address any concerns. All other photographs and diagrams in this book are by the author who holds the copyright for these materials.

Cover design and book layout by Sarah F. Jayne

ISBN 978-0-9832350-0-2

Published in 2024 by Old Garden | Oxford, Pennsylvania, U.S.A.

The author and publisher highly value accuracy and every effort has been made to ensure that the information presented herein is accurate and internet references up to date at the time of publication. Any concerns will be carefully considered, and every effort will be made to expediently correct errors or omissions. However, given the possibility of human error or updated scientific research, neither the author, nor the publisher, nor any other party who has been involved in the preparation or publication of this book is responsible or liable for any errors or omissions or results obtained from the use of the information contained herein. | All product and company names are trademarks or registered trademarks of their respective holders. Mention of them does not imply endorsement nor affiliation between them and the author or publisher of this book, nor does the author or publisher receive any financial gain. | Except as indicated, no part of this book may be reproduced, translated, stored in a retrieval system, or transmitted, in any form or by any means, electronic, mechanical, photocopying, microfilming, recording, or otherwise without written permission from the publisher. Please email publisher@oldgarden.com to request permission for use of materials contained herein. | Please note that no part of this book was written nor produced with the assistance of artificial intelligence (AI).

Library of Congress Cataloging-in-Publication Data
Names: Jayne, Sarah F., author; Tallamy, Douglas W., foreword.
Title: Nature's action guide: how to support biodiversity and your local
    ecosystem / Sarah F. Jayne; foreword by Douglas W. Tallamy.
Description: Trade paperback 2nd ed. rev. | Oxford,
    Pennsylvania: Old Garden, 2024. | Includes bibliographical references
    and index.
Identifiers: Library of Congress Control Number: 2024911138 | ISBN:
    978-0-9832350-0-2 (paperback)
LC record available at https://lccn.loc.gov/2024911138

Front Cover: With their permeable skin and diet of insects, frogs thrive in clean, viable aquatic habitats.

Author's Note:

Like the saying, "it takes a village to raise a child," it will take a village (many villages, in fact!) to restore biodiversity and local abundance to our human-dominated landscapes. My hope is that *Nature's Action Guide* will help facilitate this effort. As such, I view this book as a living, evolving document—at the center of which is you, the reader. I'd love to hear your ideas and suggestions and see photos of the actions you take. To contact me, please visit www.naturesactionguide.org. Thank you very much for being part of this journey!

Contents

Acknowledgements

For my mother, Sarah B. Jayne, with immeasurable love and admiration!

O f all the paragraphs of this entire book, these are the most difficult to write because words fall so far short for expressing the depth of my gratitude to the many people who contributed to this book. Any value you find in this book (and I truly hope it IS helpful to you!) comes not from what I've written but from the dedicated researchers, scientists, authors, gardeners, and everyday people who tirelessly do all they can to learn about and share their support of wildlife and our environment.

A glance at the Appendix shows the broad scope of organizations and people who, through an article, website, video, or photograph added to this guide in some way—I am grateful to each and every one! I sincerely appreciate the following organizations who kindly permitted me to share images of their invaluable resources: Beyond Pesticides, Biota of North America Program, Butterflies and Moths of North America, DarkSky International, Ecological Landscaping Association, Homegrown National Park, Mountain Mosses, National Wildlife Federation, Prairie Moon Nursery, Reforestation Nurseries, & Genetic Resources, Signify, U.S. Environmental Protection Agency, University of Georgia Center for Invasive Species and Ecosystem Health (Early Detection & Distribution Mapping System [EDDMapS] and Invasive Plant Atlas), Wild Ones, Wild Seed Project, and the Xerces Society of Invertebrate Conservation. The inclusion of this information was possible because the following people took time out of their busy lives to help me with the logistics of sharing these resources. I am especially indebted to the following people who added valuable perspectives to this guide: Dr. John Kartesz, the force behind the Biota of North America Program, and Misako Nishino who both went the extra mile to help me out; Jarrod Fowler and Samuel Droege for their work with native bees; Matthew Shepherd of the Xerces Society for helpful feedback from the perspective of invertebrate conservation, Annie Martin for her contribution of text and photographs featuring the use of mosses in ecological landscapes, and Becky Klukas-Brewer of Prairie Moon Nursery regarding bee lawns. I greatly appreciate, too, the generous help from Chuck Bargeron, Susan Ciarniello, Lindsay Colegrove, Aaron Ferster, Jeff France, Jess Gildea, Kayla Herriman, Heather Holm, Brandon Hough, David Kryzaniak, Aaron Lerman, Kelly Lotts, Carolyn Pike, and Catherine Ward.

Photographs are essential to this guide—they needed to go beyond being showy fillers and instead provide information. I am extremely thankful to the many people who shared their images on sites such as Wikimedia Commons. Heartfelt thanks to Will, Liana, and Alicia Jayne. This book is further enriched by the photographs of thriving designed meadows shared by Larry Weaner; bird-friendly native plantings by Sharon Sorenson; California native landscapes by Sarah B. Jayne; and the lovely prairie plantings by Roy Diblik. Roy puts the soul into gardening.

For essential feedback and encouragement from the perspective of someone not yet immersed in the world of native plants, I am sincerely grateful to Kate Hartshorn. Thanks to Anne Marie Wolfson, Mary Huey, and Shara Blagrave, of the Wild Ones Greater Cleveland Chapter and Roberta James who read the book in its ugly duckling stage and provided helpful feedback. A great big shout out to Randi Eckel (who brightens the world with her quick wit!) and to all the members of the Native Plant Society of New Jersey whose enthusiastic advance support was energizing. Many thanks, too, to Jennifer Gregan for her support—I'm not sure how I would have stayed motivated without the daily anticipation of a mug of "Velvetized" hot chocolate.

Quite simply stated: This book wouldn't exist were it not for Doug Tallamy. I deeply appreciate his steadfast support from start to finish. When my progress toward completing the book seemed interminably slow, I emailed Doug suggesting that I abandon the whole project (emancipation sounded so good!). He replied, "No emancipation for you! We need the whole book." Here it is, Doug, for better or worse!

Doug shared a breeze from the wind in his sails in the form of Cindy Tallamy. She cheered me on at every turn. No matter the size of the harvest, there will always be persimmons for you, Cindy!

If I were a pioneer traveling on a wagon trail, I'd want my husband Joe to be my wagoneer—then, now, and always.

Finally, I'd like to express my appreciation for you! Every action you take matters. As Doug sums it up tidily, YOU truly are nature's best hope!

Foreword by Douglas W. Tallamy

Every once in a while, a book comes along that meets an important need most people don't know they have. Sarah Jayne's *Nature's Action Guide* is such a book. Sarah could have called her book *Conservation for Dummies*—not that she wrote it for true dummies, but because she has identified a subject everyone needs to know but almost no one was ever taught: how to share our spaces with the natural world. I will use my own experience with conservation as an example.

When my wife Cindy and I bought a 10-acre section of a defunct farm in Oxford, Pennsylvania, our plan was to restore the eastern deciduous forest that had thrived there some 300 years earlier. We were excited about this plan for several reasons, but one was the size of the property: this was 10 times more land than we had owned before and a real chance to provide a home for many of the Piedmont plants and animals that we love. It was a good idea, but we had never restored land before, and we knew little about how to proceed. We did know that nature was on the ropes in many places, but we didn't fully understand the depth of the earth's biodiversity crisis. We didn't know, for example, that 45% of the earth's insects were already gone, that North America had lost 3 billion breeding birds in recent decades—1/3 of its total bird population—or that the planet had entered the sixth great extinction event in its history. We might have despaired had we known that the UN would soon predict that one million species—that's one million kinds of our fellow earthlings—would be forced to extinction in the next 20 years. We didn't know that light pollution was one of the major causes of insect decline, and we didn't know the extent to which neonicotinoid insecticides and mosquito fogging were impacting non-target species. Even though I was an entomologist by profession and had worked as one at the University of Delaware for 20 years, I did not fully appreciate the extent to which insects were essential components of terrestrial ecosystems or that moths and their caterpillars were the bread and butter of local food webs. We did not know that to reach a viable relationship with the natural world that supported us, our property would have to sustain a complex food web and a diverse community of native pollinators. It also would need to manage the watershed in which it lay and to remove as much carbon from the atmosphere as possible. We didn't know how extensive invasive plants and overabundant white-tailed deer were, or how those two problems intersected synergistically to degrade habitats across the country. We knew that native plants supported essential insect populations better than non-natives, but we didn't know how much better, or how extensively non-natives were used in residential landscapes. We also didn't know that just 14 percent of North American native plant species supported the food web orders of magnitude better than the rest of the native species and so were must-use choices for our restoration. There was so much we didn't know, but most of all we didn't know how to address these issues on land that had recently been mowed for hay.

As Donald Rumsfeld once said, these were unknown unknowns. Our ignorance protected us from being discouraged, so we proceeded happily, learning by trial and error, with a heavy emphasis on error. We eventually did learn how to control invasive plants, how to minimize damage from hungry deer, and how to use security lights without killing nocturnal insects. We discovered that oak trees supported more caterpillars and thus more bird food than any other plants in our ecosystem. We learned that every state had a native plant society that could help us find sources of natives, and we met talented landscape designers who could deploy native plants without running afoul of local landscaping ordinances. We have now been working on our home restoration for 23 years, and, despite our initial ignorance and missteps, we have witnessed extraordinary success. Fortunately, nature is inherently resilient, much more so than we ever thought it would be, and our early optimism has been rewarded many times over.

But how much more success could we have enjoyed, and how much easier and faster could we have reached our goals, if we had had Sarah's how-to book to guide us.

Once Cindy and I learned that nature could be restored successfully on private property, I was eager to spread this message to other people. Surely once they understood the problems, there would be many people who would be eager to create landscapes that enable rather than destroy the life around them. And so, I shared my research and the successes we have experienced on our property in *Bringing Nature Home*, *The Nature of Oaks*, and especially in *Nature's Best Hope*. In these books I explain why we have to transition from an adversarial relationship with nature to a collaborative one, and what each of us can do to make this transition. I spent little time, however, explaining exactly how to do the things I recommended. How do you reduce the area occupied by your lawn; how do you plant a tree; how can you replace your outdoor lights with insect-friendly bulbs; how can you control mosquitoes with benign biological control rather than destructive adult fogging; how do you fight invasive plants and deer overabundance; how do you plant for specialist bees and create beds beneath your trees that will enable caterpillars to complete their development? How, how, how! What was needed was a book specifically designed to guide homeowners toward meeting all of the ecological goals I have outlined over the years. Thanks to Sarah Jayne, you are holding such a book in your hands.

Sarah wrote *Nature's Action Guide* as a complement to my book *Nature's Best Hope*. My last chapter suggested 10 things homeowners could/should do to help share their property with nature. After reading my book, Sarah set about trying to enact each of these suggestions in her own yard but quickly realized that, even as an experienced gardener, she didn't know enough to be successful. And if she didn't know enough, many other budding conservationists were likely to struggle as well. Sarah's solution was to write *Nature's Action Guide*, a step-by-step, easy to use manual that explains how each of us, regardless of our background or gardening experience, can accomplish all of the goals I propose in *Nature's Best Hope*, as well as several I only hinted at!

Restoration biology is a relatively young scientific discipline a few decades old. Practicing restoration in human-dominated landscapes, in comparison, is in its infancy and we are still learning what works and what doesn't work. One of its many distinguishing features is that *Nature's Action Guide* is current, explaining state-of-the-art conservation in suburbia with the most up-to-date best-practices available. Even a half-hearted attempt to follow Sarah's action items is guaranteed to improve the biodiversity potential of your landscape and thus the productivity of your local ecosystem. For this, we all owe Sarah Jayne our heartfelt thanks and gratitude—because, whether we appreciate it or not, we all depend on those same ecosystems.

Douglas W. Tallamy

INTRODUCTION
Welcome nature where you live, work, and play!

We invite you to work alongside us as we implement the following urgent actions to restore ecologically functioning wildlife habitats in our yards and other spaces:

Action 1: **Turn off the lights**

Action 2: **Protect your wildlife habitat**

Action 3: **Shrink the lawn**

Action 4: **Remove invasive plants**

Action 5: **Identify your keystone plants**

Action 6: **Choose plants for specialist pollinators**

Action 7: **Preserve and create pupation and nesting sites**

Action 8: **Include water and protect the watershed**

Action 9: **Design a layered landscape filled with plants**

Action 10: **Propagate or procure lots of keystone plants**

Action 11: **Plant your landscape generously**

Action 12: **Use nontoxic home and yard products**

Action 13: **Manage your wildlife habitat**

Action 14: **Build acceptance for nature's natural look**

Action 15: **Share, educate, and get involved**

Whether you are brand new to the idea of restoring a wildlife ecosystem to your yard or a veteran wildlife gardener, we are thrilled to have you join us on this critical mission!

Introduction

How this action guide came to be

"*The disappearance of natural habitat is the primary cause of biological diversity loss at every level—ecosystems, species and genes, all of them. Only by the preservation of much more natural habitat than previously envisioned can extinction be brought close to a sustainable level.*"

Edward O. Wilson, "The Global Solution to Extinction," *New York Times*, March 12, 2016

This action guide is inspired by Doug Tallamy's grassroots call-to-action in his bestselling books ***Bringing Nature Home*** and ***Nature's Best Hope.*** Doug tirelessly echoes E.O. Wilson's urgent message for all of us to do what it will take to bring back the habitat required for the survival of the *"little creatures who run the world."*

The Tallamy bookshelf:

Doug's books will transform the way you think about your landscape and nature!

Bringing Nature Home: How You Can Sustain Wildlife with Native Plants (Updated and Expanded), Timber Press, 2009

Nature's Best Hope: A New Approach to Conservation That Starts in Your Yard, Timber Press, 2020

The Nature of Oaks: The Rich Ecology of Our Most Essential Trees, Timber Press, 2021

Nature's Best Hope (Young Readers' Edition): ***How You Can Save the World in Your Own Yard,*** Adapted by Sarah L. Thomson, Timber Press, 2023

Douglas W. Tallamy. *Photo by Rob Cardillo.*

Introduction

Helping our landscapes to provide essential ecological services

To sustain life on earth, our landscapes must provide essential ecological services. The actions in this guide will help our landscapes provide these services in the following specific ways:

Support wildlife food webs

Planting dense layers of native plants, especially keystone plants, to provide food, shelter, and reproduction sites for wildlife

Shrinking the lawn to make space for native plantings and to minimize the habitat disruption and destruction caused by mowing and edging

Removing invasive plants that outcompete native plants and removing introduced plants that take up critical space

Protecting wildlife by turning off lights, marking glass to prevent bird strikes, and avoiding toxins that kill wildlife or interfere with their reproduction

Allowing native plants to set seed to increase biodiversity and provide food for wildlife

Protecting pupation and nesting sites

Support pollinators

Planting for an all-season sequence of blooms

Planting the specific host plants needed by native pollen specialist bees, wasps, caterpillars, and other specialists

Leaving pithy and hollow stems to provide nesting sites for stem-nesting native bees and deadwood for cavity-nesting bees

Leaving areas of bare ground for ground-nesting bees

Monitoring blooms and pausing mowing to allow pollinators and other insects to feed

Using nontoxic lawn and yard maintenance methods that don't poison our pollinators

Opposing community-wide mosquito spraying

Not purchasing plants treated with neonicotinoids and other pesticides

Protect and manage the watershed

Replacing lawn with dense layers of plants, along with rain gardens where needed, to help keep water on the property

Avoiding the use of fertilizer and using nontoxic pest and weed control methods to prevent toxins from entering the watershed

Reducing mowing to reduce the volume of exhaust particles infiltrating the watershed

Properly disposing of home and garden chemicals, pet poop, and other toxins to prevent contamination of the watershed

Mulching new plantings with homegrown materials to conserve water

Changing water habits to reduce water usage

Build soil and sequester carbon

Leaving stumps, snags, and branches on site to store carbon

Leaving leaf litter to reduce runoff and retain soil moisture

Planting dense layers of plants to build and protect soil structure and prevent erosion

Reducing the volume of emissions by leaving leaf litter instead of using power leaf blowers

Choosing nontoxic yard maintenance methods to prevent toxins from building up in the soil

Reducing energy usage and carbon emissions by reducing mowing and turning off the lights

Sequestering and storing carbon by planting trees and other plants—lots of trees and plants!

Introduction

How to use this action guide

This action guide has been designed to provide accessible do-it-yourself strategies to encourage wildlife habitat and ecosystem restoration in your yard and other spaces.

Each action step in this guide includes clear **step-by-step checklists** that include page numbers that refer to the **illustrated guide** giving information about each step. Throughout each step, **useful resources** are recommended for further study and regional adaptations.

Step:	✔	Action Needed:	Page:
1	☐	Learn to recognize pupation and nesting sites and the different life stages of insects	7.4
2	☐	Create caterpillar pupation sites under the trees and shrubs on your property	7.6
3	☐	Protect and support caterpillar pupation sites throughout the year	7.7

Our goal is to make it easy and enjoyable to transition from an ornamental landscape to a rich, multi-purpose, nature-filled landscape. We take an **environmentally friendly**, **toward zero-waste approach** and share **cost-conscious tips** using readily available materials for those on a tight budget. We are excited to have you join us on this worthwhile journey!

In this action guide, we use the words "**your yard**" or "**your property**" to refer to **whatever space you can take action in** whether it's large or small, your own, your workplace, a community site, or an apartment balcony. We encourage you to consider every space possible from corporate landscapes and infrastructure borders to schoolyards and senior living communities.

Throughout this action guide we recommend **powerful online tools** and **explain how to use them** (see the sample step shown here). In lieu of simply providing lists of URLs, our intent is to give a tantalizing sample of the immense wealth of information that is available on these sites. The dedicated teams developing these tools are constantly making improvements and adding features to their websites or apps. The navigation of these tools may have recently changed and navigation may vary depending on your device, but the sites are all user-friendly.

For example, The Xerces Society for Invertebrate Conservation provides regional habitat assessment, installation, and management guides along with plant lists, pesticide protection, and much more through their *Pollination Conservation Resources* program (see page 6.5).

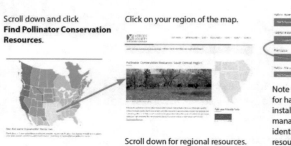
Scroll down and click **Find Pollinator Conservation Resources.**

Click on your region of the map.

Scroll down for regional resources.

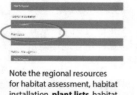
Note the regional resources for habitat assessment, habitat installation, **plant lists**, habitat management, pesticide protection, identification and monitoring resources, native seed and plant vendors, and further reading.

Websites are ever changing! If you have trouble finding any of the resources suggested in this guide, search online for [**name of the website**] [**title of the materials**], for example **xerces society pollinator conservation resources**. Typically, this will take you straight to the resource even though the navigation path may have changed.

Join Homegrown National Park and "Get on the Map"!

Homegrown National Park is a call-to-action for every one of us to take the actions needed to support biodiversity and restore our local ecosystems by removing invasive plants and planting native plants. This action guide will help you do exactly this!

Visit: **homegrownnationalpark.org**

or search online for **homegrown national park** and navigate to the site.

Click **GET ON THE MAP** to view the land area with reported native plantings.

Click **Sign up** to get on the map!

Click on the markers for local statistics.

Here, you can enter your planting goals and record your progress on one or more properties. Your firefly marker will light up on the map along with those of other community members who are supporting biodiversity where you live.

Return to the **Homegrown National Park** home page for a bounty of resources including a link to watch *What's the Rush?,* a talk by Doug Tallamy, that will get you wanting to start planting right now!

We'll visit **Homegrown National Park** in later actions. In the meantime, explore the website for a preview of the helpful tools and resources offered.

The Homegrown National Park materials shown here and elsewhere in this book are used with permission from Homegrown National Park (homegrownnationalpark.org).

Introduction

Getting started—it's worth it!

"Every oak started out as a couple of nuts who stood their ground."

Henry David Thoreau

Converting a huge expanse of lawn bereft of trees into a wildlife habitat may simply look like an impossible task. But here's the thing, once you start transitioning an area to wildlife habitat, Mother Nature steps in and helps you! A tiny speck of a seed produces a mound of blooms covered with pollinators, a jay plants an oak for you, a bare spot in the soil becomes home to native ground-nesting (non-stinging) bees. Time passes, and before you know it, there are more flowers, trees have tripled or quadrupled in height, and the landscape is filled with movement and birdsong. This really does happen!

BEFORE: This extensive lawn offered no benefits to wildlife.

BEFORE: A watershed area was covered in non-native vegetation.

BEFORE: A large expanse of front lawn was an ecological dead space.

8 months LATER: In late fall, an area of this lawn was blocked with cardboard and wood chips, then planted in spring. Pollinators (and people) enjoyed a lovely display of blooms all summer.

2 years LATER: A mix of non-native weedy growth was replaced with Joe-Pye weed (*Eutrochium*) and cup plant *(Silphium perfoliatum)*. This small valley now teems with life.

5 years LATER: Once planted, the oak grew exponentially each year. All it took was digging a hole, protecting the sapling from deer, and faith that one day it would be a tree—and now it is!

Introduction

Taking action at a level that is appropriate for you

What is wildlife habitat?

In *The Field Guide to Wildlife Habitats of the Western United States*, Janine M. Banyus describes wildlife habitat as being the place that provides animals with what they need for survival: food, water, shelter, and safe places to conduct their life activities, especially reproduction. In short, she describes habitat as being an animal's home and sanctuary.

Leaving seed heads of flowering plants provides food for birds such as the American goldfinch (*Spinus tristis*) shown here.

Some of the actions urgently needed to support wildlife can be tough and sometimes emotionally challenging. For example, you may discover that a tree that is finally old enough to provide fruit or a plant that a treasured friend gave you is an invasive species. You may be accustomed to lighting up your home and landscape at night, or you may have a broad expanse of lawn that is the pride of the neighborhood. We need to take the difficult actions for nature to survive. As your wildlife habitat starts coming alive, you'll likely find that the hard decisions become easier because you'll want to see your wild visitors sticking around and thriving!

Before stepping into action, consider which level of wildlife habitat restoration fits you:

☐ *Armchair Wildlife Habitat:* Perhaps for physical or other reasons, making changes in a landscape is not an option. Or maybe having a green thumb is not your thing—there are still many actions you can take! Turning out the lights, engaging others through conversation and dialogue, supporting community efforts, and offering financial support are vital contributions.

☐ *Landless Wildlife Habitat:* No landscape of your own to make over? Even containers make a difference. Family or friends may appreciate your help converting their landscapes. Community properties offer volunteer opportunities, or perhaps your workplace would welcome a natural and beautiful landscape makeover. You might even consider becoming an ecological landscaper!

☐ *Step-by-step Wildlife Habitat:* You would love to convert all your property to a rich wildlife habitat right now, but your time or resources are currently limited. You may want to choose which actions are most interesting to you and feasible to do now. You can then gather the resources for other actions over time.

☐ *Gung-ho! Wildlife Habitat:* You have the time, resources, and inspiration to transform your entire landscape into a thriving, natural ecosystem filled with movement and birdsong. You may be able to do every action in this guide!

Whatever level of action feels comfortable for you, we are thrilled that you are embarking on this journey with us! Let's get going!

Digging in deeper

Here are references and helpful resources related to protecting your wildlife habitat and its residents (please refer to the Appendix for publication details).

 Nature's Best Hope: A New Approach to Conservation That Starts in Your Yard by Douglas W. Tallamy. This impactful book, featuring Doug's urgent call-to-action to restore biodiversity and local abundance where we live and work, is the inspiration for this action guide. *Nature's Best Hope* will give you the inspiration—the WHY—to do the actions suggested in *Nature's Action Guide*. Read it whenever your energy flags or progress seems slow as a reminder that, even though welcoming back nature may take time and effort, it's all worth it!

Bringing Nature Home: How You Can Sustain Wildlife with Native Plants, Updated and Expanded by Douglas W. Tallamy. Like *Nature's Best Hope*, this book provides a solid argument for just how important it is that we include native plants in our landscapes, especially plants that butterflies, moths, and pollinators specialize on, to ensure the survival of the rich biodiversity of life on Earth (including human life). Filled with descriptions and photographs of insect and plant relationships, *Bringing Nature Home* is another highly recommended complement to this action guide.

Nature's Best Hope (Young Reader's Edition): How You Can Save the World in Your Own Yard by Douglas W. Tallamy and adapted by Sarah L. Thomson. The important message of *Nature's Best Hope* is presented in a format accessible to younger readers and second language learners.

The Nature of Oaks: The Rich Ecology of Our Most Essential Native Trees by Douglas W. Tallamy. In this book, Doug takes us month-by-month through the seasons with the most important plant genus when it comes to supporting biodiversity in most ecoregions of the United States—the oaks (*Quercus*).

Additional books for background reading:

Ecology: A Very Short Introduction by Jaboury Ghazoul is a pocket-sized volume that takes a comprehensive look at the basic concepts underlying the science of ecology. This foundation leads to a greater understanding of the dynamics of the looming biodiversity crisis.

The Illustrated Practical Guide to Wildlife Gardening: How to Make Wildflower Meadows, Ponds, Hedges, Flower Borders, Bird Feeders, Wildlife Shelters, Nesting Boxes, and Hibernation Sites is one of several books Christine and Michael Lavelle have written about wildlife gardening and how to attract wildlife. Although based in the United Kingdom, their step-by-step, illustrated guides for over 40 projects are universally helpful and relate to various actions in this guide. That said, no matter how closely you follow their directions for making a log pile to attract hedgehogs, if you live in North America, that little creature won't be showing up.

Now that we've reviewed the itinerary for our journey, let's get going. We'll begin with an important action that we can take today—turn out the lights!

xiv   Introduction—Welcome nature where you live, work, and play!   NATURE'S ACTION GUIDE

Introduction

Step:	✔	Action Needed:	Page:
1	☐	Turn off the lights whenever and wherever possible	1.4
2	☐	Pull drapes and blinds to block light from your home and other buildings	1.6
3	☐	Change all outdoor lights to amber, yellow, or red bulbs	1.8
4	☐	Where lighting is necessary, use the lowest level of brightness needed	1.9
5	☐	Choose lighting that has shields (or add shields) to direct light downward and to prevent light trespass	1.10
6	☐	Add motion sensors to all outdoor lights so that they shine only when being used	1.11

The moon is the best night light of all time!

Take an inventory of the lighting around your home

Use this **Dark Sky Friendly Home Lighting Inventory Form** to assess your property's lighting:

Dark Sky Friendly Home Lighting Inventory Form

Inventory Date: ....

Property Location: ....

Use the back of this form for notes, or to draw a property map indicating location of lights.

Fixture Description	Principle					Notes	Action Needed	Date Action Completed
	1	2	3	4	5			
example Front Porch	✓	☐	✓	✓	✓	Spills into neighbors yard	Need to re-aim light to fall only on stairs	
1	☐	☐	☐	☐	☐			
2	☐	☐	☐	☐	☐			
3	☐	☐	☐	☐	☐			
4	☐	☐	☐	☐	☐			
5	☐	☐	☐	☐	☐			
6	☐	☐	☐	☐	☐			
7	☐	☐	☐	☐	☐			
8	☐	☐	☐	☐	☐			
9	☐	☐	☐	☐	☐			
10	☐	☐	☐	☐	☐			

PRINCIPLES: 1. Does the light serve a *clear purpose?* **2.** Does the light *fall only where it is needed?* **3.** Is the amount of light *appropriate for the intended task?* **4.** Is the light connected to *active controls?* **5.** Is the light source *warm in color?*

Produced by The International Dark-Sky Association. April 2020. www.DarkSky.org

Note: Low-level lighting solar pathway lights do not need to be included in this inventory

©DarkSky International (darksky.org). Reproduced and used with written permission.

Action 1—GUIDE
Turn off the lights

One-third of nocturnal insects attracted to ALAN are likely to perish before sunrise.

We begin this journey with a simple but powerful action: **Turn off the lights.** Specifically, this means turning off or blocking any unnecessary artificial lights that light up the night and switching to yellow, amber, or red bulbs. This is our starting point for this action guide because it's easy to do right now!

Light pollution plays a huge role in the drastic decline in insect populations. Light attracts insects who become exhausted and dehydrated as they endlessly circle around a light source becoming prime targets for predators. Artificial light at night (ALAN) blinds insects causing them to collide with the light source which may then incinerate them. Compounding these physical dangers, night light interrupts the circadian rhythms of many insect species jeopardizing their foraging, mating, and reproduction habits and thus, their very survival.

ALAN is also having a devastating impact on bird populations. Migratory birds use gravity and the light of the moon and stars to navigate. Bright lights on buildings and skyglow from urban sprawl confuse birds causing glass strikes and exhaustion resulting in hundreds of millions of bird deaths each year! Light pollution is a leading cause of bird decline second only to predation by cats.

Insects and birds are not ALAN's only victims. ALAN interferes with the circadian rhythms and behavior of bats further threatening their survival. The impact of ALAN upon plants and their vital role in the food web is another concern. Fortunately, by taking the steps in this action and most especially by the simple act of turning off the lights, you can turn your property into your own "dark sky park" without much effort, and in so doing, help to reduce the precipitous decline in insect, bird, bat, and other animal populations.

Nightfall over the Natural Bridges National Monument in Utah, the first designated IDA Dark Sky Park.

1 Turn off the lights whenever and wherever possible

Artificial light at night has become such a normal part of modern life that we rarely consider its impacts: It obscures the stars, and sadly, 80% of Americans cannot see the Milky Way; it contributes to the increase of carbon dioxide in the atmosphere; and it's playing a devastating role in the decline of insects, bats, and migratory birds.

Turning off lights is easy yet impactful. It can take a little getting used to a less-lit home but upon realizing the tremendous hazard that night lighting poses for wildlife, the welcoming look of a brightly lit home becomes less appealing. As we'll see shortly, we can still use lights to give us a sense of security or to light our pathways—we simply need to choose our lighting and direct the light more thoughtfully.

Yellowstone National Park (*left*) and desert regions in the Southwest are some of the few places in the United States where the Milky Way is still visible.

Turning off the lights to protect insects

Light pollution is a significant contributor to insect population decline. The magnitude of this crisis is apparent as Gerhard Eisenbeiss and his colleague demonstrated in their 2009 comparison of three studies conducted in rural Germany over a span of almost 50 years. On an August night in 1949, researchers caught over 50,000 moths in one trap. In 1978, it took the entire summer to catch 50,000 moths using one trap. In the summer of 1997, researchers placed 19 traps and caught a mere 6,205 moths. The conditions for these studies varied; nevertheless, the dismal decline in the moth population is clear and shocking.

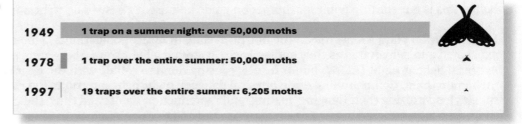

1949	1 trap on a summer night: over 50,000 moths
1978	1 trap over the entire summer: 50,000 moths
1997	19 traps over the entire summer: 6,205 moths

These studies document a staggering decline in moth populations over 50 years.

The windshield effect

If you are old enough to have been driving in the early 1990s or before, you likely recall the almost solid plastering of insects across the windshield of your car. This anecdotal observation of insect decline is backed up with alarming scientific statistics suggesting that over 75% of flying insect biomass has declined since 1990. The chore of cleaning the windshield was an unpleasant task but, oh, how welcome that task would be now given the alarming pace of insect decline.

With the simple act of turning off your lights, you are part of the solution to the worldwide insect population decline. **Every night counts—every light off counts!**

Turning off the lights to protect migratory birds

Light pollution contributes significantly to the death toll of birds—an estimated 100 million to one billion birds die each year when they become disoriented and strike glass or fly about all night until they finally land in exhaustion and become vulnerable to other hazards. Artificial light at night (ALAN) is particularly deadly to nocturnal migrants—sadly, this includes many priority bird species whose populations are already at risk.

The **National Audubon Society** and its partners are building a nationwide *Lights Out* network whose mission is to encourage building owners to turn out or block night light especially during peak migration periods in the spring and fall. (Keep in mind, glass strikes occur year-round, so lights out all year is best!)

This tragic collection of glass strike victims (*from left to right:* belted kingfisher, blue jay, indigo bunting, and three black-throated blue warblers) was collected in downtown Washington D. C. by the *Lights Out DC* group in Fall 2014.

Learn more about the *Lights Out* program by searching online for **lights out audubon** and navigate to the site. Download a 2-page fact sheet about actions you can take. Find out if there is a *Lights Out* program where you live, such as *Lights Out Cleveland, Lights Out Eugene, Lights Out Georgia, Lights Out Heartland, Lights Out Texas, Safe Passage Great Lakes*, and many more!

While on the site, consider watching the video **Lights Out: Philadelphia Darkens Its Skyline to Protect Migrating Birds**, a moving account of the glass strike problem. The video features monitors who patrol downtown streets in Philadelphia early in the morning before street cleaners begin their work. These monitors gather glass strike victims to identify particularly hazardous buildings and to help in the development of more effective preventative measures.

Peak bird migration falls on different ranges of dates depending on where you live, the weather, and resources such as food and shelter. With the help of *BirdCast*, learn when birds will be passing overhead where you live.

Exploring migratory bird populations and wildlife ecology in the air

BirdCast is a fascinating resource that provides real-time forecasting of migratory birds traveling overhead. Colorful maps show the bird population density each night during the periods of **spring migration** (Mar. 1 to June 1) and **fall migration** (Aug. 1 to Nov. 15).

BirdCast is a joint project of the Cornell Lab of Ornithology, Colorado State University, and the University of Massachusetts Amherst. To access, search **birdcast.info** and click **Live bird migration map**. Search online for **how to use birdcast** for a **Cornell Lab of Ornithology All About Birds** guide that explains how to use *BirdCast* to learn which bird species are likely to be overhead on any given night during a migration period.

While on the *BirdCast* site, click **Science-to-Action** in the top menu to learn about **aeroecology**. This emerging discipline studies the interrelationship between airborne wildlife and the airspace it occupies.

During fall migration, this warbler stopped by briefly to rest and refuel.

2 Pull drapes and blinds to block light from your home and other buildings

Another simple act can help prevent wildlife fatalities: Draw your curtains at night so that your household light is contained within your house. Pull blinds in office windows and, if possible, turn off the lights when leaving your workplace. Where window coverings don't adequately block light from escaping from your home, dim lamps and other light sources that are near windows, or even better, turn them off. As resources allow, you may wish to go one step further and replace thin curtains or blinds with window coverings that block the light more effectively.

Reducing light trespass from our homes

For interior lighting where window coverings don't adequately block out light, consider using dimmable light sources. For example, it can be as easy as placing dimmable amber, yellow, or red bulbs in compatible lamps or plugging a fixture into a plug-in dimmer switch (*left*).

Although wiring an interior light dimmer switch is pretty easy (*right*), consider watching several how-to videos before taking on this task. Search online for **how to install dimmer switches**.

Turning your property into your own (unofficial) dark sky park

So important is the need for dark skies that **DarkSky International** (formerly the **International Dark-Sky Association**) recognizes and accredits public and private properties as dark sky reserves, parks, and sanctuaries. The Natural Bridges National Monument in Utah was the first designated dark sky park. With a few changes in our habits and minimal expense, we can create unofficial dark sky parks of our own. Let's take a brief tour of the **Dark Sky International** website to learn about light pollution and get motivated to **turn off the lights!**

Visit: **darksky.org**

or search online for **darksky international** and navigate to the site.

DarkSky International restores the nighttime environment and protects communities from the harmful effects of light pollution through outreach, advocacy, and conservation.

Scroll down to:

- Learn about light pollution
- Get involved
- Visit a Dark Sky Place
- Find approved lighting products
- Find a chapter near you

Learn how to protect the night skies where you live

Visit **darksky.org.** Click **What we do.** Click **Advancing responsible outdoor lighting.** Next, scroll down to *The Five Principles for Outdoor Lighting.* Click **Learn more.**

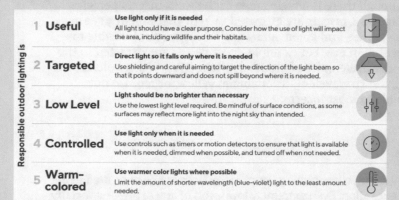

Responsible outdoor lighting is

1	**Useful**	**Use light only if it is needed** All light should have a clear purpose. Consider how the use of light will impact the area, including wildlife and their habitats.
2	**Targeted**	**Direct light so it falls only where it is needed** Use shielding and careful aiming to target the direction of the light beam so that it points downward and does not spill beyond where it is needed.
3	**Low Level**	**Light should be no brighter than necessary** Use the lowest light level required. Be mindful of surface conditions, as some surfaces may reflect more light into the night sky than intended.
4	**Controlled**	**Use light only when it is needed** Use controls such as timers or motion detectors to ensure that light is available when it is needed, dimmed when possible, and turned off when not needed.
5	**Warm-colored**	**Use warmer color lights where possible** Limit the amount of shorter wavelength (blue–violet) light to the least amount needed.

- All light should have a clear purpose
- Light should be directed only to where needed
- Light should be no brighter than necessary
- Light should be used only when it's useful
- Use warmer color lights where possible

Explore the site to learn more about each of these principles and tips for implementing them.

This 4-minute video **Dark Skies at Home** (*right*) is well worth watching. In the menu bar, click **What we do.** Click **Advancing responsible outdoor lighting.** Scroll down to **Guides and how-tos.** Click on **Home Lighting.**

Explore the **Guides and how-tos** for topics such as guidance for working with HOAs, what renters can do about light pollution, the challenges of electronic billboards, and much more.

Dark Skies Start at Home

Taking inventory of the lighting around your home

DarkSky International provides a handy *Dark Sky Friendly Home Lighting Inventory Form.* (For your convenience, a full-size blank form is reproduced with permission on page 1.2.) The inventory highlights **DarkSky's Five Principles for Outdoor Lighting.**

Consider completing the *DarkSky 101 training* and becoming a *DarkSky Advocate.* Click **Get Involved** for more information.

Find dark-sky approved lighting on the **DarkSky International** website. Visit **darksky.org.** On the home page, scroll down and click on the link **Find approved lighting products.** (**DarkSky International** does not sell lighting products.)

To get ideas for dark-sky friendly lighting, search online for **dark sky fixtures.** Big-box hardware retailers often have a category for **dark sky outdoor lighting.** Make sure that a product's design meets dark-sky guidelines described above and includes motion sensors. And, of course, be sure to install amber, yellow or red bulbs!

The DarkSky International materials shown here and elsewhere in this book are used with permission from DarkSky International (darksky.org).

3 Change all outdoor lights to amber, yellow, or red bulbs

Light pollution is especially hazardous to **nocturnal insects** (insects active at night). Given the key role moths play in the food web, the fatal attraction moths have to artificial light is of particular concern. Fortunately, this is a problem we can help to solve by changing our outdoor lighting to amber, yellow, or red bulbs. Why does this work?

Although there is a wide range in the ways insects perceive light, most insects are attracted to light that humans see as violet, blue, and green, along with wavelengths invisible to the human eye. For example, most moths are attracted to the short wavelengths of ultraviolet light (UV). Warm-colored bulbs with wavelengths of amber, yellow, or red, are not visible to most insects.

Amber or yellow bulbs protect many insects; however, fireflies are an exception. Even extremely low levels of any ALAN—**especially yellow, amber, and green**—threaten their reproductive success.

Choosing the safest bulbs for insects

Converting your lights to amber, yellow, or red (where possible) not only makes the light less attractive to most insects which is safer for them, it also makes an outdoor space more bug-free for you! Although changing your outdoor bulbs requires an initial expense, over time the energy savings from LED bulbs should help offset this cost.

The Federal Trade Commission (FTC) Energy Labeling Rule requires bulb manufacturers to include *Lighting Facts* on their product packaging. These labels make it easy to evaluate the relative insect safety of a bulb—the lower the **lumens** (lm; brightness) and the lower the **Kelvin** (K; color temperature), the better. For example, a 1900K bulb will give off a warm amber glow.

Lighting Facts Per Bulb	
Brightness	**600 lumens**
Estimated Yearly Energy Cost	**$1.14**
Based on 3 hrs/day, 11¢/kWh	
Cost depends on rates and use	
Life	
Based on 3 hrs/day	**22.8 years**
Light Appearance	
Warm — Cool	
1900°K	
Energy Used	**9.5 watts**

Bug lights vs. BUG ratings of lights

Many bulb manufacturers offer warm-colored bulbs marketed as "bug lights" which is helpful, but you may also see a **BUG rating** label on some products. A BUG rating does not relate directly to bugs! Rather, the BUG rating is used to show the quality of the light emitted from a lighting fixture. In the rating, BUG stands for **backlight, uplight,** and **glare.** The BUG rating is important during building design and construction to ensure that light fixtures, such as building lights and streetlights, are dark-sky compliant.

DISCLAIMER: *When deemed to be helpful to the reader, specific organizations, products, suppliers may be mentioned or shown in this action guide. All product and company names are trademarks or registered trademarks of their respective holders. Use of them does not imply affiliation with, endorsement by, nor association between them and the author or publisher of this book, nor does the author or publisher receive any financial gain. The goal is simply to help readers easily find the necessary resources to create functioning wildlife habitats.*

Change all outdoor lights to amber, yellow, or red bulbs, *continued*

Innovative red lighting throughout a Dutch town protects rare bat species

The town of Zuidhoek-Nieuwkoop in the Netherlands is the first town in the world to install bat-friendly, red streetlights to help preserve the breeding grounds of rare bat species. Developed by **Signify** (signify.com; formerly Philips Lighting), a worldwide supplier of lighting products, these energy-efficient LED streetlights provide enough illumination to ensure the safety of residents while emitting light perceived by bats as darkness.

A street in Zuidhoek-Nieuwkoop is lit with **Signify**'s red, bat-friendly lighting that emits a wavelength that doesn't interfere with a bat's internal compass.

Fireflies are particularly vulnerable to light pollution

Artificial light at night also interferes with the flashing signals **fireflies** (lightning bugs) use to attract mates. Green, yellow, and amber lights are especially problematic due to their spectral similarity to firefly bioluminescence. During the summer months where fireflies are present, turn off the lights whenever possible. If turning off the lights is not an option, consider replacing bulbs with dim red bulbs or cover bulbs with red gels (see page 1.12).

The **Xerces Society's** beautifully titled publication *Conserving the Jewels of the Night* (56-page PDF) gives guidelines for protecting fireflies in North America. Search online for the title to download this free guide to learn more about these beloved insects.

Where lighting is necessary, use the lowest level of brightness needed

Where outdoor lighting is needed for safety, select the lowest level of brightness required to adequately light the area. Consider the combined effect of reflected light from various surfaces. Some surfaces such as light-colored concrete, may require less lighting. Brightness levels can be lowered by adding a dimmer function or by replacing bulbs with bulbs that are less bright (lower lumens).

For outdoor locations where lighting is always needed, consider installing lighting fixtures featuring a **dual-bright** motion sensor—lights turn on at 25% brightness from dusk-to-dawn and shift to 100% for a few minutes when triggered by motion. Keep in mind that total darkness is far preferable, so, when possible, avoid dusk-to-dawn lights that remain lit beyond when motion is detected. Adding motion sensors that completely turn out lights when they're not in use is a far safer option for wildlife.

Dimmer is better! Comparing the brightness of a bulb in terms of lumens

To select a light bulb with a lower level of brightness, compare **lumens** (lm) rather than **watts** (w). Lumens measure the amount of light produced by a light source (its brightness) while watts measure the amount of energy used to produce the light. When incandescent bulbs were the primary type of bulb used, wattage was a reliable measure of brightness; however, with the growing popularity of different types of lighting, such as light-emitting diode (LED) and compact fluorescent (CFL) bulbs, comparing lumens is a more reliable measurement of brightness.

5 Choose lighting that has shields (or add shields) to direct light downward and to prevent light trespass

Poor design of many light fixtures and lighting systems contributes to light pollution. The good news is that simply by redesigning light fixtures and lighting systems, light pollution could be significantly reduced. Where turning off lights is not an option, light fixtures should be used that shield and direct light to precisely where the light is needed.

Light pollution is caused by excessive, carelessly aimed artificial lights.

Switching to wildlife-friendly lighting

Ideally, artificial light should be directed downward and shielded so that it provides useful light and nothing more.

Light shining beyond its intended target is **light pollution**. Light pollution includes **light trespass, skyglow, glare,** and **clutter.**

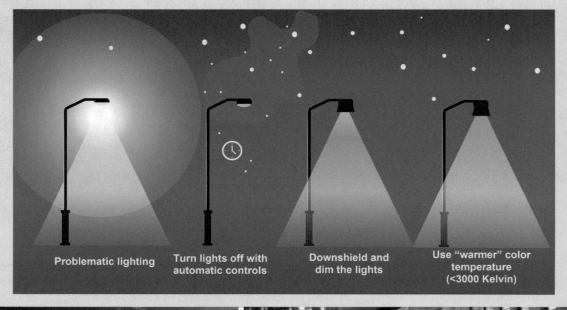

Problematic lighting

Turn lights off with automatic controls

Downshield and dim the lights

Use "warmer" color temperature (<3000 Kelvin)

Light trespass (*left*) is light that shines beyond where it's needed. If a streetlight shines into your bedroom window, you know firsthand what light trespass is! Light trespass shining upward is **skyglow. Clutter** (*right*) is the excessive grouping of bright lights resulting in **glare** that causes visual confusion.

Choosing outdoor light fixtures that help prevent light pollution

For places where outdoor lighting is necessary, reduce light pollution by choosing light fixtures that direct all exterior light downward to target the area where light is needed. When limited resources prevent the replacement of inefficient light fixtures, consider adding shields to direct the light downward.

Light fixtures that cause light pollution   Wildlife-friendlier light fixtures

Limiting the use of decorative lighting to special occasions only

An elegantly lit home is undeniably attractive; the problem is that the lights are also attractive to wildlife—often fatally so. Upward facing spotlights are particularly problematic. Directing lights downward, limiting light trespass with shields, and changing to warm-colored bulbs will help protect some insect populations; however, birds may still fly into light reflected on windows. Residential ALAN negatively affects most of the flora and fauna it shines upon. As pretty as it is, keep decorative lighting turned off as much as possible.

Using wildlife-friendly pathway lights

Just as streets and highways need adequate lighting, homeowners need lit pathways for safe passage. Luckily, with a little effort and minimal expense, pathway lighting can be more wildlife friendly. Choose pathway lighting that has these features:

- cone-shaped lamp shades or shields
- downward-directed light
- lighting limited to areas where light is needed.

To reduce light pollution, place pathway lights as low to the ground as possible. If replacement bulbs are hard to find in amber, yellow, or red, gel filters can be attached to make the light more wildlife friendly.

6 Add motion sensors to all outdoor lights so that they shine only when being used

In areas where light may be needed at night such as an entranceway, put the lights on motion sensors. In addition to protecting wildlife, motion-triggered lighting is a more effective burglar deterrent than all-night security lights. Adding a motion sensor can be as easy as screwing in an amber, yellow, or red motion-activated light bulb. In contrast to traditional dusk-to-dawn features designed to keep lights on from dusk to dawn, these bulbs have a dusk-to-dawn feature that keeps them off all day and triggers them off from dusk to dawn unless triggered on by motion. Choosing the right product requires careful review of product features to avoid accidentally installing lights that turn on at dusk and off at dawn. **The period from dusk to dawn is exactly the time period the lights need to be OFF to protect wildlife.**

Digging in deeper

Here are additional resources about turning out the lights and creating dark skies (please refer to the Appendix for publication details).

Nature's Best Hope: A New Approach to Conservation That Starts in Your Yard: Doug describes the effect on insects of their mysterious attraction to light that often spells their demise (see pages 154 - 155). He urges us to take the simple but impactful act of turning off all unnecessary lights and switching to warm-colored bulbs that attract fewer insects.

Globe at Night (*globeatnight.org*) raises awareness of light pollution through its international project that invites citizen-scientists to measure and report the brightness of the night sky where they live. Researchers use the data to analyze how light pollution affects wildlife.

Light Pollution Undermines Ecological Communities: This 2-page infographic published by the Australian government summarizes the harmful effects of light pollution across the ecosystem and stresses the importance of creating dark corridors to allow nocturnal animals safe passage between habitat patches. To read this article, search for the title online. (See page 15.5 to learn more about creating dark corridors).

Pollinator Partnership's ***Quick Reference Guide: Light Pollution*** (2-page PDF) is a handy summary of light pollution and "How You Can Help" actions along with a brief discussion about nocturnal pollination. Find this and other helpful guides in the Resources on the **Pollinator Partnership** website (*pollinator.org*).

Help protect and conserve fireflies by recording and reporting firefly sightings to the **Firefly Atlas** (*fireflyatlas.org*). Learn more about firefly conservation and research by visiting **Firefly** (*firefly.org*).

Turn the Lights Out for Fireflies and Other Insects: In this Xerces Society webinar, Avalon Owens, a firefly conservationist, presents a comprehensive view of light pollution as a conservation issue. Search online for this video's title—it's a compelling must-watch!

Installing exterior motion sensors is not difficult although some exterior lights may require a ladder to access. Before installing a motion sensor, check out one of the many videos available—search online for **how to install [motion sensor lights] video.** Note that many of the videos don't feature wildlife-friendly light fixtures!

Change the color of outdoor lights with gels. A gel is a semi-transparent sheet of colored plastic primarily used by photographers for creative color effects. In your wildlife habitat, using a gel as a filter to change the color of outdoor lighting might be an easy, economical, temporary, or even permanent solution. Color gels are available in sheets or rolls. With a little experimentation, gels can be attached to light fixtures with tape, hook and fastener stickers, or magnets. Gels can be slipped into some fixtures, for example, inside the walls of a box lantern.

Turning off or blocking artificial light at night combined with the widespread use of amber, yellow, or red bulbs in outdoor settings significantly contributes to the well-being of insects, birds, and other creatures in our wildlife habitats. Fortunately, turning off our lights is something we can do right now! Next, we'll look at many other critical actions we can take to protect the wildlife and plants that surround us.

Action 2—CHECKLIST
Protect your wildlife habitat

Step:		Action Needed:	Page:
1	☐	Monitor your property regularly for potential wildlife hazards	**2.4**
2	☐	Take precautions to prevent wildlife from becoming trapped and dying	**2.4**
3	☐	Take precautions to prevent wildlife from drowning	**2.5**
4	☐	Mark or shield glass windows and doors to prevent bird strikes	**2.6**
5	☐	Avoid burning piles of brush	**2.8**
6	☐	Constantly scan an area for wildlife as you work in your landscape to avoid accidentally harming creatures	**2.8**
7	☐	Protect wildlife while caring for your lawn	**2.9**
8	☐	Protect your wildlife habitat from pets	**2.10**
9	☐	Protect your wildlife habitat from deer and other creatures *(if present)*	**2.11**
10	☐	Protect your wildlife habitat while children are enjoying it	**2.14**
11	☐	Protect the people in your wildlife habitat	**2.14**

Leaf patterns to make bird glass-strike prevention stickers (see page 2.7).

NOTE: *Cutting out the leaf veins is optional.*

Action 2—GUIDE
Protect your wildlife habitat

The way we care for our landscape can help protect vulnerable creatures such as this baby turtle.

Before ramping up efforts to attract wildlife to our wildlife habitats, we need to take precautions to protect the creatures that may visit and take up residence. We just described how turning off lights and changing to amber, yellow, or red bulbs protect wildlife, especially moths, from exhausting themselves to death. Many of the actions we discuss in future actions also protect wildlife—adding water features prevents wildlife from dying of dehydration, preserving pupation and nesting sites supports insects through their life cycles, planting densely provides cover from predators, and so forth. In this action, we consider other measures that we can take around our home and landscape, such as the simple act of turning containers on their side to prevent creatures from becoming trapped and marking windows to prevent fatal bird strikes. Discovering a bird drowned in a container of water or lifeless on the ground beneath a window is such a depressing sight. We hope that the actions shared here will prevent you from ever having to experience these and other wildlife tragedies.

In this action, we also share strategies to protect plants from visiting wildlife such as deer who may devour an entire planting overnight.

Some of these actions take seconds and can be done right away, while others require dedicated effort. Saving a newly planted bed or preventing even one senseless wildlife casualty makes taking preventive measures all worthwhile!

As majestic as deer are, their population explosion is having a devastating impact on wildlands and biodiversity. This white-tailed deer (*Odocoileus virginianus*) enjoys this buffet of native plants.

① Monitor your property regularly for potential wildlife hazards

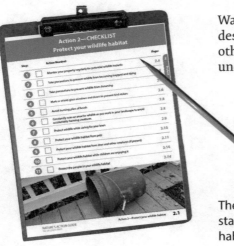

Walk around your yard and look for the potential hazards described in this action. You'll probably spot these as you do other activities, but regular, intentional walkabouts sometimes uncover dangers that are easily missed in the busyness of life.

The checklist for this action on page 2.1 provides a handy starting point for spotting potential dangers in your wildlife habitat.

② Take precautions to prevent wildlife from becoming trapped and dying

Things that are perfectly safe for people can be fatal traps for small creatures. Luckily, taking simple precautions is easy although some potential traps are hard to spot. Some outdoor enclosed light fixtures, for example, have tiny openings that insects crawl into and become trapped. Bird netting is a particularly hazardous material. While in use, netting may trap birds. Unless netting is stored in a sealed container, snakes and other animals may become hopelessly entangled in stored netting, often dying as they try wriggling their way out.

Cover basement window wells to prevent creatures from becoming trapped. Basement window wells are a death trap for frogs, toads, lizards, and other small creatures who may fall into them as they make their daily or nightly rounds. Plastic window well covers are readily available for under $15. Fancier options (for fancier prices) are also available. Make sure to seal the sides of the cover so that it sits snugly against the exterior wall or siding. Recycled foam can be stuffed in the gaps, or foam packaging can be carved to fit and fill the gaps between the cover and the wall.

Turn empty containers on their side to prevent creatures from becoming trapped. Always leave empty containers of all sizes on their side to prevent small creatures such as baby birds from becoming trapped. This also prevents water from collecting in the container helping to eliminate potential mosquito breeding grounds.

Even small containers are hazardous if left standing upright.

Keep the doors of the garage and other outbuildings closed whenever possible to avoid trapping bees, birds, and butterflies that fly in and frogs and toads that hop in. Small creatures may enter and die before they can find an exit. Insects and spiders may enter your house and become trapped. Small creatures can easily be removed safely. Carefully pop a glass jar over the creature and gently slide a piece of stiff paper under the jar while nudging the creature to walk onto the paper. Invert the jar holding the paper firmly to seal the jar. Carry it outside and release the critter.

2

Protect

③ Take precautions to prevent wildlife from drowning

It's devastating to find a bird or other creature drowned in a bucket of water or pond. Hopefully, you'll never

Cover open containers of water to prevent creatures from drowning. If a container is holding water for future use, cover it so that birds, chipmunks, native bees, beetles, and other creatures don't become trapped and drown. Or at a minimum, put a wide flat stick in the container to give insects and other creatures an escape ramp.

Place animal escape ramps in swimming pools and ponds to prevent small creatures from drowning. Even ponds intended for wildlife can become death traps for frogs and creatures that accidentally fall in if the sides are too steep or the overhang too wide for them to exit. Be sure to place animal escape ramps in all water features.

In ponds, add places for frogs to land or scramble onto such as lily pads. Adding lily pads provides landing places for frogs. If growing lily pads in your pond is not an option, consider adding your own fake ones such as the homemade one shown above (see below for directions to make one). A long, flat stone leaned up on the side of the pond makes a good escape ramp.

How to make a fake lily pad

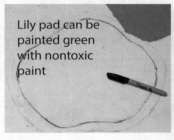

Lily pad can be painted green with nontoxic paint

serrated knife

cut at angle

sand

sand washed

fishing line

bread clip or button

bread clip

two holes

fishing line

bottom side of floating lily pad

Step 1: Draw a lily pad on a flat, 1-inch thick or so sheet of foam packaging. Draw a second outer line about 5/8 Inches away from the first line.

Step 2: Cut along the inner line at an angle from the inner line to the width of the outer line. A serrated knife works well here.

Step 3: Fill an old jar with sand or gravel for a weight. Tie a piece of fishing line around the jar's top. Cut the line 10" longer than the pond's depth.

Step 4: Poke two holes in the center of the pad. Poke the line from the bottom to the top of the pad and back to the bottom. Tie a plastic bread tag to the line on the bottom side.

Swimming pools are deadly for frogs and toads. Unless they can quickly escape, frogs and toads will drown, or pool chemicals will poison them. **The Humane Society** recommends securing one or more water-exit devices to the edge of a pool (or steep-sided pond) such as the *Froglog* shown here (visit *froglog.us* to learn more). If you have a pool, search online for **pool safety for wildlife** to learn more about this dangerous hazard.

4 Mark or shield glass windows and doors to prevent bird strikes

In the United States alone, **nearly one billion birds per year** are killed when they fly into glass windows! Researcher Scott R. Loss and his colleagues estimate that 44 percent of these **glass strikes happen at our homes—equating to over one million per day!** After striking glass, a bird may appear to recover and fly off, but it's likely to die later from internal injuries. We can all take precautions that together could significantly reduce this number.

Some species of birds have a greater incidence of glass strikes such as the ovenbird (*Seiurus aurocapilla*) shown here.

Keeping curtains and blinds closed helps. Reflections are reduced but not eliminated (compare the photos above and below).

Move house plants away from unmarked, unscreened windows. The plants shown here are too close to a hazardous window.

Place bird feeders and baths less than 3 feet or more than 30 feet away from windows.

Put screens on plate glass windows even though windows don't open. This may seem extreme, but it can be a solution for particularly hazardous windows. Also, screen or mark any dangerous windows of outbuildings.

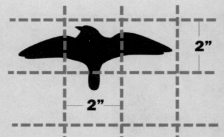

Remember, the 2 x 2 rule! Stickers and other markings need to be spaced so that the gaps between them are no greater than 2 inches high by 2 inches wide. Single stickers or larger gaps will **NOT** offer sufficient protection.

Paint designs on the outside of windows using tempera paint, UV reflective liquid, or bar soap. Remember the 2 x 2 rule. Make sure the markings are easily seen from 10 feet away. This is the easiest method!

Read an in-depth article about window collisions by Cornell Lab All About Birds (*allaboutbirds.org*). Search online for *Why Birds Hit Windows—And How You Can Help Prevent It.*

The **American Bird Conservancy** (*abcbirds.org*) provides many helpful resources for protecting birds. Visit **abcbirds.org**. In the top menu, click **Threats**. In the top picture menu, click **Bird Collisions**. Scroll down and click **Learn More** to read about *Preventing Bird Collisions at Home*. Review the different solutions and products. Scroll down and read the section **Ensure That Your Window Solutions Are Effective** for helpful (and important!) tips. On the **Bird Collisions** page is the **Products & Solution Database**, a comprehensive list and efficacy review of products and solutions to the bird collision crisis. A Threat Factor (TF) score is assigned to each entry—the *lower* the TF score, the *more effective* the prevention product or method is.

Mark or shield glass windows and doors to prevent bird strikes, *continued*

Apply vinyl tape to the outside of windows.

Attractive tapes and adhesive dots are available for glass located in fancy places. White, vinyl electrical tape is an economical choice. Space the tape horizontally every 2 inches and vertically every 2 inches on the **outside** of the window.

Apply stickers, decals, or clings to the outside of windows.

Stickers can be homemade (*above*) from adhesive vinyl such as peel-and-stick wallpaper. Draw designs on the paper back of the vinyl. (See page 2.2 for leaf patterns.) Cut out and apply to the outside of a window. Stickers, decals, or clings can be bought; search online for **anti-collision window cling** [or stickers]. To be effective, they must be stuck to the **outside** of windows* and arranged so that the gaps between them are **less than 2 inches high and 2 inches wide**. Make sure the markings are easily seen from 10 feet away. (*Confirm that products can be applied to the outside of windows—indoor stickers do not provide protection.)

Hang parachute cording spaced vertically every 2 inches. Parachute cording is a good collision deterrent in part because it has movement. Here's an easy DIY method for hanging it.

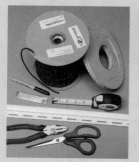
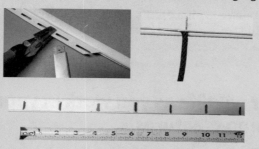

double-stick tape

side-view of undersill

knot

Step 1: Gather supplies: tools, inexpensive 550-pound parachute cord, undersill (available where vinyl siding is sold), double-stick tape.

Step 2: Cut undersill to width of window. Trim off bottom edge by scoring with a razor blade and snapping off. Mark the back every 2 inches.

Step 3: Cut cord about 4 inches longer than the height of the window. Tie small knots at both ends. Slip one end into the undersill. Repeat.

Step 4: The undersill strip is attached above the window with double-sided tape or self-adhesive hook and loop fastener.

What to do if a bird is still alive after striking glass: This is one of the rare instances when bringing in and caring for an injured wild animal IS recommended because a bird's dazed or comatose state makes it extremely vulnerable to predators such as cats. Although victims of glass strikes are unlikely to survive, their chances are improved if they are gently transported to a small, towel-lined box and placed in a warm, quiet location. Close the box (add airholes if needed). The box can be placed partially on a heating pad set on a low setting. In one hour, check on the bird. If it is alert, active, and able to fly, release it at once. If it is still ailing, take it to a wildlife rehabilitator as quickly as possible. Search online for **wildlife rehabilitation [city, state]**.

Contribute to research by reporting dead birds. Make an important contribution to bird mortality research by reporting any dead birds that you find to *dbird.org*, a project of NYC Bird Alliance (formerly NYC Audubon). Visit **NYC Bird Alliance** (*nycbirdalliance.org*) to learn more about **dBird** and how to care for injured birds.

All glass windows are hazardous for birds. Windows lit up at night, window reflections, and windows where birds can see through to vegetation or sky are deceptively dangerous. Assess all the buildings on your property and in your community. Are there windows that need treatment to prevent glass strikes?

⑤ Avoid burning piles of brush

Burning a pile of brush not only contributes to air pollution, but it also kills insects that may have nested within it along with any lichen or fungi. It may also kill the small animals and insects that use it for shelter. Instead, think of brush as a valuable renewable resource. Consider these uses for brush:

Leave piles of brush to provide habitat for birds and other creatures. While the shrub layer of the landscape is filling in, brush piles provide protection from some predators.

Use pruned or dead branches to create "fake tree" perches for birds. Find an attractive branch, stick it in the ground (away from windows unless they are screened or treated to prevent bird collisions) and enjoy watching the birds that perch on it. Here, a young ruby-throated hummingbird (*Archilochus colubris*) pauses on a "fake-tree" branch.

Chip any brush that exceeds the available space for brush piles. Chippers can be rented for a reasonable rate. The resulting wood chips are a useful blocking material or pathway topping which creates a rich habitat for soil micro life. *Before chipping brush, check brush carefully for insects and small critters.*

⑥ Constantly scan an area for wildlife as you work in your landscape to avoid accidentally harming creatures

Garden tools can become accidental weapons. Before and while digging, keep a watchful eye out for baby turtles such as this one. They blend in well with the soil and are easy to miss!

Our activity in a landscape can injure or kill wildlife. Power tools are particularly lethal, but even hand tools such as hoes, trowels, or hori hori garden knives are hazardous for small creatures. Some creatures, such as toads and baby turtles, bury themselves in the top layer of soil and **duff** (plant litter). In fact, young turtles spend most of their life underground. Probe first, then dig, and continue to check the area as you work.

Avoid walking on caterpillar pupation sites or on areas where soil has been intentionally left bare for ground-nesting bees. Although difficult to do, limiting our footsteps to paths and stepping stones is the best way to protect soil structure and the world of micro life it contains. Bordering beds with logs or other edging materials can serve as a guide as to where to step.

How you mow any remaining lawn can significantly affect the wildlife on your property. With knife-sharp blades spinning at high speeds, lawn mowers inadvertently maim or kill wildlife. To protect wildlife, mow slowly, scan for wildlife, and pause mowing to give a bumblebee or moth time to fly out of your path. Following are more guidelines to protect wildlife while caring for your lawn.

7 Protect wildlife while caring for your lawn

4" or higher ↑

Always set your mower blades to their highest cutting height. Although you may have to adjust your visual standards for your lawn, this gives small creatures a better chance of survival if they can't avoid the mower's path.

Before starting to mow or string trim, walk around the area to scare off wildlife. Before edging a bed, gently run a rake or glide your foot across it to rustle away sunning lizards or toads.

Start mowing after the sun has dried the dew and finish mowing before dusk. Amphibians, nocturnal insects, and other nocturnal creatures become active as night approaches.

Plant "island beds" to provide shelter from mowing. Until you can replace lawn with plantings, create safe zones in the middle of lawns by adding island beds. Frogs, toads, and other creatures can flee to these beds for protection from mowing.

Mow in a pattern that starts in the interior of the lawn and works concentrically outward toward planted beds OR in a pattern (*above*) **that moves increasingly toward an island bed**. These two patterns help wildlife to move away from areas that have yet to be mowed and instead toward planted beds. In contrast, if the mowing pattern works from the outer perimeter inward and there is no island bed, fleeing wildlife ends up corralled in the center of the lawn—subject to the mower's final deadly pass.

↓ compacts soil ↓

Mow only when the grass is dry. When it's wet, frogs and toads are likely to be active because their skin can remain moist. Also, the weight of a lawn mower quickly compacts wet soil destroying its structure and killing soil micro life. On the plus side, when the grass is dry, your mower won't get plastered with clumps of wet grass!

Avoid senseless mowing. Instead of simply mowing on the same day each week, mow only when the grass is at a height that requires mowing. Avoid double mowing the same area. Resist mowing in a fancy pattern if it requires double mowing. These are luxuries our ecosystem can no longer afford.

Stop and pick up frogs and toads and move them to a planted area away from the mower's blades. If you are likely to encounter many frogs or toads, you may wish to bring along a container with holes poked in the lid to gather any that you spot. Remember to release them when you're done mowing!

8   Protect your wildlife habitat from pets

One of the most emotionally challenging considerations for protecting the wildlife in your natural landscape is choosing how much to limit your pet's access to your wildlife habitat.

Protect your wildlife habitat from pet cats

In the United States alone, researchers Scott Loss and colleagues estimate that outdoor cats kill between 1.3 to 4 billion birds every year. Of these, our **pet cats kill between 320 million to 1 billion birds each year!** Free-ranging cats, such as barnyard cats, strays, and feral cats, kill three times as many additional birds. These shocking statistics show that the way we care for our cats makes a difference.

Give your cat a welcoming home indoors. An indoor home can be a wonderland for kitties filled with toys and a cozy spot by a window. Or consider an outdoor "catio," keeping cats safe from coyotes and raccoons.

Take your cat for walks on a leash. With a little time and patience, cats can be leash trained. Walking cats on a leash gives them (and the birds) a safe way to enjoy the outdoors.

Place birdbaths and feeders thoughtfully. Keep them at least 10 feet from shrubs or other places where cats may hide.

Visit **American Bird Conservancy** (*abcbirds.org*) for many more solutions. In the top menu, click **Solutions**. In the top menu, click **Cats Indoors**. Scroll down and click on *Check out ABC's Solutions for Pet Cats page.* Here you will find information about cat enclosures, harnesses, strollers, indoor play, and anti-predation devices.

Protect your wildlife habitat from pet dogs

Stray dogs and free-to-roam dogs pose another one of the greatest risks to wildlife habitat. Worldwide, dogs threaten almost 200 species of animals including mammals, birds, reptiles, and amphibians that are classified as critically endangered, endangered, and vulnerable. Fortunately, pet dogs can be managed to minimize the negative impact dogs have on wildlife. Consider these strategies:

- Don't allow your dog to roam freely outside of a fenced area.
- Set aside at least some of your property as being off-limits to pet dogs, especially in places where ground-nesting birds and turtles may live.
- Erect temporary fencing to protect new plantings until they are established.

Remove and properly dispose of pet poop

Pet poop is considered hazardous material and should be collected and properly disposed of to avoid exposing people and pets to sickness-causing bacteria and parasites. Proper poop disposal also helps to prevent contamination of the watershed and your wildlife habitat. As the **Center for Disease Control and Prevention** (*cdc.gov*) advises:

Practice responsible pet poop habits to keep yourself, your family, and the environment healthy!

⑨ Protect your wildlife habitat from deer and other creatures *(if present)*

Deer may be a welcome sight in your landscape, but as many gardeners have experienced, deer can devour an entire planting in one night. In regions where their populations are exploding, deer pose one of the most serious risks to biodiversity. Their browsing removes keystone trees, shrubs, and other plants that wildlife and insects depend upon for survival. Exclosures, which we'll look at in a moment, are the most effective way to protect your wildlife habitat from deer and other critters. Exclosures can require a significant upfront investment of time and money; but where deer pressure is heavy, they are liberating for the wildlife gardener. Unfortunately, not all neighborhoods look kindly upon exclosures. If that's the case in your neighborhood, consider a combination of the following strategies:

Deer repellent strategies that offer variable protection:

Plant deer resistant plants. If deer pressure is heavy, few plants are completely safe. A plant that goes untouched in one landscape, may be devoured by deer in another. Search online for **deer resistant native plants [ZIP Code™]**. Make it a priority to grow as many deer resistant *keystone* plants as possible (see *Action 5: Identify your keystone plants*).

Install a motion-activated sprinkler. Setting it to spray only at night spares the delivery person an unexpected shower. The *Orbit 62100 Yard Enforcer® Motion-Activated Sprinkler* (*right*) is an example of this effective deer deterrent that is second only to exclosures in the protection it offers. Bringing it in for winter, if needed, and changing its batteries are the only tasks required to care for this *Orbit™* model.

Mix two or more of these ingredients in 1 gallon of water:
  4 Tbsp cayenne pepper
  3 Tbsp garlic powder
  1 egg
  1/4 tsp peppermint oil
  (or more)
Strain. Spray weekly.

Spray deer's favorite plants with homemade (*above*) **or commercial deer repellents.** An online search for **deer repellents** yields a variety of brands, such as the nontoxic *Deer Out®* or *Deer Scram™*. Read the labels carefully to verify that all the ingredients are nontoxic.

Deer repellent strategies to avoid:

Don't hang scented fabric softener dryer sheets. Most brands of dryer sheets contain extremely toxic chemicals (see page 12.11). I hung dryer sheets in small evergreen trees, and later, wherever they had been, there were 1-foot spheres of dead branches that never recovered.

Don't hang bars of fragrant soaps randomly around the garden. As with dryer sheets, soap bars (especially the fragrant ones recommended to repel deer) may contain toxic chemicals that will contaminate the soil and watershed.

Don't erect a single fence under 8 feet in height. Unfortunately, a single short fence takes considerable time to erect. Although it may deter deer momentarily, one night they'll inevitably hop over the fence and enjoy a lovely feast—at your expense!

Protect your wildlife habitat from deer and other creatures, *continued*

So innocent and oh so cute!

In contrast to fenced enclosures designed to keep animals in, **exclosures** are intended to keep animals out. The type of animal you are trying to keep out will determine the height of the exclosure as well as the most suitable materials for construction. Here, we provide directions for building exclosures to prevent deer browsing with an option for including a lower fence dug into the ground to exclude rabbits and other medium-sized creatures. Unfortunately, a lower fence poses the ecological concern of preventing turtles from freely roaming to and from your wildlife habitat.

How to erect simple exclosures to protect individual shrubs or trees

Enclose a newly planted or prized shrub or tree with a circle of garden fencing. Cut a length of garden fencing (2 x 3-inch mesh welded wire) long enough to encircle the plant. The height of the fencing should be sufficient to stand at least 18 inches above the plant's height. Drive in two stakes to hold up the fencing. If the exclosure is in the front yard, consider using decorative stakes. This approach can be used to protect smaller plants from rabbit browsing but use chicken wire and bamboo stakes instead.

Make an invisible fence using nylon fishing line. Fishing line (30-lb) can be used to erect a fence or add height above a short fence. Tie fishing line to posts 15 to 20 feet apart. A **Seed Savers Exchange** (*seedsaver.org*) blogpost gives clear directions. Search online for **inexpensive but effective deer fence seed savers exchange**. Following the same procedure, fishing line can be used to extend the height of an existing fence. This method often works surprisingly well and is visually less bothersome to neighbors than wire fences.

What is the deer population in your state? For a state-by-state analysis of deer species and their estimated populations, check out a blogpost from **Wildlife Informer** (*wildlifeinformer.com*) or search online for **wildlife informer deer populations by state**. This article considers the populations of black-tailed deer, mule deer, and white-tailed deer. As stated in the blogpost, these are population estimates only. Refer to the sources linked in the post for additional information.

How to erect double exclosures to protect large areas

Where deer pressure is heavy, fencing must be at least 8 feet high to keep deer out. The materials for such a tall fence are expensive, harder to come by, and the installation is difficult for the average DIYer. An easier alternative is to construct a 5-foot-high fence and add a second fence or obstacle. If you want to exclude rabbits and other small mammals from the area, run chicken wire along the base of the fence dug in at least 6 inches below ground level.

Primary fence: 5-foot-high fence that requires a secondary fence to exclude deer

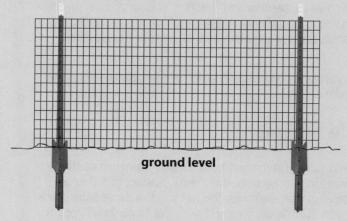

ground level

- One 50-foot roll of 5-foot-high, 2 x 3-inch mesh welded wire for each 50 feet of fence length. Green or black fencing readily blends into the landscape.

- One 8-foot metal stake for each 10 feet of fence length

- Single strand wire to tie the wire to the stakes

- Dual-handled steel fence post driver OR sledgehammer to pound in the stakes

The post driver (*right*) makes short work of stake installation enabling a person of average (or even below average) strength to easily install the stakes single-handedly.

OPTIONAL: One 50-foot roll of 3-foot high, galvanized steel chicken wire with 1-inch hexagonal openings for each 50 feet of fence length. If pressure from rabbits or other animals is heavy, you might consider 4-foot-high chicken wire dug in 12 inches.

NOTE: *Chicken wire in contact with moist soil tends to break down within about 3 years requiring monitoring and likely replacement.*

Secondary fence: Consider the following options (or a combination of these):

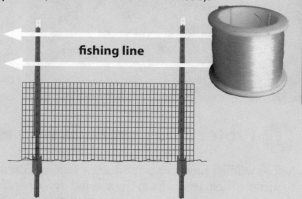

fishing line

- Two strands of 30-lb fishing line directly above the primary fence 12 to 18 inches apart (*above*)

  NOTE: *If 6-foot-high fencing is used for the primary fence, a single strand of fishing line 18 inches above the primary fence should be sufficient. Add another strand above if deer pressure is extreme.*

- Single strand of visible wire strung about 4 feet above the ground and 5 feet inside the primary fence on 5-foot stakes spaced 20 feet apart. Deer typically do not jump into enclosed spaces. Severe deer pressure may require that the secondary fence be constructed of mesh wire. In this case, 4-foot-high mesh wire can be used.

- Wide (and/or high) brush pile built lengthwise along the inside of the primary fence line leaving only enough room to walk between the pile and the fence. The average horizontal jumping distance for deer is about 10 to 15 feet. The point here is to prevent deer from perceiving there to be a safe landing place if they jump over the primary fence. A brush pile on the external side of the fence needs to be wider.

- A single strand of electric wire strung about 4 feet above the ground and 4 feet from the primary fence. Electric wire is an effective secondary fence for areas with extreme deer pressure. To prevent people from being accidentally shocked, plug the fence into an outdoor timer set to turn on only at night.

10 Protect your wildlife habitat while children are enjoying it

Sharing your wildlife habitat with children can be a strong motivator for creating a wildlife habitat . . . but there are precautions worth taking to protect the wildlife habitat from the exuberant curiosity of childhood.

Encourage children to look at small animals and insects without touching them. Not only does this protect the wildlife, but in some cases, it may protect the child as well! Encourage observation rather than collection of fascinating insects such as butterflies and fireflies. Taking photos can be a good substitute for collecting. Foster a love of nature through nature crafts, science experiments, and other nature-based projects.

Creating wildlife landscapes offers rich opportunities to engage children with nature.

11 Protect the people in your wildlife habitat

Just as wildlife needs to be protected from children, children (and grown-ups) need to take some precautions to protect themselves from the natural defenses of some our small creatures and plants. Shown together as they are here, the various dangers may give the false impression that your wildlife habitat is a dangerous place to be. In reality, these dangers are seldom encountered. If you familiarize yourself with the hazards where you live and take precautions to avoid them, you are all the more unlikely to experience firsthand their potentially painful defense mechanisms.

Learn to identify these creatures and give them a wide berth

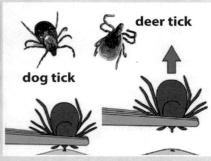

The spines of the saddleback and tussock moth caterpillars (*above*) can deliver a wallop of an itching, burning sting. To identify other toxic caterpillars, do a search with the terms **poisonous caterpillars [your state].** For example, the **Florida Poison Information Center** describes 10 stinging caterpillars along with possible symptoms and recommended treatment protocol. Get to know the poisonous caterpillars in your region so you can give them a wide berth!

Most of the snakes you may encounter in your garden such as the common garter snake (*above left*) are harmless. Although your first reaction might be to jump back with a shriek, sighting most snakes is cause for celebration as they are garden allies who control insect pests and rodent populations. That said, play it safe and learn to identify venomous snakes such as the copperhead (*above right*). Do a search with the terms **venomous snakes [your state].**

Ticks, such as the dog tick and deer tick (*above*), may be a serious concern where you live. Visit the CDC for tick ID and distribution maps (search **cdc regions where ticks live**). Do proactive prevention—suit up before heading outside; while outside, routinely scan yourself for ticks; once inside, meticulously check every body surface; make a tick removal kit to have handy.

DIY Tick Removal Kit: tweezers, clear tape (wrap tick up in tape without touching it and seal in a plastic bag for identification and/or disposal), rubbing alcohol or soap and water, triple antibiotic cream.

Protect the people in your wildlife habitat, *continued*

Poison ivy (*left*), poison oak (*middle*), and poison sumac (*right*) are a trio of native plants notorious for causing itchy, blistering rashes. Interestingly, some people can work with these plants and be unaffected; of course, for those who are allergic, it's a whole different story!

Wherever there is enough space away from human activity, allowing these plants to grow provides great benefit to wildlife. Insects feed on the flowers, and mammals, reptiles, amphibians, and birds eat the leaves and berries which provide nourishment in the fall and winter.

Here are more native plants that should be placed carefully if planted:

Prickly or thorny plants or plants with burs: holly (*Ilex; left*), hawthorn (*Crataegus*), white avens (*Geum canadense*)
Rash-causing plants: Virginia creeper (*Parthenocissus quinquefolia*), trumpet creeper (*Campsis radicans; middle*)
Poisonous plants, if ingested: pokeweed (*Phytolacca americana; right*), raw elderberries (*Sambucus canadensis*), milkweed sap (*Asclepias*)

To learn more, do an online search with the terms: **toxic native plants [your state].**

2
Protect

How to safely remove single plants or very small patches of poison ivy, oak, or sumac:

Step 1: Gather used plastic bags and a gardening knife or shovel. Loosen the soil where the plant is growing.

Step 2: Open a bag wide and set it on the ground. Grab another bag and put it over your dominant hand.

Step 3: Reach for the base of the plant and pull. Do this carefully to avoid coming in contact with any part of the plant.

Step 4: Use additional bags to contain any straggling plant parts. Put the plant and bags in the open bag from *Step 2* for disposal.

Prepare yourself for action!

Before heading outside, consider protecting yourself from head to toe:

Extra-long brimmed hat (worn over the hoodie) and sunglasses

Lightweight, long-sleeved, UV-protection hoodie and sunscreen

Work gloves such as these compostable gloves

Tucked in pants or rubber bands around pant cuffs (especially in tick-infested regions)

Digging in deeper

Here are additional helpful resources about protecting your wildlife habitat and its residents (please refer to the Appendix for publication details).

Nature's Best Hope: A New Approach to Conservation That Starts in Your Yard: Doug describes potential hazards to wildlife and the safeguards needed to protect wildlife (see pages 208 - 209).

In ***The Humane Gardener: Nurturing a Backyard Habitat for Wildlife: How to Create a Sustainable and Ethical Garden that Promotes Native Wildlife, Plants, and Biodiversity,*** Nancy Lawson promotes a gentle and conscientious approach to caring for our landscapes.

The magnitude of the crisis of bird glass-strikes: A leading expert on the mortality of birds due to glass windows, Daniel Klem Jr. has dedicated this entire book (as well as his professional career) to building awareness and finding solutions to this bird population decimator. His book ***Solid Air: Invisible Killer—Saving Billions of Birds from Windows*** takes a scientific deep dive into both the problem and what happens physically to the bird victims. Klem then takes an equally comprehensive look at what can be done to solve this modern-day crisis.

Are deer devouring your landscape? In ***Deer-Resistant Design: Fence-free Gardens That Thrive Despite Deer***, Karen Chapman offers palettes of 10 deer-resistant plants for various regions in the U.S. The book features a variety of gardens that remain lovely despite deer pressure along with practical advice and inspiring tips. Many books offer deer-resistant plant lists, but so often their suggestions include introduced and even invasive plants—deer's distaste for invasive plants is a primary reason for their success! Ruth Clausen and Gregory Tepper, in ***Deer-Resistant Native Plants for the Northeast,*** profile deer resistant plants of the northeastern United States. For other regions, searching online for **deer resistant native plants [region/state]** yields useful lists of deer-resistant native plants.

In ***5 Surprising Things that Could Be Preventing Your Backyard from Serving as a Wildlife Sanctuary,*** Doug Tallamy, Daniel Klem, and Jim Cubie give a short, but impactful, punch list of actions (also discussed in this guide) that must be taken BEFORE attracting wildlife to your landscape.

The **Humane Society of the United States'**s *Pool safety for wild animals: Simple ways to save the lives of your wild neighbors* provides tips for protecting wildlife around pools. Search online for **humane society pool safety.**

A crash course in deer behavior, deterrents, and landscaping tips, the Master Gardeners of Northern Virginia's video ***Browsers of the Garden Buffet: Deer*** presented by Kathie Clements has it all. Search for its title online. If deer are a problem in your landscape, this video is a must-watch!

Have you ever thought about rehabilitating wildlife? The Pennsylvania Association of Wildlife Rehabilitators offers a free 2-hour series of videos *Introduction to Wildlife Rehabilitation* that covers the nitty-gritty details of becoming a wildlife rehabilitator. Visit **pawr.com**. In the left menu, click on **Becoming a Wildlife Rehabilitator in Pennsylvania. Is it for you?** Regardless of where you live, this introduction will give you a front-line perspective of what it takes to be a wildlife rehabilitator. Is wildlife rehabilitation for you?

Water-exit devices to help prevent animal drownings: *Froglog* (froglog.us); *Skamper-Ramp®* (skamper-ramp-store.com)

Glass-strike prevention product database: American Bird Conservancy (abcbirds.org)

Motion-activated sprinkler to deter deer: Yard Enforcer® Motion-Activated Sprinkler (orbitonline.com)

We've explored many ways to protect your wildlife habitat and the creatures and people within it. Later in this guide, we'll look at an important action that not only protects wildlife habitat but also our personal health—avoiding the use of toxic chemicals in our landscape and in our homes. But next, we'll look at shrinking the lawn so that we can replace it with ecologically beneficial plants.

Action 3—CHECKLIST
Shrink the lawn

Step:	✔	Action Needed:	Page:
1	☐	Check if there is a lawn conversion rebate program in your area	3.4
2	☐	Make a plan to shrink your lawn in stages	3.4
3	☐	Decide which area(s) of your lawn to shrink first	3.5
4	☐	Review nontoxic methods for removing lawn	3.5
5	☐	Choose which lawn removal method(s) to use	3.14
6	☐	Start collecting the materials needed for removing lawn	3.14
7	☐	CAUTION: Before digging, call 811 to get your utility lines marked	3.15
8	☐	Shrink your lawn!	3.15

BEFORE: Extensive lawn provides no hazard-free wildlife habitat.

AFTER: Native trees, shrubs, and herbaceous plants begin to offer safe habitat.

3

Lawn

Coming soon . . . .

WILDLIFE HABITAT!

Action 3—GUIDE

Shrink the lawn

Limiting grass to useful places such as pathways frees up space to plant ecologically beneficial plants.

Since lawn demands significant resources, negatively affects the environment, and does little (and often nothing) to support wildlife, our goal here is to limit lawn to the areas where lawn is truly needed. In this action, we first explain how to check if there is a lawn conversion rebate program in your area. Next, we look at how to choose which areas of lawn to keep and which to remove. Then, we look at nontoxic methods for removing lawn. For each method, we consider the pros and cons, list the materials needed, and provide a step-by-step how-to guide.

In later actions, we'll share options for areas of your landscape where you would like to preserve the visual effect of lawn but increase its ecological services. Although few of these alternatives tolerate the typical traffic of a turf lawn, we'll discuss replacing lawn with native grasses and sedges (*Carex*), pollinator-friendly bee lawns, mosses, meadows, and prairie gardens. When thinking about what to do with areas where lawn is removed, remember that the best replacement for lawn is a landscape filled from ground to sky with keystone plants as we'll explain later.

For lawn that stays, be sure to practice the eco-friendly mowing and lawn care methods that we discussed in the previous action. These will protect the wild visitors and residents of your wildlife habitat.

The only good thing about endless lawn is the endless potential it holds for becoming wildlife habitat!

① Check if there is a lawn conversion rebate program in your area

Some municipalities sponsor lawn conversion or landscaping rebate programs for property owners who convert their lawns to drought tolerant or wildlife plantings. Lawn conversion programs may provide you with expertise specific to your region, rebates, or other resources. If there is a program in your area, the extra support it provides may mean you'll be able to shrink a larger portion of your lawn sooner. Be sure to find out the requirements for a program BEFORE starting work on removing lawn as some programs require pre-approval and won't support projects in progress.

Rebate programs are offered by a variety of agencies. The more drought-prone your region is, the more options there may be due to the need to conserve water. For example, a utility district in Northern California offers landscape design assistance and higher rebates for residents who follow ecological best practices; in Southern California, a water district gives generous per-foot rebates along with design resources and plant lists; and a county in Florida offers residents an incentive for participating in a class about landscaping basics.

To find out if a lawn conversion rebate program is available where you live, search online for **lawn conversion rebate [your city or state]** or **landscaping rebate [your city or state].**

Is there a rebate program currently available in your area? Check it out!

② Make a plan to shrink your lawn in stages

It may be tempting to remove a huge expanse of lawn all in one go. Instead, consider your resources carefully. When transitioning conventional landscapes to wildlife-rich habitats, the early years require time both to install and maintain plantings. The action steps in this guide will help you to get an idea of what is realistic without becoming overwhelmed. Let's get started!

Draw a rough sketch of your property. Later, we'll look at making detailed plans for your wildlife habitat. For now, a quick sketch is fine. (See pages 8.2 and 15.2 for extra blank grids.)

Mark your plan with the areas of lawn that you want to keep. This might include:

- areas where your family or pets play
- sections of your lawn that you want to keep for aesthetic reasons
- grass pathways between current and future landscape beds.

At this point, you may not know which areas of lawn you want to keep or remove. That's just fine! These decisions will become easier as you create your wildlife habitat. For example, as you add landscape beds, your network of paths will evolve along with your wildlife habitat. We'll be discussing landscape design in later actions.

③ Decide which area(s) of your lawn to shrink first

You may know exactly which area of your lawn to remove first, but if you're unsure, consider the following factors. It makes sense to start by removing lawn in areas that are:

In the middle of the lawn and could become an island bed (*above*) to serve as a refuge for small creatures fleeing for safety during mowing.

Time-consuming to mow such as around individual trees. A kidney-shaped bed planted with natives would be much easier to mow around than these three solo trees!

Growing poorly and looking crummy anyway. Many native plant species thrive in poor soil like this.

Under trees where soft landings are needed to encourage caterpillar pupation. Plus, not mowing is better for the trees.

Other areas to consider removing lawn from first include areas that are:

- **hidden from public view**—Consider starting with places on your property where transitioning to wildlife-friendly plantings is easier such as areas hidden from public view that can sport a wilder look.

- **dangerous to mow**—Why take the risk of mowing areas that are dangerous to mow, such as slopes or along heavily traveled roads, when you could have a lovely display of native plants instead?

④ Review nontoxic methods for removing lawn

Now, let's take a close look at some ways lawn can be removed without resorting to toxic chemicals. Get ready to hone your lawn-shrinking superpowers.

Shrink the lawn: METHOD A—Block it!

This low-cost method of converting lawn to garden beds uses cardboard or other blocking materials and mulching materials to smother the lawn. This is a good project any time of the year but avoid doing this on a windy day!

PROs	CONs
• No digging is needed unless the soil is compacted. • Disrupting the soil and its micro life is avoided, unless digging is needed to loosen compacted soil. • Blocking will kill most lawns. • Materials that otherwise may end up in a landfill are reused. • This method is inexpensive or free. • No harmful chemicals are used.	• Usually, a full growing season is needed to kill the lawn before the area is ready for planting. • Lots of blocking and mulching materials must be gathered. • The area may look unattractive unless you have access to a top layer of attractive mulch. • Care must be taken when walking on the laid-out materials to avoid injuring toads, lizards, and other creatures that may have taken shelter underneath. • **Rhizomatous** grasses and invasives (species with long, string-like runner roots) may be weakened but not killed. A longer blocking period or a supplemental method such as the *Dig it!* method may be required.

MATERIALS:

Biodegradable **blocking materials**: plain cardboard and/or newspaper. Remove any staples, stickers, or tape from the cardboard and avoid wax-coated and color-printed materials (unless you can confirm that the ink is eco-friendly). Old rugs made of natural fibers are a good blocking material for uneven surfaces such as rocky areas or brush piles that are overrun with invasive vines.

NOTE: *Non-biodegradable materials such as old plastic, tarps, or synthetic fiber rugs can be used as a blocking material and removed when the area is ready for planting; however, the beneficial interaction between the soil and mulching material is lost.*

Biodegradable **mulching materials**: wood chips, mulch, leaves, grass clippings, trimmings from your yard, and the like. To get a large quantity of wood chips, check out *chipdrop.com* (see page 3.16). For smaller quantities, contact local arborists who often welcome a place to dump their chips.

NOTE: *Avoid rubberized mulches. Use commercial mulch only as a last resort after verifying its composition (see page 7.9).*

3

Lawn

Shrink the lawn: METHOD A—Block it!, *continued*

Plan and mark the area and shape of the bed. A hose or rope is helpful here. Or mark the perimeter by sprinkling flour or sand.

String trim the weeds. This is optional, but it does help the blocking material to lie flat.

Collect enough **blocking** material to cover the area without gaps AND enough **mulching** materials to cover the blocked area 2 to 3 inches deep.

Soak the **blocking** materials overnight or longer (unless rain is forecast). Don't soak newspaper ahead of time because it clumps together and becomes difficult to separate. (This step is optional.)

Lay out the blocking material, so that pieces overlap and there are no gaps except for spots left open for immediate planting of trees, shrubs, or accent plants (optional). If using newspaper, use sections at least 10 sheets thick and water it in place.

Spread the mulching material over the blocking material to a depth of 2 to 3 inches. Make sure there is a thick enough layer of mulching material to hold down the blocking material in case of heavy winds.

Water the area unless rain is forecast (optional). This helps hold the materials in place but is unnecessary if the layers feel stable.

If spots were left open for trees, shrubs, or accent plants, these can be planted now. Dig as little as possible to avoid damaging the underground network of microorganisms.

Wait one growing season or more until the blocking material has smothered the grass. Plant the bed, digging minimally to avoid soil disturbance. Here an old rug has readied an area for planting.

Shrink the lawn: METHOD B—Bake it!

Cover an area with clear plastic. This process is called **solarization** since it uses the sun's rays to increase the soil temperature. Especially during hot summer months, solarization may kill soil pathogens, nematodes, and weed seeds to a depth of 6 inches as well as most small weeds growing in the area.

PROs	CONs
• Minimal labor is required, the sun does most the work.	• Full sun is required for this method to be effective.
• Disrupting the soil and its micro life is avoided, unless digging is needed to loosen compacted soil.	• Depending upon the vigor of the lawn underneath and the amount of sunlight, this method may take time.
• This method is free.	• The plastic looks unattractive in the landscape.
• No harmful chemicals are used.	• Unless the plastic is reused and otherwise would have gone to the landfill, this approach should be avoided.
	• Heat from solarization may kill beneficial microorganisms, but they will recolonize.

MATERIALS:

Used clear plastic that otherwise would go to the landfill, such as old shower curtains or paint drop cloths. Sturdy, clear plastic bags or pieces of bubble wrap can be repurposed by stitching them together to form a large sheet.

NOTE: *This method is most effective during sunny, hot weather when the sun's rays are trapped by the clear plastic generating heat that helps kill the lawn. In cooler weather, clear plastic may act as a greenhouse and protect the unwanted plants instead of killing them.*

Weights to hold down the plastic, such as stones, bricks, or logs

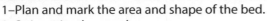

1–Plan and mark the area and shape of the bed.
2–String trim the weeds.
3–Collect weights and enough used clear plastic to cover the area without gaps (*above*).

4–Lay out the plastic so that pieces overlap without gaps (*above*).
5–Secure the plastic with enough stones, bricks, or logs so that it will stay in place even in heavy wind (*above*).
6–Wait through a growing season or longer until the plants underneath the blocking material are dead.
7–Plant the bed, digging as little as possible to avoid soil disturbance.

Shrink the lawn: METHOD C—No-dig it!

No-till farming and no-dig gardening is gaining popularity. This approach minimizes soil disturbance protecting the delicate soil structure and beneficial soil microorganisms. For heavily compacted soils, a single initial digging can be done to break up compaction; however, usually even with the most barren soil, soil disturbance can be avoided with a little patience (OK, a lot of patience!). The trick is to allow your plants' roots to do the work of loosening compaction. Here, we explain how to use biodegradable blocking materials and topsoil to make a no-dig bed of your own so that your plants can do the work for you.

PROs	CONs
• Poor soil that is hard to dig can be converted to a garden bed without backbreaking manual labor.	• Unless you have topsoil leftover from a project, getting enough topsoil may be expensive, and a high-quality source of topsoil may be hard to find.
• A bed can be ready to plant as soon as you've laid down cardboard and spread topsoil over it.	• Rhizomatous grasses are likely to survive underneath the bed and infiltrate the planted bed.
• This approach shares a raised bed's advantage of being instantly ready to plant but without the cost and possible toxicity of the frame materials, plus it requires less topsoil than a raised bed.	• If the soil underneath is poor, you may be limited to planting annuals and small perennials for a year or more, but you can use the *Dig it!* method for spots in the bed where you would like to place a shrub or tree right away.

3

Lawn

MATERIALS:

Cardboard or other biodegradable material, enough to cover the area well

Topsoil, enough to cover the area at least 6 inches deep

Optional: **Spading or digging fork** (4 sturdy tines) **or broad fork** (5 or more sturdy tines) for loosening severely compacted soil. This is only necessary if soil is severely compacted soil.

NOTE: *Pitch forks and stable forks lack the strength to loosen soil compaction.*

1–Plan and mark the area and shape of the bed (*above*).
2–String trim the weeds (*above*).
3–Collect enough cardboard to cover the area overlapping the pieces of cardboard at least 4 inches without any gaps.

4–Cover the cardboard with topsoil at least 6 inches deep. Once the topsoil is in place, the bed is ready to plant with small plants (forbs, grasses, sedges, mosses, or ferns). Choose tough native plants that have a reputation for being easy to grow.

5–If the weather is not ideal for planting, cover the area with mulch or wood chips. With time, underlying good soil will become better and poor soil will become more friable making it possible to plant shrubs and trees with less effort.

Shrink the lawn: METHOD D—Let it creep!

With this method, your existing plants do most of the work! As the plants in your garden beds expand in width, rather than trimming them to fit the bed, allow them to cast shade over the lawn. As the grass weakens or dies, it's easy to pull out. If there is a border, such as loosely placed flat stones or bricks, simply move the border out making a new border for the bed. This method works especially well in areas where overhead trees cast added shade. This is not a speedy method, but it's gentle and allows nature to take its course.

PROs	CONs
• No materials are needed other than thriving plants.	• Patience is required as it takes time for plants to grow.
• Minimal labor is required since the existing plants do the work for you.	• Lush growth is required to shade the grass underneath.
• Disrupting the soil and its micro life is avoided, unless digging is needed to loosen compacted soil.	• Hardscape borders (such as mortared stone borders) prevent the use of this method.
• No harmful chemicals are used.	

MATERIALS:

Happy plants thriving in your landscape beds

As the plants in your garden beds expand in width, allow them to hang over the lawn, rather than trimming them to fit the bed.

After the shaded area of grass weakens, pull it out if needed. In many cases, the shade from the creeping plants kills the grass, doing the work for you!

If there is a border of stones or bricks, simply move the stones or bricks out to form a new border for the bed.

Collateral damage from mowing

Although lawn offers few ecological services, animals nevertheless travel across the lawn or make their homes among the grass blades. Inevitably, these unsuspecting creatures become collateral damage as lawn mowers pass overhead.

One potential victim is the American grass spider (*Agelenopsis*). These spiders build a funnel-shaped web with a platform in front of it and a web of threads above it. Insects fly into the web above and fall onto the platform. The very speedy grass spider quickly captures its prey.

Shrink the lawn: METHOD E—Let it grow!

Although this method sounds like a suggestion to simply stop mowing an area, doing that usually leads to a tangled mess of non-native grasses and invasive volunteers. Nor is this method synonymous with converting lawn to meadow. (For more about meadows, see pages 11.17 - 11.18.) This method is useful where native plants are trying to grow but are continually held back by regular mowing.

This method need not be limited to low-growing plants. In one area of my yard (*right*), 6-foot-tall Joe-Pye weed (*Eutrochium purpureum*) and evening primrose (*Oenothera biennis*) that I originally planted from packets of seed have seeded themselves and replaced lawn with a sturdy stand of pollinator and butterfly magnets. In partially shaded areas of my lawn, violet (*Viola*; see photos below) sows itself. When I stop mowing such areas, violets broadly take over and only occasional weeding is needed.

PROs	CONs
• No materials are needed other than thriving plants.	• Neighbors may object to nature's wildness.
• Minimal labor is required, unless there is a heavy intrusion of invasive plants.	• Along with the desired native species, invasive plants may self-sow and require removal.
• Disrupting the soil and its micro life is avoided, unless digging is needed to loosen compacted soil.	• This method may not be an option in arid regions where fire risk is high.

MATERIALS:

Aggressive native plants already growing in the lawn

Here, violets are starting to establish a presence in the lawn. Since violets are a low-growing plant, mowing may continue until the violets dominate the area. Set the mower to its maximum height and pause mowing or use a string trimmer during bloom and seed production.

Stop regular mowing when the native plants have outcompeted the grass. Monitor the area for invasives and remove them at once. This will save you future work! Above, the invasive creeping Charlie (*Glechoma hederacea*) needs removal.

If an occasional trimming is needed, cut the area with a string trimmer to 6 inches or higher. The higher trimming height gives desired plants the opportunity to flower and produce seed. It also helps to avoid disrupting insect life cycles and injuring or killing frogs, toads, turtles, and other small creatures.

NOTE: *You may wish to add native trees, shrubs, and other plants to these areas.*

Shrink the lawn: METHOD F—Stop watering it!

In arid regions, removing your lawn in preparation for replacing it with native vegetation may be as simple as not watering it. But beware of grass species that go dormant and burst forth with growth as soon as watering is resumed. Removal of such species will likely require a different method (and persistence!).

PROs	CONs
• There is no cost as no materials are needed. • Minimal labor is required since the lack of water does the work for you. • No harmful chemicals are used.	• Neighbors may not appreciate the dry period as the lawn is transitioned to native plantings. • Some grass species may appear dead but spring forth with life when watering resumes. • This method may not be an option in arid regions where there is a risk of fire.

1 Choose an area where the lawn will die if it doesn't receive regular water.

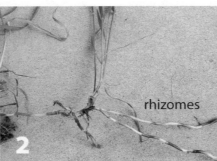
rhizomes

2 If possible, identify the grass species growing in the lawn to determine if the roots are rhizomatous and will need to be removed using a different method.

Coming soon . . .
WILDLIFE HABITAT!

3 For this method and the others, you may wish to put up temporary signage to let neighbors know that your landscape is in transition. (See page 3.2 for a full-size copy of the sign above.)

Shrink the lawn: METHOD G—Dig it!

This free—but labor-intensive—method involves digging up the living grass with its roots. Once the grass layer is removed, depending on the condition of the soil underneath, you may be able to plant right away. This method should be considered a last resort. When possible, soil disturbance should be avoided because it destroys the soil structure and disrupts the microorganisms that bring life to the soil. Reserve this method for:

• areas filled with invasive plants whose roots must be removed to prevent regrowth

• areas where the soil is heavily compacted (soil surface is not easily penetrated with a shovel) or where there is hard layer several inches below the surface that is impenetrable

• situations when a landscape bed needs to be installed quickly and other methods such as *Block it!* may take too long or be impractical, for example, when strict homeowners association (HOA) rules are in place.

PROs	CONs
• This method is a quick way to convert a small area of lawn into a bed ready for planting. • There is no cost as no materials are needed. • No harmful chemicals are used. • The removed **sod** (combination of grass, roots, and soil attached to roots) can be composted or turned upside down and piled elsewhere to create a mound that can be planted later, or the fully decomposed sod can be used later where topsoil is needed.	• Physical labor (and a strong back!) is needed. • Soil disturbance destroys soil structure and disrupts the soil micro life. • Soil disturbance exposes the **seed bank** (see page 4.5) which is likely to be mostly invasive species in the early years of transitioning to native plantings. • Plants with rhizomatous roots such as Bermuda grass are difficult to control with this method as every last piece of root must be removed.

1–Plan and mark the area and shape of the bed.
2–String trim the weeds.
3–With a shovel, slice the perimeter of the area (red arrows).

4–Cut strips approximately 7 - 8 inches wide in both directions (red arrows). This creates "chunks of sod" that are easy to handle.

5–Lift out a sod chunk taking as little soil as possible with it. Put your shovel blade on its side and beat the chunk of sod against the edge of the shovel to shake off the soil. This helps keep the topsoil on site and reduces the amount of material needing removal.

6–Pile the removed material in an out-of-the-way place to decompose. Once all the sod is removed, avoid additional digging unless the soil is heavily compacted.

7–If the soil is heavily compacted, you may need to thrust a shovel or a sturdy multi-tine digging fork (see page 3.9) into the soil in a grid pattern. Heave the soil upward without turning it. This aerates the soil and shouldn't need to be done again.

8–The area can be planted right away. If it's not an ideal time to plant, instead immediately cover the ground (at least temporarily) with a 2-inch layer of mulch (see page 11.9) until conditions permit planting.

3

Lawn

5 Choose which lawn removal method(s) to use

Consider which methods for shrinking your lawn will work best for different areas of your lawn. Put a check by the method(s) that you'll use and note the areas where you'll use them:

✔	Method	Area(s) to use this method
☐	Method A—**Block it!**	
☐	Method B—**Bake it!**	
☐	Method C—**No-dig it!**	
☐	Method D—**Let it creep!**	
☐	Method E—**Let it grow!**	
☐	Method F—**Stop watering!**	
☐	Method G—**Dig it!**	

6 Start collecting the materials needed for removing lawn

It can take time to accumulate enough blocking and mulching material, so start piling up these materials now in a hidden corner of your property:

Cardboard boxes can be flattened and stored outside for several months with a heavy block on the stack, so they don't blow away. After storing cardboard, be careful when picking it up as toads and snakes may be appreciating the shelter.

Leaves can be stored in a cage made from a circle of fencing and several stakes. Keeping leaves slightly moist will help them decompose and form **leaf mold** (decomposed leaves) more quickly, although leaves are a good mulching material at any stage of decomposition.

Wood chip piles can heat up as they start to decompose. Monitor your pile. Turning a pile helps prevent it from overheating. If it's heating up, turn it with a pitchfork or with a 16-tine stable fork which makes the task easier. High levels of heat can cause a wood chip pile to internally combust.

7 CAUTION: Before digging, call 811 to get your utility lines marked

Before digging, **call 811**, the national call-before-you-dig phone number. Allow several days prior to the start of digging for utility companies to come to your property to mark the approximate location of buried utilities. Prevent property damage, costly repairs, injuries, and even death by making this important call!

Call before you dig! Visit **call811.com**

Call 811 before digging!

Learn more by visiting the website: **call811.com** or by calling **811 In Your State.**

On the website, click on your state for phone number(s) and website(s) specific to your state.

RED:	Electric Power Lines, Cables, Conduit and Lighting Cables
YELLOW:	Gas, Oil, Steam, Petroleum or Gaseous Materials
ORANGE:	Communication, Alarm or Signal Lines, Cables or Conduit
BLUE:	Potable Water
PURPLE:	Reclaimed Water, Irrigation and Slurry Lines
GREEN:	Sewer and Drain Lines

Utility lines are marked with color-coded flags and/or painted lines.

8 Shrink your lawn!

Use the "how-to" steps shown earlier to implement the lawn removal methods you chose (or develop a creative method of your own) and start shrinking your lawn!

BEFORE: This area was an uninteresting expanse of lawn requiring mowing.

AFTER: The perennial native plants now growing here require little care—and no mowing!

Each time I shrink the lawn, even by the smallest amount such as by letting a bed creep out or blocking a small section to plant a shrub, I calculate the square footage of lawn that has been reduced and appreciate the slow but steady progress I am making.

Over time each square foot adds up. What once was a barren, endless lawn is now a functioning ecosystem filled with dense layers of plants and a wildlife community alive with movement and song.

Digging in deeper

Here are additional helpful resources for shrinking your lawn (please refer to the Appendix for publication details).

Nature's Best Hope: A New Approach to Conservation That Starts in Your Yard: Doug focuses on shrinking the lawn and explains why this is such a critical step toward supporting biodiversity (see pages 51 - 59 and 205). He also discusses the sociocultural perspectives that keep our home landscapes blanketed in a monoculture of lawn and offers an inspiring call for us to act before it's too late for our actions to matter.

In ***Lawns into Meadows: Growing a Regenerative Landscape***, landscape designer Owen Wormser provides an easy-to-read introduction to converting lawns to meadows. He explains the basics of establishing a meadow and includes color photos and 21 profiles of meadow plants such as butterfly weed, smooth blue aster, wild bergamot, and switchgrass.

Bee City USA (*beecityusa.org*): An initiative of the Xerces Society, *Bee City USA* provides resources to help people shrink their lawns and reduce mowing of remaining lawn areas. Learn how to support bees coming out of hibernation by providing them with a well-timed sequence of blooms. View past webinars and videos.

In the video ***Kill Your Lawn with Dan Jaffe Wilder***, ecologist, horticulturist, and botanist Dan Jaffe Wilder gives an entertaining and compelling argument urging people to replace their lawns with native plants. To watch, search online for the title. His practical firsthand advice and examples are inspiring.

Wood chips: Quantities of wood chips are nice to have on hand for pathways and for blocking large areas of lawn. **ChipDrop** (*getchipdrop.com*) connects people who want wood chips with the arborists and landscapers needing a place to dump them. To determine if this would work for you, search online for two videos produced by **ChipDrop**: *Why CHIPDROP Probably Is NOT for You* and *So You Really DO Want a ChipDrop*. If you would like a load of chips, sign up is free on the **ChipDrop** website.

Now that the process of shrinking the lawn is well underway, we'll shift our attention to the next critical step toward restoring biodiversity: removing invasive plants.

Action 4—CHECKLIST
Remove invasive plants

Step:	✔	Action Needed:	Page:
1	☐	Don't purchase, share, or plant invasive plant species	4.6
2	☐	Note the locations of invasive plants growing on your property	4.7
3	☐	Learn to identify invasive plant species so that you can help eradicate them • Use plant identification apps to identify invasive plant species • Use the ***National Invasive Species Information Center*** **(NISIC)** to learn about the most problematic invasive plants • Use **EDDMapS** to view the distribution of invasive plant species in your region • Use the ***Invasive Plant Atlas*** **(*Invasive.org*)** to learn more about invasive plant species	4.8
4	☐	Remove invasives—NOW is the time to start removing invasive plants from your property!	4.16
5	☐	Get involved with local and regional organizations to help remove invasive species from natural areas	4.21

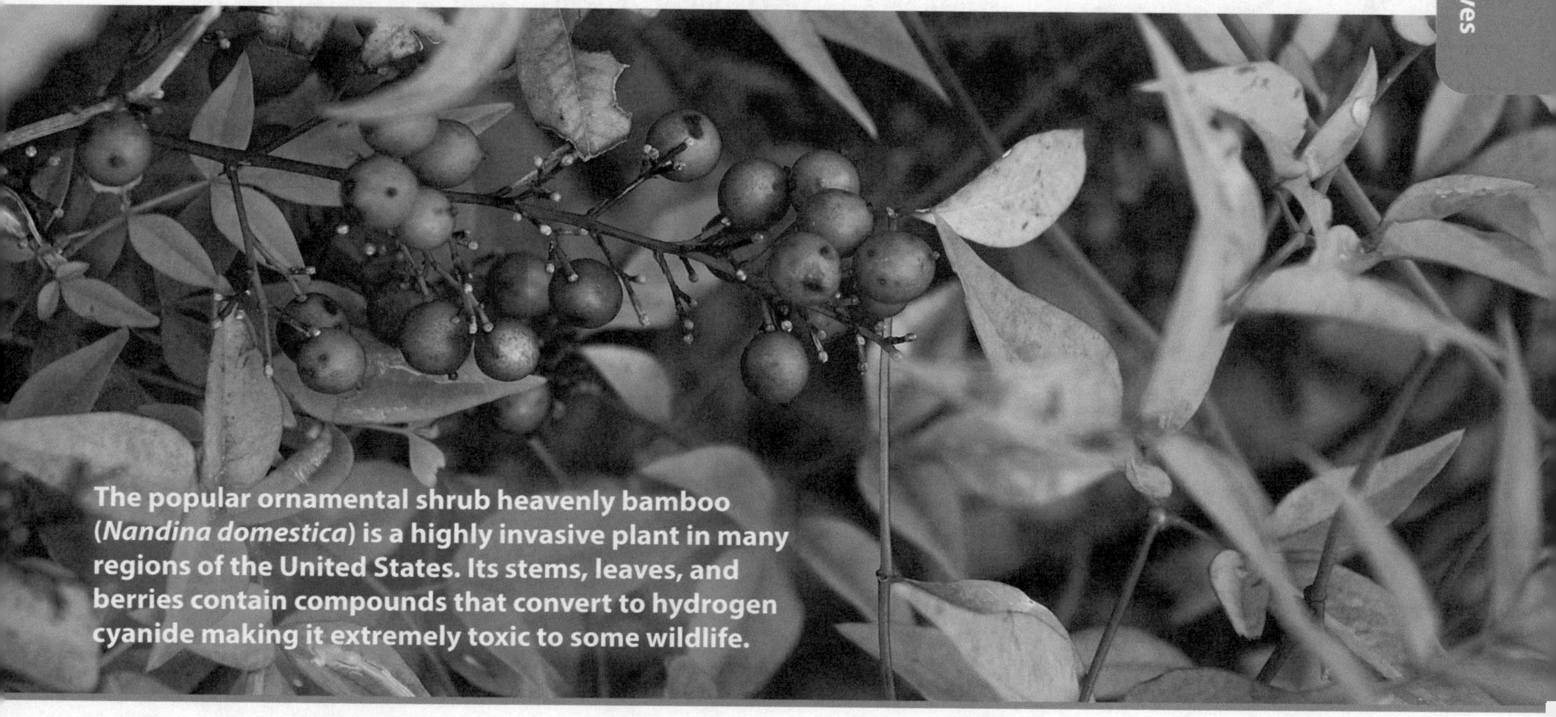

The popular ornamental shrub heavenly bamboo (*Nandina domestica*) is a highly invasive plant in many regions of the United States. Its stems, leaves, and berries contain compounds that convert to hydrogen cyanide making it extremely toxic to some wildlife.

Removing invasive plants from your property helps to protect wildlands

Our nation's forests, our coastlines, and our regional and national parks are at risk from invasive plants that escape from our home landscapes. These invasive species stress the woodlands, prairies, deserts, and waterways that are our greatest natural resources. The good news is that when you remove invasive plants from your property, you help to prevent the spread of these invaders and help to protect your local wildlands.

Still widely planted: The Norway maple (*Acer platanoides; left*) outcompetes native saplings preventing native forest regeneration. Roots that grow close to the surface inhibit the forest's native understory growth along with the populations of animals and organisms that depend on a rich, native plant-filled ecosystem.

Fast food joint for butterflies? As its name implies, butterfly-bush (*Buddleja davidii aka Buddleia davidii; right*) is a butterfly magnet. The jury appears to be out regarding the quality of the nectar, but the troubling concern is this plant's tendency to escape our home landscapes and invade forests displacing native plant communities. Luckily, the many beautiful native alternatives make eliminating butterfly-bush from our landscapes an easy decision.

Beauty and the (lack of) beasts: It is hard to deny the visual appeal of purple loosestrife (*Lythrum salicaria aka L. virgatum; left and below*), but its rampant spread has a devastating impact on wetlands and waterways smothering large areas of native grasses, cattails, and rare aquatic plants that wildlife depends on. Without a source of food, cover, and reproduction sites, native communities of animals and micro life cannot survive.

Action 4—GUIDE
Remove invasive plants

Alas, although it's a symbol of love and friendship, ivy (*Hedera*) is no friend to our wildlife habitats where it aggressively smothers the natural plant communities that it overtakes.

Plants that are **introduced** to a country or region are considered **non-native**, **alien**, or **exotic** species. When restoring landscapes to wildlife habitat, introduced plants occupy space in the landscape that otherwise could be used by native plants that offer significantly more wildlife support. Far more worrisome are the introduced plants that compete aggressively and cause extreme damage to the natural ecosystems they invade. These aggressive plants are called **invasive** species.

Invasive plant species outcompete and often kill the native plants they overtake. When a native plant species disappears from an ecosystem, the wildlife depending upon it will also disappear. Unfortunately, there are numerous species of invasive plants including many that are still available for purchase. In this action, we share tools to help you identify the invasive species you are most likely to encounter and offer ways to remove them to make room for native plants that will welcome and support the wildlife in your yard.

Asiatic bittersweet (*Celastrus orbiculatus*) is an aggressive, invasive vine that climbs up trees weighing down and breaking branches and strangling trees to death.

Why are invasive plants so successful?

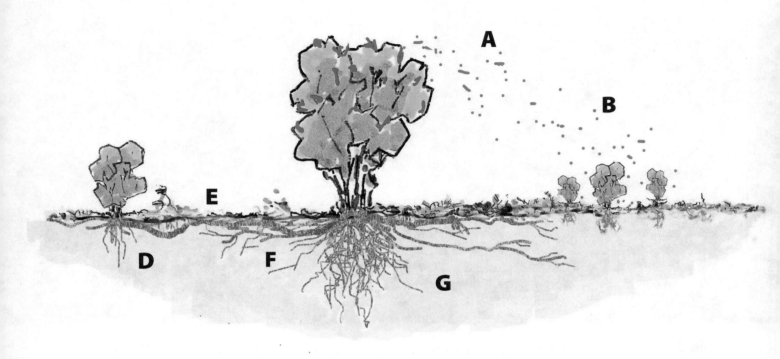

Invasive plant species have **one or more** of these qualities:

A Plants produce **large quantities of seeds**

B Seeds are **easily dispersed** by wind or water

C Seeds are **transported near and far by animals or people**

D **Aggressive root systems** spread long distances from the parent plant and send up new plants

E Plants **grow well in disturbed soil** (soil that is recently dug or left bare)

F **Dense root systems** crowd out the roots of nearby plants

G Roots and leaves produce **allelopathic chemicals** that inhibit the growth of other plants

H Plants reach out with **vines that strangle** native vegetation

I Plants grow rapidly shading out or **smothering the native vegetation** underneath

J Plants **lack natural predators, parasites, or competitors**

K Plants have a **longer growing season** than native species greening up earlier and staying green longer helping the species to outcompete native species

L Control methods are limited, and **eradication is extremely difficult** to achieve due to resistance to chemical herbicides, aggressive regrowth, or other factors

M Plants have beautiful flowers, evergreen foliage, or delicious fruit, so **humans buy and plant them!**

4

Invasives

Why are invasive plants so successful?, *continued*

NOTE: *The letters in the photographs below correspond to the diagram on the previous page.*

A single plant of stiltgrass (*Microstegium vimineum*) can produce up to 1,000 seeds that are **viable** (alive and able to germinate) for 3 years or more. Such prodigious seed production makes it very hard to keep up with removal.

Some plants in the Aster family (*Asteraceae*) such as thistles produce **pappus** (fluffy tufts attached to each seed) that work like a parachute to carry the seed away in the wind.

Birds feast on the berries of invasive plants such as this Amur honeysuckle (*Lonicera maackii*). Later the birds fly away and deposit the seeds elsewhere.

People and lawn mowers spread seeds embedded in the mud on their shoes and tires. Some invasive plants have seeds that stick to clothing and animal fur.

Invasive plants that spread by **rhizomes** (underground stems that root) or **stolons** (horizontally growing stems that may root and form new plants) can quickly dominate an area. Removal is challenging because even a tiny piece of the plant may produce a new plant.

Disturbed soil is an invitation for invasive plants to take over. Disruption exposes seeds in the **seed bank** (an accumulation of viable seeds stored in the soil) to sunlight causing germination. Invasive plant species often outcompete any native species seeds that germinate.

Allelopathic plants such as garlic mustard (*Alliaria petiolata*) release biochemicals in the soil that inhibit the growth and survival of surrounding plants.

Year-round foliage offering privacy and ornamental interest spurs the distribution of many invasive species. Laws are increasingly in place to ban their sale.

Ornamental plants with beautiful flowers have been the driving force in landscape design for centuries resulting in the widespread dispersal of invasives.

① Don't purchase, share, or plant invasive plant species

Sadly, many invasive species are still widely propagated and sold in wholesale and retail nurseries. In a 2021 study, Evelyn M. Beaury and colleagues analyzed the U.S. plant trade and found that 60% of the invasive plant species in the United States were still available for purchase! Even worse, 50% of the species that states have identified as especially problematic and 20% of federally identified noxious weeds were still offered for sale!

Many invasive plants are still available for purchase!

Invasive plant species in the United States

over 1200

Invasive plant species still sold in the United States

over 700

Learning to identify which common ornamental plants are invasive will help you to avoid inadvertently planting these invasive plants in your landscape. By not buying invasive plants that are still being offered in retail nurseries, you will help send the strong message that wholesale growers need to hear:

PLEASE STOP PROPAGATING INVASIVE PLANT SPECIES!

Help prevent the spread of invasive plants

Don't buy an invasive plant species! The average homeowner is unknowingly buying and planting invasive species. Refuse to be part of the distribution of invasive plants by getting to know the invasive plants in your region!

Verify that your plant source, especially if it's an online nursery, is certified and sells only healthy and clean plants. Get to know your local nurseries, research online plant and seed suppliers, and read the reviews.

Be extremely cautious when transporting plants from other regions. Insects and the seeds of invasive plants may be hitching a ride. If an out-of-state friend gives you a plant, or if you are moving and bringing along some favorite plants, examine the plants very carefully to ensure there are no hitchhiking pests or weeds. After planting, regularly check these plants for insect damage or sprouted seeds.

Research plants before accepting them from neighbors or local plant shares. Often plants that are shared are aggressive growers (which is why there are plenty to share!). Make sure to accurately identify these freebies to make sure you don't introduce an exotic plant pest into your wildlife landscape.

After purchasing some native plants, I was excited when a seedling came up in a pot along with one of my new plants. I nursed it along, eager about the possibility of a new native. When it was large enough to identify, I snapped a photo, used my plant ID app, and identified it as common buckthorn (*Rhamnus cathartica*), an extremely invasive plant that is not common where I live . . . at least not yet!

② Note the locations of invasive plants growing on your property

Although transitioning our landscapes to 100% native plants is ideal, a more realistic initial goal for most of us is to strive for mostly native plants growing alongside introduced plants that are not invasive. In a multi-year study comparing chickadee nesting success in residential landscapes with varying percentages of introduced versus native plants, Desiree Narango, Douglas Tallamy, and Peter Marra (2017) found that as the percent of native plants increased in the landscape, the probability that chickadees would nest increased. Among those that nested, the number of eggs laid increased, and the likelihood of the nestlings surviving also increased. What an incentive this provides for removing introduced plants, especially invasive ones, to make room for native plants!

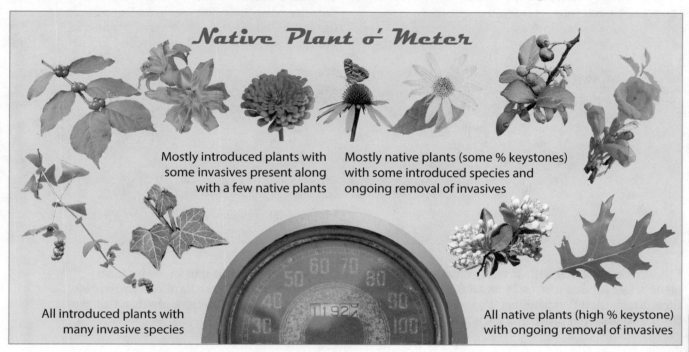

Native Plant o' Meter

Mostly introduced plants with some invasives present along with a few native plants

Mostly native plants (some % keystones) with some introduced species and ongoing removal of invasives

All introduced plants with many invasive species

All native plants (high % keystone) with ongoing removal of invasives

You may already recognize some of the invasive plant species growing on your property. As you transition to native plants, your landscape will fall somewhere along the continuum above. Use the tools and resources described in this action and those in the next action to help you identify any plants that are unfamiliar. Are there any pesty invasive plants growing on your property?

Walk around your property and note the locations of invasive plants that need removal. If you drew a map of your property earlier, you could use a copy of that. A rough sketch of the shape of your property is all that's needed. You can draw a plan freehand on a blank grid (see pages 8.2 or 15.2), trace your property from real estate documents, or use *Google Earth* to zoom in and trace it from the computer screen. Save time by assigning identifying letters or symbols to plant names.

Consider also noting the **non-invasive** introduced plants growing on your property that could be removed to free up space for native plants that provide more ecological services. Once you've reviewed your property, make an estimate as to where your property currently falls on the continuum above.

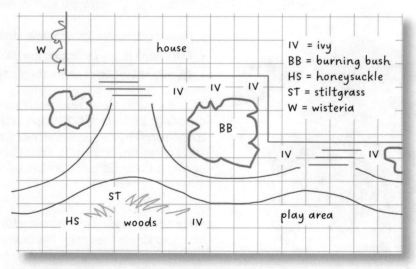

IV = ivy
BB = burning bush
HS = honeysuckle
ST = stiltgrass
W = wisteria

③ Learn to identify invasive plant species so that you can help eradicate them

In this guide, we focus on easy-to-identify invasive plants that you are likely to find in your yard. The more you can learn about the invasive plants in your region, the better prepared you will be to eradicate them from your wildlife habitat. Invasive plants in your landscape come from two primary sources:

Intentionally planted invasive species
Plants people have bought from a nursery, been given, propagated themselves, or acquired as part of an established landscape

Volunteer invasive species
Plants that have grown from seeds and nuts brought in by wildlife, blown in by the wind, or attached to shoes, clothing, vehicles, and so forth

Ivy (*Hedera*)   Forsythia (*Forsythia*)   Porcelain berry (*Ampelopsis*)   Foxtail (*Setaria*)

Familiarizing yourself with as many invasive species as possible will allow you to spot a new invasive plant before it takes root and sets seed. Since many invasive plants are sold in retail locations nationwide, their distribution is expanding. It's a good idea to become familiar with the top invasive plants across the United States, even those that are not in your area . . . yet!

Online resources to help you identify and learn about invasive plant species

When you come across an unfamiliar plant, it's super important to identify it before allowing it to grow or yanking it out. Although in the early stages of building your wildlife habitat, the plant is likely to be an invasive species, just maybe, it will be a native plant brought in by animals or the wind. Luckily, with an increasing selection of handy plant identification resources available, you no longer need to be an expert botanist to identify most plants. To help you identify the plants you discover growing on your property, we'll first review some popular plant identification apps, then we'll look at several websites including:

* *National Invasive Species Information Center* **(NISIC)**
* **EDDMapS** *(Early Detection and Distribution Mapping System)*
* *Invasive Plant Atlas of the United States* (*Invasive.org*)

As you explore these resources, you will notice that they share each other's links. In fact, **EDDMapS** and the *Invasive Plant Atlas* are both coordinated by the University of Georgia Center for Invasive Species and Ecosystem Health. The sites have handy links for navigating between these different resources.

Amur honeysuckle (*Lonicera maackii*) is one of the most invasive bush honeysuckles in the Pacific Northwest and Eastern United States. It is rapidly spread by birds (for a photo of its berries, see page 4.5).

Use plant identification apps to identify invasive plant species

First, we'll look briefly at some general plant identification apps that are useful for identifying invasive plants and which later will be useful for identifying native plants. Then, we'll explore several websites designed specifically to help identify and report invasive species.

General plant identification apps

There are numerous plant identification apps. Here are a few:

iNaturalist – Users share observations and identifications world-wide

Seek (*iNaturalist*) – An identification app for plants and animals. Developed by the iNaturalist Team, jointly with the California Academy of Sciences and the National Geographic Society. Take photos of plants, animals, and insects. Participate in challenges and earn badges. Record and share your sightings. Free

PictureThis – A popular, user-friendly app with a large database of plants. It requires a subscription although it can be used on a limited basis for free.

PlantNet – A "citizen science project on biodiversity." Contribute photos to confirm the identity of a plant. Sign in and create a profile for maximum benefit. Free

LeafSnap – Uses AI to identify plants by their leaves. Developed by Columbia University, University of Maryland, and the Smithsonian Institute. Free or premium service for a fee

 Search for **plant identification** apps or the app's name on a cell phone. To evaluate the ease of use and accuracy of an app, play around with each app using plants for which you already have an accurate identification.

Invasive plant identification apps

Some apps are designed specifically to help you identify and report invasive species such as the mobile version of the **EDDMapS** website that we discuss on pages 4.12 - 4.13. The *National Invasive Species Information Center* (**NISIC**) that we discuss next (see pages 4.10 - 4.11) is a go-to resource for finding descriptions and links for smartphone apps related to the identification and reporting of invasive species identification. Search online for **nisic smartphone apps**.

 To evaluate additional apps, including ones that may be specific to your region, search online for **invasive plants mobile apps [state]** or search on a cell phone for **invasive plants**. Examples of apps that may come up include *Invasive Plants of Arizona, Alaska Invasives ID,* and *Washington Invasives*.

 Although not a plant identification app per se, *Google Lens* is an easy starting point for narrowing down the identification of a plant (or insect). Download the app to a phone. Open the app and snap a photo of the plant you are wondering about. Explore the suggested search results to verify the identification.

Keep in mind that accurate identification depends on the size of an app's database of plants. Also, you will find that many of the general plant identification apps are geared toward non-native, ornamental species.

Next, we'll explain how to efficiently use several websites that are very helpful for identifying, learning about, and in some cases, reporting invasive species. In this guide, we focus on invasive plants but some of these sites also provide fascinating information about invasive microorganisms, insects, fish, amphibians, reptiles, mammals, and other invasive species.

Use the *National Invasive Species Information Center* (NISIC) to learn about the most problematic invasive species

The *National Invasive Species Information Center* (**NISIC**) site is an ideal place to get to know the worst of the invasive plant bullies. In addition to thorough descriptions, distribution maps are presented for each plant. The limited number of plant profiles* features some of the most problematic invasive species in the United States. (*For a comprehensive list of invasive plant species, visit the ***Invasive Plant Atlas*** (*Invasive.org*) described later in this chapter.) Especially nice are the informative videos about each plant. If you identify one of these species on your property, use the various resources in this action to determine the best method for removing it ASAP!

First, let's look at using the **NISIC** to learn about an invasive plant species; then, we'll explore its extensive resources.

Visit: **invasivespeciesinfo.gov**

or search online for **invasive species nisic** and navigate to the site.

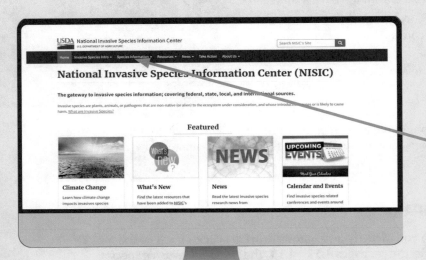

Click **Species Information**.

Click **Terrestrial Invasives**.

Click **Terrestrial Plants**.

Use the *National Invasive Species Information Center* (NISIC) to learn about the most problematic invasive species, *continued*

Learn more about specific species

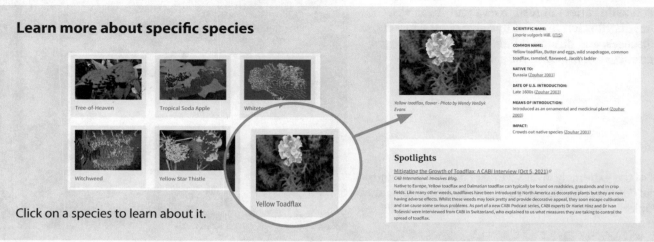

Yellow toadflax, flower - Photo by Wendy VanDyk Evans

SCIENTIFIC NAME:
Linaria vulgaris Mill. (ITIS)

COMMON NAME:
Yellow toadflax, Butter and eggs, wild snapdragon, common toadflax, ramsted, flaxweed, Jacob's ladder

NATIVE TO:
Eurasia (Zouhar 2003)

DATE OF U.S. INTRODUCTION:
Late 1600s (Zouhar 2003)

MEANS OF INTRODUCTION:
Introduced as an ornamental and medicinal plant (Zouhar 2003)

IMPACT:
Crowds out native species (Zouhar 2003)

Spotlights

Mitigating the Growth of Toadflax: A CABI Interview (Oct 5, 2021)
CAB International. Invasives Blog.
Native to Europe, Yellow toadflax and Dalmatian toadflax can typically be found on roadsides, grasslands and in crop fields. Like many other weeds, toadflaxes have been introduced to North America as decorative plants but they are now having adverse effects. Whilst these weeds may look pretty and provide decorative appeal, they soon escape cultivation and can cause some serious problems. As part of a new CABI Podcast series, CABI experts Dr Hariet Hinz and Dr Ivan Toševski were interviewed from CABI in Switzerland, who explained to us what measures they are taking to control the spread of toadflax.

Click on a species to learn about it.

Get resources specific to your location worldwide

Click **Resources** in the top menu bar.

Then click **Resources by Location** in the menu.

Click on the United States.

Click on your state for regionally relevant information.

Check out this super handy resource to help you find native plants and native plant organizations.

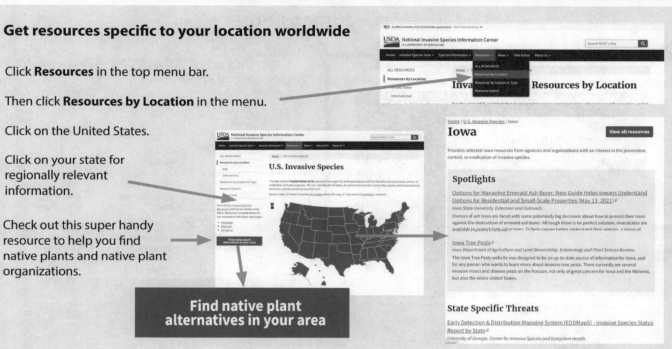

Find native plant alternatives in your area

Iowa

[View all resources]

Provides selected Iowa resources from agencies and organizations with an interest in the prevention, control, or eradication of invasive species.

Spotlights

Options for Managing Emerald Ash Borer: New Guide Helps Iowans Understand Options for Residential and Small-Scale Properties (May 13, 2021)
Iowa State University. Extension and Outreach.
Owners of ash trees are faced with some potentially big decisions about how to protect their trees against the destruction of emerald ash borer. Although there is no perfect solution, insecticides are available to protect high-value trees. To help Iowans better understand their options, a group of

Iowa Tree Pests
Iowa Department of Agriculture and Land Stewardship. Entomology and Plant Science Bureau.
The Iowa Tree Pests website was designed to be an up-to-date source of information for Iowa, and for any person who wants to learn more about invasive tree pests. There currently are several invasive insect and disease pests on the horizon, not only of great concern for Iowa and the Midwest, but also the entire United States.

State Specific Threats

Early Detection & Distribution Mapping System (EDDMapS) - Invasive Species Status Report by State
University of Georgia. Center for Invasive Species and Ecosystem Health.

Get resources specific to your location worldwide

Click **Resources** in the top menu bar.

Then click **Resources by Subject or Type** in the menu.

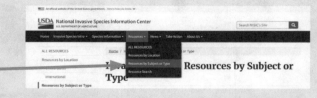

Here you will find smartphone applications related to invasive species identification, community action opportunities, education and outreach, an image gallery, grants and funding, impact reports, laws and regulations, management resources, and much more!

SOURCE: *National Invasive Species Information Center* (NISIC), U.S. Department of Agriculture. Available online at https://www.invasivespeciesinfo.gov.

4

Invasives

Use EDDMapS to view the distribution of invasive species in your region

Take some time to explore the **EDDMapS** website to discover a wide variety of resources about invasives, including distribution maps of invasive plants, insects, fungi, diseases, and other wildlife. Information, images, and references are provided for each species.

Control of the extremely invasive tree of heaven (*Ailanthus altissima; right*) is complicated by its similarity in appearance to ecologically beneficial native plants such as sumac (*Rhus*).

Visit: eddmaps.org

Scroll down to see all the **EDDMapS Features**. Then click on **Species Info**.

Features

Report Sightings
Report invasive species sightings to a national network of expert verifiers

Maps
Data visualization at state, county and individual population view

Species Info
Taxonomy, descriptions, images, and distribution maps of invasive species

EDDMapS Apps
Apps for iOS and Android smartphone devices providing mobile reporting

EDDMapS Query
Advanced search and filter tool to download verified data and maps based on specified

Dashboard & Tools
Create and access statistics, graphs, charts, projects, manage data, and

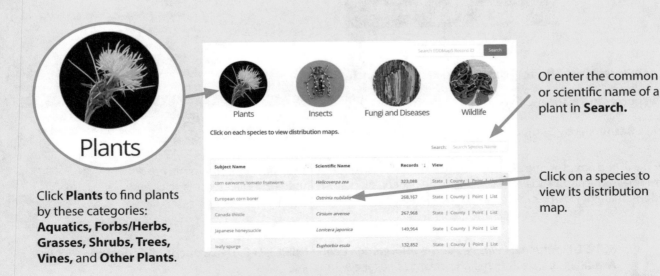

Click **Plants** to find plants by these categories: **Aquatics, Forbs/Herbs, Grasses, Shrubs, Trees, Vines,** and **Other Plants**.

Or enter the common or scientific name of a plant in **Search.**

Click on a species to view its distribution map.

Subject Name	Scientific Name	Records	View
corn earworm, tomato fruitworm	*Helicoverpa zea*	323,088	State | County | Point | List
European corn borer	*Ostrinia nubilalis*	268,167	State | County | Point | List
Canada thistle	*Cirsium arvense*	267,968	State | County | Point | List
Japanese honeysuckle	*Lonicera japonica*	149,964	State | County | Point | List
leafy spurge	*Euphorbia esula*	132,852	State | County | Point | List

Click on each species to view distribution maps.

Plants   Insects   Fungi and Diseases   Wildlife

Click **Counties** to view distribution maps at the county level.

Click **Points** to get an idea of the population size and relative strength of this plant's invasion in your region. Each red dot shows the number of times this plant species has been reported in this location.

Click **Species Info** for resources, images, state invasive species lists, taxonomic rank, common names, and synonyms.

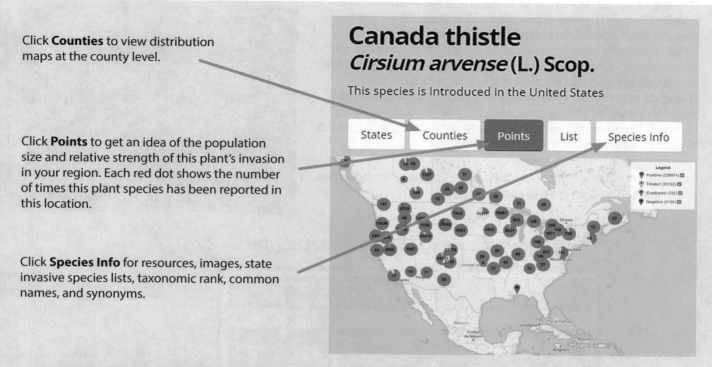

NOTE: *The content of the EDDMapS species information varies from species to species. In some cases, control methods are recommended which is particularly helpful. Chemical controls are listed; however, in this action guide, we advocate avoiding the use of toxic chemicals (see Action 12: Use nontoxic home and yard products).*

EDDMapS encourages citizen interaction, for example, by reporting sightings. Explore the extensive training materials that explain how to take part in this important project.

In the EDDMapS top menu, click **Training.**

Here you will find **EDDMapS Training Materials. Learn how** to enter data and how to use the data. Watch videos to learn about becoming an EDDMapS volunteer or partner. Explore the wide variety of additional materials including such topics as **Herbarium Collecting Guidelines.**

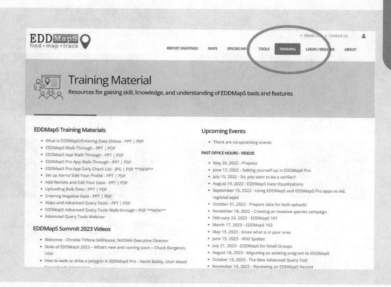

The EDDMapS materials shown here and elsewhere in this book are used with permission from EDDMapS (eddmaps.org). EDDMapS. 2024. Early Detection & Distribution Mapping System. The University of Georgia–Center for Invasive Species and Ecosystem Health. Available online at http://www.eddmaps.org.

Use the *Invasive Plant Atlas* (*Invasive.org*) to learn about invasive plant species

Developed by the University of Georgia and the National Park Service along with other environmental organizations, the ***Invasive Plant Atlas of the United States*** (***invasiveplantatlas.org***) helps users with identification, early detection, prevention, and management of invasive plants by providing species information, images, interactive distribution maps, and early detection reporting procedures. The list of plants included is exhaustive, making this an invaluable resource not only for learning about common invasive species, but also for finding critical information about less common but problematic invasives.

Japanese knotweed (*Reynoutria japonica* aka *Fallopia japonica*) is one of the most difficult invasive plants to eradicate.

Visit: **invasive.org** (or invasiveplantatlas.org)

Click **Plants**.

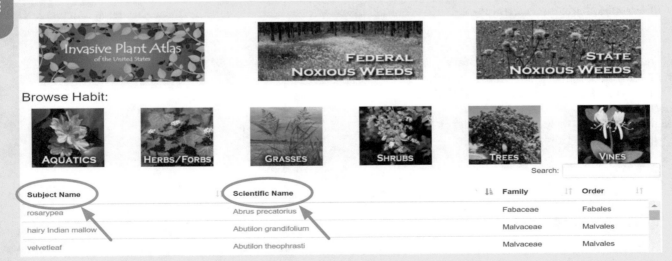

Click on a plant category (such as **Aquatics, Herb/Forbs**, and so on.). Then, click on a plant's **Subject Name** (common name) or **Scientific Name** to go to its profile. Click the arrows next to a column title to sort the column. Click again to reverse the order. Or click on the tiles above to browse by legal status or growth habit.

Use the *Invasive Plant Atlas* (*Invasive.org*) to learn about invasive plant species, *continued*

Here is a sample profile showing the invasive velvetleaf (*Abutilon theophrasti*). Many of the plant profiles include a gallery of images along with resources and distribution maps.

Subject Name	⬆⬇	Scientific Name
rosarypea		Abrus precatorius
hairy Indian mallow		Abutilon grandifolium
velvetleaf		Abutilon theophrasti

A particularly helpful feature on some profiles is the inclusion of photographs of the different life stages of the plant, such as seed heads, seeds, and seedlings.

Scroll down to view an **EDDMapS** map showing the presence of this species by county. When applicable, another map displays the states where this species is regulated or on a state invasive species list.

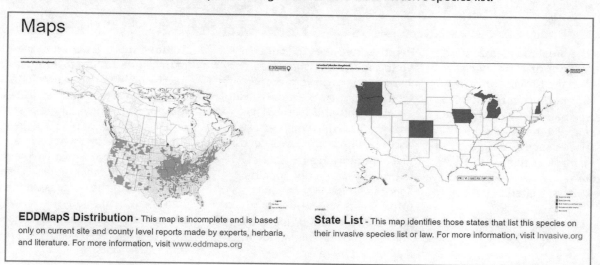

EDDMapS Distribution - This map is incomplete and is based only on current site and county level reports made by experts, herbaria, and literature. For more information, visit www.eddmaps.org

State List - This map identifies those states that list this species on their invasive species list or law. For more information, visit Invasive.org

For extremely helpful images and in-depth information about the plants in this database, further sleuthing is well worth the effort. For example, from the ***Invasive.org*** home page, search a plant's name and click on the plant's common or scientific name. On the plant's profile, click the **Go to Host Page** tab (not available for all species). This takes you to the **View Subject List** where you can explore the images for this species. Images include everything from propagation and cultivation practices to close-up images of the insects and pathogens related to a species.

NOTE: *Some of the plants in the **Invasive.org** database are **native** species in the United States. For example, ponderosa pine (Pinus ponderosa) is a native tree widely distributed in mountainous western states. (In contrast, ponderosa pine is a weedy, introduced, invasive species in New Zealand and Australia.)*

The Invasive Plant Atlas (Invasive.org) materials shown here are used with permission from Invasive Plant Atlas (Invasive.org). Joint effort of University of Georgia Center for Invasive Species and Ecosystem Health, USDA Animal and Plant Health Inspection Service, and USDA Forest Service, Agriculture. Available online at http://www.invasive.org.

4

Invasives

④ Remove invasives—NOW is the time to start removing invasive plants from your property!

Most large-scale efforts in public and private wildlands rely on herbicides to remove invasive plants. This action guide strongly advocates against using toxic herbicides. Because of the smaller scale of a typical yard, a chemical-free approach is possible by implementing strategic management practices and thoughtful landscape design. While establishing your wildlife habitat, the pressure from invasives will be greater. However, with time, there will be fewer and fewer invasives producing seed. Instead, the native plants will be crowding out the seedlings of invasives that do sprout and building up a native species seed bank.

Which invasive plants should be removed first?

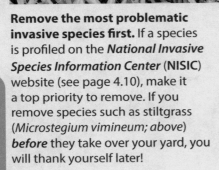

Remove the most problematic invasive species first. If a species is profiled on the *National Invasive Species Information Center* (NISIC) website (see page 4.10), make it a top priority to remove. If you remove species such as stiltgrass (*Microstegium vimineum; above*) *before* they take over your yard, you will thank yourself later!

Remove invasives BEFORE they go to seed! Learn *when* the worst invasive plants on your property set seed. If two species are overtaking a garden bed, and *Species A* has finished flowering while *Species B* is just beginning to flower, focus first on removing all of *Species A* to prevent seed production by *Species A*. This will save you years of future weeding. The mile-a-minute (*Persicaria perfoliata*) vine above is about to provide this landowner with a whole lot more work!

Remove small, isolated patches of invasives before tackling large patches. It's human nature to tackle a heavily infested area first. Instead, look for and remove single or small patches of invasive plants in areas that otherwise are invasive-free. By removing single invasive plants scattered about in otherwise clean areas, such as the stiltgrass in the flower bed above, you establish invasive-free zones and prevent the development of seed banks or the proliferation of aggressive roots.

How to safely dispose of removed invasive plants

Once you've done the hard work of removing invasive plants, care must be taken to prevent accidentally spreading the plant during disposal. Get to know your invasive plants and how they spread—many plants regrow from cut pieces of root, and seeds may ripen even after removal. Some municipalities consider invasive plant species to be controlled waste. Check the policies for your waste collection service and follow their guidelines for disposal.

Many invasive plants can simply be placed in a shallow pile on pavement, a tarp, or a pallet until they dry out and die within a couple of weeks (see page 7.9) Then, the plant waste can be placed in a hidden pile to decompose and monitored in case of regrowth. But some invasive plants require strict precautions; for example, Japanese knotweed and some honeysuckles will regrow from tiny fragments of stems or roots. For tough invasives like these and for plants that have already gone to seed, remove any plant parts that may grow or sprout, such as rhizomatous roots, mature flowers, seeds, and fruits; and seal them in a plastic bag. Place the bag in the sun to bake for at least 3 weeks, longer in cooler seasons. After "baking" the waste in a bag or on hot pavement, place it in a hidden, isolated pile used only for invasive plant waste. Over time, the bottom layers of the pile will decompose into rich organic matter, but due to the potential presence of viable seed, this waste is best left in a pile and monitored. Subsequent layers of newly removed invasive plants and/or cardboard laid over the pile will help to smother any regrowth.

Invasives 4

More strategies to effectively remove and keep out invasive plants

The strategies we just discussed for deciding which invasives to tackle first are also the most important strategies for efficient invasive plant management, so they top the list here and bear repeating:

- Remove the most problematic invasive species first.
- Remove invasive plants BEFORE they go to seed!
- Remove small, isolated patches of invasive plants before tackling large patches.

Now, let's look at some more strategies.

More strategies to effectively remove and keep out invasive plants

Learn to identify invasive plants, especially their seedling stages. This knowledge makes it easier to eliminate invasive plants and encourage native ones. For images of the seedling stage of invasive plants, visit the two websites discussed earlier: *National Invasive Species Information Center* (NISIC; invasivespeciesinfo.gov) and the *Invasive Plant Atlas of the United States* (invasiveplantatlas.org). The plant ID apps and other resources discussed earlier are also helpful here. Often the easiest time to identify a plant is when it is flowering or by its seed or fruit. Getting to know the look and feel of different stems is helpful for selectively removing invasive plants at their base, especially when they're growing among desirable native plants.

Remove invasives when they first appear as soon as you've identified them. This is the best and most important habit to develop (called *Early Detection and Rapid Response*—EDRR). For example, a tiny patch of weedy grass can be completely removed before it infests an entire area; a first season Callery pear (*Pyrus calleryana*) can be pulled out by hand while anything older must be individually dug out; an invasive honeysuckle is best removed before birds distribute the seeds, and so forth! If not removed soon, the single vine of honeysuckle (*above*) will overtake and quickly fill in this area of the woodland floor like it has already done below.

Tackle one species at a time. Different species require different tools and methods of removal. You may find it more efficient to move around the landscape with the tools for a single method to remove all the invasives that require that method. This approach makes it easy to focus on a species that is about to go to seed. For most herbaceous perennials, a pair of garden gloves, a hori hori knife, and a basket or big tub for gathering waste is all that is needed. Woody invasives may require pruners or loppers. If the diameter of the stem is greater than about 2 inches, anything from a battery-powered saws-all (reciprocating saw) to a full-size chainsaw may be needed.

The old proverb "*A stitch in time saves nine*" is quite apt when it comes to controlling invasive plant species. Continue reading for more strategies to make short work of removing invasive plants followed by a summary of methods for removing them.

More strategies to effectively remove and keep out invasive plants, *continued*

Learn which method most effectively eliminates each invasive species on your property. Use the resources described earlier to figure out the most effective way to eliminate a specific invasive species. When an herbicide is recommended, search online for [name of invasive species] control without chemicals. Most invasive plants can be controlled without the use of toxic herbicides.

Time your invasive plant removal with the weather conditions. After several days of heavy rain, prioritize digging out deeply rooted tree seedlings before the ground dries out. On a hot day, refrain from removing an expanse of invasives to avoid causing sunburn on any native plants growing beneath them.

Avoid using plastic or woven landscape fabric except as described below for stump control. Although landscape fabric will temporarily block weeds, over time weeds grow over or root through the material making it tedious to garden around and difficult to remove. See page 7.9 to learn why landscape fabric (weed barrier cloth) is particularly problematic both environmentally and management-wise.

Roll up mat-forming invasive plants, such as creeping Charlie (*Glechoma hederacea*; see page 11.13) or ivy *(Hedera)*. Sometimes (not always, unfortunately!) conditions will make it possible to roll up a dense patch of an invasive plant. Try it when the plant is in full growth after a rain. Lift, pull up, push, and roll. The trick is getting on a roll when the conditions are right. (That's life too, isn't it?) Plant or mulch right away.

Cover and tie stumps of shrubs and trees with landscape fabric to prevent resprouting. Herbicides are often painted on freshly cut stumps to prevent resprouting, but for many tree and shrub species, herbicide use can be effectively avoided by draping a double layer of landscape cloth over the stump and tying it around the base of the stump and leaving it covered for about 6 – 12 months or until the stump is completely dead and depleted. Any regrowth from the stump base should be cut off and covered with barrier cloth. If not already present, herbaceous plants can be planted in this area to hide the covered stump from view.

To dig or not to dig—that is the question!

There are differing points of view about digging to remove invasives. Whenever cutting a plant off at soil level will kill it, do that instead of digging. This will reduce weed seed germination and protect the soil structure and its micro life. Any soil disturbance promotes the germination of seeds which likely will be invasive species if these have been the dominant plants in the area. But, some invasives will simply regrow when their roots (or even tiny pieces of their roots!) remain in the ground. For aggressive species like Japanese honeysuckle (*Lonicera japonica*), consider these options: Dig the roots out very carefully, limiting soil disturbance to the extent possible; use the *Block It!* method, replenishing the blocking material until the invasive plant has exhausted its resources (and probably yours as well!); or continue to cut the plant at ground level until it no longer regrows. These are the difficult species that make you wish that herbicides didn't poison frogs, children, and other living things!

Next, we'll look at effective methods for removing invasive plants followed by management practices that can help prevent invasives from taking over in the first place.

4

Invasives

Effective methods for removing invasive plants

 HAND PULL

Hand pull–Works best with young plants and shallow-rooted plants. Always aim to disturb the soil as little as possible.

 TRIM

Whack with string trimmer or cut with pruning shears–Repeat until the plant has used up its reserves and does not regrow.

 BURN

Burn with propane torch–This setup uses a portable propane tank equipped with a propane torch. It is most effective when used at the seedling stage for large-scale removal of non-rhizomatous plants in areas where there is no risk of fire.

 SMOTHER

Smother (block)–Many invasives can be controlled using the *Block It!* method (see page 3.6). It may be necessary to reapply the blocking materials for some of the more persistent species such as rhizomatous grasses. For trees and shrubs, covering the stumps with landscape cloth and tying it around the base is an effective alternative to herbicides (see page 4.18).

 DIG

Dig to remove roots–A sturdy trowel or hori hori garden knife is sufficient for small plants; larger plants will likely require a shovel. It's best to limit the use of this method to invasives that will readily regrow if their roots are left in the ground, such as rhizomatous grasses, tree seedlings, or honeysuckle. Soil disturbance exposes seeds and usually results in a new generation of invasive growth. After removing roots, immediately install a dense planting including ground layer plants, and apply a 2-inch deep layer of leaves, garden trimmings, or wood chips until the area fills in with plants.

 CHOP

Chop with a hoe–Hoeing is much easier when invasive plants are young—for both plants and people!

Chop with a reciprocating saw, hand saw, or a chain saw–Large shrubs and trees will require sawing to remove.

Chop 'n drop–Use the invasive plant waste to build the soil right where you are working (or gather as you go for use as a mulch elsewhere). CAUTION: Be sure to remove any plant parts that may sprout or regrow if left on the ground, such as seed heads, English ivy, honeysuckle, or rhizomatous grasses. Consider spreading trimmings out on pavement until they are thoroughly dry before cautiously piling them somewhere inhospitable to decompose further. In cool, moist weather, this may take months.

4

Invasives

Proactive management practices to help prevent invasive plants from taking over in the first place

How we manage our landscape helps determine the magnitude of invasive plant pressure. Consider adopting the practices below to help prevent invasives from getting a foothold in the first place.

If invasive plants continue to reinfest an area, find the underlying source of each invasive. Make eliminating that source a top priority. For example, I have a small area that I call my woods. It's heavily infested with young Callery pear trees (*Pyrus calleryana* 'Bradford', also known as Bradford pear). The source of these seedlings was five mature Callery pear trees (one of them is shown at right) that lined the driveway and have since been cut down. Although I'll be removing Callery pear seedlings for some time to come, now that the parent trees are gone, the seed bank will eventually expire.

Plant densely to create "green mulch." Closely spaced plants form a canopy of leaves that blocks the germination of invasive seeds.

Plant aggressive native plants to suppress invasive plant growth. Aggressive native plants, such as native ferns or Joe-Pye weed (*Eutrochium purpureum*) can be planted into areas dominated by invasives. Initially the area will need weeding, but with time, an aggressive native plant can dominate the invasive-infested area. For example, where stiltgrass (*Microstegium vimineum*) and garlic mustard (*Alliaria petiolata*) run rampant, a patch of golden ragwort (*Packera aurea*) can outcompete these two invasives with minimal weeding required.

Mulch gaps between newly planted plants with a 2-inch layer of leaf litter, compost, or wood chips. Avoid mulching areas where fine seeds have been sown or where existing native plants may disperse seeds that you would like to grow. Once established, the **leaf canopy** (leaf cover) should make mulching unnecessary. If gaps remain in the planting, plant more plants!

Reevaluate what is and isn't a weed. Sometimes what we view as a weed is a wildlife ally, but sometimes not so much. An online search for "worst weeds" often includes violets, clover, and dandelions. Violets are a valuable native plant. Clover definitely doesn't belong in a strictly native planting, but it offers more ecological value than lawn. Dandelions (*Taraxacum officinale*), a non-native, invasive species, are sometimes promoted as an early spring nectar source for bees. Although some native bees may feed on dandelion nectar, its pollen lacks the nutritional value needed to nourish bee larvae.

Violets (*Viola*) provide various ecoservices: fritillary butterflies use them as host plants; rabbits devour their leaves; mason bees and pollinating flies feed on their flowers; and their seeds nourish wild turkeys, doves, mice, ants, and other creatures.

Clover (*Trifolium*) provides abundant nectar and pollen for generalist pollinators while fixing nitrogen in the soil; songbirds eat clover seed; deer, rabbits, squirrels, gophers, and other small mammals feed on clover leaves and flower pods.

Dandelions penetrate and break up compacted soil with their deep taproots, and birds eat the flowers and seeds; but unfortunately, the entire dandelion plant is allelopathic including its pollen. This may reduce growth and seed set among neighboring native plants.

5 Get involved with local and regional organizations to help remove invasive species from natural areas

Getting involved in community efforts to eradicate invasive plants is an extremely worthy and important activity. The reality is that the battle to eradicate invasives will only succeed if more of us get involved at all levels while applying pressure on the various powers that be to help us with this monumental challenge that threatens the biodiversity of our planet. Because of the importance of getting involved, we mention it here as an action step, but we focus on the topic of getting involved in *Action 15: Share, educate, and get involved.* Hiking about wild lands in the fresh air, spotting and removing invasive plants, and joining in with other dedicated individuals can be a satisfying way to spend a day.

The **National Invasive Species Information Center (NISIC)** that we visited on pages 4.10 - 4.11 lists community action opportunities. Visit **invasivespeciesinfo.org.** Click **Resources** in the top menu bar. Then click **Resources by Subject or Type** in the dropdown menu. In the category **Resources by Subject**, click **Community Action** and **What You Can Do** for a variety of opportunities to participate in invasive species monitoring and control. While there, explore the **Education and Outreach** resources.

Coming to terms with our "legacy plants"

Having spent my childhood in Pennsylvania where summer days were filled with the fragrance of honeysuckle, I was excited to plant honeysuckle upon finally having my own garden in California. I promptly bought some from a mail-order nursery and eagerly planted it. I no longer live on that property, and I hope that the honeysuckle is no longer there either. As an avid gardener, it was never my wish to do harm, and it troubles me to think of the many invasive plants I have introduced to my past gardens. Now, I spend many a summer evening removing honeysuckle from the wood's edge. As you begin to inventory your existing plantings, you may find, as I did, that some of your old favorites are *not* beneficial to wildlife. Many are likely to be introduced plants, and some may even be invasive.

Perhaps the biggest challenge of removing invasives is pulling out the plants for which you have happy memories! The prospect of removing these "legacy plants" may bring up strong emotions since these plants might be a plant handed down for several generations, a tree planted to honor your child's birth, or a fruit tree that is finally producing after years of patient care. It can be heart-wrenching even to think about cutting down a tree or digging out a beloved plant. Although it may not be native, a treasured legacy plant that is not invasive can be left to grow in your landscape among the native plants you are adding. And just think, the native plants you grow can become your legacy!

Digging in deeper

Listed here are references and examples of some handy resources for identifying invasive plants species and learning how to remove them (please refer to the Appendix for publication details).

Nature's Best Hope: A New Approach to Conservation That Starts in Your Yard: Doug explains what "invasive" means and why invasive plants fail to support wildlife in the way that native plants do (see pages 89 - 123 and 206). He also explains the ways in which invasive plants degrade local ecosystems by reducing the diversity and population size of native species of animals and plants and decreasing the diversity of ecological interactions. Armed with this understanding comes a renewed sense of urgency to fill our landscapes with native plants.

Invasive Plants: Guide to Identification and the Impacts and Control of Common North American Species: Sylvan and Wallace Kaufman provide profiles of more than 250 invasive plants including their environmental impact and control methods.

Native Alternatives to Invasive Plants: C. Colston Burrell helps make the transition to native plants easier by suggesting native plant alternatives to widely planted invasive species.

Plant Invaders of Mid-Atlantic Natural Areas (free 168-page PDF): Wherever you live, this is a must-have resource since many of the invasives featured are distributed across the United States and still available for purchase. This National Park Service and U.S. Fish and Wildlife Service resource by Jil Swearingen and colleagues incudes almost 60 invasive plant profiles featuring each plant's origin, distribution, ecological threat, prevention and control methods, and native alternatives. If you live outside of the Mid-Atlantic area, don't be misled by the title; instead, find this title on the **Invasive.org** website or search online for the title and get well-acquainted with these pests.

Mistaken Identity? Invasive Plants and Their Native Look-Alikes an Identification Guide for the Mid-Atlantic (free 68-page PDF): Matthew Sarver and colleagues present clear comparisons between 20 highly invasive species and native look-alikes. Although the focus is the Mid-Atlantic region, many of these invasives are widely distributed across the U.S. Search online for this title to check out this handy reference!

Don't Plant a Pest! The **California Invasive Pest Council** (*cal-ipc.org*) ***Don't plant a pest!*** program offers resources to identify invasive plants and help stop their spread across California and elsewhere. To access this resource, search online for **don't plant a pest**. Along with a wealth of other resources, you'll find plant profiles with exquisite photos and data sheets that include non-chemical control methods.

The ***MGNV Illustrated Glossary*** offered by the **Master Gardeners of Northern Virginia** is a masterful compilation of the horticultural and botanical terms likely to be encountered when exploring plants. Each entry includes a definition of the term, its pronunciation, high quality descriptive photos, in-depth background information, and journal references for further study. Explore this fascinating resource by searching online for **mgnv glossary**.

Managing Invasive Plants by Mike Bald (Pollinator Pathway of Addison County, online video, April 30, 2023). This video features Mike Bald, the owner of ***Got Weeds?***, who refuses to believe that herbicides are ever a good solution, and his actions align with this belief. A collective agreement by all of us to not use toxic chemicals will force innovation and safe alternatives. Bald is a role model for this new perspective. He takes the extra effort required to control invasive plants without resorting to toxic chemicals.

Learn about the invasive plants where you live by searching online for **invasive plants video [your state]**. Learn more about a specific species by searching for its common or scientific name. As always, consider the source and experiment to find out what works for you.

Now that we have started removing invasive plants, it's time to start filling our landscapes with keystone plants. That's what the next action is all about!

Action 5—CHECKLIST
Identify your keystone plants

Step:	✔	Action Needed:	Page:
1	☐	Identify and learn about the keystone plants found in your region with these handy online tools: • Use the **NWF** *Keystone Plants by Ecoregion* tool to identify keystone and host plant species in your ecoregion • Use the **NWF** *Native Plant Finder* tool to identify native plants by ZIP Code™	**5.4**
2	☐	Start a plant list for your wildlife habitat to guide your planting choices	**5.6**
3	☐	Note the locations of familiar plants that are keystone species already growing on your property	**5.10**
4	☐	Use the **BONAP** *Maps* to determine the status of a plant in your region	**5.12**
5	☐	Explore the **EPA** *Ecoregion Maps* to get to know your region's wildlife habitats	**5.18**
6	☐	Identify the host plants for caterpillars (Lepidoptera) that specialize on specific plants	**5.22**

In most of the United States, oaks (*Quercus*) are the most valuable plant for supporting biodiversity because they host so many caterpillar species.

5

Keystones

What does a plant's scientific name tell us?

Keystone plant recommendations are often listed by their scientific name and organized by **genus** (group of species) rather than individual plant species. Let's clarify this terminology.

A plant may have many common names, but each has its own botanical name. This name, consisting of the plant's genus and species, not only uniquely identifies the plant but also shows its classification giving us clues about the plant's characteristics. Consider these examples:

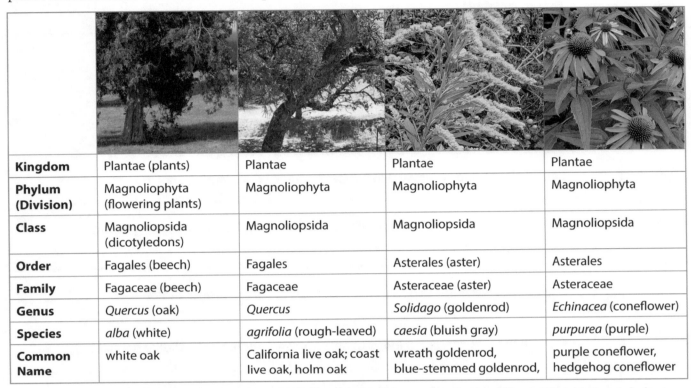

Kingdom	Plantae (plants)	Plantae	Plantae	Plantae
Phylum (Division)	Magnoliophyta (flowering plants)	Magnoliophyta	Magnoliophyta	Magnoliophyta
Class	Magnoliopsida (dicotyledons)	Magnoliopsida	Magnoliopsida	Magnoliopsida
Order	Fagales (beech)	Fagales	Asterales (aster)	Asterales
Family	Fagaceae (beech)	Fagaceae	Asteraceae (aster)	Asteraceae
Genus	*Quercus* (oak)	*Quercus*	*Solidago* (goldenrod)	*Echinacea* (coneflower)
Species	*alba* (white)	*agrifolia* (rough-leaved)	*caesia* (bluish gray)	*purpurea* (purple)
Common Name	white oak	California live oak; coast live oak, holm oak	wreath goldenrod, blue-stemmed goldenrod,	purple coneflower, hedgehog coneflower

Since oaks, asters, and goldenrods are in the Magnoliopsida class, we know that their seedlings all have two **cotyledons** (embryonic leaves; see page 10.17). *Quercus alba* and *Q. agrifolia* look very different and come from different parts of the United States, but they share characteristics with beech and chestnut trees, other members of the Fagaceae family. Likewise, because both *Solidago caesia* and *Echinacea purpurea* are in the Asteraceae family, we know that they both have composite flower heads made up of many small flowers in a flat, disc-like flowerhead. Plus, if a friend recommends that you plant blue-stemmed goldenrod and another friend recommends wreath goldenrod, you know they are the same plant! The species shown above are **straight species** (the original species as it would be found in the wild without the human interventions of cultivation or hybridization). Straight species can be reliably propagated by seed.

A few more important classification terms

Subspecies: An isolated population that differs from the straight species (*Prunella vulgaris* ssp. *lanceolata,* a subspecies native to the U.S.)

Natural selection (or **nativar** *if parents are native species*): Naturally occurring variation selected for its desired traits (*Phlox paniculata* 'Jeana')

Cultivar (or **nativar**, *when parents are native*): Intended or accidental crossbreeding of two selections (*Echinacea purpurea* 'Razzmatazz')

Hybrid: Two or more plants interbred from different species within the same genus (*Prunella vulgaris* x P. *laciniata*)

Action 5—GUIDE
Identify your keystone plants

Plants in the aster family (Asteraceae) are one of the most valuable herbaceous plants for preserving biodiversity.

With the very real possibility of extinction facing many species of plants and animals, more and more people are feeling a sense of urgency to do their part to save wildlife. Due to the media awareness of the plight of monarch butterflies, planting milkweed has been a starting point for many of us to fill our gardens with wildflowers. Flowers such as milkweed, echinacea, asters, and clumps of native grasses planted alongside pretty patches of non-native zinnias, cosmos, and daisies reward us with engaging views of butterflies and pollinators buzzing about our garden. Without a doubt, such plantings are a step in the right direction; however, with little added effort, we can significantly increase our support of wildlife by carefully choosing the plants we grow, specifically by choosing **keystone plants**. Keystone plants are those native plants that provide the greatest support to wildlife. The survival of wildlife depends upon increased populations of keystone plants.

Keystone species are the MOST IMPORTANT native plants on your property! Online tools and maps are now available to identify the keystone plants for specific regions. In this action, we show how to use these tools and maps so that you can select keystone plants that will support the most wildlife species possible on your property.

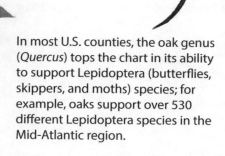

In most U.S. counties, the oak genus (*Quercus*) tops the chart in its ability to support Lepidoptera (butterflies, skippers, and moths) species; for example, oaks support over 530 different Lepidoptera species in the Mid-Atlantic region.

5

Keystones

① Identify and learn about the keystone plants found in your ecoregion with these handy online tools

Keystone plants are NOT a one-size-fits-all choice; instead, wildlife-plant relationships are unique to specific **ecosystems**. Ecosystems are a community of animals and other organisms that live in and interact with a physical environment. It's helpful to get a feel for the ecosystem characteristics of your region by identifying and learning about the **ecoregion** in which you live. This can help guide your decisions as you build your wildlife habitat.

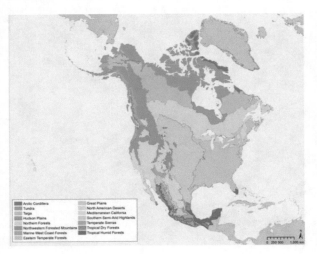

So, what is an ecoregion? **Ecoregions** are geographical areas that have similarly functioning ecosystems that broadly define the characteristics of a region. The boundaries of ecosystems are determined by an area's vegetation, geology, soil, water systems, climate, wildlife, and land use.

In this action, we look at tools helpful in identifying native vegetation, specifically keystone plants. We also take an in-depth look at the different mapped levels of ecoregions which provide a glimpse of the plants and wildlife you can expect to find in a specific area.

This *EPA Ecoregion Map of North America—Level I* presents the broadest division of ecoregions.

Handy tools to help you identify your keystone plants

Thanks to the hard work of researchers and dedicated volunteers, we now have powerful online tools making it easy to choose keystone plant species for your wildlife habitat. Let's take a close look at how to use some of these tools to further refine your keystone plant choices:

- *National Wildlife Federation* (NWF) *Keystone Plants by Ecoregion* and *Host Plants by Ecoregion*—Use to identify keystone and host plants native to your broader ecoregion. The NWF developed this tool with the help of Doug Tallamy and wildlife biologist and native bee expert Sam Droege.
- *National Wildlife Federation* (NWF) *Native Plant Finder*—Use to identify keystone plants native to your ZIP Code™ area. The NWF teamed up with Doug Tallamy and his research collaborator Kimberley Shropshire to create this super handy resource based on over 3,200 references.
- *Biota of North America Project* (BONAP) *North American Plant Atlas* (NAPA) plant distribution maps—Led by Dr. John T. Kartesz, this project and the resulting maps are extremely helpful for evaluating and selecting plants native to your county.

Increased populations of keystone plants are urgently needed for wildlife survival. **Planting native plants is important, but planting native keystone plants is crucial!**

Caterpillars of most fritillary butterfly species depend exclusively upon the keystone plant violet *(Viola)* as their larval food.

Use the NWF *Keystone Plants by Ecoregion* to identify keystone plants in your ecoregion

Visit **nwf.org/keystoneplants**

or search online for **nwf keystone plants by ecoregion.**

Scroll down. Click on your region.

This takes you directly to a printable PDF list of the top keystone plants for your region along with host plant lists for both caterpillars and specialist native bees.

Here we've selected *Marine West Coast Forest—Ecoregion 7*.

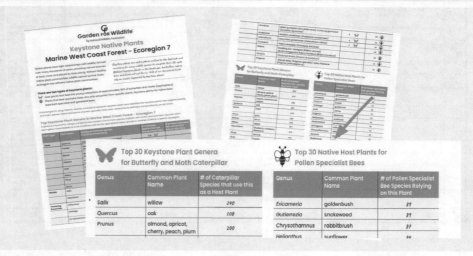

Genus	Common Plant Name	# of Caterpillar Species that use this as a Host Plant
Salix	willow	290
Quercus	oak	208
Prunus	almond, apricot, cherry, peach, plum	200

Top 30 Keystone Plant Genera for Butterfly and Moth Caterpillar

Genus	Common Plant Name	# of Pollen Specialist Bee Species Relying on this Plant
Ericameria	goldenbush	89
Gutierrezia	snakeweed	89
Chrysothamnus	rabbitbrush	87
Helianthus	sunflower	90

Top 30 Native Host Plants for Pollen Specialist Bees

Use the NWF *Host Plants by Ecoregion* to identify host plants in your ecoregion

Search online for **nwf host plants by ecoregion.**

Scroll down below the map to select your ecoregion for a handy list of commercially available host plants for butterflies and moths.

The second page is a helpful list of **Regional Plant Suppliers.**

2 Start a plant list for your wildlife habitat to guide your planting choices

It's a good idea to keep a list of the native plants you have growing on your property as well as those you would like to add to your wildlife habitat. As you identify keystone plants already growing on your property or plant new ones, this list is a handy place to record when and where a species is planted. The lists from the **NWF *Keystone Plants by Ecoregion, Host Species by Ecoregion,* and *Native Plant Finder*** are good starting points. Many government agencies, university extensions, and native plant organizations also provide regional lists of native plants that you can print and use as a checklist. Or you may wish to create your own list. This can be jotted down on paper or recorded on a basic computer spreadsheet like the sample list shown here.

Have	Source	Location	BOTANICAL NAME	Common Name	De	Germ	Sh	F	c	V	M	Dry	Notes	Group	Sub
			Acer negundo	Boxelder									weedy		
✓	on property		Acer rubrum	Red Maple									Acer 297 spp	Shrub	Decid
			Actaea pachypoda	White Baneberry; Doll's Eyes	⊘	F diff	shade	part			moist		poisonous; rich soil	Forb	
	FK		Adiantum pedatum	Maidenhair Fern	⊘		shade	part			moist		unfurling single single leaves closely spaced	Fern	Decid
			Aesculus										spp. Rx Darke?		
✓	FK	Redbud terrace	Aesculus pavia 'humilis'	Dwarf Red Buckeye									NOT NATIVE in PA--NC & south		
			Agalinis purpurea	Purple False Foxglove					sun	wet	moist			Forb	
✓			Agastache foeniculum	Anise Hyssop										Forb	
✓	volunteer 18 seed late Oct	21-trans to many places	Ageratina altissima (Eupatorium rugosum)	White Snakeroot	⊘		shade	part	sun		moist	dry	poisonous	Forb	
			Agrostis perennans	Autumn Bentgrass			shade	part	sun	wet	moist	dry		Grass	
			Allium cernuum	Nodding Onion	⊘	C60		part	sun		moist	dry	JunA 18" pollinator	Forb	
✓	CSF 21		Alnus rugosa	Speckled Alder; Gray Alder									Alnus 255 spp		Decd
			Alnus serrulata	Hazel Alder					sun	wet	moist			Shrub	Decid
✓			Amelanchier stolonifera	Serviceberry										Tree	Decid
		deer territory	Amorpha fructosa	Indigo Bush	⊘	C10-innoculant		part	sun		moist	dry	23 spp	Forb	
✓	MSG21x6		Amorpha nana	Fragrant False Indigo	⊘				sun		moist	dry	2' frangrant pllinator	Forb	
			Amsonia tabernaemontana	Eastern Blue Star; Willow Leaf Bluestar		C60 EZ		part	sun		moist		easy & self-sow	Forb	
			Anaphalis margaritacea	Pearly Everlasting	⊘	C30		part	sun		moist	DRY	butterfly, dry flower	Forb	
✓	BWC plant		Andropogon gerardii	Big Bluestem				part	sun	wet	moist	dry	Andropogen 14 spp	Grass	
			Andropogon glomeratus	Bushy Bluestem				part	sun	wet	moist			Grass	
			Andropogon virginicus	Broomsedge					sun	wet	moist	dry		Grass	
✓	MSG 21 x5		Anemone canadensis	Canadian Anemone	⊘	Z*F40-70 X2		part	sun		moist		2 yr to germ; Weaner Rx; can mow later; aggressive	Forb	Lawn
✓	seed-Oct		Anemone virginiana	Thimbleweed				part	sun		moist	dry		Forb	

If you opt to create a spreadsheet for your plant list like the one above, save yourself the tedious task of typing all the botanical and common names of plants by searching for a regional list of native plants in your region in a format that you can copy and paste the plant names along with other useful data.

Use online search terms such as ***native plant list xls [your region]***. Including "xls" in your search terms increases the chance that the list will copy into a table as rows and columns instead of one long string of data. You will likely need to experiment with several of the search results until you find a list that has the information you want and will copy-and-paste into columns and rows on a spreadsheet.

For starters, there is a blank, reproducible, plant list template on the following page. We'll be adding plants to this plant list in future action steps.

Wildlife Habitat Native Plant List

Have	Source	Location	SCIENTIFIC NAME	Common Name	Deer	Germ Code	Shade	Part	Sun	Wet	Moist	Dry	Notes	Group

5

Keystones

Use the NWF *Native Plant Finder* tool to identify native plants by ZIP Code™

Visit **nwf.org/nativeplantfinder**

or search online for **nwf native plant finder** and click on **Home - Native Plants Finder** or a similar result.

Click **Find Native Plants** for a list of plants suited to your geographic location that host butterfly, skipper, and moth caterpillars.

Find Native Plants

Flowers and Grasses *Trees and Shrubs*

Enter your ZIP Code™.

The results are presented in two categories which helps with planning:

Shown here are profiles for the Denver area *ZIP Code*™ 80013.

The profiles feature plant **genera** (groups of plant species; the singular form is **genus**) ranked by the number of caterpillar species each genus supports.

goldenrod
Solidago
Asterales

The **greater** the caterpillar species number, the more likely this plant genus is to attract a diversity of Lepidoptera species.

Click SAVE to sign in and start a customized list of plants for your wildlife habitat.

Click on a plant profile to learn more about the top 15 caterpillars that use this plant genus as a host plant.

Here are two plant genera profiles:

Some of the plant profiles include a list of plant species within a plant genus that are native to your specific region. For example, *Salix exigua* (see red arrow; above right) is a *Salix* species native to the Denver area.

Each caterpillar (Lepidoptera) profile shows the number of plants available as a host plant for this caterpillar in your area. A low number indicates that a caterpillar is a specialist (in human terms—a picky eater!).

The **lower** the number, the more this Lepidoptera species needs this host plant for survival.

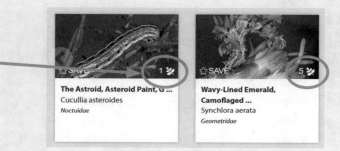

Once you have saved some plants to your list, you may want to print your list.

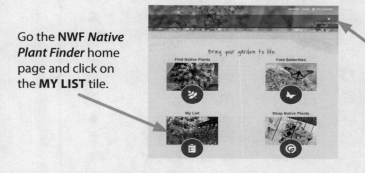

Go the **NWF *Native Plant Finder*** home page and click on the **MY LIST** tile.

Or click on **MY LIST** in the top menu bar.

NOTE: *You'll need to log in (free) to save and print your list.*

Available in many states, the **NWF *Garden for Wildlife*™** program offers plant collections selected for specific ZIP Codes™. The plants are non-GMO and grown without **neonicotinoids** (see page 10.23). Plant care and garden design ideas are included. If your budget allows, this is a convenient way to add keystone plants to your landscape.

Hummingbird Heroes
6-Plant Collection II
(Part Shade)

Monarch Munchables
12-Plant Collection II
(Full Sun)

Butterfly Buffet 3-Shrub
Collection (Part
Sun/Part Shade)

5

Keystones

3 Note the locations of familiar plants that are keystone species already growing on your property

Many keystone species are familiar plants that you likely already know. Take a look at this table compiled in 2018 by Doug Tallamy and his colleagues for the mid-Atlantic region. Using the **NWF** *Keystone Plants by Ecoregion Tool* (see page 5.5), you'll be able to identify a similar list specific to where you live.

20 most valuable woody and perennial native plant genera
for supporting biodiversity in the mid-Atlantic region

WOODY PLANTS				PERENNIAL PLANTS		
Plant Genus	Common Name	Lepidoptera species		Plant Genus	Common Name	Lepidoptera species
Quercus	oak	534		Solidago	goldenrod	115
Prunus	black cherry	456		Aster	asters	112
Salix	willow	455		Helianthus	sunflower	73
Betula	birch	413		Eupatorium	Joe-Pye weed	42
Populus	poplar	368		Ipomoea	morning glory	39
Malus	crabapple	311		Carex	sedges	36
Vaccinium	blueberry	288		Lonicera	honeysuckle	36
Acer	maple	285		Lupinus	lupine	33
Ulmus	elm	213		Viola	violets	29
Pinus	pine	203		Geranium	geraniums	23
Carya	hickory	200		Rudbeckia	black-eyed Susan	17
Crataegus	hawthorn	159		Iris	iris	17
Picea	spruce	156		Oenothera	evening primrose	16
Alnus	alder	156		Asclepias	milkweed	12
Tilia	basswood	150		Verbena	verbena	11
Fraxinus	ash	150		Penstemon	beardtongue	8
Rosa	rose	139		Phlox	phlox	8
Corylus	filbert	131		Monarda	bee balm	7
Juglans	walnut	130		Veronica	veronica	6
Fagus	beech	126		Schizachyrium	little bluestem	6
Castanea	chestnut	125		Lobelia	cardinal flower	4

If you recognize plants from these plant families and have them growing on your property, go ahead and check them off here or on the list you generated for your region, and note their planting locations on your plant list (see page 5.6). If you're not sure of a plant's identification, the plant apps reviewed in the previous action can help with identification (see page 4.9). Spending time exploring the **NWF** *Keystone Plants by Ecoregion, Host Species by Ecoregion,* and *Native Plant Finder* tools that we just looked at will be helpful in getting to know your keystone plants and zeroing in on a plant's identity.

In a moment, we'll explain how to use the *Biota of North America Program* (**BONAP**) maps. Once you have identified a plant, you can use the **BONAP** maps to determine the status of a plant in your region to assess whether a plant is truly native to your county.

5

Keystones

We need to plant more native trees and shrubs!

To appreciate the importance of careful plant choices for our wildlife habitats, consider the table compiled for the mid-Atlantic region by Doug Tallamy and his colleagues (see page 5.10). Compare the number of Lepidoptera species supported by genera of **woody plants** (trees and shrubs) to the number supported by genera of **herbaceous plants** (forbs, ferns, and grasses). Notice that the oak genus (*Quercus*) supports almost five times more than the top herbaceous genus (*Solidago*).

Native pines (*Pinus*) support 203 Lepidoptera species in the mid-Atlantic region and add a welcome evergreen element to the landscape.

Also, notice that even the lowest ranking woody plant genus on this list, chestnut (*Castanea*), supports 10 more Lepidoptera species than the top herbaceous plant genus, goldenrod (*Solidago*). This data gives a very clear message: ***We need to plant more native trees and shrubs!***

Goldenrod is often mistaken for an allergen because it blooms at the same time as ragweed; fortunately, goldenrod doesn't cause allergies.

Visit Homegrown National Park to find keystone trees and shrubs for your ecoregion

Visit homegrownnationalpark.org.

In the top menu, click **Resources.** In the drop-down menu, click **Keystone Plant Guides.** Click **Keystone Trees & Shrubs.**

Scroll down and click your location on the map to identify your Ecoregion Level II.

Click on the tile for your region. We have clicked on the tile for *Ecoregion 5.2 Mixed Wood Shield.*

View the informative profiles of keystone trees and shrubs for your region.

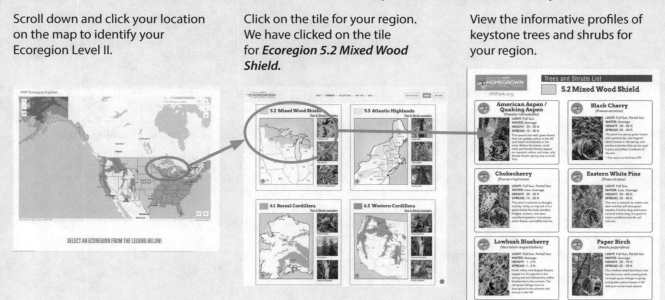

Action 5—Identify your keystone plants **5.11**

4 Use the BONAP maps to determine the status of a plant in your region

Is this plant native? The BONAP maps will help you quickly determine if a plant you have just identified in your landscape is (dare we hope!) native. Developed by the *Biota of North America Program* (**BONAP**), the *North American Plant Atlas* (**NAPA**) is an online series of maps. The **BONAP** maps show the distribution of all the plants growing in the United States and Canada. The maps represent the status of a plant down to the county level! They are color-coded to show the geographic occurrence of a species and its status, for example, native, exotic, noxious, rare, or even extinct. Once you have positively identified a plant, **BONAP** maps are a very helpful tool to determine if the plant is native or invasive in your county.

Here is the **BONAP** map for the highly invasive Japanese honeysuckle (*Lonicera japonica*), a perennial vine growing across the United States. It's difficult to eradicate and can quickly take over gardens and wildlands.

Here is the **BONAP** map for another member of the honeysuckle family, twinberry honeysuckle (*Lonicera involucrata*). Unlike the vining Japanese honeysuckle, twinberry honeysuckle is a welcome shrub in the western United States.

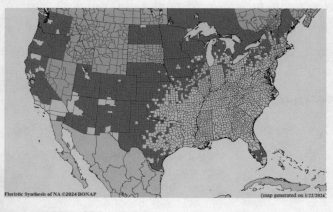

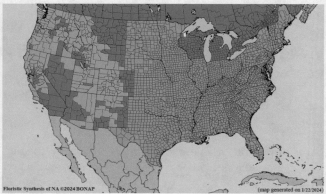

 Species is present and **exotic** in state

Species is present and **exotic** in county

 Species is **noxious** and listed on a state or county noxious plant list

Species is present and **native** in state

Species is present and **native** in county; not rare

 Species is present and **native** in county; but rare

With the help of the **BONAP** maps, we have confirmed that Japanese honeysuckle is an exotic and noxious plant in many parts of the United States. Here is an invasive foe that needs immediate removal!

With the help of the **BONAP** maps, we have identified a welcome native plant that definitely should not be yanked out!

Using the BONAP color key to identify the geographical occurrence of plants

Earlier in this action, we defined native plants as *"plants needed for survival by the wildlife in the region."* Native plants form intricate, supportive relationships with the native wildlife. Now, to clarify additional plant classification vocabulary, let's use the **BONAP** map color key to explore terms that describe the geographical occurrence of plants. Understanding the color key will make the maps much more useful to you.

Color Key	Status of Plant Species	Status of Geographical Occurrence
STATE-WIDE STATUS		
	Present and **native in state**	Species is present in the *state* and native (plants needed by wildlife for survival).
	Present but **exotic in state**	Species is non-native (also called 'introduced' or 'alien'); similar to adventive species, but the term exotic implies that the species originated in a different continent and was introduced to the state intentionally or accidentally.
	Not present in *state*	This one is pretty clear!
COUNTY-WIDE STATUS		
	Present and **native in county**; not rare	Species is present and plentiful in this county and native. This is a welcome status as it indicates a healthy population of a native species in your county.
	Extinct species	Species used to live in this county but no longer exists anywhere.
	Present but **adventive** in this area	Species is not native in this county, but it is native in a neighboring county, state, or region.
	Waif species	Species is an unusual occurrence in this county; either it cannot reproduce without human help, or it only survives for one to several seasons.
	Present and native but **rare**	Species is native but present only in small numbers.
	Noxious species on state or county list	Species is on a noxious plant list or law as it can cause economic or environmental harm or endanger public health in this region [Plant Protection Act (Public Law 106-224)]. **Do not plant these and remove any plants you encounter!**
	Species **eradicated**	Humans have completely removed this species from this county.
	Species **extirpated** (historic)	Species historically has grown in this county, but it is now locally extinct. It still grows elsewhere.
	Species present and **exotic in *county***	Species is non-native; this is similar to an adventive species, but the term exotic implies that the species originated on a different continent and was introduced to the county intentionally or accidentally. **Do not plant these species!**
	Questionable presence	This one speaks for itself!

How to use the BONAP maps to determine the status of a plant species

There are various ways to search the **BONAP** maps. Let's look at how to determine the status of a specific plant species in your county. For example, let's say you find a plant you have never seen before growing in one of your landscape beds. You use one of the plant identification apps and confidently identify the plant as wild bergamot (*Monarda fistulosa*). Follow these steps to figure out the status of this plant in your county.

A patch of wild bergamot *(Monarda fistulosa; right)*

Visit: bonap.net/napa

or search online for **bonap maps** and navigate to the site. (The home page may look different.)

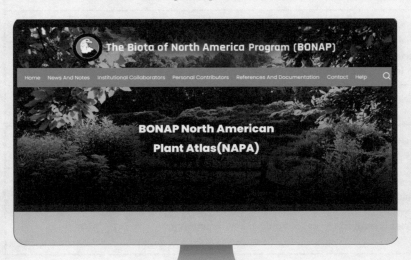

Scroll down to select the way you would like to view the maps. For our purposes, click on **Alphabetically by Genus** in the **US County Maps** section:

PHYTOGEOGRAPHIC MAPS

1. US County Maps

- Alphabetically by Genus
- In Traditional family Arrangement
- In APG family Arrangement
- In Phylogenetic family Arrangement
- BONAP Maps by States and Provinces

Click on the first letter of the genus of a plant. We've clicked on '**M**' for *Monarda*.

Click on the genus (they are arranged alphabetically **across the rows**) which in our case is *Monarda*.

How to use the BONAP maps to determine the status of a plant species, *continued*

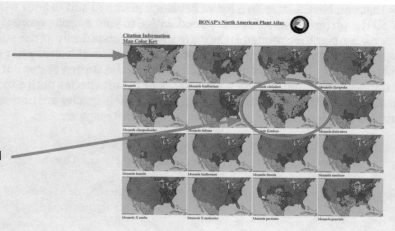

The first map in the top left corner shows the combined geographical occurrence of all the species of this genus in the United States.

The following maps show the distribution of individual species within this genus organized alphabetically by the species name.

Scroll through the maps and find the individual species, in our case, *Monarda fistulosa*.

Click on the map for a close-up view of your region.

Use the color key to interpret the map:

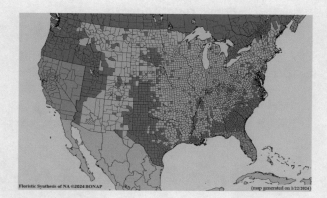

 Species is present and **native** in state

 Species is present and **native** in county; not rare

We see that wild bergamot is a welcome native plant growing throughout much of the United States.

In contrast, if the plant you identified had been stiltgrass (*Microstegium vimineum*), the color keys would be quite different:

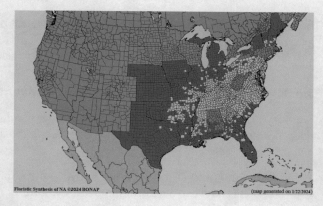

 Species is present and **exotic** in state

 Species is present and **exotic** in county

 Species is **noxious** and listed on a state or county noxious plant list

With the help of the **BONAP** maps, we see that stiltgrass is an exotic and noxious pest in many parts of the United States. We have identified another invasive plant that needs immediate removal!

 The BONAP materials shown here and elsewhere in this book are used with permission from Dr. John T. Kartesz. Kartesz, J.T., The Biota of North America Program (BONAP). 2015. North American Plant Atlas. (http://bonap.net/napa). Chapel Hill, N.C. [maps generated from Kartesz, J.T. 2015. Floristic Synthesis of North America, Version 1.0 Biota of North America, Version 1.0 Biota of North America Program (BONAP). (in press)].

Use the BONAP maps to confirm your keystone plant choices

Now that you have a start on a list of keystone plants to add to your wildlife habitat, it's a good idea to confirm that all the plants on your list are indeed native to **your specific ecoregion**. This can take a bit of detective work. Often native plant recommendations are made geographically at the state level. Given the potentially very distinct ecoregions within a state, a native plant from a state-level list may not actually be native to your ecoregion. Retail nurseries and big box stores offer plants native to the United States but not necessarily native at the local level, and online seed suppliers offer a wide variety of plant species native to different regions throughout the United States. The **BONAP** maps make it easy to check which species are native to where you live. Let's look at some examples that demonstrate how helpful the **BONAP** maps are.

Are these plants native in my county? Should I grow them?

Suppose you live in Kentucky, and a local nursery is offering two species of oaks for sale: *Quercus incana* and *Quercus imbricaria*. With the BONAP maps, you can easily check if these oak species are native to your county.

 Access the **BONAP** maps as we did on page 5.14, or simply search online for **bonap county quercus**.

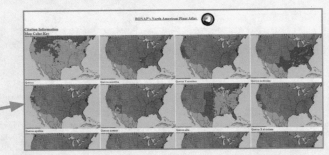

Scroll through the maps of the *Quercus* species to find the species of oaks. Click on each map for a closer view.

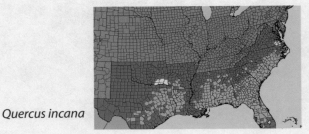

Quercus incana

Quercus imbricaria

These maps make it clear that *Quercus incana* (*left*) is not native to Kentucky, however, for most counties in Kentucky, *Quercus imbricaria* (*right*) would be a good addition to a wildlife habitat.

The BONAP map shows this plant as being adventive where I live. Should I grow it?

Suppose you live in Salt Lake City, Utah. In their native plant section, a local nursery is offering lovely California poppy (Eschscholzia californica) in full bloom.

 Adventive—Species is not native in this county, but it is native in a neighboring county, state, or region

A quick glance at the county-level **BONAP** map for California poppy shows that, indeed, this plant is native to parts of the United States, including California, of course. However, the teal green color of the counties in the Salt Lake City area shows that California poppy is **adventive** in this region. In other words, where a plant is adventive, it is not native.

Given this distinction, it's best to avoid planting adventive plants since the local native wildlife has not coevolved with this plant.

Use the BONAP maps to confirm your keystone plant choices, *continued*

You have likely seen goldenrod or "*Solidago* spp." ("spp." stands for more than one species) as a highly recommended keystone genus. But which goldenrod species should you plant? To identify species within a genus that are native to your county, the **BONAP** maps come in handy again, but we'll interpret the results in a slightly different way.

Which species within a keystone genus are native to my county?

Access the BONAP maps for the *Solidago* genus by entering the search terms **bonap county solidago**.

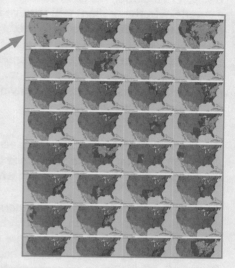

The first map in the top left corner shows the combined geographical occurrence of all the species of the genus *Solidago* in the United States.

Each of the following maps shows the distribution of an individual species of goldenrod organized alphabetically by the species name.

NOTE: *Shown here is just a small portion of the 76 maps of different species within the Solidago genus.*

Scroll through the maps of all the *Solidago* species looking for these colors in your region:

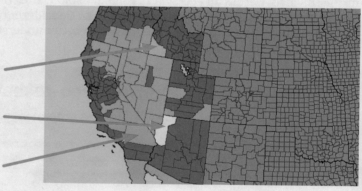

 Species used to grow in this county but is no longer present (extirpated)

 Species is present and native in this county but rare

 Species is present and native in this county and not rare

When your county is color-coded with one of the colors above, this plant species is native to your county. The dark green shows that the species is native and present in the state but not present in this county. In the map above, the light brown color to the east of the areas in green shows that the species is not present in the state.

Interpreting the BONAP maps accurately

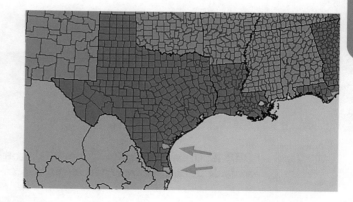

When first using the maps, it's easy to misinterpret the dark green color code on the map and conclude that this species grows throughout the state. Dark green areas show that this species is native somewhere in this state but *not* in these counties. Look at this map showing the range of red mangrove (*Rhizophora mangle*), a coastal tree that grows at sea level. Red mangrove can be found in a couple of areas along the Texas Gulf Coast but certainly not in the state's North Central Plains!

5 Explore the EPA *Ecoregion Maps* to get to know your region's wildlife habitats

You are probably familiar with a hardiness zone map such as this one:

Traditionally, gardeners have referred to the **USDA Hardiness Zone Map** to determine if a plant will grow well in their region. This map addresses only a fraction of a plant's needs primarily indicating, for example, whether a plant will survive in the winter or receive enough chill hours to produce fruit. This map does not consider a plant's relationship within an ecosystem. Fortunately, as the urgency of planting for wildlife becomes increasingly apparent, a much more useful series of maps is now available—the **EPA** *Ecoregion Maps of North America.*

The USDA Plant Hardiness Zone Map was updated in 2023. Visit *planthardiness.ars.usda.gov* to identify and learn more about the hardiness zone where you live.

The **EPA** *Ecoregion Maps of North America* clearly delineate geographical areas with similarly functioning ecosystems. The ecoregion maps represent four levels: **Level I** presents the broadest divisions of ecoregions and **Level IV** presents the smallest unique regional divisions. With each increasing level of ecoregion divisions, the characteristics of a wildlife habitat become more defined. Yet even within **Level IV**, the ecoregions can often be further divided. Within an ecoregion's general habitat, sites that share similar characteristics form unique but consistent wildlife habitats called **microhabitats**. Considering the microhabitat of a site when choosing plants will give a plant the best chance for survival. To better understand ecoregions and their microhabitats, let's explore the ecoregion maps.

Visit: epa/gov/eco-research/ecoregions

or search online for **epa ecoregions** and navigate to the site.

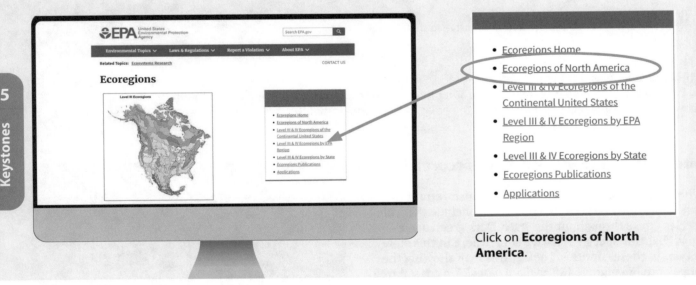

Click on **Ecoregions of North America**.

SOURCE: United States Environmental Protection Agency, *Ecoregions of North America.* Available online at https://www.epa.gov/eco-research/ecoregions.

Explore the EPA *Ecoregions Maps* to get to know your region's wildlife habitats, *continued*

Compare the four levels of EPA Ecoregion Maps:

Level I - Continental United States

To get a feel for the differences between the four map levels, let's look at the ecoregions of Nevada.

At **Level I**, almost all of Nevada is in ecoregion **10.0 North American Deserts** with a tiny western edge of the state in **6.0 Northwestern Forested Mountains.**

Level II - Continental United States

At **Level II**, Nevada is divided into three regions:

6.2 Western Cordillera (the tiny western edge)

10.1 Cold Deserts

10.2 Deserts

Level III - Continental United States

At **Level III**, Nevada is divided into four regions:

6.2.12 Sierra Nevada (the tiny edge)

10.1.3 Northern Basin and Range

10.2 Central Basin and Range

10.2.1 Mojave Basin and Range

Level IV - Oklahoma (example)

The **Level IV** maps use a different numbering system from Levels I - III. The maps are accompanied by informative descriptions of each Level IV ecoregion.

At **Level IV**, Nevada is divided into 43 different ecoregions!

Identify your Level I, Level II, Level III, and Level IV Ecoregions

As mentioned earlier, native plant recommendations are often made at the state level which can be misleading. After viewing the ecoregion maps of Nevada, it's clear that a list of recommended native plants for the state of Nevada could include plants that would thrive in the cold desert regions but perish in the warmer southern deserts or vice versa. Getting to know your local ecoregions can help you choose native plants that are best adapted to the growing conditions where you live.

At all four levels of the EPA **Ecoregions of North America** maps, each ecoregion is color-coded, and each map includes a color key identifying the ecoregion's habitat. For example, let's identify the Level II ecoregion for El Reno, Oklahoma:

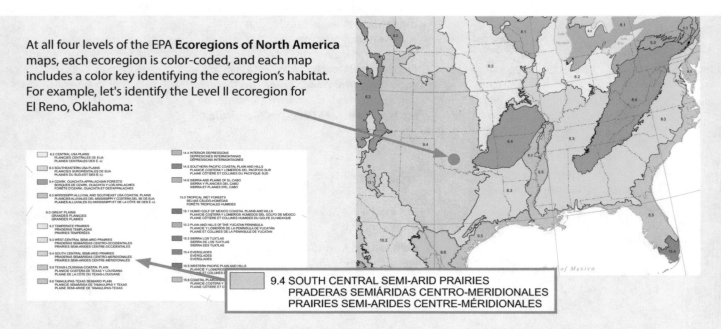

Referring to the color key for the **Level II** map for El Reno, we can see that the salmon color represents the **9.4 South Central Semi-Arid Prairies** ecoregion.

Identify your local ecoregions

Following the steps we just went through, find your location on each level of the **EPA Ecoregions of North America** maps.

Note the **Level I** ecoregion for your property: _____

Note the **Level II** ecoregion for your property: _____

Note the **Level III** ecoregion for your property: _____

As mentioned earlier, the **Level IV** ecoregion maps are state based. They use a different numbering system with color keys that make it easy to identify each region. Many of the **Level IV** ecoregion maps include downloadable PDF maps that include informative profiles of each ecoregion like the one shown here for El Reno, Oklahoma. Check out your **Level IV** resources!

Note the **Level IV** ecoregion for your property: _____

Get to know the characteristic microhabitats of your ecoregion

Consider your property. Are there different microhabitats within your wildlife landscape? For example, several large trees growing near one another may begin to form a woodland habitat that will support similar species of plants and animals to those found in woodland habitats throughout your ecoregion. Elsewhere on your property, a sunny, open area may attract similar species to those found in meadows in your ecoregion. Getting to know the characteristic habitats of your ecoregion, all the way down to its microhabitats, will help you to design, choose plants, and install habitat features that will support a predictable population of wildlife visitors and residents.

Example A: On a property near Asheville, North Carolina in the *Blue Ridge Level IV Ecoregion 66d, Southern Crystalline Ridges and Mountains* (*left*), you could expect to see a community of plants living along a stream (*middle*) that would be different from those living in a sunny meadow of a mountainside forest clearing (*right*) on the same property.

Example B: Similarly, much of Orange County, California is in the *Southern California Level IV Ecoregion 85d, Los Angeles Plain* (*left*), yet the plant and wildlife community in the Upper Newport Bay (*middle*), an inland delta, will be different from that of the coastal sage scrub (CSS) that blankets much of the surrounding foothills. Some characteristic plants of this soft chaparral community (*right*) include California sagebrush (*Artemesia californica*), black sage (*Salvia mellifera*), California buckwheat (*Erigeron fasciculatum*), toyon (*Heteromeles arbutifolia*), and lemonade berry (*Rhus integrifolia*).

On your own property, you will find that the wildlife habitats that are characteristic of your ecoregion will determine the appropriate plants as well as the wildlife species likely to visit or reside in your landscape. You will also discover unique conditions in different areas of your property even if you live on a small urban lot. These conditions will further refine your choice of plants, and thus, the creatures you can expect to see.

5

Keystones

6   Identify the host plants for caterpillars (Lepidoptera) that specialize on specific plants

Earlier in this action (see pages 5.8 - 5.9), we looked at how to use the **NWF** *Native Plant Finder* to find native plants in your area that are host plants for Lepidoptera species (butterflies, skippers, and moths). Here, we'll use this same tool in reverse to find Lepidoptera species native to your area and the host plants they rely on for reproduction. By doing this, we can identify specialist Lepidoptera species whose survival depends on just one or a small number of specific plants. For example, the caterpillar of the familiar monarch butterfly is a specialist that depends upon plants in the milkweed genus (*Asclepias*) for its survival. Although some of these host plants may not be keystone plants (because the surrounding ecosystem would not change significantly without them), growing plants from the resulting list will help encourage biodiversity where you live by supporting specialist species.

Visit **nwf.org/nativeplantfinder**

or search online for **nwf native plant finder** and navigate to the site.

Click **Find Butterflies** for a list of butterflies and moths native to your ZIP Code™.

Find Native Plants

The resulting profiles feature butterflies and moths native to your area.

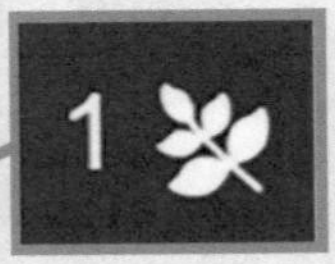

Each Lepidoptera profile shows the number of host plant species available in this region.

Great Spangled Fritillary, Var
...
Speyeria cybele
Nymphalidae

Hackberry Emperor
Asterocampa celtis
Nymphalidae

Monarch
Danaus plexippus
Nymphalidae

Olive Hairstreak, Juniper Hair
...
Callophrys gryneus
Lycaenidae

Showy Emerald
Dichorda iridaria
Geometridae

The Astroid, Asteroid Paint, G
...
Cucullia asteroides
Noctuidae

Unexpected Cycnia
Cycnia inopinatus
Erebidae

Zebra Swallowtail
Eurytides marcellus
Papilionidae

As explained on page 5.9, the **lower** the number of host plant species, the more critical it is to plant this host plant to ensure the survival of this caterpillar species. **Remember, if this caterpillar cannot find the plant species it needs to survive, this caterpillar species cannot survive in your area!**

5 Keystones

Use the NWF *Native Plant Finder* to identify the host plants for caterpillars (Lepidoptera) that specialize on specific plants, *continued*

Click the name in each profile for a list of the specific host plant(s) the caterpillar can eat.

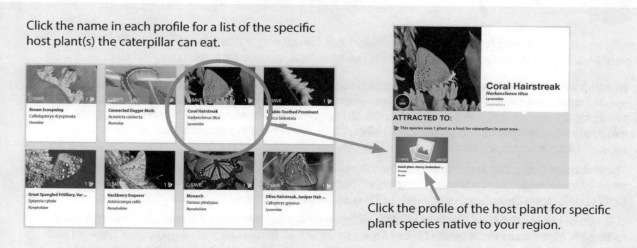

Click the profile of the host plant for specific plant species native to your region.

Click SAVE to create a customized list of Lepidoptera you are likely to attract to your wildlife habitat.

Dare to plant oaks and other trees—they really will grow!

Oaks and other trees are valuable host plants for caterpillars. At first, a tree seedling is often hidden in the herbaceous layer and almost invisible. Here, an oak gets a small but earnest start as fall approaches. I marked its location and keep it weeded.

After several years of growth, a sapling has more presence but is still lost in the busyness of the landscape in early fall. Protected from deer its entire life, this hickory is slowly making progress.

One day you look out and realize that the acorn or seedling you planted is now a tree! Planted as a seedling from a 1-gallon pot 6 years ago, this scarlet oak (*Quercus coccinea*) is now a 20-foot-tall tree.

5

Keystones

Digging in deeper

Here are more resources for learning about your ecoregion and identifying native plants—especially keystone plants—and the caterpillars they host (please refer to the Appendix for publication details).

Nature's Best Hope: A New Approach to Conservation That Starts in Your Yard: Doug's discussion about specialization (see pages 99 - 106) clarifies why introduced plants simply cannot take the place of native plants for the vast majority of our native insects. Doug goes on to explain why planting native plants, especially keystone plants (see pages 125 - 144 and 206), is the most important action we can take to support biodiversity. You'll come away from this chapter informed and inspired!

The Nature of Oaks: The Rich Ecology of Our Most Essential Trees: The oaks (*Quercus*) reign supreme among keystone plants, supporting more Lepidoptera species than many other native species combined. In this book, Doug describes the rich web of life supported by oak trees throughout the seasons.

This duo of books, ***The Field Guide to Wildlife Habitats of the Eastern United States*** and ***The Field Guide to Wildlife Habitats of the Western United States*** by Janine M. Benyus, provide a glimpse of the flora and fauna characteristic of different types of habitats, such as cattail marshes, shrub-sapling edges, grassy fields, Appalachian cove forests, sagebrush desert, redwood forest, and many more.

Regional books about native plants complement the online resources mentioned in this action and on page 9.5. Once you have identified the keystone plants for your ecoregion, it's nice to have a good regional native plant book to reference. Here are just a few examples:

- Northeast: ***Native Plants of the Northeast: A Guide for Gardening and Conservation*** by Donald J. Leopold
- Southeast: ***Native Plants of the Southeast: A Comprehensive Guide to the Best 460 Species for the Garden*** by Larry Mellichamp
- Midwest and Eastern U.S.: ***The Gardener's Guide to Prairie Plants*** by Neil Diboll and Hilary Cox
- West Coast: ***The Drought-Defying California Garden: 230 Native Plants for a Lush, Low-Water Landscape*** by Greg Rubin and Lucy Warren

Field guides to help identify the caterpillars and the host plants they depend upon:

- North America: ***Caterpillars in the Field and Garden: A Guide to the Butterfly Caterpillars of North America*** by Thomas J. Allen, James P. Brock, and Jeffrey Glassberg. Numerous photos and clear descriptions make this a handy resource for identifying the caterpillars of butterflies and skippers.

- Eastern U.S.: ***Caterpillars of Eastern North America: A Guide to Identification and Natural History*** by David L. Wagner. This comprehensive guide will help you identify the caterpillars that support life within your wildlife habitat.

The **MGNV Illustrated Glossary** (*mgnv.org/plants/glossary*) offered by the **Master Gardeners of Northern Virginia** is a helpful tool for identifying keystone plants (see page 4.22 for a detailed description).

Discover Life (*www.discoverlife.org*) is another amazing online resource to help identify not only plants but also vertebrates, fungi, and insects. Designed by **The Polistes Corporation** and served by **Sam Houston State University** in Huntsville, Texas, this site features over 1.4 million species pages and over 820,000 shareable worldwide maps making this a resource well worth exploring!

We now have a good idea about what keystone plants are and which keystone species we want to add to the landscape. In addition, we looked at how to identify plants needed by Lepidoptera species (butterflies, skippers, and moths) that specialize on certain plants. Next, we'll look at choosing plants for specialist pollinators such as native pollen specialist bees that require specific plant groups or even a single plant species for survival.

Action 6—CHECKSHEET
Choose plants for specialist pollinators

Step:	✔	Action Needed:	Page:
1	☐	Identify native plant species that will provide a continuous sequence of blooms to support pollinators	6.4
2	☐	Refine your wildlife habitat plant list to include plants for specialists	6.6
3	☐	Identify the specific plants that support native pollen specialist bees in your region	6.7
4	☐	Identify the specific plants that support native bumble bees	6.10

The blueberry digger bee (*Habropoda laboriosa*), a native pollen specialist bee, specializes on redbud (*Cercis*) and blueberry (*Vaccinium*) for its survival.

In contrast, the two-spotted bumble bee (*Bombus bimaculatus*) is a generalist that forages on a wide selection of plants.

6

Pollinators

Challenges pollinators face and the actions we can take to help them

Habitat loss:

Create a wildlife habitat filled with the plant genera that support native bees along with ample nesting sites (plant stems, bare ground, leaf litter, branches, deadwood) and water sources.

Fragmentated habitat:

Connect your plantings with neighboring plantings wherever possible to create **wildlife corridors** (connected habitats).

Monoculture planting such as lawn causing lack of plant diversity:

Shrink the lawn and replace it with a variety of native plants that fill your landscape from ground to sky.

Specialists lacking the plants they specialize on:

Identify and plant the native plants native pollen specialist bees and other specialists need to survive.

Periods when bees emerge where nothing is in bloom:

Plan and plant for a succession of blooms. Plant in groups of 3 to 5 plants to attract pollinators and other foragers.

Nesting sites lacking or disturbed:

Leave areas of bare ground for ground-nesting bees. Leave pithy and hollow stems for stem-nesting bees. When safe, leave dead trees and fallen wood for cavity-nesting bees.

Plants treated with toxic chemicals:

Don't use toxic pesticides, herbicides, or fertilizers. Don't buy plants treated with neonicotinoids!

Predators, pathogens, and parasites:

Practice bee-friendly management and good hygiene if providing homemade or artificial bee nests. Better yet, grow the plants native bees need for nesting.

Disrupted bloom timing, temperature, and precipitation due to climate change:

Plant trees and keep dead woody materials on your property. Do what you can to reduce your carbon footprint.

Pollinators 6

Action 6—GUIDE
Choose plants for specialist pollinators

Many species of mining bees (*Andrena*) are native pollen specialist bees that depend upon willow (*Salix*) for survival.

Planting keystone plants meets the needs of many native pollen specialist bee species, host-specific caterpillars, and other specialist animals. Yet, there are many unique animal-plant relationships in which a particular animal species depends upon a specific plant species without which it cannot complete its life cycle. Although a plant may not be a keystone plant that many species depend on, it may be critical for the survival of the few species that it nourishes or hosts. **If the plant species required by a specialist is not present, that animal will not be present.**

Doug Tallamy along with native bee experts Jarrod Fowler and Sam Droege recommend that we plant with specialists in mind because these plants will also support the generalists. Take heart, choosing plants for specialists is not as daunting a task as it may seem. Fortunately, keystone plants meet the needs of many specialists. Plus, the contributions of these tireless researchers have provided us with data-based plant recommendations and planting guides for help identifying needed plants.

As your landscape grows and your experience builds, learning about the unique specialist relationships and including the plants that support these relationships is an essential next step toward supporting vulnerable species and welcoming even greater biodiversity to your wildlife habitat.

Evening primrose (*Oenothera biennis*) is a source of pollen for some native pollen specialist bees.

6

Pollinators

① Identify native plant species that will provide a continuous sequence of blooms to support pollinators

As Doug Tallamy points out in *Nature's Best Hope*, pollen must be available from a continuous sequence of blooms. If there is even a short gap in blooms lasting only two to three weeks, the native bees that depend upon this pollen source may perish. In this action, we'll use the **Xerces Society** *Pollinator Conservation Program* resources to identify native pollinator plants and their bloom periods for your region. These plants can then be added to your plant list with their bloom times noted.

Pussy willow (*Salix discolor*) provides an essential source of pollen for both specialist and generalist bees.

Exploring the Xerces Society *Pollinator Conservation Program* resources

If you're not already familiar with the **Xerces Society for Invertebrate Conservation,** you're in for a pleasant surprise. For over 50 years, this international, non-profit organization has been working to *"protect the natural world through the conservation of invertebrates and their habitats."* Their three key program areas are **pollinator protection, endangered species conservation,** and **reducing pesticide use and impacts.** Here, we'll point out the extensive resources available in their *Pollinator Conservation Program*. Then, we'll access the plant lists available for different regions of North America to identify pollinator plants for your region.

Native long-horned bees (*Melissodes*) specialize on pollen from the aster family (Asteraceae), such as aster, black-eyed Susan, goldenrod, and sunflowers.

Visit: xerces.org

Before delving into the **Xerces Society** *Pollinator Conservation Program,* you may wish to explore the many resources offered by the **Xerces Society**. Here, you will find ways to get involved through webinars, workshops, and community science projects along with a wealth of resources including informative publications, the **Xerces Society** *Wings* magazine, educational resources, and so much more.

Now, let's explore the **Xerces Society** *Pollinator Conservation Program* resources.

Websites are ever changing! If you have trouble finding any of these materials from the **Xerces Society**, do an online search for **xerces [title of materials]**, for example: **xerces pollinator conservation resources**. You will likely find all these materials though perhaps in a different location, along with exciting new resources.

Exploring the Xerces Society *Pollinator Conservation Program* resources, *continued*

On the **xerces.org** website, find **Our Work** in the top menu. Click **Protecting Pollinators** to view the **Pollinator Conservation Program** resources.

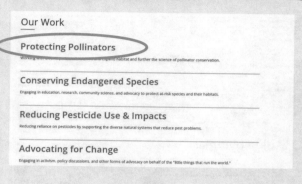

Here, you can read about the **Pollinator Conservation Program.**

Scroll down and click **Find Pollinator Conservation Resources**.

Click on your region of the map.

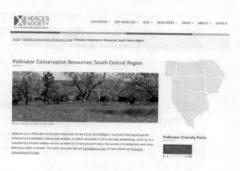

Scroll down for regional resources.

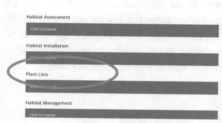

Note the regional resources for habitat assessment, habitat installation, **plant lists**, habitat management, pesticide protection, identification and monitoring resources, native seed and plant vendors, and further reading.

From the regional resources list, click **Plant Lists**.

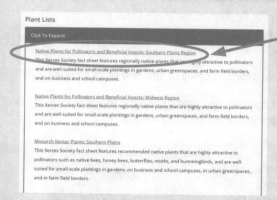

Here, we've selected the list for the Southern Plains.

Scan the lists until you come across **Pollinator Plants [your region]**. Click on the title for a web or printer-friendly guide or list of pollinator plants in your region.

These handy resources include plant information, such as height, flower color, bloom period, water needs, ecological services, deer resistance, and more—all of which will be helpful as you design your landscape beds.

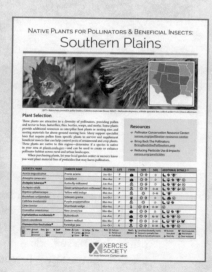

The Xerces Society materials shown here and elsewhere in this book are used with permission from the Xerces Society of Invertebrate Conservation (xerces.org).

6

Pollinators

2 Refine your wildlife habitat plant list to include plants for specialists

Now, let's add the plant suggestions from the **Xerces Society** *Pollinator Conservation Program* lists to your plant list. On your list, note the plant bloom times so that you can procure plants that ensure a continuous succession of bloom. By now, your plant list may be getting pretty long, which is good because this will give you plenty of options when procuring plants.

When reading lists of native plant suggestions, keep in mind that the top recommendations will vary depending on the focus of the list. For example, the primary focus of the pollinator plant lists from the **Xerces Society** *Pollinator Conservation Program* is the survival of native bees. In contrast, the **NWF** *Native Plant Finder* is especially helpful for identifying keystone plants essential for supporting caterpillars, and the **Audubon Native Plant Database** (*below*) focuses on plants that support birds. As you explore these resources, you'll find that some of the plants are already on your list since many of them are keystone plants!

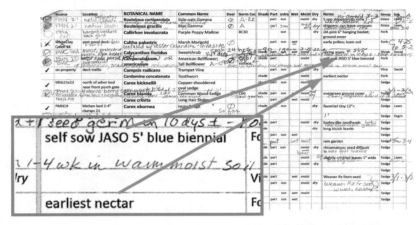

Noting the ecological service that a plant offers is a helpful reminder. For example, the letters JASO indicate that bellflower (*Campanula americana*) blooms from July to October, and toothwort (*Cardamine concatenata*) is an early source of nectar.

Making a note of how a plant helps your wildlife habitat will help you determine which plants to procure first. Place a priority on plants that show up on more than one list. For example, in the mid-Atlantic region, highbrush blueberry (*Vaccinium corymbosum*) is at the top of many plant lists because:

- It's a keystone plant supporting **281 Lepidoptera species.**
- It **blooms early** in the season when blooms are less abundant.
- Its leaves are used by leafcutter **bees to build their nests.**
- It's a **source of pollen for native bees.**
- Its **berries** are happily devoured by birds (and people!).
- It even has **pretty fall color.**

"Must-grow" plants like this deserve to be at the top of your wish list!

Blueberry (*Vaccinium*) offers many ecological benefits if the planting site has moisture and a low pH for these acid-loving shrubs.

The **National Audubon** *Native Plant Database* is an invaluable resource for bird lovers. This online tool will help you find native plants that your local bird species depend upon for survival. Search online for **audubon native plant database** and navigate to the site. Enter your ZIP Code™ to generate a list of plants native to your region that includes profiles of bird families that each plant may attract. Click on a bird family for profiles of bird species within this family to find birds that live in your ecoregion. Each bird profile provides information about the bird's habitat, diet, eggs, nesting, natural range, recordings of its song and calls along with a map that predicts the change in the bird's range due to climate change.

Ruby-throated hummingbird baby (*Archilochus colubris*)

③ Identify the specific plants that support native pollen specialist bees in your region

Adult bees eat both nectar and pollen, but their larval young develop solely on pollen. Many native bees are generalists when it comes to nectar, so they can get nectar from a wide variety of plants including some introduced plants. In contrast, the pollen gathering anatomy of native bees is exclusively adapted to the botanical structure of their host plants.

Horticulturalist and conservationist Jarrod Fowler and wildlife biologist Sam Droege conducted extensive research into native bee species and the plants they visit. Their painstaking research, which they have generously given permission to share in this book, allows us to identify the specific plant species that will contribute to the survival of native bee species in a region. Summarized below are their findings showing the top five plant **genera** (groups of species) visited by native pollen specialist bees:

Plant genera supporting native pollen specialist bees by U.S. regions

According to Fowler and Droege's research, the top five plant genera visited by native pollen specialist bees in the following regions are:

☐ **Western United States**	☐ **Central United States**	☐ **Eastern United States**
Helianthus (101 bee species)	Helianthus (101 bee species)	Solidago (39 bee species)
Gutierrezia (94)	Grindelia (67)	Helianthus (35)
Ericameria (93)	Heterotheca (63)	Symphyotrichum (32)
Chrysothamnus (91)	Solidago (57)	Rudbeckia (26)
Grindelia (84)	Verbesina (54)	Chrysopsis (19)
SOURCE: Western U.S.: Fowler, J. (2020). *Pollen Specialist Bees of the Western United States*	SOURCE: Central U.S.: Fowler, J. (2020). *Pollen Specialist Bees of the Central United States*	SOURCE: Eastern U.S.: Fowler, J. & Droege, S. (2020). *Pollen Specialist Bees of the Eastern United States*

Making a concerted effort to include plants from all these genera and especially the plants recommended in the resources on page 6.9 could help to provide a threatened bee species in your region with the specific plants it needs for survival.

Look at the table above and put a check mark for the region in which you live.

Are any species from these genera already on your plant list?

TOP GENERA # of species already on plant list:

Helianthus _____   _____

_____   _____

_____   _____

_____   _____

Next, we'll use the **BONAP** maps to identify some species for each of the top plant genera for your region (as listed in the table above) that are native to the ecoregion where you live.

6

Pollinators

Identify the specific plants that support native pollen specialist bees in your region, *continued*

Now that we have identified the top genera of host plant species for native pollen specialist bees in your region, let's use the **BONAP** maps to identify specific plant species within the top five genera. (For a review about how to access and use the **BONAP** maps, see pages 5.14 - 5. 15.)

Search online for **bonap county [genus]**.

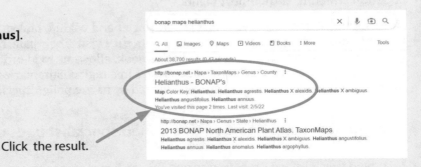

Since *Helianthus* is an important genus across the United States, we'll look for species in this genus using the search terms: **bonap county helianthus.**

Click the result.

Remember that the first map in the top left corner shows the combined geographical occurrence of all the species of the genus *Helianthus* in the United States. Here, the first map is not really useful for our purposes. Instead, scroll through the rest of the maps which show the distribution of individual species of *Helianthus* organized alphabetically.

Make a note of the species where your region is light green or yellow:

Species is present and native in county and not rare

Species is present and native in county but rare

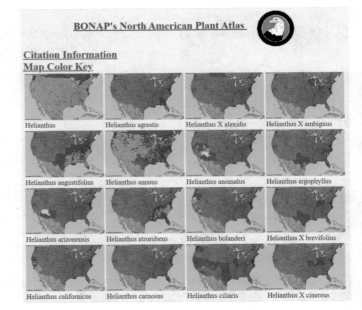

Avoid species that have areas in pink because this shows that a species is noxious or regulated as an invasive plant in this region. For example, although *Helianthus ciliaris* is native to parts of the United States and is of value to bees and birds, it's considered a noxious weed in Texas, and Washington state has banned its sale and distribution due to the plant's aggressive growth habits.

Typically, the more areas in light green that a species has, the easier it will be to find a source for this species. For example, a source for *Helianthus maximiliani* (*left*) would likely be easier to find than for *H. salcifolius* (*right*).

Identify the specific plants that support native pollen specialist bees in your region, *continued*

It's worth making the effort to identify the plants required by native bees considering that almost 60 percent of our native bees are listed as rare (Fowler, 2020). **Sixty percent is an astounding number!** Planting a pollinator garden in your wildlife habitat is a concrete step that you can take to reverse these species' trajectories toward extinction.

Depending on where you live in the United States, approximately 25 to 35 percent of the native bees are pollen specialists. Consider the data for your region:

- *Western United States:* Approximately 1,050 of 3,000 native bee species are specialists (**35%**)
- *Central United States:* Approximately 480 of 1,800 native bee species are specialists (**almost 30%**)
- *Eastern United States:* Approximately 190 of 770 native bee species are specialists (**almost 25%**)

This means that for approximately one-third of our native bees, pollen must come from specific plant species or genera for these native bee species to survive. Hopefully, you have been able to identify some plants that will help support these imperiled native bees. If you would like to dig in even deeper, Jarrod Fowler and Sam Droege have got you covered! Check out the following resources shown here with their permission.

Western United States:

Visit jarrodfowler.com/pollen_specialist.html OR search online for **pollen specialist bees western us.**

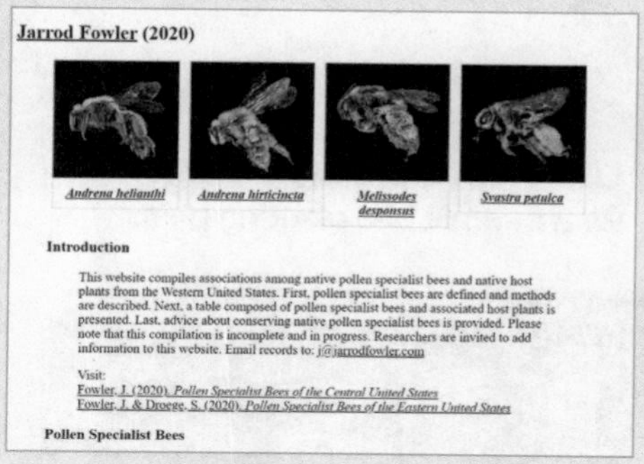

Jarrod Fowler (2020)

Andrena helianthi *Andrena hirticincta* *Melissodes desponsus* *Svastra petulca*

Introduction

This website compiles associations among native pollen specialist bees and native host plants from the Western United States. First, pollen specialist bees are defined and methods are described. Next, a table composed of pollen specialist bees and associated host plants is presented. Last, advice about conserving native pollen specialist bees is provided. Please note that this compilation is incomplete and in progress. Researchers are invited to add information to this website. Email records to j@jarrodfowler.com

Visit:
Fowler, J. (2020), *Pollen Specialist Bees of the Central United States*
Fowler, J. & Droege, S. (2020), *Pollen Specialist Bees of the Eastern United States*

Pollen Specialist Bees

Central United States:

Visit jarrodfowler.com/bees_pollen.html OR search online for **pollen specialist bees central us.**

After the very long list of bees and helpful details about each bee species, scroll way down to **Recommendations.** The first paragraph lists plant genera that pollen specialist bees need. Use the **BONAP** maps to zero in on species for your specific region.

When tracking down a source for plants mentioned in these reports, keep in mind that due to developments in plant **taxonomy** (classification), some of the scientific names of the plants may have changed since the date of these reports. A quick online search will provide a plant's updated scientific name.

Eastern United States:

Visit jarrodfowler.com/specialist_bees.html OR search online for **pollen specialist bees eastern us.**

Essential plants for native pollen specialist bees (Eastern United States)

Visit jarrodfowler.com/host_plants.html OR search online for **host plants specialist bees eastern us.**

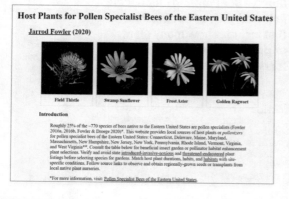

Host Plants for Pollen Specialist Bees of the Eastern United States

Jarrod Fowler (2020)

Field Thistle   Swamp Sunflower   Frost Aster   Golden Ragwort

Introduction

Roughly 25% of the ~770 species of bees native to the Eastern United States are pollen specialists (Fowler 2016a, 2016b, Fowler & Droege 2020)*. This website provides local sources of host plants or *pollenizers* for pollen specialist bees of the Eastern United States: Connecticut, Delaware, Maine, Maryland, Massachusetts, New Hampshire, New Jersey, New York, Pennsylvania, Rhode Island, Vermont, Virginia, and West Virginia**. Consult the table below for beneficial insect garden or pollinator habitat enhancement plant selections. Verify and avoid state introduced-invasive-noxious and threatened-endangered plant listings before selecting species for gardens. Match host plant durations, habits, and habitats with site-specific conditions. Follow source links to observe and obtain regionally-grown seeds or transplants from local native plant nurseries.

*For more information, visit: Pollen Specialist Bees of the Eastern United States

On this site, Jarrod Fowler provides two important plant lists for the Eastern U.S. The first is a list of host plants for native pollen specialist bees that includes links to suppliers of seeds or transplants for each plant species. The second list (*right*) features plants that are not readily available and for which propagation should be prioritized. The plants most critically needing to be planted are underlined.

Fabaceae: Faboideae: Diocleae - *Galactia regula[...]* (L.) Britton, Sterns & Poggenb. - Eastern milkpea Perennial - Forb - FAC
Fabaceae: Faboideae: Diocleae - *Galactia volubil[...]* (L.) Britton - Downy milkpea - Perennial - Forb [...]
Fabaceae: Papilionoideae: Phaseoleae - *Strophost[...] leiosperma* (Torr. & A. Gray) Piper - Slickseed fuzzybean - Annual - Forb - FAC
Geraniaceae - *Geranium carolinianum* [...] geranium - Biennial - Forb - FACU
Geraniaceae - *Geranium robertianum* L[...] geranium - Biennial - Forb - FACU
Hydrophyllaceae: Hydrophylloideae - *[...] appendiculatum* Michx. - Great waterle[...] Forb - FAC

6
Pollinators

Identify the specific plants that support native bumble bees

Here, we'll use the amazing *Bumble Bee Flower Finder**, compiled by Jarrod Fowler (2022), engineered by James Edwards, and supported by **The Polistes Foundation**, to identify bumble bees and the plants they need for survival. (**The Bumble Bee Flower Finder currently features bumble bees of the Eastern United States.*)

Visit: bumblebeeflowerfinder.info

or search online for **bumble bee flower finder** and navigate to the site.

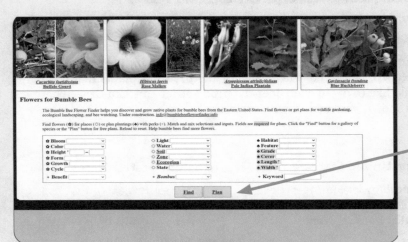

Enter search criteria such as: *bloom, color, height, form, soil, zone, ecoregion, habitat*, and more.

Click **Find**.

Add criteria for *grade (flat, gentle, steep)*, *cover (weak, strong)*, *length* and *width of area*. Click **Plan**.

Find — Click **Find** for profiles of flowering plants that support bumble bees.

Click a profile for a helpful fact page including bloom times.

Identify and learn about bumble bee species:

Scroll down on the home page (without clicking **Find** or **Plan**).

Click **Click Here to Identify Bumble Bees**. Enter bee characteristics.

Click each bee for a detailed fact sheet.

Plan — Click **Plan** for profiles of plants for a bumble bee planting plan.

Profiles of plants used in the ***Bumble Bee Planting Planner*** are followed with a *Planting Plan* that includes how many plants or pounds of seed are needed for each plant species.

A. *Salix discolor*: 3 patches, 21 plants, < 0.01 lb seeds
B. *Amsonia tabernaemontana*: 3 patches, 30 plants, 0.08 ll
C. *Cercis canadensis*: 3 patches, 21 plants, 0.10 lb seeds
D. *Vaccinium corymbosum*: 3 patches, 21 plants, < 0.01 lb
E. *Ilex verticillata*: 3 patches, 21 plants, 0.02 lb seeds
F. *Rubus idaeus*: 3 patches, 21 plants, 0.01 lb seeds
G. *Liriodendron tulipifera*: 3 patches, 21 plants, 0.14 lb se

	1	2	3
1	B	F	K
2	F	G	F
3	C	B	C
4	K	C	L
5	B	L	G
6	J	H	J
7	L	J	D
8	E	D	A
9	I	E	D
10	E	A	G
11	K	H	A
12	I	H	I

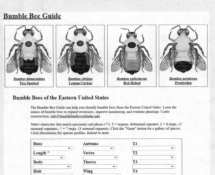

Pollinators   6

Bumble bee resources for other regions in the United States

The *Bumble Bee Flower Finder* that we just looked at focuses on bumble bees of Eastern United States. Fortunately, there are helpful resources for other parts of the country. The **U.S. Forest Service** and the **Pollinator Partnership** guide *Bumble Bees of the Western United States* is a free PDF readily accessible on the **Xerces Society** website. (*Bumble Bees of the Eastern United States* is also available.) To download this guide, search online for **xerces bumble bees western** [or **eastern**] **us** and navigate to the **Xerces Society** site.

For the Midwest and other regions, consider surveying bumble bee activity and contributing data online through the *Bumble Bee Atlas* science project:

Visit: bumblebeeatlas.org

or search online for **bumble bee atlas** and navigate to the site.

In the top menu, click **Get Involved** to learn how to participate. Then, click **Find Your Atlas.** (Not all states have an atlas.)

Some of the states that have an active Bumble Bee Atlas offer the opportunity to **Adopt a Grid Cell**. Participants commit to completing at least two **Atlas surveys** in their grid cell during the field season. Explore the *Bumble Bee Atlas* website to learn more.

SOURCE: The Bumble Bee Atlas is a Xerces Society project in collaboration with diverse partners and funders. Used with permission from The Xerces Society of Invertebrate Conservation (xerces.org).

Carpenter bees (*Xylocopa*) are often mistaken for bumblebees, but their **shiny abdomen** makes it easy to tell them apart since bumblebees have fuzzy abdomens. Carpenter bees are valuable pollinators that need our protection. They are sometimes considered pests because they excavate cavities in wood (hence their name). Painting, staining, or applying an annual coat of almond oil can help to prevent carpenter bees from starting nests in wood. To learn about nontoxic and least-toxic control methods, visit **Beyond Pesticides** (*beyondpesticides.org*); click **Resources**; click **ManageSafe™**; click **carpenter bees**, or search online for **least-toxic control of carpenter bees PDF**, a Beyond Pesticides article.

Developed by *The Pollinator Lab* at Kansas State University, the **Bee Machine** is a nifty app for identifying bees as well as flies, wasps, and other insects that are often confused with bees. It works like the plant identification apps shown on page 4.9. Download the **Bee Machine** app to a phone. Open the app and upload or snap a photo of the bee you are wondering about. Suggested identifications include quality photos, informative descriptions, and distribution maps. Learn more by visiting *www.beemachine.ai*.

6

Pollinators

Digging in deeper

Here are references and additional handy resources for identifying pollinators and their host plants (please refer to the Appendix for publication details).

Nature's Best Hope: A New Approach to Conservation That Starts in Your Yard: Doug discusses the habitat and vegetation needed to restore native bee populations along with a simple way to attract queen bumble bees to build nests using only a roll of toilet paper (see pages 155 - 168, and page 207). Get inspired to encourage pollinators to visit and reside on your property!

Attracting Native Pollinators, Protecting North America's Bees and Butterflies: The Xerces Society Guide: Filled with helpful diagrams and photos, this informative book by The **Xerces Society** provides a solid foundation for understanding who the pollinators are and why they matter, their biology, their life cycles, and the threats they face. Strategies for helping pollinators are described for homes, schools, farms, golf courses, and more. Read this for an in-depth understanding of pollinators and how to help them.

Pollinator, bee, and wasp identification books:
A leading pollinator conservationist, Heather Holm writes must-have books for budding and serious pollinator stewards. For these and additional useful pollinator resources, visit Heather Holm's website: **pollinatorsnativeplants.com.**

  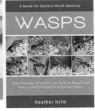

Creating a Pollinator Garden for Native Specialist Bees of New York and the Northeast (*free 35-page PDF*) by Maria van Dyke, Kristine Boys, Rosemarie Parker, Robert Wesley, and Bryan Danforth: This guide provides information fundamental to supporting specialist bees beyond the scope of this book. Find it by searching online for **danforth lab creating a pollinator garden.**

Wild bee conservation (*webpage*): This **Xerces Society** webpage provides a hub of useful links. Search **wild bee conservation xerces** and navigate to the site.

Bee City USA (*beecityusa.org*): An initiative of the **Xerces Society**, *Bee City USA* "*provides a framework for communities to work together to conserve native pollinators by increasing the abundance of native plants, providing nest sites, and reducing the use of pesticides*" through their outreach, training, citizen participation, and resources.

Pollinator Pathway (*pollinator-pathway.org*) is a grassroots effort to identify and protect pathways on high conservation value land. Check out the toolkit for starting a pollinator pathway in your community.

Pollinator Partnership (*pollinator.org*) helps bring awareness to the plight of pollinators. Check out their pollinator programs and other resources. Consider displaying one of their **garden signs** (*free signs to print*).

Pollinator habitat signs: These lovely signs are available for purchase from the Xerces Society. Purchase includes a one-year membership in the Xerces Society. Search **xerces pollinator habitat sign**. Help spread awareness about pollinator habitat in your neighborhood or community while helping to support the **Xerces Society's** science-based conservation work.

In this action, we focused on providing food sources for native pollen specialist bees and other specialist pollinators. Next, we'll delve into another important requirement for every wildlife habitat: safe places to reproduce and raise future generations.

Pollinators 6

Step:	✔	Action Needed:	Page:
1	☐	Learn to recognize pupation and nesting sites and the different life stages of insects	**7.4**
2	☐	Create caterpillar pupation sites under the trees and shrubs on your property	**7.6**
3	☐	Protect and support caterpillar pupation sites throughout the year	**7.7**
4	☐	Leave the leaf litter!	**7.8**
5	☐	Cover the ground with plants or organic material (except for some areas left bare for ground-nesting bees)	**7.9**
6	☐	Leave stumps and dead trees (when safe) and place wood stacks, brush piles, logs, and large rocks all around your property	**7.10**
7	☐	Supply safe nesting places for native bees: deadwood, bare ground, and pithy and hollow plant stems	**7.11**
8	☐	Manage and plant your landscape strategically to encourage birds to feed and nest in your wildlife habitat	**7.14**

Ensure your wild visitors become permanent residents by providing the habitat they need to reproduce

The way in which we set up and manage our wildlife landscape determines whether our wild visitors have what they need to reproduce. Let's look at how we can support the life cycles of visiting creatures to welcome them as permanent residents.

Most caterpillars burrow into leaf litter on the ground or underground to pupate.

Many native bees require pithy or hollow stems in which to lay their eggs while others lay their eggs in cavities in deadwood.

Still other native bees require bare ground to burrow into and lay their eggs.

Ground-dwelling creatures such as beetles need plant litter and dead logs for shelter and reproduction.

Amphibians need safe and accessible water sources in which to reproduce. Some species need water for their entire life cycle.

Most reptiles need dark, moist sites such as under woodpiles and shrubs or in areas of tall grass.

Significant numbers of birds require cavities in which to build their nests. One such cavity-nester is this pileated woodpecker.

Other bird species require dense shrubs or tall trees in which to build their nests. Ground-nesting birds need safe areas to build their nests.

Birds need cover to raise their young. Stems camouflage this sparrow for safety from free-roaming cats and dogs.

Action 7—GUIDE
Preserve and create pupation and nesting sites

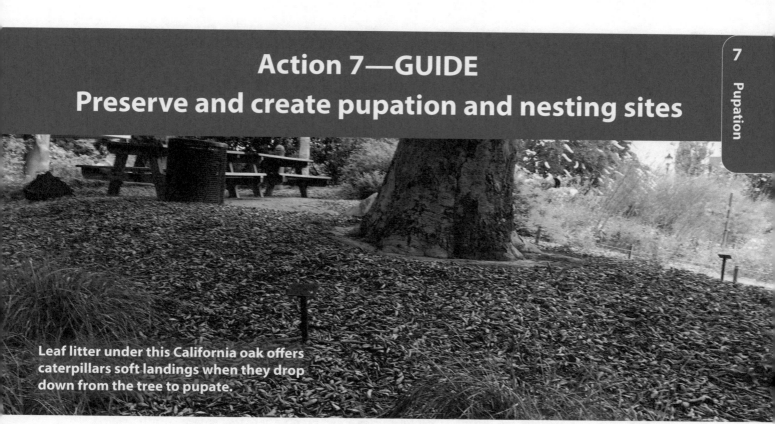

Leaf litter under this California oak offers caterpillars soft landings when they drop down from the tree to pupate.

Planting native plants, especially keystone species, invites insects and other wildlife to our wildlife landscapes. As these plants become established in our landscapes, we can see the truth in the saying, *"Plant them and they will come!"* But how can we encourage our new visitors to remain and become thriving residents in our wildlife habitats? It's actually rather simple: **Provide wildlife with food, water, shelter, and places to reproduce.**

In this action, we focus on *places to reproduce* including how to preserve and create pupation sites for caterpillars, wasps, beetles, and other insects and how to encourage nesting sites for bees, birds, and other creatures throughout your landscape.

Pupation sites also called **soft landings,** are planted areas under trees where caterpillars drop to the ground and pupate along with other beneficial insects. The true measure of a rich, supportive wildlife habitat is the presence of pupating and nesting creatures!

Native plants, leaf litter, and logs (*left*) create a welcoming habitat for pupating insects and micro life.

The area under this tulip poplar (*Liriodendron tulipifera; right*) is not mowed allowing for soft landings.

① Learn to recognize pupation and nesting sites and the different life stages of insects

If you come from a background of vegetable or fruit gardening, then every grub-like creature you encounter may mistakenly be perceived to be an unwelcome pest. The challenge is that many beneficial native insects resemble garden pests in the early stages of their lives. To be a good wildlife steward, it's important to be able to recognize the different life cycle stages of insects and their pupation and nesting sites. Here are some resources that will help you do exactly that! (Please refer to the Appendix for publication details.)

Nesting & Overwintering Habitat (*free, 12-page PDF*): Produced by the **Xerces Society**, this informative guide shows clear images of the different stages of the life cycles of pollinators and other beneficial insects along with illustrated steps for creating nesting and overwintering habitat. To find this guide, visit the **Xerces Society** website (xerces.org). In the search bar, enter **nesting & overwintering habitat**. Scroll through the results until you see this title and click on it, or search online for **xerces nesting & overwintering habitat**.

Bumble bees: For an illustrated diagram of the life cycle of bumble bees, visit the **Xerces Society** website (xerces.org). In the search bar, enter **life cycle bumble bee**. Click the article *About Bumble Bees* for an illustrated diagram of the bumble bee life cycle and click *Bumble Bees: Nesting and Overwintering* for exquisite photos of nesting bumble bees. While on this site, check out the other helpful articles about bumble bees that are well worth reading.

Butterflies and moths: Different life stages of a single species of Lepidoptera may have completely different appearances. Consider, for example, the black swallowtail whose young caterpillar is black with orange dots and spots and a white saddle (*far left*). It develops into a smooth bright green and black striped caterpillar with yellow spots (*left*); later it becomes a black and white butterfly that even has some blue markings (*right*).

Life cycles of other insects and creatures: Search online for **images** with the terms **life cycle [animal's name]**, for example "life cycle dragon fly." Typically, both diagrams and photographs will come up. Shown at left is a dragonfly **exuvia** (the cast-off skin of a dragonfly larva). A fascinating book *The Secret Lives of Backyard Bugs: Discover Amazing Butterflies, Moths, Spiders, Dragonflies, and Other Insects!* by Judy Burris and Wayne Richards is an engaging resource when it comes to getting familiar with the life cycles of insects such as butterflies, moths, beetles, ants, grasshoppers, aphids, and even the black widow spider.

Recognizing nesting sites of insects and creatures: Search online for **nesting site [animal's name]**. Typically, the first result will describe the preferred nesting site or habitat for this creature. For photos or diagrams, search for images using the same search terms.

(top right tab)

7

Pupation

Explore the *Butterflies and Moths of North America* (BAMONA) website to learn to recognize the different life cycle stages of Lepidoptera species

Now, we'll take a close look at the *Butterflies and Moths of North America* (**BAMONA**) website. Here, you'll find informative profiles of Lepidoptera (butterflies, skippers, and moths) that include historic and current range maps, life history, caterpillar host plants, adult food sources, habitat, conservation status, and much more including numerous photos of documented sightings and high-quality images of caterpillars. BAMONA will even help you identify a butterfly or moth. This is a remarkable resource!

Visit: butterfliesandmoths.org

or search online for **bamona** OR **butterflies and moths of north america** and navigate to the site.

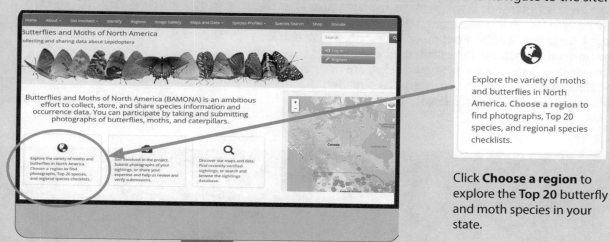

Explore the variety of moths and butterflies in North America. **Choose a region** to find photographs, Top 20 species, and regional species checklists.

Click **Choose a region** to explore the **Top 20** butterfly and moth species in your state.

Click United States.

Click on your state for clickable profiles of the **Top 20** species.

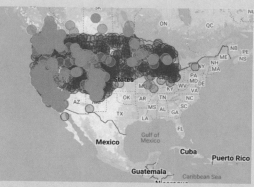

Next, click on the **scientific name** of one of the **Top 20** species for a description, life history, habitat needs, and a range map along with numerous photos documenting sightings (*right*) of the species.

NOTE: Websites are ever changing! The navigation for the BAMONA website may have changed. Spend a little time exploring and you will likely find all of these materials, though perhaps in a different location, along with exciting new resources.

Used with permission from Kelly Lotts and Thomas Naberhaus, Coordinators. 2024. Butterflies and Moths of North America. http://www.butterfliesandmoths.org/ (Version 04272024).

NATURE'S ACTION GUIDE   Action 7—Preserve and create pupation and nesting sites   **7.5**

2 Create caterpillar pupation sites under the trees and shrubs on your property

When a fully grown caterpillar drops to the ground, it will either spin a cocoon in the leaf litter under the tree, or it will burrow into the soil to pupate underground. The soil must be loose and protected from disturbance until the pupa emerges as an adult. Landscape beds can serve as pupation sites; in contrast, the soil under a tree located in the middle of a mowed lawn is compacted and inhospitable to caterpillars. Luckily, it's not difficult to create pupation sites under trees and shrubs.

If you have an existing tree or shrub, remove any lawn to at least the tree's **drip line** (an imaginary line around the farthest reaches of the leaf canopy). Choose a lawn removal method described in *Action 3: Shrink the Lawn* other than the *Bake It!* method which could overheat the surface roots of trees or shrubs. Shown below are the steps for using the *Block It!* method to create a caterpillar pupation site around a tree growing in the middle of the lawn.

The **drip line** of a tree (red line).

Step 1: Identify the tree (or shrub) under which you want to create a pupation site.

Step 2: Lay out the shape of the pupation site. Be sure it extends at least to the drip line of the tree. Gather leaves and trimmings for mulch.

Step 3: Cover the area with cardboard and enough mulch to hold down the cardboard.

Step 4: Keep the area mulched with a 2-inch layer of leaf litter, trimmings, or other organic matter to help the soil remain friable and to block out persistent weeds.

Step 5: As soon as resources permit, densely plant the area with keystone plants and plants needed by specialists. While waiting for plantings to get established, fill in any gaps with leaf litter or regionally appropriate mulch. Any cardboard that remains will break down over time and mix in with the mulch.

③ Protect and support caterpillar pupation sites throughout the year

Once you've set up a pupation site, take these important actions to support caterpillars throughout their pupation:

 Grow native plants and maintain a layer of leaf litter on all your pupation sites to provide critically needed shelter for pupating caterpillars.

 Add and arrange some rocks and logs or branches in a pleasing design. Include piles of rocks and stacks of logs wherever possible.

 Avoid disturbing the leaf litter and plants growing in pupation sites.

 Avoid walking on pupation sites. Borders help prevent people from accidentally trampling on pupation sites.

 Don't mow pupation sites. Mowing not only crushes pupae, but it also compacts the soil making it impossible for caterpillars to burrow into the soil.

Increase the size of the caterpillar pupation site as a tree grows and the leaf canopy expands so that there is always a welcoming bed of duff extending to at least the drip line of the tree. Here, this oak has outgrown the current protected pupation site (red line). The caterpillar pupation site needs to be extended out to the tree's current drip line (green line).

Avoid the use of artificial lights at night, especially near pupation sites. See *Action 1: Turn off the lights* for tips to reduce night light.

Consider adding a border of logs (or a fancier material) around a pupation site. A border provides a visual edge that delineates the pupation site. This helps to prevent people from stepping on the pupation site.

Generously plant caterpillar pupation sites as soon as possible to ensure soft landings for caterpillars dropping to the ground to pupate.

Leave the leaf litter!

When the leaves drop from your trees, wherever possible, leave the leaf litter. Leaf litter is nutrient-rich "gold" in a wildlife habitat. Some caterpillar species feed on fallen leaves. As leaves decompose, they form a rich layer of **duff** (decaying organic matter) that provides an ideal habitat for pupating caterpillars, overwintering native bee larvae, and many other small creatures. A layer of duff keeps the soil moist and loose for caterpillars that pupate below the soil surface and bees that excavate underground nests.

Wherever possible, leave a tree's **own** fallen leaves in place extending all the way out to the tree's drip line to a depth of about 2 inches. Avoid raking the leaves into a pile around the base of a tree trunk!

Composted leaf litter, called **leaf mold**, is a rich soil amendment that supports micro life. Adding moisture to a leaf pile and turning it every so often is all that's required to produce leaf mold—your bucket of gold!

Caution: To prevent smothering of plants, clear leaf litter away from low-growing ground covers such as mosses, sedges (*Carex*), pussytoes (*Antennaria*), and moss pink (*Phlox subulata*) and away from plants with basal rosettes such as cardinal flower (*Lobelia cardinalis*).

Leaf litter is aptly named—great big leaves from a native magnolia tree really do look like litter on the lawn, but what welcome litter it is!

Gaining neighborhood acceptance

Some neighborhood standards may prohibit leaving leaf litter where it falls. If that is the case where you live, consider gathering the leaves and composting them in a hidden area. A circle of wire fencing makes a handy container for a pile (see page 3.14). Although some leaves, such as oaks or sycamores, take longer to break down, once leaves have decomposed, the resulting leaf mold makes an attractive mulch.

Leave
THE
Leaves

PROVIDE FOOD & SHELTER FOR OVERWINTERING CREATURES
INSULATE PLANT ROOTS
BUILD LIVING SOIL

Wild Seed Project   LEARN MORE AT wildseedproject.net

Putting up a "Leave the Leaves" yard sign can help to build neighborhood acceptance for leaving leaf litter. For free yard signs to print, search online with the terms **leave the leaves free yard sign.**

Wild Seed Project (wildseedproject.net) offers this attractive yard sign as a free download. Find it by searching online for **wild seed project leave the leaves**. Not only will you find the sign, but there is a wealth of information about the value of leaf litter along with strategies for dealing with large volumes of leaves. While on the site, take a look at the photo of luna moth pupae that demonstrates how well pupae can blend in with leaf litter and how easy it is to overlook the life in leaf litter.

5 Cover the ground with plants or organic material (except for some areas left bare for ground-nesting bees)

As we discuss throughout this action guide, how we manage our landscapes can positively affect the survival of our local wildlife. One such management practice is that of being diligent about keeping all the ground in your landscape covered with plants or organic materials except for areas purposefully left bare for ground-nesting bees. (We'll look at the needs of ground-nesting bees later in this action.)

A **green mulch** (a tight matrix of growing plants) is an ideal ground cover. If resources for acquiring plants are limited or while waiting for plants to grow, place a 2-inch layer of leaf litter, grass clippings, trimmings from your yard, wood chips, or other organic material. Where regionally appropriate (see page 11.9), a 1-inch layer of crushed stone may be a good interim option. Covering the ground offers multiple benefits. Most important here is the need to keep the soil loose and **friable** (easily crumbled) to provide shelter for caterpillars, native bees, beetles, salamanders, and numerous other creatures that pupate or nest above the surface or burrow underground.

Process weeds before using them as mulch

You can even use piles of invasive plants that you have removed as mulch to cover the ground, but first make sure they have not gone to seed and are dead!

1. Put a pile of removed invasive plants on pavement or on a tarp in the hot sun to quickly dry them out.

2. Make sure that the reproductive parts of the plant, such as seeds or rhizomes, are not present (or you will be kicking yourself later!).

3. Once the removed invasives are completely dead, move the pile to an out of the way place until the pile decomposes.

Avoid covering ground with these materials:

- **Landscape fabric**—See the serious downsides described below.
- **Rubberized mulch**—This releases high levels of zinc along with heavy metals and rubber leachates which contaminate the soil and watershed.
- **Commercial mulches**—Be sure to verify the components to prevent introducing toxins to your landscape.
- **Contaminated leaf litter or leaf mold**—Be vigilant when gathering leafy material from outside sources as it may contain invasive plants or grass that has pesticide or herbicide residues.

Landscape fabric (weed barrier cloth) is particularly problematic

- Caterpillars and other small creatures cannot burrow into the ground to pupate or nest.
- Circulation of air, water, and micro life is restricted damaging micro life and soil vitality.
- Underlying soil structure and soil quality decline as organic matter no longer mixes into the soil.
- Native plants are unable to self-seed and clumping plants are prevented from expanding.
- Over time rhizomatous weeds often creep in through holes creating a weeding nightmare.
- Eventually landscape fabric breaks down and releases microplastic particles into the environment.

6 Leave stumps and dead trees (when safe) and place wood stacks, brush piles, logs, and large rocks all around your property

Wherever possible and when it's safe to do so, leave dead branches and **snags** (dead trees) standing and leave fallen trees and stumps in place on the ground. Many insects and other organisms that play a critical role in the food web feed and reproduce on deadwood. For example, the pileated woodpecker shown here depends primarily upon carpenter ants and other wood-boring insects who inhabit deadwood. Deadwood also offers reproduction sites for species of cavity-nesting birds and some species of native bees and other creatures. The very survival of these animals depends on the availability of rotting wood, deadwood, or existing cavities!

With a mature height measuring 16 to 19 inches, the pileated woodpecker (*Dryocopus pileatus*) is the largest woodpecker in North America. Deadwood provides the insects and shelter this woodpecker needs to survive.

We had a dead tree in the front yard, so we could not leave it for deadwood. Right after we cut the tree down and placed a birdbath on the stump (shown at left temporarily uncovered), carpenter ants (*above*) occupied it and have been there ever since.

There is nothing like a wood stack or pile of branches to provide shelter for insects, small birds, and other creatures along with habitat for fungi and micro life in the soil. Place the pile somewhere hidden from view at least ten feet away from any buildings. Consider planting a screen around the pile to hide it from view. The **Xerces Society** suggests highlighting your pile with a **Pollinator Friendly Habitat** sign "*to advertise your good intentions to your neighbors*" (see page 6.12). Not every property can accommodate the invaluable wildlife resource of deadwood, but hopefully yours can!

In the less visible areas of my yard, borders of logs around my landscape beds create a sense of order and remind me where not to step. The best thing is that using logs as borders provides an opportunity to place logs throughout my landscape. These log borders store carbon and contribute to rich habitats teeming with microorganisms, beetles, carpenter ants, and other insects which in turn support birds and other animals.

7 Supply safe nesting places for native bees: deadwood, bare ground, and pithy and hollow plant stems

Ensuring that native bees in your wildlife habitat have safe nesting places, though not difficult, requires some planning. Unfortunately, mismanaged artificial bee nests can lead to predation and disease in native bee populations. By providing deadwood, bare ground, and pithy or hollow plant stems, artificial bee nests are unnecessary (and Mother Nature does the housekeeping for you!)

Types of nesting habitat required by native bees

deadwood

bare ground

pithy stems

hollow stems

Provide deadwood, brush piles, and stones as habitat for cavity-nesting bees. As we just discussed, deadwood is a critical resource for cavity-nesting native bees, some bumble bee species, and many other animals.

Supply well-situated bare ground for ground-nesting native bees. Sparse vegetation is fine as long as bees have access to bare soil. We'll discuss the needs of ground-nesting bees next.

Grow plants with pithy and hollow stems for stem-nesting bees and leave the stems standing. Shortly, we'll explain how to manage stems to benefit native bees with examples of plants that produce ideal stems.

Supply well-situated bare ground for ground-nesting native bees

Approximately 70% of native bees are ground-nesters that excavate burrows underground. To support these bees, find an out-of-the-way place on your property where they can nest undisturbed. Ideally, the area should be well-drained with sparse vegetation and sandy or loamy soil that is **friable** (you could scoop it with a spoon—if you had to for some reason!), although some native bees readily nest in compacted soil. Patches of thin layers of small pebbles or a few small rocks create attractive crevices. A gently sloped site is especially attractive to some bee species. Keep an eye out for small mounds of soil and bee activity.

Unlike ground-nesting yellow jackets, which are a species of wasp, ground-nesting native bees don't sting unless they are seriously provoked at their nesting site. Mostly it is male native bees that hover around the nest, and they don't even have stingers. Discovering native bees nesting in your wildlife habitat is cause for celebration!

A patch of native grass clumps with ample bare ground between them is an acceptable look for most neighborhoods.

Manage pithy and hollow plant stems to optimize safe nesting places for native bees

When the urge hits to clean up the garden in the fall and spring, resist the temptation to clear out the garden debris. Instead, help ensure the survival of native bees by leaving the stems and canes of perennial plants to provide nesting sites for native bees. Here's how to do this:

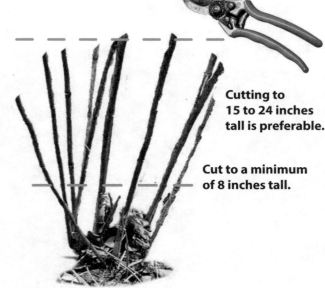

Cutting to 15 to 24 inches tall is preferable.

Cut to a minimum of 8 inches tall.

YEAR 1—Fall and winter: Leave as many stems and flower stalks as the aesthetics of your neighborhood will allow. Shown here are stems of Joe-Pye weed (*Eutrochium*) after a full growing season. Some bee species overwinter in stems.

YEAR 2—Spring: Using a sharp tool, cut stems back to varying heights. Leave at least 8 inches of stem. Cutting stems to 15 to 24 inches tall is preferable. Some bee species nest in the spring.

YEAR 2—Summer and beyond: Foliage will begin to cover the cut stems. Be on the lookout for signs of bees excavating the pith from stems (*above right*). Different bee species will nest and emerge at different times of the year, so be sure to leave the dead stems standing.

YEAR 3: Continue to leave the Year 1 stems (cut in Year 2) standing until they decompose naturally. By now several generations of stem-nesting bee species may have used these stems. Some bee species reuse the stems from previous years. Decomposition of the stems helps to naturally prevent the spread of disease that could come from continual reuse. In spring, cut the stems of Year 2 growth—thus, the cycle begins anew!

Leaving stems is much easier than it sounds!

Simply:

- Wait until spring to cut back stems.
- Cut stems to various heights, ideally between 15 to 24 inches and no shorter than 8 inches.
- Leave the stems in the garden until they decompose (or stack them in a hidden place).
- Repeat annually.

If you live in a neighborhood with rigid aesthetic standards, you may have no choice but to cut stems to 8 inches. This looks tidy and new foliage will quickly cover last year's stems. If possible, take the cut pieces of stem and stack them upright in a hidden area of your property—the bees may still use them.

A treasure trove of pollinator resources:

For exquisite photos and an illustrated chart showing the life cycle of stem-nesting bees, visit Heather Holm's website: **pollinatorsnativeplants.com** and click on **Plant Lists & Posters**. Here you will also find wasp fact sheets and other high-quality charts such as *Trees and Shrubs for Pollinators*.

Grow native plants that produce pithy or hollow stems for stem-nesting bees

Approximately 30% of native bees excavate cavities or use existing cavities in deadwood, stone crevices, or plant stems. Intentionally planting native plants that have pithy or hollow stems will go a long way toward attracting and supporting these native bees. As we just discussed, the other half of the equation is proper management of the stems. Here are examples of plants that provide pithy or hollow stems:

Native forbs:

Echinacea species (coneflower)

Helianthus species (sunflower)

Eutrochium species (Joe-Pye weed)

Monarda species (bee balm, wild bergamot)

Native grasses:

Silphium species (cup plant, compass plant, rosinweed, prairie dock)

Solidago species (goldenrod)

Symphyotrichum species (aster)

Schizachyrium scoparium (little bluestem), *Panicum virgatum* (switchgrass)

Native vines: Native shrubs:

Rubus species (blackberry, raspberry, dewberry)

Hydrangea species (oakleaf or smooth hydrangea)

Rhus species (staghorn sumac, lemonade berry)

Sambucus species (elderberry)

 The **Lady Bird Johnson and Xerces Society Plant Database for Pollinators** offers a handy list of plants that provide nesting materials for native bees. Visit *wildflower.org/project/pollinator-conservation*. Scroll down to **Resources**. Click on **Plants of Special Value to Beneficial Insects**. Click on **Provides Nesting Materials/ Structures for Native Bees**. Use the filters to narrow your search.

You will recognize many of these plants as keystone plants. They hold the promise of becoming luxurious multi-unit housing for stem-nesting bees. Next, we'll look at managing and planting your landscape to encourage birds to stay and nest.

8 Manage and plant your landscape strategically to encourage birds to feed and nest in your wildlife habitat

Like native bees and caterpillars, birds may be generalists or specialists in terms of their diet. Generalist birds may eat seeds, nectar, fruit, insects, spiders, fish, mollusks, small vertebrates, and even other birds. In contrast, some birds are specialists, such as the hummingbird whose beak has adapted to feed on the nectar of flowers or the whip-poor-will whose beak has adapted to catch flying insects. Yet, aside from seabirds, **96 percent of bird species in the United States rely on insects to feed their young**. It's no surprise that with the precipitous decline in insect populations worldwide, the biodiversity of bird species is threatened, especially those species that specialize on insects throughout their life cycle.

To attract and keep birds in your wildlife habitat, choose native plants that:

	Attract and support insects	Insect-eating birds are facing the steepest population declines. Encouraging insect populations in general is especially critical for the survival of these insectivores.
	Attract and support caterpillars	Since caterpillars are the primary food source for baby birds, plants that specifically support caterpillars are essential for bird reproduction.
	Attract and support pollinators	Many plants require pollinators to produce seed and seed is a primary food source for many bird species, so planting to support pollinators is also essential for the survival of seed-eating bird species.
	Produce seeds and fruit	Seeds and fruits are an important dietary component for most bird species, especially species that feed exclusively on these foods.
	Provide nesting sites	Trees, densely branched shrubs, and clumping native grasses are an invitation to nesting birds.

Along with your native plants, be sure to **provide water.** Access to a year-round supply of clean water is critical for bird survival. Plus, water sources may offer you a glimpse of birds rarely seen otherwise.

On a cold, winter day, mourning doves and a junco cluster together on this heated birdbath.

Encourage birds to nest in your wildlife landscape

Finding a bird nest in your wildlife habitat is always exciting. Plus, it's a sign that your ecosystem is functioning! Employing bird-friendly ecological management practices, such as leaving deadwood standing and growing native plants, will encourage birds (and the insects they depend on) to live on your property. Cavity-nesting birds often reject human-made cavity nest boxes. If a cavity-nesting bird cannot find a suitable nesting site, it will fail to breed that season.

The shortage of cavity sites is exacerbated by the presence of invasive species of birds, such as the house sparrow (*Passer domesticus*) and European starling (*Sturnus vulgaris*), that attack some cavity-nesting bird species further reducing their reproductive success.

This cavity-nesting red-bellied woodpecker (*Melanerpes carolinus*) relies on soft or deadwood to excavate its nest. Even when it finds deadwood large enough to accommodate its cavity, it must fend off attacks from sparrows and flocks of starlings to protect its eggs and raise its young.

Strategies for inviting nesting birds to your wildlife landscape:

Leave dead trees if they don't pose a danger. **Snags** (dead trees) provide ideal nesting opportunities for cavity-nesting birds that mostly reject human-made cavity nests.

Plant densely branched native trees and shrubs, such as holly or viburnum. A tight network of branches provides protection and a solid foundation for nest-building.

Also, plant open-branched native trees and shrubs which some birds prefer. Hummingbirds and orioles, for example, will nest in sycamore trees.

Plant clumping grasses. The clumps provide sheltered places for ground-nesting birds to build their nests, and the grass seed provides food.

Allow shrubs to **sucker** (shoots growing at the base of a shrub). These suckers create safe shelter for nesting birds.

Grow native fruit-bearing shrubs and caterpillar host plants close to nesting sites. These provide a ready supply of food for birds.

Digging in deeper

Here are additional useful resources for help creating a rich environment for pupation and nesting sites and for learning about the likely visitors to your wildlife habitat (please refer to the Appendix for publication details).

Nature's Best Hope: A New Approach to Conservation That Starts in Your Yard: Doug explains what caterpillar pupation sites are and why they are critical to the survival of caterpillars. (See pages 148 - 151 and 209 - 210). It's not enough that we provide host plants for caterpillars, we must also protect their reproduction sites.

Bird lovers' guide to creating a native plant wonderland for birds: Sharon Sorenson's *Planting Native to Attract Birds to Your Yard* is a must-have book for birders in the eastern half of the United States. Reading this book is like taking a stroll with the author through her landscape marveling at the many bird sightings as she shares her knowledge about the native plants creating this bird paradise.

A birds-eye view of a corner of Sharon's bird paradise with Missouri coneflower (*Rudbeckia missouriensis*) in the foreground and short-toothed mountain mint (*Pycanthemum muticum*) behind it, backed with a mix of native plants including sweet black-eyed Susan (*Rudbeckia subtomentosa*), rattlesnake master (*Eryngium yuccifolium L.*), royal catchfly (*Silene regia*), coral honeysuckle (*Lonicera sempervirens*), joe-pye weed (*Eutrochium*), and others. *Photo courtesy of Sharon Sorenson.*

Welcoming Wildlife to the Garden: Creating Backyard & Balcony Habitats for Wildlife by Catherine J. Johnson, Susan McDiarmid, and Edward R. Turner offers illustrated plans that include measurements, tools, and materials *"for housing and feeding birds, bees, butterflies, and more."* One project is the Peterson Style Bluebird Box. We previously had no bluebirds residing on our property; within 10 minutes of installing one of these bluebird boxes, five bluebirds circled around it and a pair claimed it as their own. Bluebirds have been nesting and roosting on our property ever since.

Explore the Merlin® app to identify the birds and birdsong in your wildlife habitat. Observing the birds who visit or reside in a wildlife habitat is a great pleasure. **The Cornell Lab of Ornithology's *Merlin*®** app is an incredibly helpful bird identification aid especially for furtive birds that may be heard but rarely seen. You can download the app from a cell phone.

- When you spot an unfamiliar bird, open the app and tap **Start Bird ID**. If you hear unfamiliar birdsong, tap **Sound ID**. Follow the prompts to identify the bird.

- After you enter the size, colors, and location of your sighting, profiles of possible identifications will appear. You can add new birds or sightings to your life list.

- After recording birdsong, a list of the birds that were recorded is generated. You can explore each bird's profile and select birds to add to your life list.

When you include pupation and nesting sites as you establish or expand your wildlife landscape, it benefits multiple aspects of the surrounding ecosystem. Native trees, shrubs, and herbaceous plants host caterpillars. Protected pupation sites help caterpillars to reproduce, yielding an abundant supply of food for birds and other creatures. Deadwood, bare ground, and pithy and hollow stems provide nesting sites for native bees that pollinate the native plants that are the foundation of the food web. Next, we'll add a critical element for wildlife survival—water. Your wildlife landscape will fill with movement and birdsong and take on a life of its own!

Action 8—CHECKLIST
Include water and protect the watershed

Step:	✔	Action Needed:	Page:
1	☐	Include ground-level and elevated year-round water sources situated for easy care	**8.4**
2	☐	Add as many additional year-round water features as possible	**8.5**
3	☐	Carefully maintain water features on a regular basis to prevent algae buildup and spread of disease	**8.7**
4	☐	Get to know the watershed of your property and the surrounding region	**8.8**
5	☐	Conserve water and protect the watershed on your property	**8.10**

Several months after planting, this mainly native bed is filling in, and the invasive bugleweed (*Ajuga reptans*) temporarily providing erosion control can be removed.

Action 8—GUIDE
Include water and protect the watershed

A dry streambed has been tastefully lined with local stone, gravel, and pots, and planted with species that can tolerate occasional flooding.

Water is central not only to human survival but to the survival of all life on earth. Like so many of our planet's resources, the earth's water supply is under siege as human activity races forward. In this action, we focus on two aspects of water: supplying water sources for wildlife and protecting the watershed.

First, we consider the need to supply water and water features for the flora and fauna in the landscape. We describe several types of water features along with tips for maintaining them on a regular basis to safeguard both creatures and humans.

Second, we explain what the watershed is, how to find the status of your local watershed, and why it needs your protective stewardship. Finally, we share handy tips for conserving water and protecting the watershed where you live.

Landscapes can be designed to provide wildlife with essential water and protect the watershed. Natural water sources such as this stream in the Pacific Northwest need our support and protection.

① Include ground-level and elevated year-round water sources situated for easy care

Year-round water sources are one of the easiest and most direct ways to support wildlife. Be sure your wildlife habitat includes at least one ground-level and one elevated water source.

Ground-level water sources

8
Water

A shallow drinking hole will attract a wide variety of creatures. This can be as simple as a shallow dish dug into the ground or the top of a birdbath placed on the ground or something more elaborate such as a chiseled rock basin. Slope the surface so that creatures can easily exit or place flat rocks to serve as exit ramps.

Filling a shallow dish with mud and keeping it moist will give mud dauber and potter wasps a supply of building material for their nests. Take it one step further and add some sand or small gravel to the mud and perhaps some overripe fruit and you may get to see butterflies **puddling** (drinking water and gathering nutrients).

A fountain made to look like a gnarled log provides a ground-level source of water (*left*).

Elevated water sources

Birdbaths are a good option for providing elevated water sources. Consider their placement carefully to ensure they are easily accessed for maintenance. Place them away from glass windows and if cats are present, at least 10 feet away from their potential hiding places.

Many birdbaths are dangerously deep. This is easily remedied by placing flat rocks so that the water is about ½-inch deep at the edge and sloping to a maximum of 2 inches deep in the middle of the basin. If there is space, flat rocks can be placed to create various water levels in the basin.

With a birdbath in place, you are likely to see birds you otherwise would never see. Plus, birds taking baths is an amusing and joyful sight!

This elevated birdbath (*right*) includes a small, floating, 1.4 watts solar fountain set to the lowest possible spray option.

Add as many additional year-round water features as possible

Once your landscape has ground-level and elevated water sources, add as many additional water features as your enthusiasm and resources can support. Small additions that add movement to a water feature attract creatures. For instance, an inexpensive solar fountain can be added to a birdbath as a bubbler, or a drip irrigation line can be set up to create a slow drip that will attract birds. Additional tiny, ground-level ponds can be hidden in landscape beds for frogs and toads to visit.

If you're feeling industrious, adding a small pond may attract resident frogs. See below for the basic steps for installing a small pond. Dragonflies are likely to perch on sticks placed around a pond and poked in at an angle. Adding a waterfall takes water features to a whole new level—the movement will attract creatures and the beauty will please humans!

Search online for a wide array of water feature ideas, products, and how-to videos. Here, I carved a fake rock from foam, faux painted it, and placed it over a solar fountain (*left*) to give a more natural look to this bubbler.

Basic steps for installing a small pond

Plan the dimensions of your pond. Remove the soil and keep it nearby for backfilling later. If using a pre-formed liner (*shown below*), ensure that the soil "floor" is level. Contour the soil as you wish for flexible liners.

Line the bottom of the basin with sand and tamp down. Pre-formed liners require solid support for their base and sides. For flexible liners, sand provides a supportive surface free of rocks and sharp objects.

Drop the pre-formed liner or flexible liner sheet in place. Thoroughly backfill the sides of a pre-formed liner. Secure the sides of a flexible liner.

Place rocks around the perimeter and plant the surrounding area. Plant native aquatic plants or install a filtration system to prevent algae buildup and mosquito breeding. (See page 8.7 for pond care tips.)

Install a rain garden to direct and collect stormwater

Rain gardens are a valuable tool for collecting stormwater allowing it to soak into the ground and stay on your property. An established rain garden can help prevent the loss of valuable topsoil. Furthermore, the deep roots of plants suitable for rain gardens filter out pollutants and other contaminants from the watershed in a process called **phytoremediation**.

8

Water

Native plants should be carefully selected for their ability to tolerate occasional flooding and standing water during periods of heavy rainfall **and** dry conditions in between periods of rain. The deep roots of grasses, sedges, and rushes make these plants particularly well suited to a rain garden. Other plants that work well include understory trees and shrubs, such as willow (*Salix*) and elderberry (*Sambucus*), and herbaceous plants, such as rose mallow (*Hibiscus moscheutos*), bee balm (*Monarda*), Joe-Pye weed (*Eutrochium*), and many others.

After heavy rainfall, stormwater collects in this rain garden.

A low-lying area of landscape in front of a public library has been transformed into a rain garden filled with swaths of locally native plants (*above*).

Learn more about rain gardens

Before installing a rain garden, search online for **rain garden design** to learn everything you can about designing and installing them. Also search for **rain garden diagrams** to view diagrams that are especially helpful for gaining an understanding of how rain gardens work. Here are some examples of the available resources:

It Starts with a Raindrop: Planning Your Rain Garden is a particularly informative online video presented by **Amanda Arnold** and hosted by **The Conservation Foundation** in Illinois. All aspects of rain garden installation and design are discussed in detail. Arnold explains complex principles in an easy-to-understand way and suggests many invaluable resources. Consider watching this video for a crash course in rain gardens.

For free sample rain garden designs, visit **Three Rivers Rain Garden Alliance** (*raingardenalliance.org*). Click on **Planting a Rain Garden**, then click on **Garden Design**. Plans are included for both sun and partial sun/shade. Click on **Plant List** to get an idea of the types of plants that work well in rain gardens.

Some municipalities, such as Arlington, Virginia, offer stormwater utility fee credits when homeowners install a rain garden (*left*). Search online for **arlington va rain garden** to learn about this model program and explore the other useful rain garden resources on this site.

See page 8.12 for more resources about rain gardens.

③ Carefully maintain water features on a regular basis to prevent algae buildup and spread of disease

Maintaining water features is not time-consuming, but regular care is necessary to maintain water quality and prevent disease to ensure the safety of wildlife and humans.

Care tips for shallow water features such as birdbaths

Refresh the water—Dump out old water. If possible, rinse with a high-pressure hose. Refill with fresh water. Do this daily or every other day.

Scrub the basin—Scrub the basin with a mixture of 9 parts water to 1 part vinegar using a stiff scrub brush. Rinse thoroughly with a high-pressure hose. Refill with fresh water. Do this weekly or whenever debris or slimy film remains in the basin after the daily refresh.

Heat the water in cold climates—In cold climates, seasonally place a water heater in at least one water source. The **K & H Pet Products Super Ice Eliminator Birdbath Deicer** (*right*) is one option (search online with the product's name). Mel Hinton of the San Diego Audubon Society chapter designed a DIY solar-powered birdbath. Search online for **build your own solar birdbath mel hinton** for directions.

Discourage algae—Place copper pennies (from 1982 or before) in birdbaths. Five to seven pennies in a regular-sized birdbath may help to inhibit algae.

Care tips for larger water features such as small ponds

Without care, larger water features will quickly fill with algae and mosquito larvae (*below left*). Since refreshing the water and scrubbing the basin regularly is impractical, it's tempting to use algaecide (*right*), but these often contain harmful toxins. Instead, address the underlying causes of algae growth and mosquito breeding. Some people have success using native plants to keep pond water clear. A helpful reference is Robert Pavlis' book *Building Natural Ponds: Create a Clean Algae-free Pond without Pumps, Filters, or Chemicals* (see page 8.12).

Add native aquatic plants—Algae starts filling a pond when there is an imbalance in the water. Plants help to balance the pond water by absorbing excess nutrients in the water.

NOTE: *Prior to installing a pond, do research to identify native aquatic plant species for your region. Some of the readily available aquatic plants are highly invasive. Refer to the resources in* **Action 4: Remove invasive plants.**

Many algaecides contain chemicals toxic to wildlife.

Add a fountain or waterfall—Algae and mosquitoes thrive where there is a lack of air and no movement in the water. Movement from a fountain or waterfall helps to aerate the water and discourage these pests.

Shade 40 to 60% of the pond surface area—Algae needs sunlight to grow. Floating plants offer shade. Tall plants placed on the south and west sides in and around the pond may also help.

Install a filtration system—If growing plants in your pond is not enough to prevent algae buildup, your pond will likely require a filtration system. *Mechanical filtration systems* remove debris from a pond and aerate the water as it cycles through the system. *Biological filtration systems* include a separate storage box outside of the pond that contains filter media (such as short sections of ridged plastic tubing) on which beneficial bacteria colonize.

Get to know the watershed of your property and the surrounding region

What is the watershed?

This 1847 engraving shows the high starting point of a watershed as it flows downward toward a body of water.

The **watershed** is the land area where surface water (from rain and snow) and underlying groundwater collects and flows into lakes, streams, creeks, wetlands, and other bodies of water. Watersheds are identified by the tributaries of regional primary sources of water, such as the Mississippi River watershed (*right*) and the Colorado River watershed (*below left*). In the United States there are approximately 160,000 watersheds.

An 1823 map shows the western section of the Mississippi River watershed.

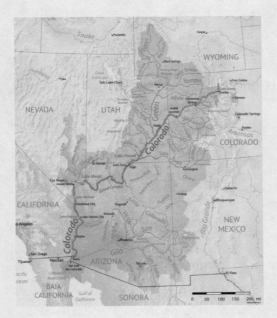

Watersheds are the source of the water that we and our wildlife ecosystems depend upon for survival. Melting snow dripping off a roof and rainwater flowing down a driveway, along with any contaminants they contain, flow into the watershed. This is why it's so important to get to know your local watershed and learn how to protect it and keep it clean!

The Grand Canyon is located within the Colorado River watershed (*left*).

Next, we'll look at using the **EPA** *How's My Waterway* online tool to identify and learn about the condition of your local watershed.

Get to know the watershed of your property and the surrounding region, *continued*

Now, let's use the United States *Environmental Protection Agency (EPA) How's My Waterway* to learn about the condition of your local watershed.

Visit: **epa.gov/waterdata/hows-my-waterway**
or search online for **hows my waterway** and navigate to the site.

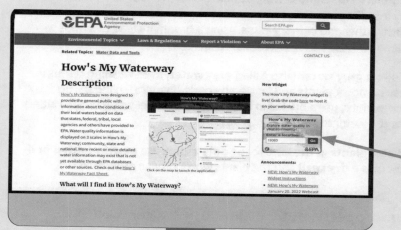

To see the status of your local watershed, enter your address. (*This is more precise than using your ZIP Code™.*)

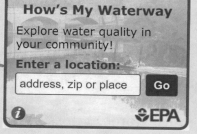

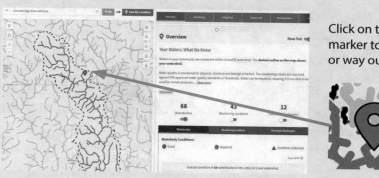

Click on the location marker to zoom in (*right*) or way out (*below*).

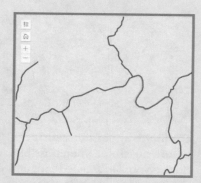

The result is an in-depth overview of your region's watershed. (*If a map isn't visible on the left, open the window wider.*) Click on the blue tabs at the top right of the page for useful information. For example, way over on the right is **Protect**. Here you can get a watershed health score for your area, find locations of designated *Wild and Scenic Rivers*, and find out if there are watershed protection projects or protected areas in your watershed.

SOURCE: United States Environmental Protection Agency, How's My Waterway. Available online at https://www.epa.gov/waterdata/hows-my-waterway.

⑤ Conserve water and protect the watershed on your property

When water is plentiful, it's easy to take it for granted. A power outage or drought is a quick reminder of how central water is to our very existence. Getting to know the watershed of a property and becoming its steward gives us the knowledge and opportunity to do what we can to help ensure that our water supply remains clean and free flowing.

Look for ways to conserve water in and around your home

Conserve household water. Look for ways to reduce water usage by installing low-flow toilets, taking shorter showers, running fewer dishwasher and laundry loads, using a broom instead of a hose to clean outdoor surfaces, and so forth.

Collect grey water (also called **gray water**) from washing dishes for use on houseplants and landscape beds. If you're feeling particularly industrious, use a bucket in the shower to collect water while waiting for the water to warm up.

Water plants in the landscape only if they are newly planted or if there is a dry spell and the plants won't survive otherwise.

Keep as much water as possible on your property, but consider using a car wash

Eliminate impervious surfaces where possible. When possible, design your landscape to minimize the area of paved surfaces and other impervious hardscape features. This allows water to absorb into the soil and stay on your property. Obviously, your home's roof needs to be impervious, but there are attractive options for permeable driveways and sidewalks.

Collect rooftop runoff in rain barrels for later use in your landscape. Many styles of rain barrels are available.

Direct downspouts to landscape beds and rain gardens to water plants and help your property to absorb water.

Take your car to a commercial car wash. Car washes use an average of 70 gallons less water per wash, and they are required to send their wastewater to a treatment facility where the water is treated prior to being released into waterways. If you wash your vehicle at home, do so on the lawn or other permeable surface with biodegradable, phosphate-free soap. Keep in mind that the dirty water will contain exhaust and gas residues and heavy metals.

Water conservation is not a new goal as this U.S. postage stamp from 1960 shows—it's just become a lot more urgent!

Protect the watershed on your property:

Leave an unmown buffer and plant native trees and shrubs along stream banks (if you're fortunate to have a stream!). This **riparian buffer** (or stream buffer) filters runoff and prevents erosion.

Plant native plants. Many have deep roots that help remove contaminants from the soil through phytoremediation; they require less water; and they don't require the application of fertilizers or toxic pesticides.

Avoid using toxic household and landscape chemicals. These enter the water and contaminate the watershed (see *Action 12: Use nontoxic home and yard products*).

Avoid applying fertilizer and soil amendments. Excess nutrients can cause algae growth in waterways (see page 12.10).

Safely dispose of toxic household chemicals and automotive fluids (see page 12.11).

Scoop the poop. Not a fun task, but proper disposal of pet waste helps to prevent disease-causing microorganisms from contaminating water sources (see page 12.10).

Get your septic system inspected and pumped regularly to prevent leakage that can contaminate the watershed.

Get involved with your local watershed organization

Find your local watershed organization. With a quick online search, you are likely to find a watershed association near you. Try using the terms **watershed association [your county, state]**. Look through the results. You may be surprised by how many watershed associations (or alliances) there are. Some state extension programs, such as those in Arkansas, Pennsylvania, and Texas, offer watershed stewardship programs which train participants to be watershed stewards who volunteer to educate their communities about watershed protection and care. Search online for **watershed steward program [your state]**.

Volunteer in community cleanups and other activities that support the watershed. Find volunteer opportunities by visiting your local watershed organizations.

Caring for our watersheds ensures the survival of animals that depend upon aquatic habitats such as this green heron (*Butorides virescens*).

Digging in deeper

Listed here are references and additional resources related to providing water for wildlife, installing rain gardens, and protecting the watershed (please refer to the Appendix for publication details).

Nature's Best Hope: A New Approach to Conservation That Starts in Your Yard: Throughout Doug's work, he stresses that our landscapes must provide four essential ecological services (see pages ix and III of this guide). One of these essential services is protecting and managing the watershed. Through a story about how one couple transformed their yard into a wildlife oasis (see pages 202 - 203), Doug stresses the importance (and ease) of providing water for wildlife.

In ***Building Natural Ponds: Create a Clean, Algae-free Pond without Pumps, Filters, or Chemicals***, Robert Pavlis explains how to build ponds for wildlife and suggests using plants to avoid the need for pump or filtration systems and toxic chemicals.

Learn more about rain gardens. Here are several helpful books when it comes to designing and installing rain gardens:

- ***Rain Gardens: Sustainable Landscaping for a Beautiful Yard and Healthy World*** by Lynn M. Steiner
- ***Creating Rain Gardens: Capturing the Rain for Your Own Water-Efficient Garden*** by Apryl Uncapher and Cleo Woelfle-Erskine
- ***Rain Gardens for the Pacific Northwest: Design and Build Your Own*** by Zsofia Pasztor, Keri DeTore, and Jill Nenemaker

Online searches for **best books on water conservation** and **best books on water-saving gardening** yield many enticing reads!

Shreya Ramachandran launched **The Grey Water Project** when she was just 13 years old. Since then, her efforts have resulted in an impressive, go-to resource for water conservation. Visit ***thegreywaterproject.org*** for grey water how-tos, volunteer opportunities, K-12 curriculum, and much more.

Watershed-Friendly PA (*watershedfriendlypa.org*) is a project of the Penn State Extension's Master Watershed Steward Program and the local Nurture Nature Center. Along with many helpful resources, Pennsylvania residents may apply for Watershed-Friendly Certification. It can serve as model for developing a watershed program wherever you live!

Three Rivers Rain Garden Alliance (*raingardenalliance.org*; mentioned on page 8.6) is a good example of the many online resources about rain gardens. Although based in western Pennsylvania, this website offers a wealth of information about rain gardens regardless of where you live. From technical information that includes a calculator to determine the right size for your property's rain garden to sample rain garden designs, this website covers it all.

In cold climates where bird baths and other water features may freeze, products such as the **K & H Pet Products Super Ice Eliminator Birdbath Deicer** (see page 8.7) come in handy.

Creatures and people are attracted to water, so it's not surprising that including water features in your wildlife habitat may bring more joy and entertainment than any other addition. Water is an essential resource to conserve and protect; indeed, water may be the most important feature in your landscape for wildlife survival.

Action 9—CHECKLIST
Design a layered landscape filled with plants

Step:	✔	Action Needed:	Page:
1	☐	Gain an understanding of the vertical layers of your landscape	**9.4**
2	☐	Get to know your palette of plants	**9.5**
3	☐	Begin to develop a vision for your wildlife habitat	**9.6**
4	☐	Identify a manageable area of your property to transform into wildlife habitat and choose a design approach to use for this area	**9.7**
5	☐	Design a wildlife planting that matches your resources and skill level	**9.8**
6	☐	Design your landscape to maximize its benefits to wildlife	**9.21**
7	☐	Design your landscape to minimize future maintenance needs	**9.23**
8	☐	Design your landscape to comply with local ordinances and HOA policies	**9.24**
9	☐	Design your landscape to optimize your property's watershed	**9.25**
10	☐	Design your landscape to optimize your property's potential for carbon sequestration and storage	**9.25**
11	☐	Fill containers with native plants for more opportunities to benefit wildlife	**9.26**

9

Design

A layered landscape fills this space from ground to sky.

Native Plant Information Sheet

Scientific Name_____ Family_____ Keystone ☐

Common Names_____ Habitat_____

Related Plants (i.e., genus, cultivars)_____

TREE SHRUB VINE FORB GRASS FERN   ☙   LAYER: canopy understory shrub herbaceous ground layer

Description:

Growth habit (i.e. clumping, upright, etc.)_____

Evergreen | Semi | Deciduous | Ephemeral   Perennial | Biennial | Annual

PHOTO or

BOOKS _____
_____

Book_____
Page _____

Native to_____ Conservation status_____

DEER: ☠ | never | rarely | sometimes | often | EAT!

GROWTH: slow   1   2   3   4   5   fast   AGGRESSIVE

height _____   width _____   spacing _____

ZONES _____   TEMPERATURE _____°F to _____°F

WATER: wet | > | moist | > | dry   DROUGHT TOLERANT

LIGHT: ☺ deep | > | part | > | full ☼

SOIL: _____ WELL-DRAINED pH:____

PROPAGATION Best: _____

SEEDING: Germination code _____ easy | hard
Days to germinate: _____   Require: DARK or LIGHT
Transplant out:

Cuttings | Division | Layering

PRUNING:

DATES (bloom/fruit dates, collect seed, propagation):

JAN	FEB	MAR
APR	MAY	JUN
JUL	AUG	SEP
OCT	NOV	DEC

☐ Lepidoptera	☐ Pollinators	☐ Birds	☐ Other Wildlife	☐ People	☐ Pests/Diseases
				☠	edible	yummy	
		Landscape Services		Plant with:	*have

My experience growing it: easy | > | med | > | hard   Observations:

Source	Propagation	Planting Date	Notes	Location	Map on back:
_____	_____	_____	_____	_____	Y	N
_____	_____	_____	_____	_____	Y	N
_____	_____	_____	_____	_____	Y	N

Action 9—GUIDE
Design a layered landscape filled with plants

Natural plantings provide a symphony of beauty as in this prairie planting designed by Roy Diblik. *Photo courtesy of Roy Diblik.*

Now, it's time to design your garden beds in preparation for acquiring plants and planting them. In this action, we cover the basic landscape design principles that maximize ecological services and benefits to wildlife. We consider the landscape layers that make up a rich wildlife habitat. Plus, we share some flexible landscape design plans that can be adapted to your ecoregion, your property, your skill level and resources, and your personal preferences.

Start thinking about how you would like your wildlife habitat to look. Does your neighborhood require a formal landscape design or is a more natural look acceptable? Do you have specific goals for your landscape, such as attracting birds, pollinators, or aquatic wildlife? We explain a step-by-step approach for designing wildlife habitat landscape beds. We also provide resources for finding native garden designs already created for your ecoregion and tips for hiring and working with landscape professionals.

Flexible landscape bed designs can accommodate a family's landscape needs while still creating a rich, functional ecosystem for local wildlife.

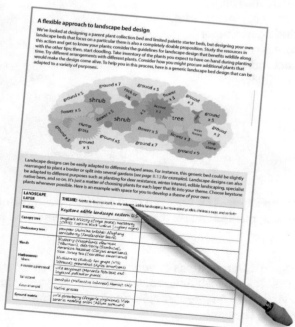

Gain an understanding of the vertical layers of your landscape

Wherever possible, design your landscape beds to accommodate all five vertical layers: **canopy tree**, **understory tree**, **shrub**, **herbaceous**, and **ground layer**. Note that not all plant communities include all five vertical layers.

The 5 vertical layers of the landscape:

Including native plants from each vertical layer will ensure that your landscape becomes a dense network of plants that supports wildlife.

Understory Tree Layer - Mature understory tree species are shorter than canopy species and typically either tolerate or require shade. It's important to note that this layer also includes young canopy trees that one day may replace old or ailing canopy trees.

Herbaceous Layer - Most familiar to gardeners, the herbaceous layer includes plants without woody stems: ferns, grasses, sedges, rushes, and **forbs** (non-woody flowering plants). This layer offers a broad diversity of plant species, including pollinator favorites such as goldenrod, aster, and sunflower.

Canopy Tree Layer - The canopy is filled with the branches and leaves of mature species of tall trees, such as oaks, maples, and pines.

Shrub Layer - Mature shrubs typically have single or multiple woody stems. Some shrubs may grow 20 feet or taller. Underappreciated in traditional landscaping, shrubs are an essential landscape component. They provide wildlife with shelter from the elements, cover for nesting, protection from predators, and food including foliage, fruits, pollen, nectar, seeds, and nuts.

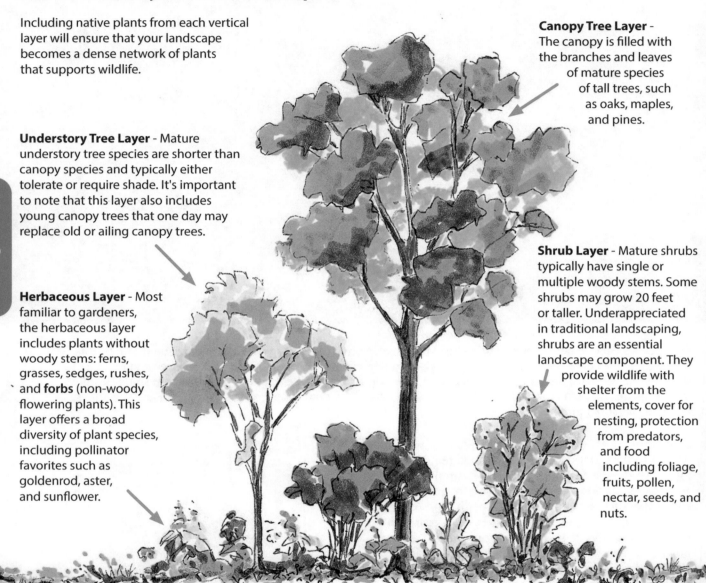

Ground Layer - This layer not only includes low-growing, shade-tolerant plants, such as sedges (*Carex*), mosses, and creeping plants, but also the rich layer of leaf litter and other organic matter that teems with microscopic life.

Observe different areas of your property. Are there areas where plants are missing from one or more of the layers? If so, revisit **Action 5: Identify your keystone plants** to identify keystone plants to fill these layers and see **Action 10: Propagate or procure lots of keystone plants** to learn different ways to get a lot of plants without breaking the bank.

② Get to know your palette of plants

Get to know a small number of plants really well. This sage advice is a message that internationally acclaimed perennial garden designer Roy Diblik shares in his book *The Know Maintenance Perennial Garden.* Roy convincingly makes the case that by really knowing your plants, you can envision how they fit into a legible, attractive design. When you place plants in conditions where they are happy, they thrive. They fill in and block out weeds reducing the need for maintenance. This gives you time to putter about and enjoy the beauty of your garden.

This prairie planting designed by Roy Diblik demonstrates how drifts of a limited number of plant species can make a simple but lovely impression. *Photo courtesy of Roy Diblik.*

Get to know a plant by growing it, observing it, and being curious about it!

The best way to get to know a plant is to grow it and observe it. There's no substitution for this, but you can boost this knowing beforehand with curiosity and a little research.

Roy Diblik's book and his online videos will help you get a feeling for plants and their unique characteristics. Additional handy online resources include:

- **Lady Bird Johnson Wildflower Center** (*wildflower.org/plants*)

- **Missouri Botanical Garden Plant Finder** Search online for **missouri botanical garden plant finder**.

- **USDA Plant Database** (*plants.usda.gov*)
- **Native plant nursery catalogs**

Filling out a *Native Plant Information Sheet* for each of the plants in your plant palette may help you get to know your plants (see page 9.2 for a blank reproducible sheet). Use books (see page 5.24 for regional recommendations), plant catalogs, online resources, and your own observations. Draw the plant or cut out photos from plant catalogs. After filling in a sheet even partially, you'll likely feel a stronger relationship with this plant. Plus, the information sheets are a handy place to record your experiences with your plants.

Choose a limited palette of plants

Limiting yourself to a small number of plants is a challenge since there are so many wondrous plants to choose from. Here are some basic guidelines for choosing plants for your wildlife habitat:

- ☐ Plant is **native** to your ecoregion.
- ☐ Plant is a **keystone** plant.
- ☐ Plant has a reputation for being **easy to grow and propagate** (or easy to procure in bulk).
- ☐ Plants are included from each of the **five layers of the landscape** (see diagram on page 9.4).
- ☐ Plants that will be placed together share **similar requirements** for light, water, and soil.

For help choosing plants, refer to the plant list created in earlier actions (see pages 5.6 - 5.7).

③ Begin to develop a vision for your wildlife habitat

First, let's consider the type of wildlife habitat you envision. The design may vary from formally designed to wild and natural. Different areas of your property may call for different approaches. By now, you likely have a feeling for which design approach appeals to you given your resources, your experience level, and your property's location.

Which of these design approaches do you envision for your wildlife habitat?

☐ **Formally designed** with the use of eco-beneficial plants and management approaches to meet the needs of some wildlife while still meeting the requirements of a strict HOA

☐ **Semi-designed** and well organized but still natural enough to support more wildlife while also fitting into a more traditional neighborhood

☐ **Semi-wild and natural** appearance with some intentional design while providing a rich wildlife habitat with paths and other structures to gain neighborhood acceptance

☐ **Wild and natural** appearance providing maximum wildlife support with no limits imposed by neighbors or a homeowners association (HOA)

Your property may be large enough that you can use a combination of these approaches in different areas of the landscape. Formal landscape designs require more advanced design skills, more extensive plant knowledge, and larger quantities of specific plants. Considering the design of a bed and choosing plants that are likely to look attractive together gives a bed a semi-designed and acceptable look for most front yards. Less visible areas of your property are suitable places to plant a landscape bed if you are just starting out because you can plant whatever plant materials you can procure even if their heights are mismatched or their colors clash. In an area hidden from view, you might experiment with plantings that focus exclusively on the ecological benefits of different plants without needing to consider the aesthetics of the bed.

4 Identify a manageable area of your property to transform into wildlife habitat and choose a design approach to use for this area

As you think about which portion of your property to tackle first, consider your current level of native plant knowledge and design skills as well as your available resources including time, budget, and plants you already have. Start small so that you can have success while you learn.

Select an area with a size that matches your current skill level and available resources. Note the area here:

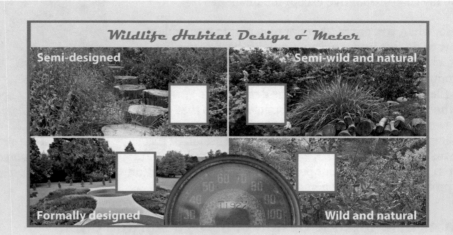

Review the design approaches on page 9.6. Check the box for the design approach that will best suit your current resources and your site:

Describe or draw a rough sketch of what you envision for this area:

If you are unsure about a vision for the area, leave this blank for now. Just keep on working through this action and others. Your landscape will grow and evolve along with your growing expertise.

⑤ Design a wildlife planting that matches your resources and skill level

Landscape designs often specify plant species and the quantities needed for each. If you have the resources and a good local native plant source, it might be possible to stay true to such a design; however, when you're on a tight budget, planting according to a landscape design plan is usually cost-prohibitive except for small areas.

Also, when you propagate your own plants (we explain how to do this in the next action), it's hard to predict which cuttings will root or which seeds will germinate and produce plantable plugs in time for planting. This makes it challenging to follow a landscape design plan. Furthermore, rather than specifying **straight species** plants that can be grown from seed, many designs specify **cultivars** or **nativars** that require **clonal propagation** (for a discussion of these terms, see pages 5.2, 10.9, and 10.21). These cultivars are often patented (or patent pending), and their propagation is prohibited—even for personal use.

A cultivar of the straight species purple coneflower (*Echinacea purpurea*), 'Pas702918' Powwow® White is patented thus prohibiting its propagation—even for personal use.

Think of landscape design plans as a starting point

Given these circumstances, consider using a landscape design as a starting point rather than a recipe that must be followed to the tee. Study a landscape that appeals to you. Think about what makes it strong. Figure out the structure (its "bones") and components (plant choices and hardscape) that make this landscape attractive. Try to capture the structure of this landscape and approximate its components in your design.

Decide upon the location for a planting, then use your notes to help flesh out your vision and decide where to place a tree, position several shrubs, plant drifts of perennials, place an accent plant, add ground layer plants, and so on. Fill in your design with plants that mimic the components of the attractive landscapes you have observed. Then, let it be okay that your landscape beds may not be perfect.

Planting many single plant species vs. multiples of a limited number of species

A planting of many single species of plants reads as a plant collection rather than a legible design. Indeed, since strong design relies in large part upon rhythm and repetition, many single plants may create chaos rather than harmony.

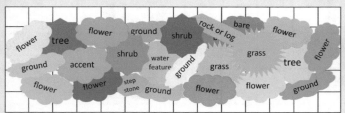

Planting one-of-each-species—Although individual plants may be beautiful, the variation in color, foliage, heights, and plant architecture often gives one-of-each-species plantings a chaotic look.

Planting in multiples—In contrast, planting in multiples of the same species provides the opportunity to create rhythm and repetition which leads to an organized, more attractive look.

When you're starting out, you may not have the resources to plant multiples of the same species. That's okay! In a moment, we'll explain how to be intentional about your plant collection and create a **parent plant collection bed**—a one-of-each-species trial bed that can be a source of plants for future plantings.

Tips for designing and growing a native plant landscape bed

Lower your expectations so that you can be happy with how ever your plants grow! Whether this is your first or fortieth garden, the primary goals are to provide the plants your local wildlife needs and get to know your chosen palette of plants. What you learn and what you grow here will lead to beautiful gardens in the future!

YEAR 1: Start small. Consider planting a **parent plant collection bed** or **starter bed** as explained on the following pages. For all the suggested bed layout designs, consider using an existing tree or shrub as a starting point for your design. If your resources permit, add multiples of plants to achieve a denser planting. If that's not possible, plan to keep gaps covered with regionally appropriate mulch (see page 11.9) until the plants fill in (leaving some area bare for ground-nesting native bees).

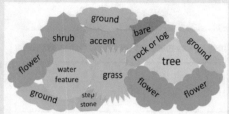

Many landscape design plans (such as the ones we've presented here) give the false impression of a full planting. Actually, some of the plants likely will take several years to fill in.

A newly planted bed will look more like the diagram above. The gaps allow plenty of opportunities for invasive plants to take hold, so maintaining a layer of regionally appropriate mulch and diligent weeding will be required.

If you can propagate or buy ground layer plants in bulk, plant them! A tight ground matrix of plants (the red x's above) will form a green mulch that will help prevent invasive plants from getting established.

Regular maintenance during the early years of a native planting is key to an easy-to-maintain future landscape. After your plants are established, begin propagating any plants that thrive (see *Action 10: Propagate or procure lots of keystone plants*). For example, collect seeds of flowering plants and identify the best time to take cuttings or divide plants that grow well. Propagating as many plants as you can helps to set your landscape up nicely for future years. Later in this action, in addition to explaining how to design a parent plant collection bed and a starter bed, we provide a seven-step approach for planning and sketching a landscape bed design.

YEARS 2 and 3: You probably learned a lot in Year 1. Some of the plants likely thrived and others . . . well, maybe some didn't make it. That's just how it goes—don't beat yourself up! If propagation was successful, use these plants (or plants purchased in flats) to design additional landscape beds. Here's a flexible approach to designing attractive beds that work well in wildlife habitats:

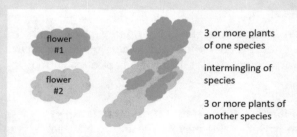

Observe your planted landscape beds. Identify potential **plant communities** (plant groupings) by noting combinations of plants that look good and grow well together. Group multiples of each species together so that each species stands out (this gives a species presence and helps insects find it), but also place some of each species intermingled with each other to give the design an attractive, natural look.

Plant the mixed plant groups in **drifts** (narrow, elongated groups) along with drifts of tall grasses and sedges (*Carex*). Fill spaces between the drifts with low-growing ground layer plants—the contrast in height will add **legibility** to your design (see page 9.18). Repeat these designed mixed groups of plants within a bed or in various beds around your property to create rhythm and repetition. Place accent plants randomly throughout the plantings. Add a water feature, logs, rocks, and of course, leave a bare spot for bees—voilà, you have an inviting oasis for wildlife!

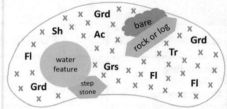

9

Design

Grow a parent plant collection bed (10 plants)

If you are starting out with limited resources, growing a one-of-each-species parent plant collection bed is an ideal approach. As the plants grow, they become the source of plant material to propagate more plants to populate your landscape. Keep in mind that the intent of the parent plant collection bed is functionality—not a stunning design. Since single plants of different species planted together tend to lack cohesion and a sense of design (see page 9.8), place this bed in a less prominent location. Plus, an out-of-view location will give you the freedom to experiment and learn. Stick with a limited palette of plant species (see page 9.5 for help with plant choices). Here, we show bed layouts for 10- or 20-plant palettes. Choose a different species for each plant. For the 10-plant palette, along with one each of a tree, shrub, tall accent plant, and grass, you would choose three *different* flowering perennials and three *different* ground layer species. As you make your plant choices, remember to choose plants whose requirements for light, water, and soil match the growing conditions for your site. Also, plan for protection from deer and other hungry visitors if needed.

LANDSCAPE LAYER	10	PLANTS: Native to ecoregion, keystone, easy to grow, easy to propagate, share similar growing requirements
Canopy tree OR Understory tree	1	
Shrub	1	
Herbaceous: Flowering perennial	3	
Tall accent	1	
Grass (clumps)	1	
Ground matrix	3	

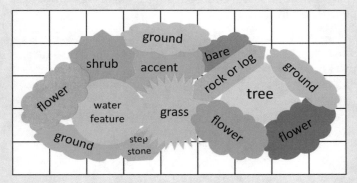

Parent plant collection bed—10-plant palette—island bed layout: Here 10 plants, each a different species, are laid out in an island bed. When including a tree or shrub, situate your parent plant collection bed in the location where you ultimately want the tree or shrub to grow. As the tree grows, this plant community will shift toward shade plants.

Sometimes within a bed, there will be different growing conditions, for example a neighboring tree may shade half the bed. Choose plants whose growing requirements meet the growing conditions for their specific location within the bed.

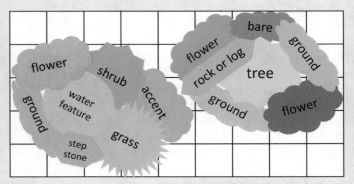

Parent plant collection bed—10-plant palette—split bed layout: Depending on your site and your available time and budget, you may want to split your plant palette into two (or more) beds. For example, you might plant a tree with a pupation site around it and plant the rest of the plants in a separate bed in a different area.

Note that all the plans include a water feature (*see Action 8: Include water to support wildlife*), a stepping stone for access to maintain the water feature, and a rock or log. Adding additional rocks and logs is recommended.

Grow a parent plant collection bed (20 plants)

As with the 10-plant palette, choose single plants of different species. For example, here you would choose two *different* trees, two *different* shrubs, eight *different* flowering perennials, and so forth.

LANDSCAPE LAYER	20	PLANTS: Native to ecoregion, keystone, easy to grow, easy to propagate, share similar growing requirements
Canopy tree **OR** **Understory tree**	2	
Shrub	2	
Herbaceous: Flowering perennial	8	
Tall accent	1	
Grass (clumps)	2	
Ground matrix	5	

Design

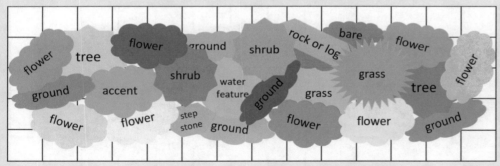

Parent collection plant bed—20-plant palette—island bed layout: In your parent plant collection bed, if your resources allow, add more plants of the same species to achieve a denser planting. If that's not possible, sow native annuals, grasses, or sedges or keep the gaps covered with mulch until the planting fills in.

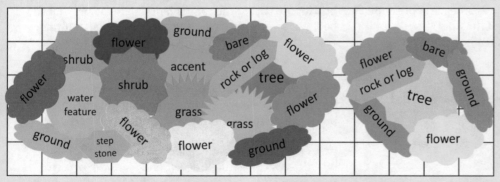

Parent collection plant bed—20-plant palette—split bed layout: The 20-plant palette plan (*left*) is split in two to accommodate two separate beds that each contain a tree and plants beneath them for pupation sites. Leave an area bare for ground-nesting bees if this is not provided elsewhere on your property.

NOTE: *The squares in these plans and those shown elsewhere represent approximately one square foot. When a bed is first planted, it will look quite sparse (as explained on page 9.9). If resources permit, fill in the gaps with regionally appropriate mulch, or better yet, additional ground layer plants.*

Grow a small starter bed (10 plants)

Growing a small starter bed is another handy approach if you are starting out and have limited resources. As with the parent plant collection bed, we'll stick with a limited palette of plant species, but in contrast to the parent plant collection bed, this bed uses multiples of the same species, for example, *three of the same* flowering perennials and *three of the same* ground layer plant species. The advantage of a starter bed is three-fold—there are fewer plants to get to know, buying plants in multiples can be more economical, and the design is more likely to be pleasing. As you make your plant choices, remember to choose plants whose growing requirements match the growing conditions of your site. Also, prepare in advance for any needed protection from deer or other dangers.

LANDSCAPE LAYER	10	PLANTS: Native to ecoregion, keystone, easy to grow, easy to propagate, share similar growing requirements
Canopy tree OR Understory tree	1	
Shrub	1	
Herbaceous: Flowering perennial	3	
Tall accent	1	
Grass (clumps)	1	
Ground matrix	3	

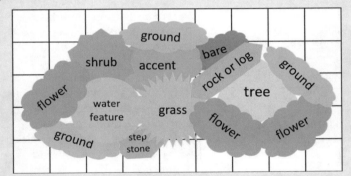

Small starter bed—10 plants (6-plant palette)—island bed layout: All the layers of the landscape are represented in this small island bed. Multiples of the flowering perennials and ground layer plants offer rhythm and repetition.

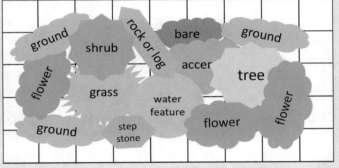

Small starter bed—10 plants (6-plant palette)—border bed layout: Using the same plant palette as the island bed, this arrangement lends itself to a border planting. The arrangement can be repeated for a longer border.

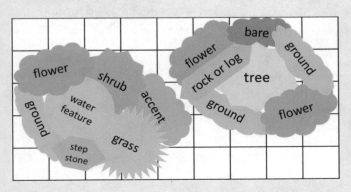

Small starter bed—10 plants (6-plant palette)—split bed layout: Here again, the same plant palette is used but this time the plants are split among two beds.

As with the parent plant collection bed, all the plans include a water feature (*see Action 8: Include water to support wildlife*), a stepping stone for access to maintain the water feature, and a rock or log. Additional rocks and logs are recommended along with additional ground layer plants if resources permit.

Grow a larger starter bed (20 plants)

The same approach used for a small starter bed also works for a larger bed. These layouts use 20 plants. You may wish to limit yourself to a 6-plant palette and use multiples of the same species for each landscape layer or expand your palette. For example, you could include two different shrubs or trees. Or you may consider two different species of flowering perennials. Consider including a native vine. Just remember that if you use too many different species for the 20 plants, the bed will lack rhythm and repetition and will likely convey a feeling of disorganization. If resources permit, add additional plants of the same species of perennials and ground layer plants to fill in the gaps until the bed gets established and fills in. Remember to choose plants whose growing requirements match the growing conditions of your site and plan in advance for any needed protection from deer or pests.

LANDSCAPE LAYER	20	PLANTS: Native to ecoregion, keystone, easy to grow, easy to propagate, share similar growing requirements
Canopy tree **OR** **Understory tree**	2	
Shrub	2	
Herbaceous: Flowering perennial	8	
Tall accent	1	
Grass (clumps)	2	
Ground matrix	5	

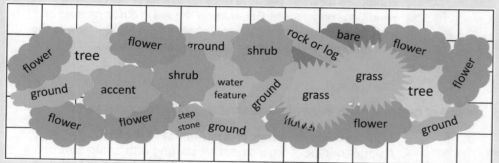

Large starter bed—20 plants (6 or more-plant palette)—border bed layout: Multiples of the flowering perennials and ground layer plants offer rhythm and repetition. Keep in mind that as trees grow, their pupation sites will need to be extended to ensure that caterpillars have soft landings.

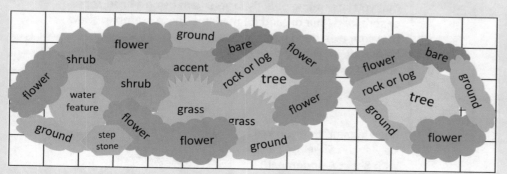

Large starter bed—20 plants (6 or more-plant palette)—split beds: This 20-plant plan is split in two to accommodate an island bed and a smaller bed. Both include a tree and its pupation site.

Sketch your landscape bed design in seven steps

When you are ready to finalize your plans in preparation for planting, these seven steps will provide a step-by-step guide. This is where you'll bring all your ideas together and sketch a plan that focuses on the area you plan to start with. In a moment, we'll discuss additional resources for developing your vision along with guidelines for optimizing the ecological and wildlife benefits of your design, so review those before returning here to finalize your bed design. A reproducible sheet of grid paper follows on page 9.16. The plan will be easier to sketch on three layered sheets. Tracing paper and a pencil or upcycled clear sheets of plastic packaging and a permanent marker work well for drawing the top two layers.

PLAN SHEET A: (*bottom*) Immobile features of the property, utility lines, and growing conditions

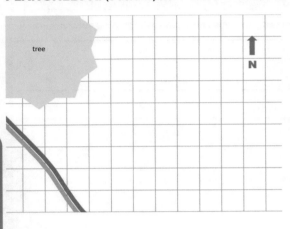

STEP 1: Mark the locations of significant features of the area making sure to mark where utility lines run through the area. Mark the locations of existing trees, water sources, and hardscape features, such as patios, pathways, and fences. Note any planned additions, such as water sources and hardscape features that will require plumbing or electrical work. In preparation for digging, call to have your property's utility lines marked. See page 3.15 for more information about this free service. ***Know what's below. Call 811 before you dig*** (or visit ***call811.com***). Determine how much area each block on your grid represents. Here, each block is equal to approximately one square foot.

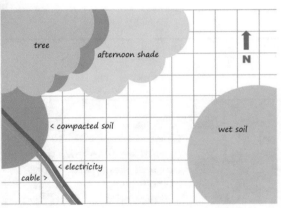

STEP 2: Observe and note the growing conditions of the area. You may already know the growing conditions for the area you plan to start with. If not, observe the area several times each day over time (ideally over a year if time permits). Record the sun and shade patterns. A shortcut for determining which plants are likely to thrive is to identify any existing plants (including weeds) that are growing well on the site. Then, look up the ideal growing conditions for these plants to get a good idea of the growing conditions on your site. Get to know the soil in different areas of your property: Is it sandy, loamy, or heavy clay? Make a note of the different soils and the sunny, shady, dry, and wet areas.

PLAN SHEET B: (*middle*) Shape and size of bed and placement of trees, shrubs, and herbaceous layer

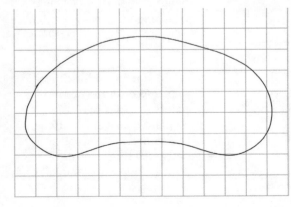

STEP 3: Define the shape and perimeter of the bed. A simple outline of the area you are starting with is sufficient. You may wish to draw a detailed plan, or it can be a rough plan that you later refine directly in your yard using a hose, rope, or sprinkled flour or sand for marking. These examples show that your plan need not be grandiose, simply clear enough to guide your efforts.

Keep in mind that you will be viewing Sheet B (*above*) with Sheet A underneath it (*right*).

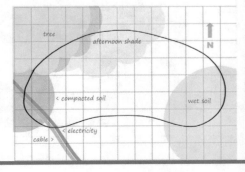

Sketch your landscape bed design in seven steps, *continued*

PLAN SHEET B: (*middle*), *continued*

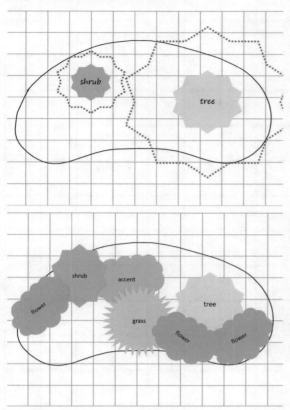

STEP 4: Mark the spots for keystone trees and shrubs.

If you are including a tree, place it first; then, place shrubs. Consider the mature circumference of trees (and shrubs). Allow sufficient area for the landscape bed to expand to accommodate caterpillar pupation sites beneath a fully mature tree. For the next several years, the bed can be small since the tree will be small. The bed can be expanded to accommodate larger pupation sites as the tree expands its canopy and as you propagate or procure more plants to plant generously around the tree as it grows.

STEP 5: Mark the spots for keystone herbaceous plants, pollinator plants, and native grasses.

Place multiples of the same species to make the plants more attractive to insects (and people). Intermingle plants where two species meet (see page 9.9). When deciding which herbaceous plants to place around trees and shrubs, choose plants that meet the current site conditions. As trees and shrubs mature and the site conditions change, shade-adapted plants can be planted. Place plants as densely as resources permit. This will help control invasives, protect the soil, and provide a richer wildlife habitat.

PLAN SHEET C: (*top*) Placement of logs, stones, water features, bare ground, and ground layer plants

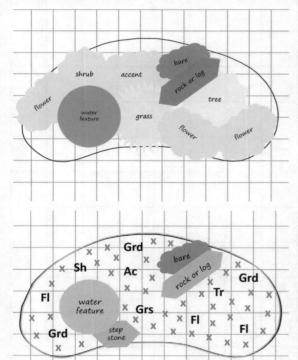

STEP 6: Mark the spots for several logs or large stones, additional water features, and bare ground for native bees.

Logs and large stones will serve as pupation sites and hiding places for all kinds of small creatures. Determine the placement for additional water sources, such as elevated and ground-level birdbaths. Mark a spot which can be left bare for ground-nesting, native bees if this has not been adequately provided elsewhere on your property.

Sheet C shown with Sheet B underneath it (*left*)

STEP 7: Mark the spots for low-growing ground layer plants.

Fill in gaps with low-growing plants (red x's). Place *sun adapted,* low-growing plants in gaps or open areas. Under any existing large shrubs and trees, tuck in *shade-tolerant* plants, such as low-growing sedges (*Carex*), mosses, and native creeping plants, to establish a matrix of ground layer plants. Your landscape bed design is ready to go!

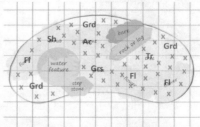

Sheets A, B, and C stacked (*right*)

9

Design

A flexible approach to landscape bed design

We've looked at designing parent plant collection and limited palette starter beds, but designing your own landscape beds that focus on a particular theme is another completely doable proposition. Study the resources in this action and get to know your plants. Consider the guidelines for landscape design that benefit wildlife on page 9.21 along with the other tips throughout this book, then start doodling. Take inventory of the plants you expect to have on hand during planting time. Try different arrangements with different plants. Consider how you might procure additional plants that would make the design come alive. To help you in this process, here is a generic landscape bed design that can be adapted for a variety of purposes.

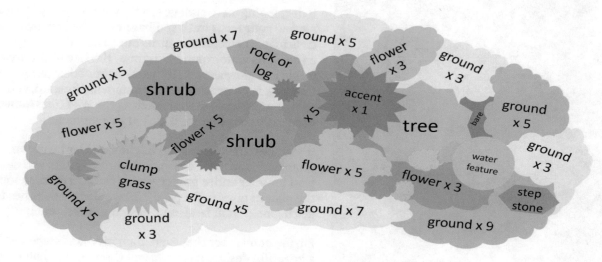

Landscape designs can be adapted to different shaped areas. For instance, this generic bed can easily be rearranged to accommodate a border bed or split into two gardens as we saw with the parent plant collection and starter beds (see pages 9.12 - 9.13 and 10.8 for additional examples). Designs can also be adapted for different purposes, such as planting for deer resistance, winter interest, native pollen specialist bees, or edible landscaping. Choose native plants for each layer that fit into your theme and match the growing conditions of the site. Here is an example with space for you to develop a theme of your own:

LANDSCAPE LAYER	THEME: Keystone deer resistant, winter interest, edible landscaping, hummingbird garden, children's oasis, and so forth	
THEME:	Keystone edible landscape eastern U.S.	
Canopy tree	shagbark hickory (Carya ovata); hackberry (Celtis); Eastern black walnut (Juglans nigra)	
Understory tree	pawpaw (Asimina triloba); Allegheny serviceberry (Amelanchier laevis)	
Shrub	blueberry (Vaccinium); viburnum (Viburnum); elderberry (Sambucus); American hazelnut (Corylus americana); New Jersey tea (Ceanothus americanus)	
Herbaceous: Vines:	blackberries (Rubus); fox grape (Vitis labrusca); groundnut (Apios americana)	
Flowering perennial	wild bergamot (Monarda fistulosa) and keystone pollinator plants	
Tall accent	sunchoke (Helianthus tuberosa) Harvest this!	
Grass (clumps)	Native grasses	
Ground matrix	wild strawberry (Fragaria virginiana); Viola sororia; nodding onion (Allium cernuum)	

Developing a vision for your wildlife habitat when it seems overwhelming

Get ideas by driving around and looking at people's landscapes, visiting public gardens, hiking through natural areas, finding images online of regional native plantings, and studying books about landscaping with natives. Notice designs that you find attractive and consider how you could incorporate them into your vision. Find native plants to replace introduced plants in appealing designs.

If developing an overall vision for your property is daunting, narrow your focus until you have identified an area that feels manageable. If this turns out to be a tiny area, let that be okay. As your experience grows, the size of the area you tackle can grow as well. If the thought of designing even a tiny area is preventing you from moving forward, consider using professional designs such as the *Wild Ones Native Garden Designs* that we'll look at in a moment.

If you have the means, you might consider hiring an ecological landscape designer. Some designers will develop a plan for your entire property with the goal of implementing the plan in phases. On page 9.20 we share guidelines for getting help from landscape design professionals.

Finally, remember that even if a native landscape bed lacks a beautiful design, creatures will thrive in the habitat you've created!

Gardens at Chicago's Shedd Aquarium are a combination of native and rugged prairie perennials designed to appeal to wildlife and people. *Photo courtesy of Roy Diblik.*

Natural plantings work in formal landscapes

If your neighborhood or your personal aesthetics call for it, planning a formal design does not prevent you from incorporating native plants and wildlife habitat into your landscape. For a more traditional look, you'll typically want to design with:

- straight lines and a more angular design
- crisp edges, clipped hedges, and tidy plants overall
- defined paths and clear patterns of plants.

A formal garden is likely to have clearly defined paths in contrast to those that might meander through a natural wildlife habitat. These design approaches add definition and organization, giving a planting **legibility** (an understandable and pleasing design) and helping viewers to comprehend the landscape. Despite these more constrained design approaches, wildlife ecosystems can come alive through:

- plant choices
- hardscape structures that support wildlife (such as water features)
- nature-friendly management routines.

Orderly frames and **cues to care**, that we discuss in *Action 14: Build acceptance for nature's natural look*, become especially important when striving for a formal aesthetic.

How to find Wild Ones *Native Garden Designs* by professional landscape designers

The downloadable *Native Garden Designs* shared by **Wild Ones** are an amazing free resource. You can use these designs in your landscape, learn about the featured native plants, study the design process, and explore different approaches to landscape design. Often video interviews with the designers are included. These are especially helpful if you live in ecoregions such as arid desert regions whose climates often require approaches to native garden installation that are different from those broadly recommended elsewhere in the United States. Studying these plans and watching the interviews will give you ideas for designing a flourishing native garden.

Visit: wildones.org

or search online for **native garden designs wild ones** and navigate to the site.

Click on **Programs.**

In the dropdown menu, click on **Native Garden Plans.**

Here are links for garden plans for many regions of the United States. First, you may wish to click on **Why Native Plants** which leads to a series of informative web pages: **Create Your Garden Plan, Work Your Plan, Keep it Beautiful**, and finally back to the **Garden Designs** listing described below.

Click the tiles to view the downloadable, free native garden designs available for many regions of the United States.

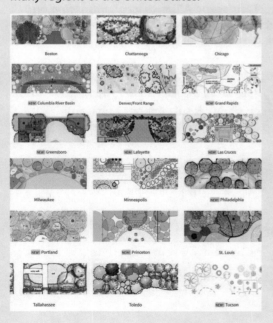

These professionally designed native garden designs include detailed drawings to scale (*right*) and photos of the native plants used in the design (*below*). Click plant photos for detailed plant information.

Many of the plans feature video interviews with the designers (*right*).

The Wild Ones materials shown here and elsewhere in this book are used with permission from Wild Ones (wildones.org).

Getting help from ecological landscape professionals

While hiring landscape professionals is not required for the actions suggested in this guide, you may wish to enlist the services of a landscape professional. For plans that require electrical wiring, grading, retaining walls, heavy-duty stormwater management, or other types of construction, the help of a **landscape architect** or **landscape contractor** will ensure compliance with building codes and ordinances. For sites that require complex or formal landscape design, say to meet the requirements of a demanding homeowners association (HOA), the plant knowledge and design skills of a **landscape designer** will help to ensure the success of your project. Once your wildlife habitat is planted, you may wish to hire a **landscaping maintenance service** to maintain your property on a regular basis. See below for general tips about choosing eco-friendly landscape professionals.

National organizations that provide directories for finding ecological landscape professionals:

Homegrown National Park (*homegrownnationalpark.org*)
Find consultation, design, installation, gardening, and native plant sources in the *Resource Directory*.

Ecological Landscape Alliance (*ecolandscaping.org*)
Check out ELA's *Eco-Directory* to find an ecological landscaping professional in your area.

 Finding an ecological landscaper in your region may require further research. If so, search online for **native plant landscape [architect/designer/maintenance] near me** OR **sustainable landscape [architect/designer/maintenance]**. Your state or local native plant society or **Wild Ones** websites may also list eco-friendly landscape professionals.

When choosing a landscape professional to help you with your wildlife habitat project, carefully review their website and request to see a portfolio of their work if one is not readily available online. Ensure that the professional:

- has experience with native plants
- has the know-how to manage your property as a natural wildlife habitat
- will agree NOT to use pesticides, herbicides, fertilizers, and other toxic chemicals on your property
- is licensed, if required. For example, all states require landscape architects to have earned a bachelor's degree in landscape architecture from an accredited school, gained internship experience, and passed the Landscape Architect Registration Examination.

Request a phone interview to explain your vision and requirements. If the landscape professional seems like a good match, arrange a consultation visit to your property.

6 Design your landscape to maximize its benefits to wildlife

As you design your landscape, keep the following guidelines in mind to maximize the benefits to wildlife.

Plant generously rather than waiting to make the perfect plant choices. As your landscape evolves, you'll be able to edit your plant palette.

Plant Selection

These plants are attractive to a diversity of pollinators, providing pollen and nectar to bees, butterflies, flies, beetles, wasps, and moths. Some plants provide additional resources as caterpillar host plants or nesting sites and nesting materials for above-ground nesting bees. Many support specialist bees that require pollen from specific plants to survive and supplement beneficial insects that can help control pests of ornamental and crop plants. These plants are native to this region—determine if a species is native in your area at plants.usda.gov—and can be used to create or enhance pollinator habitat across rural and urban landscapes.

When purchasing plants, let your local garden center or nursery know you want plant material free of pesticides that may harm pollinators.

Resources
→ Pollinator Conservation Resource Center: xerces.org/pollinator-resource-center
→ Bring Back The Pollinators: BringBackThePollinators.org
→ Reducing Pesticide Use & Impacts: xerces.org/pesticides

Plant for a sequence of blooms to ensure the survival of specialist bees. Especially needed are plants that bloom very early and very late in the season. See the *Xerces Society* plant lists (see page 6.5) and the **Pollinator Partnership** *Garden Cards* (under Resources at pollinator.org) for help with planning flowering sequences.

Group plants of the same species rather than planting single isolated plants. Pollinators and other insects are more likely to visit when there is at least a 3-foot x 3-foot mass planting of their preferred species. Groups of plants (also called **drifts** or **swaths**) intermingled on the edges with each other tend to contribute greater power to garden design as well. At first, your budget may not allow for planting multiples, but with time, your plants will mature, and you'll be able to propagate them and plant more abundantly.

Include native sedges (*Carex*) and grasses in your landscape beds (see pages 11.10 - 11.11 and 11.19.) Not only do sedges and grasses (*above*) provide seed for mammals and birds, many are also caterpillar host plants. Plus, their dense root structures prevent erosion and filter pollutants in the watershed.

Plant high value nectar plants together with host plants for butterfly and moth caterpillars. This saves travel time for these creatures allowing them to conserve energy. A skipper (*below*) is feeding on wild ageratum (*Conoclinium coelestinum*) which is planted right next to a swath of native grass—the skipper's host plant.

Design your landscape beds to allow sufficient area for caterpillar pupation sites under trees and shrubs. Place logs and rocks for additional pupation and nesting sites.

Include ground-level and elevated water features.

Include island beds in the middle of your lawn, especially if you have a large lawn. These islands give pollinators and other small creatures a place to escape from the path of a lawn mower.

Plant fruit- and nut-bearing plants along with dense shrubbery nearby to attract birds and to provide nesting sites and shelter. When planting fruit for human consumption, plant extra so that you won't mind when a catbird or some other feathered friend shares your harvest!

9

Design

For areas that need to look like lawn, consider options that offer more ecological benefits than traditional lawn offers

Wherever possible, it's best to fill your wildlife landscape with plants from ground to sky, but there may be some areas of your property where you need to keep lawn for aesthetic reasons. Here, we focus on options for areas where you would like to create the visual effect of lawn. Although most of these lawn alternatives cannot tolerate the typical wear-and-tear that a turf lawn can, they have the tremendous advantage that, in addition to requiring little or no mowing, they provide ecological services, such as food for wildlife in the form of pollen, nectar, foliage, and seed; host plants for caterpillars; shelter for small creatures; water and air filtration; erosion control; soil improvement and carbon sequestration.

For areas where you would like to replace your lawn, yet keep the visual effect of lawn, consider these alternatives:

- planting a sedge (*Carex*) lawn
- planting a pollinator-friendly bee lawn
- planting mosses or encourage an existing mossy area
- planting a native meadow or prairie garden.

Plant a sedge (*Carex*) lawn.

Plant a pollinator-friendly bee lawn.

Plant mosses or encourage an existing mossy area.

Plant a native meadow or prairie garden.

You may have other areas of lawn that are not heavily used that you would like to keep in lawn. In these areas, you may consider replacing conventional turf with low- or no-mow eco-friendly grasses that can tolerate some traffic (see page 11.18).

For all these options, removing conventional turf prior to planting will yield the best results. Refer to the lawn removal methods described in *Action 3: Shrink the lawn.* We'll explain how to plant each of these lawn alternatives in *Action 11: Plant your landscape generously.*

Design your landscape to minimize future maintenance needs

You will thank your future self if you consider future maintenance needs during the design stage of a landscape. The tips below can help you dramatically reduce the amount of maintenance your landscape will require. Several of these tips are mentioned in other actions, but they are worth repeating here.

Start small! As you transition your landscape to wildlife plantings, it may be tempting to tackle your entire property in one go. To avoid getting overwhelmed, start with an area that is smaller than you would like. This will give you enough time during the establishment phase of a landscape to proactively remove invasives before they set seed or spread.

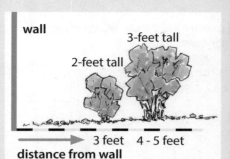

Leave space between plantings and exterior walls. This provides access to walls and windows, reduces fire risk, and helps to prevent roots from invading the foundation of a building.

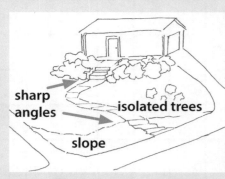

Design the shapes of your planting beds to make maintenance and mowing around them easier. Avoid leaving lawn areas that have sharp corners, isolated trees, or steep slopes.

Plant the ground layer densely in a tight matrix using low-growing sedges (*Carex*), mosses, creeping natives, and other gap-filling plants.

Plant densely. By densely planting a bed, your desired plants will fill in more quickly and block out invasive weeds. Sow seed of **ruderal plants** (fast-growing, short-lived plants that thrive on soil disturbance such as *Rudbeckia hirta*) between newly planted perennials, shrubs, and trees.

Carefully choose the location of poisonous, prickly, or stinging native plants or plants with burs. If they can be safely situated, some plants with these qualities are still worth including in your landscape for the eco-services they provide. A skin irritant, meadow rue (for example, *Thalictrum fendleri*; *above*) is a beneficial host plant for some specialist caterpillars.

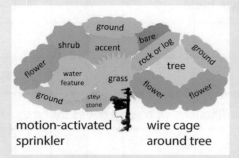

Plan ahead for how you will protect a planting from deer browsing or other dangers. For example, grow deer-resistant plants and install protective fencing or sprinkler deterrents. This will spare you a lot of headaches later!

Space plants to allow for an extended period of blocking persistent invasive plants. If a difficult to remove invasive plant has infested an area, plant trees, non-suckering shrubs, or large, single-stemmed perennials. This makes the area easy to block with cardboard covered with a layer of organic matter. Remove any invasives that sneak through the cardboard and continue to block them until they have exhausted their resources and been eradicated.

Sow annual seed over the entire area. Observe where people and pets walk.

Place paths where the annual plants were trampled.

Place paths where traffic goes. Avoid wasting time replacing trampled plants. Instead, before landscaping an area, observe where people and pets walk. Align your paths with these natural traffic patterns.
Year 1–Sow an annual cover crop in the area and observe for a season to see where people naturally walk.
Year 2–Place paths along these natural paths (known as **desire lines**). Sometimes a path will be needed in a specific location to guide people to a scenic view or other destination but wherever possible, put paths where people and pets will walk anyway.

⑧ Design your landscape to comply with local ordinances and HOA policies

Review your local ordinances and homeowners association (HOA) policy if your property has one. Researching potential restrictions on your property *before* installing your wildlife habitat could spare you anguish and expense later. For example, there may be rules that limit grass height, prohibit planting milkweed, or even prohibit hanging a birdhouse.

In *Action 15: Share, educate, and get involved*, we'll look at how to help change local policies to be more wildlife-friendly but until they are updated, you'll want to keep the policies in mind as you plan and install your wildlife habitat. If you have a project in mind that may conflict with these rules, apply for a variance.

Large lawns like this one are a drain on resources and offer few ecological services.

Some HOAs require excessive front lawns such as the one shown here. If this is the case for your property, you might consider one of the lawn-like alternatives introduced on page 9.22 and discussed further on pages 11.10 – 11.18.

 To determine if there are local ordinances or zoning codes for your property, do an online search for **landscape ordinances [zip code]**. This will likely yield zoning codes primarily relevant to builders and commercial properties, but it may be worth a quick read-through.

Are there HOA policies, local ordinances or zoning codes that may affect your landscape design?

Does your property have an HOA? YES or NO

If yes, note the contact info for the HOA here:

Note applicable HOA policies, local ordinances, or zoning codes that may affect your plans:

Design your landscape to optimize your property's watershed

Rather than fighting wet areas of your property or the impact of stormwater, design your landscape to optimize boggy areas and your property's watershed. Refer to *Action 8: Include water and protect the watershed* for a discussion about watersheds and how to protect them. If you have a wet area, you may want to design a bed for plants that thrive in boggy conditions. Or you might have an area of your property where stormwater collects making it an ideal location for a rain garden. Here's a grid to help with planning a moisture loving garden bed or rain garden:

Plant Palette	#	PLANTS: Native to ecoregion, keystone, easy to grow, easy to propagate, share similar requirements
Canopy tree OR Understory tree		
Shrub		
Herbaceous: Flowering perennial		
Tall accent		
Grass (clumping)		
Ground matrix		

Design your landscape to optimize your property's potential for carbon sequestration and storage

The terms carbon sequestration and carbon storage are often used interchangeably; however, they are slightly different. **Carbon sequestration** is the *process* of removing carbon from the atmosphere, an ecoservice provided by trees and other growing plants. **Carbon storage**, as the name implies, is the *storage* of carbon such as that stored in trunks, branches, roots, and soil.

Designing your landscape to include as many trees, shrubs, and other plants as possible optimizes your property's ability to sequester carbon. Keeping the organic matter that plants produce—wood, leaves, roots, and other organic materials—on your property contributes to carbon storage. As scientists strive to develop sophisticated solutions to the carbon emissions crisis, why not fill the landscape with native plants of every size to maximize carbon storage now?

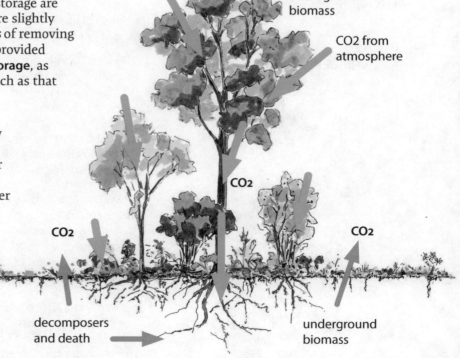

aboveground biomass

CO2 from atmosphere

CO2

CO2

CO2

decomposers and death

underground biomass

(11) Fill containers with native plants for more opportunities to benefit wildlife

Incorporating native plants into your container planting may seem like an insignificant contribution toward helping wildlife, yet every action taken to help wildlife no matter how small contributes to nature's well-being. Have some fun by adding some native plant-filled containers to your space.

Plant a container with a solo species or a thriller-filler-spiller trio

Here are two easy ways to plant containers that are both eye-catching and eco-beneficial.

Materials Needed:

Container: 12 to 16-inch diameter that is approximately 14 inches tall. Or use any size container and simply adjust the recommended quantities.

Pot bottom fill: Gravel, decomposing wood chips, old branches or twigs, chunks of foam from packaging

Potting mix: See page 10.13 for potting mix suggestions

Water

Plants for single species containers:

A single species of plant. Depending on the growth habit of the plant and the size of the pot, you may wish to plant three or more individual plants so that the container fills out more quickly. *Suggested plants*: The plants recommended in the **Homegrown National Park** *Container Gardening with Keystones* guide (see page 9.27) are ideal. You might consider medium height native sedges and grasses. Choose a plant whose height is approximately double the width of the pot.

Plants for thriller-filler-spiller trio:

THRILLER

FILLER

SPILLER

Choose plants with contrasting yet harmonious foliage, color, and bloom time.

Thriller: A "thriller" gives pizazz to the container. This can be a tall, attractive plant whose height is double the width of the pot or any plant with visual interest. *Suggested plants: Solidago, Echinacea, Monarda, Rudbeckia, Zizia,* a flowering vine on a mini-trellis, young shrubs (*Cornus, Spirea*), or non-natives such as dill, parsley, fennel, or sage. The plants recommended in the **Homegrown National Park** *Container Gardening with Keystones* guide (see page 9.27) work well as thrillers or fillers.

Filler: Three to five plants of the same species (depending on the size of the container) to fill in the space between the thriller and the spiller plants. *Suggested plants*: Native perennials, such as *Carex, Heuchera,* or low-growing flowering natives. Choose a species whose height is about a half or third of the height of the thriller or one that contrasts with the thriller.

Spiller: Three to five plants that will spill over the perimeter of the pot. *Suggested plants*: Creeping ground layer plants, such as wild strawberry (*Fragaria*) and *Phlox stolonifera* and sedges with a droopy growth habit such as *Carex bromoides.*

Fill containers with native plants for more opportunities to benefit wildlife, *continued*

Steps to assemble the container

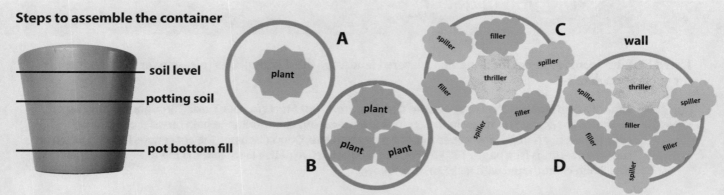

A

plant

B

plant
plant plant

C

spiller filler
spiller
thriller
filler spiller
filler
spiller filler

D

wall

spiller
thriller
spiller
filler
filler
filler
spiller

Fill the bottom one-fourth of the container with "pot bottom fill" to promote drainage and reduce the amount of potting soil needed. Add potting mix to about two-thirds full.

With your plants still in their pots, arrange them in your container.

For solo containers, place one plant in the middle of the container (see **A** above) or 3 plants in a triangle in the center of the container a few inches apart (**B**).

Remove the plants from their pots one at a time and replace them in the container. Make sure that each plant **crown** (point where the stem meets the roots) is about one inch below the top of the container.

Add potting mix to all the spaces between the plants. Make sure that the potting mix does not cover the crown of the plants.

Water the container.

*For mixed species, if your container will be viewed from all sides (**C**),* place the "thriller" plant in the middle. Set "spiller" plants at equal distances around the perimeter of the container. Place "filler" plants in the gaps.

*If your container will have its back to a wall (**D**),* place the "thriller" plant in the back middle of the container. Set "spillers" in an arc from the back left side, across the front, and to the back right side but not in the center back. Place "filler" plants in the remaining spaces.

9
Design

Use Homegrown National Park guide to identify keystone plants suitable for containers

Visit **HomegrownNationalPark.org**.

In the top menu, click **Resources**. Click **Keystone Plant Guide**. Click **Keystone Flowering Plants (Container-Friendly)**.

Or search online for **container gardening with keystone plants** and navigate to the site.

Scroll down and click on the tile for your region to see profiles of plants that work well in containers.

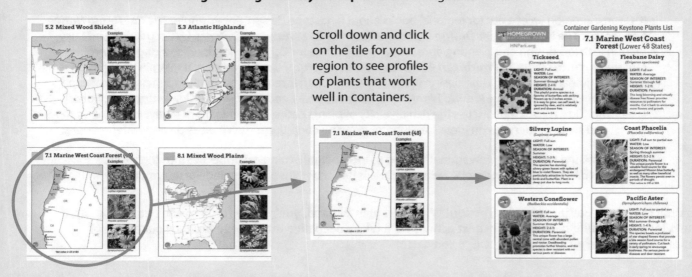

Digging in deeper

Design

9

Listed here are more resources for designing a layered landscape filled with plants (please refer to the Appendix for publication details).

Nature's Best Hope: A New Approach to Conservation That Starts in Your Yard: Throughout Doug's work, he shares the concern of many in the ecological landscaping community: To gain broader community acceptance, our natural landscapes must also be attractive. Doug discusses the challenges faced in urban and suburban settings (see pages 185 - 201). Designing attractive native landscapes is the topic of an earlier book that Doug co-authored with Rick Darke as follows.

The Living Landscape: Designing for Beauty and Biodiversity in the Home Garden is a marriage of ecological principles and compelling landscape design. Rick Darke and Doug Tallamy teamed up to take an in-depth look at landscape layers and the importance of establishing functioning ecosystems within these layers to support biodiversity. This book includes strategies for increasing the ecological value of visually appealing landscapes.

An invaluable resource for understanding landscape layers and plant communities and designing attractive natural plantings, ***Planting in a Post-Wild World: Designing Plant Communities for Resilient Landscapes*** by Thomas Rainer and Claudia West is a must-read for a basic understanding about creating ecologically functional, layered landscapes that are also beautiful.

Planting: A New Perspective by Piet Oudolf and Noel Kingsbury is a richly illustrated glimpse into the design process of an internationally renowned landscape designer. Not only is this book a showcase for the modern landscapes of Piet Oudolf, but the book also provides a broad understanding of landscape design along with planting plans, diagrams, and photographs. Different approaches to achieving natural beauty through thoughtful landscape design are explained. Despite this book's international audience and inclusion of plants from ecoregions worldwide, it includes many U.S. natives, and its concepts can be universally applied.

In ***The Know Maintenance Perennial Garden***, Roy Diblik not only gives us 62 ready-to-go designs. He also explains a friendly, doable approach to landscape design based on grid patterns featuring plant communities. Included are plant profiles featuring native and tough perennial prairie plants.

The Essential Garden Design Workbook: Completely Revised and Expanded is a comprehensive guide to professional garden design. Rosemary Alexander and Rachel Myers guide readers through each phase of landscape design—pre-design, concept, layout, planning, planting, and maintenance. This is an ideal resource for homeowners wanting to design their own landscape as well as for people considering a future in professional landscape design.

It's worth keeping an eye out for regional books about landscape design. For example, ***The California Native Landscape: The Homeowner's Design Guide to Restoring Its Beauty and Balance*** by Greg Rubin and Lucy Warren features design and planting approaches appropriate for California landscapes along with profiles of regionally native plants. In ***Prairie Up: An Introduction to Natural Garden Design***, Benjamin Vogt provides excellent guidance for landscape design in the Midwest. Another regional book, although not a landscape design book per se, is ***Native Florida Plants: Low Maintenance Landscaping and Gardening***. In it, Robert Haehle and Joan Brookwell discuss the rich diversity of plants native to Florida (third in diversity among the 50 states) and share garden design ideas for different growing conditions, such as seaside and water gardens.

For the aspiring landscape professional looking to incorporate ecological principles into their work, ***Principles of Ecological Landscape Design*** by Travis Beck contains a mother lode of information.

It's time to put all your planning into action! With your plan in hand, you're now ready to start procuring the plants for your wildlife habitat. In the next action, we'll take a deep dive into how to produce quantities of plants even if you're on a tight budget. See you there!

Action 10—CHECKLIST
Propagate or procure lots of keystone plants

Step:	✔	Action Needed:	Page:
1	☐	Match the size of the area you plan to transition to native plantings with your available time and resources	**10.4**
2	☐	Propagate or procure lots of plants (even on a tight budget!)	**10.6**
3	☐	Hone your propagation skills—propagation is surprisingly easy!	**10.9**
4	☐	Review your landscape design plans to estimate your native plant requirements	**10.21**
5	☐	Decide whether you will propagate or purchase each plant species and locate sources for seeds and plants	**10.21**

Calendar of Propagation Events Note when plants should be propagated: seeds sown, cuttings made, etc.

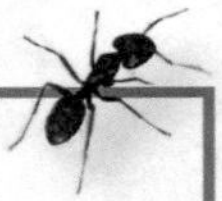

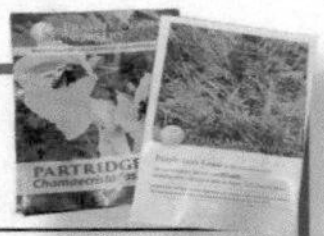

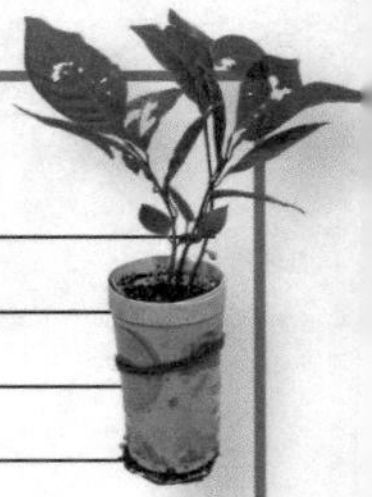

JANUARY
Stratify seeds

FEBRUARY

MARCH

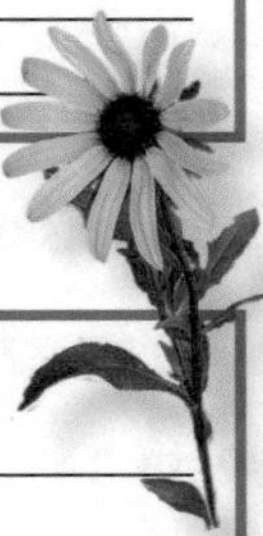

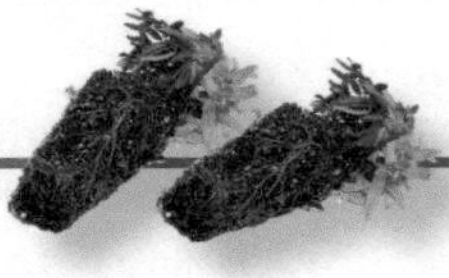

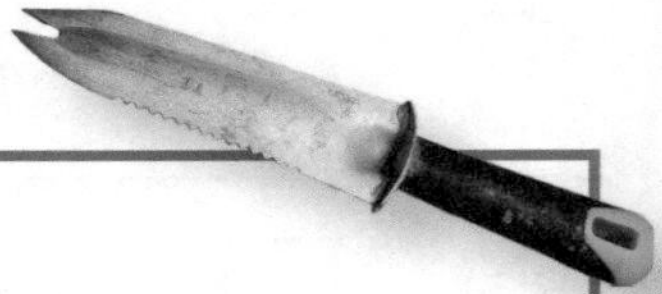

APRIL

MAY

JUNE

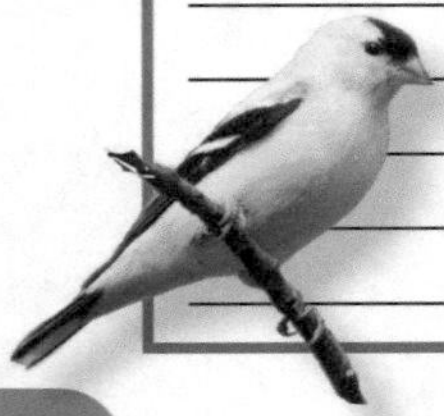

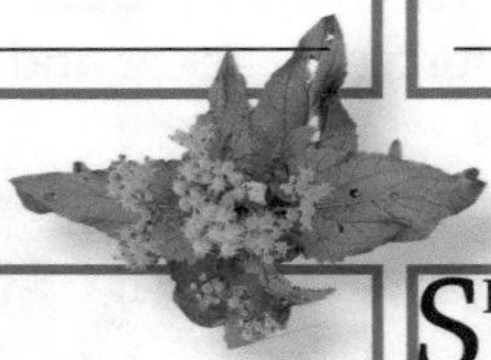

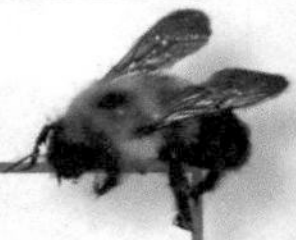

JULY

AUGUST

SEPTEMBER

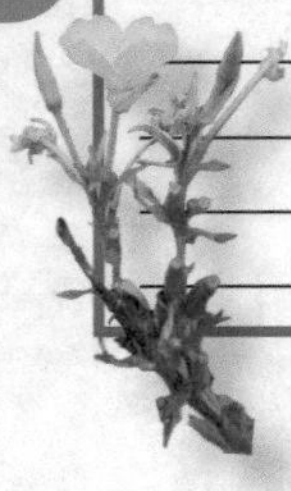

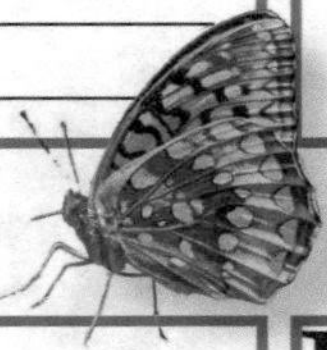

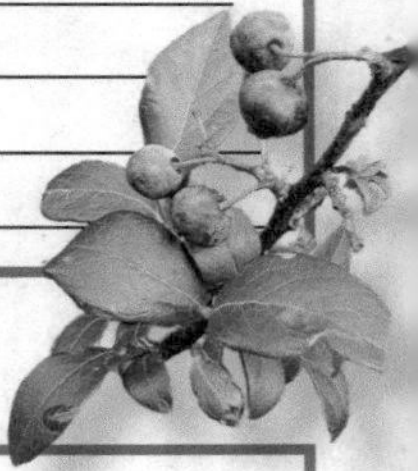

OCTOBER

NOVEMBER

DECEMBER

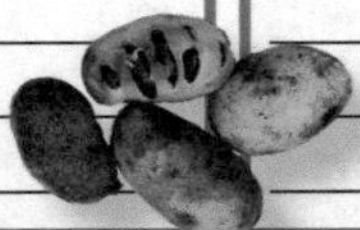

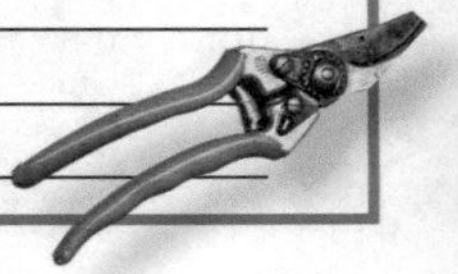

Action 10—GUIDE
Propagate or procure lots of keystone plants

In this lovely meadow designed by LWLA, the flowers will be allowed to set seed to build the seed bank ensuring years of future blooms. *Photo courtesy of Larry Weaner.*

It takes a lot of plants to create an ecologically functional wildlife habitat. By now, you likely have a good idea of the plants you would like to add to your property to enliven your wildlife habitat. With the help of the plant list we started earlier; the next step is to begin procuring plants. In this action, we share budget-friendly strategies and techniques for propagating large quantities of native plants so that you are able to generously plant all the layers of your landscape . . . from ground to sky.

If you have an adequate budget, then getting plants is a simple process of locating suppliers of native plants—ideally plants that are **local ecotypes** (populations within a species that have genetically adapted to the local environmental conditions) of **straight species** (original wild species not altered by humans). In this action, we share guidelines for purchasing native plants.

On the other hand, if you're on a tight budget, with patience and a little ingenuity, you can still plant generously. Here, we look at ethical and inexpensive—even free—ways to procure plants. In fact, with some basic supplies and knowing just a few simple propagation techniques, it's possible to produce hundreds of plants for under $100!

We'll show you how, so let's get started!

1 Match the size of the area you plan to transition to native plantings with your available time and resources

Now is the time when all our planning begins to come together! By now, your plant wish list is likely way larger than what your time and budget will permit. The temptation may be huge to take on much more than you can feasibly care for unless you have a team of landscapers or willing friends and family to help you out. Evaluate how large an area is reasonable for you to tackle given your resources. Take advantage of the tips in this action to get the most bang for your bucks (and effort!).

The transition from newly installed plants to dense native plantings takes time—your time and nature's time. It especially takes time for trees to grow, shrubs to fill out, and groundcovers to spread. Select a manageable area to convert to wildlife habitat. If you undertake transforming your entire property in one go, you may become overwhelmed by the magnitude of the project. Your transition will go more smoothly if you have enough time and resources to care for a specific area. The following strategies will help you to bridge this transitional time in your landscape.

Start small and transform your property in increments

YEAR 1: Oak seedling is planted with a small bed of herbaceous perennials around it.

YEAR 2: Beds with a mix of herbaceous perennials and shrubs are planted around the house.

YEAR 3: Using cuttings and volunteers from Years 1 and 2, the bed around the oak is extended and connected to the Year 2 beds.

Starting out . . .

Later on

In full public view, this area of my property would be far more beneficial to wildlife if I could have removed all the lawn in one go and filled it with native plantings ground to sky. But my finite resources force me to transform limited areas each year to ensure that I can keep up on its care (and not be booted out of the neighborhood!).

Later, a dead tree in the front yard had to be removed to comply with neighborhood standards. There are still large areas of grass slated for removal, but island beds with native forbs, grasses, shrubs, and saplings are filled with wildlife. In less visible areas where less grooming is required, 95% of the lawn is now filling up with natives from ground to sky.

Achieve plant density in the early years while new plantings become established

This introduced conifer can remain for the time being. It provides shelter for birds and it's not invasive.

Likewise, this daylily can remain—it's not invasive and it provides beauty and builds neighborhood acceptance.

Violets, a host plant for fritillary butterflies, happily spread when they get regular water and light shade.

Downy wood mint (*Blephilia ciliata*) is an aggressive native, a pollinator magnet, and deer usually leave it alone.

If the species is not invasive, consider leaving an introduced (non-native) plant in place until you have the resources to replace it. While new plantings are getting established, you may wish to leave some of the existing introduced plants in place to provide nesting sites and shelter IF the plants are not invasive species. (BUT keep in mind the importance of removing invasive plant species!) Later, you can replace introduced plants with native ones or remove them when the surrounding native plants have filled in.

Choose easy-to-grow plants that cover the ground quickly. Such plants are typically described as "vigorous" or "aggressive." Often, these will be plants that reproduce easily by seed or vegetatively by **rhizomes** (underground stems that root) or **stolons** (horizontally growing stems that may root and form new plants). Aggressive natives can be used to quickly fill in an area where you are not also attempting to get less vigorous native species established.

Just 3 months after planting closely spaced homegrown plugs, this woodland planting has filled in. Later, it will need thinning which happily will provide plants for other areas of the landscape.

If your budget permits, plant plugs or pots rather than seeds. Seeds are far more economical than plugs or pots; however, plugs or pots fill in bare ground more quickly and are visually more impactful. With herbaceous plants such as perennials, the larger the plant, the sooner the planting will look established. In contrast, woody plants (shrubs and trees) establish more readily when planted very young, such as from seeds, nuts, or 1- to 2-year-old bareroot or potted seedlings. R-pots (see page 10.10) are ideal for starting seeds and nuts of woody plants because they are long and narrow.

Plant densely with tight spacing. In nature, plants grow in close-knit communities occupying different root depths, plant heights, and growth cycles. Mimic nature's approach. Fill the space around newly planted trees and shrubs with herbaceous plants (forbs, ferns, mosses, grasses, *Carex*, or rushes) with tight spacing. As the plants fill out, some can be selectively removed and transplanted to other beds or simply cut off at their base.

② Propagate or procure lots of plants (even on a tight budget!)

Obviously, planting densely requires a lot of plants. First, we'll look at how two of the tips we just shared for helping bridge the transition from traditional to more eco-friendly landscapes are also helpful strategies for planting generously when on a tight budget. Then, we'll look at additional strategies for procuring plants on a tight budget so that it's easy to plant generously.

Keep introduced (non-native) plants in place as long as they're not invasive until you have the resources to replace them with native alternatives. If an introduced plant is not invasive, it's better left in place until it can be replaced with a native. Although native plants will do so much more, as you gather resources to transition your property to a wildlife habitat, a non-invasive introduced plant can provide shelter for wildlife, sequester carbon, and perhaps add appeal to your property for neighborhood acceptance.

Choose easy-to-grow native plants that cover the ground quickly. Buy a single plant of a native plant described as "vigorous" or "aggressive," and it will likely fill in an area and provide transplants to fill in other areas. Try out a variety of plants and soon you'll know which ones are your easy-to-grow "go to" plants to quickly and economically fill an area.

How to procure plants on a tight budget so that it's easy to plant generously

Here are additional tips for procuring an abundance of plants when you're on a tight budget (or even if you're not!).

Learn how to grow plants from seeds and nuts and grow your own plugs! You'll save a tidy sum and have a wider selection of plants from which to choose.

Learn how to propagate plants from cuttings, division, and layering. Many native plants are quite easy to propagate with these methods!

Collect seeds, nuts, and cuttings instead of buying them whenever possible. As your plants become established, you'll be able to collect seeds, take cuttings, and make divisions.

Native seed and plant material collection etiquette

When you find opportunities to collect seeds and nuts OR take cuttings or other plant material on public or privately owned lands, keep native plant collection etiquette in mind:

- Be sure you have correctly identified the plant material you are collecting so that you never accidentally collect rare or endangered species!
- Ask permission of property owners before collecting any plant material.
- Only collect seeds, nuts, and other plant material in places where a species is growing abundantly.
- Limit harvest to a very small percentage of the existing plant population.

How to procure plants on a limited budget so that it's easy to plant generously, *continued*

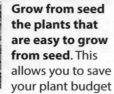

Grow from seed the plants that are easy to grow from seed. This allows you to save your plant budget for hard-to-propagate plants. Most seed catalogs note easy-to-grow seeds, such as this spotted beebalm (*Monarda punctata*) that blooms in its first year.

Buy single "parent plants" of easy to propagate species. Choose parent plants that are easy to propagate by seed, division, or cuttings. For example, the native trumpet honeysuckle (*Lonicera sempervirens*) is a rampant grower that is quite easy to propagate by taking cuttings or layering.

Exchange native plants with friends and neighbors. A word of caution: Be sure that you can accurately identify all plants that you exchange to avoid giving or receiving invasive plants. Cup plant (*Silphium perfoliatum*), a pollinator magnet, is an aggressive native plant that happily volunteers all over the place. Despite its being native, this eagerness to grow has earned cup plant a place on noxious lists in New York and Connecticut.

Buy one species in bulk to broadly fill an area instead of many single plants of different species. Native species that are already doing well in your landscape are good choices for mass plantings. Consider purchasing 6-packs, 8-packs, 12-packs, or flats (when available). These are much more economical than single pots. Plus, insects find what they need more easily when plants are grown in drifts or masses. Later, you can add plant diversity as time and resources permit.

Learn to identify the seedlings that volunteer from your native plantings so that you don't accidentally weed them out. When allowed space to do so, Mother Nature will help with propagation. These volunteers can be left to grow or moved to fill in other areas. When I grow plants from seed, I take a picture of the seedlings a couple of weeks after germination. This helps me train my eye to spot these welcome seedlings in the landscape.

Encourage native plants to volunteer. Allow plants to self-sow by not cutting off the flower heads of desirable plants so that they can go to seed. In spring, monitor the leaf litter or mulch below your plants to be sure it's loose enough so that seedlings can come up through it. As soon as you spot a native tree seedling, protect it from deer and other hazards (such as the lawn mower). These seedlings are nature's succession plan. Shown above is an oak volunteer likely planted by a squirrel or blue jay.

10

Propagate

How to procure plants on a limited budget so that it's easy to plant generously, *continued*

15,000 seeds

500 seeds

LANDSCAPE LAYER	THEME: Keystone deer resistant, winter
THEME:	*Keystone edible landscape east*
Canopy tree	shagbark hickory (Carya ovata); ha (Celtis); Eastern black walnut (Jugl
Understory tree	pawpaw (Asimina triloba); Allegher serviceberry (Amelanchier laevis)
Shrub	blueberry (Vaccinium); viburnum (Viburnum); elderberry (Sambucus) American hazelnut (Corylus americ New Jersey tea (Ceanothus americ
Herbaceous: Vines:	blackberries (Rubus); fox grape (Vit labrusca); groundnut (Apios americ
Flowering perennial	wild bergamot (Monarda fistulosa) keystone pollinator plants
Tall accent	sunchoke (Helianthus tuberosa) Har
Grass (clumps)	Native grasses

Buy just one or two of a plant to test it out in your landscape before investing in more. Existing native species that are doing well make good choices for mass plantings. If your budget permits, consider buying several of one species and planting it in various locations to see where it will grow best (or if it will grow at all). Despite its reputation as being deer resistant, after much experimentation where I live, woodland phlox (*Phlox divaricata, above*) thrives only in areas protected from deer.

Cover large areas by planting with seeds purchased in bulk. Compare the seed packet prices with the price per ounce. For example, a nursery may offer a seed packet containing 500 seeds of little bluestem (*Schizachyrium scoparium*) and an ounce containing 15,000 seeds for only a dollar more. Buying seed in bulk gives you the opportunity to grow thousands of plants for the price of just one 3-inch potted plant!

Limit your plant palette. If you're on a tight budget or if you have a large area to cover, consider focusing on a limited number of keystone species. Pick easy to propagate plants and propagate multiples or sow seed of your selected species. Then, repeat different combinations of the species throughout your landscape. For larger properties, propagate or sow seed in higher quantities of each species. This approach is explained below.

Planting with a limited palette of plant species

In *Action 9: Design a layered landscape* we discussed getting to know a limited palette of plants to use in different landscape bed designs. This same approach makes it easy to plant generously on a shoestring budget.

Decide on the 10 plant species you want to focus on. The reproducible form on page 9.10 is a handy place to record your plant choices (see sample at right). The species will vary by ecoregion, so use the resources in *Action 5: Identify your keystone plants* to identify the best choices for each category.

Consider the different places you would like to plant. For example, perhaps you would like to add an island bed to replace some lawn, create a pupation site under a tree, fill a corner with native plants, and plant around your mailbox. The same ten plant species can be used in different configurations to meet all these needs.

LANDSCAPE LAYER	10	PLANTS: Native to ecoregion, keystone, easy to grow, easy to propagate, share similar growing requirements
Canopy tree OR Understory tree	1	
Shrub	1	
Herbaceous: Flowering perennial	3	
Tall accent	1	
Grass (clumps)	1	
Ground matrix	3	

This form for a 10-plant palette may be helpful for planning.

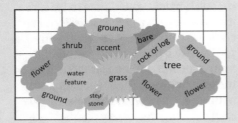

Large island bed

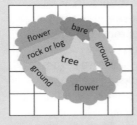

Small island bed

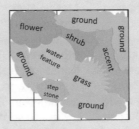

Small corner bed

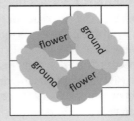

Bed around mailbox post

③ Hone your propagation skills—propagation is surprisingly easy!

Propagating your own plants is surprisingly easy. With minimal supplies and some patience, you'll likely have more plants than you'll know what to do with. Here, we explain the basics of collecting and sowing native seeds and nuts, taking cuttings for rooting, dividing perennials, and layering branches for rooting. We also suggest useful resources if you would like to take on the challenge of propagating more finicky species. Get ready to experience the thrill of discovering seedlings as they first poke up and the excitement of brushing off soil from cuttings to find newly formed roots!

The biggest hurdle to growing plants from seed, especially when it comes to shrubs and trees, may be the psychological notion that it is complicated to do. But it really isn't. Many native plants, including shrubs and trees are extremely easy to grow from seed. Others just need a little pre-treatment, such as **scarification** (scratching of the hard seed coat) or **stratification** (moist chilling or warming for a specific time period). As you decide which plants to grow from seed, be sure to include shrubs and trees on your seed sowing list.

Some shrubs such as nine-bark (*Physocarpus opulifolius*) are surprisingly easy to grow from seed!

Growing plants from seeds and nuts offers many advantages

Growing plants from seed preserves a diverse and resilient genetic pool since individual plants have different genetic profiles. In the event of disease, climate change, or other adversities, some individual plants may offer resistance or be able to adapt to changing conditions allowing a species to survive. In contrast, **vegetative propagation** (asexual propagation by cuttings or other vegetative means) creates offspring with identical **genotypes** (genetic profiles) or **clones**. Clonal propagation is the norm for mass propagation of native plants for the retail market. Growing plants from **straight species seed** (seed from the original species that has not been bred for specific traits; see pages 5. 2 and 10.21) helps preserve the genetic diversity of the native plant gene pool.

Shrubs grown from seed, as well as those grown from plugs or young bareroot seedlings, often outperform larger-sized specimens. At first this seems counterintuitive, but given the extreme transplant shock that plants experience, it makes sense. A seed, plug, or bareroot seedling starts its life IN its future home spared of transplant shock.

Growing plants from seeds is significantly more economical than purchasing plugs or potted plants. This is especially true for shrubs and trees which tend to be priced higher than herbaceous plants. A handful of seeds can produce a small forest's worth of plants for a fraction of the price of one plant.

10
Propagate

Some species of shrubs when grown from seed will form colonies that block invasives

Larry Weaner, in his and Thomas Christopher's milestone book *Garden Revolution: How Our Landscapes Can Be a Source of Environmental Change*, explains that many shrub species (such as *Aronia, Clethra,* and *Spirea*) when grown from seed will **sucker** (send up shoots from their roots) to form lovely thickets that suppress invasive plant growth. In contrast, **clonally propagated plants** (plants propagated asexually, for example by stem or root cuttings) of these same shrub species tend to grow as distinct shrubs with single trunks. Learn more about this and much more in *Garden Revolution*—a must-read for anyone passionate about encouraging functioning ecosystems in our landscapes.

The berries of red chokeberry (*Aronia arbutifolia*), native from Maine to Texas, are a winter source of food for birds and other animals. Despite being tart and pithy when raw, chokeberries make delicious jellies and jams (or so I've heard!).

How to make your own do-it-yourself propagation supplies

Propagation supplies need not be fancy. In fact, most of the necessary supplies can be found around the house or from a recycle bin. Seeds and fertilizer-free potting soil are the only expenses needed for a basic setup other than the one-time purchase of lighting (if you choose to propagate indoors and don't have bright light from a window). Here are some budget-friendly, do-it-yourself supplies for propagation:

Seed-starting cells: Recycled plastic containers of all shapes are useful. Egg cartons provide handy cells that make potting up easy. Punch holes in the bottom of each cell, fill with potting soil, and sow seeds.

 Reuse cell packs, pots, and flats from purchased plants. To disinfect, soak containers for 30 minutes in a 1 : 1 vinegar to water solution. Rinse well.

Plant labels: Plastic containers and their lids (which often are not recyclable) can be cut into strips for plant labels. Print the name of the plant with a permanent marker. Lids can also be left whole and used to mark soil mixes.

Pots for transplanting seedlings into: Plastic containers such as 1-quart yogurt containers make nifty, adjustable pots. Mark and cut the container in half with sturdy scissors or clippers. Cut as shown below. Wrap the cut half into a cylinder and secure with a rubber band. I call these **R-pots** (R = repurposed). R-pots make deep and narrow plugs—a pot size that's not readily available for purchase.

bottom

R-pots are easy to mass produce.

 NOTE: *Product containers vary in their suitability. Some plastics are brittle or difficult to cut, especially across the bottom. Experiment with containers from the recycle bin to find ones that cut relatively easily without splitting.*

Larger R-pots: The same system works well to make wider cylindrical pots ideal for shrub and tree seedlings. Mark as shown (*right*) and cut down only one side of the container. Cut one bottom circle. Secure with a rubber band.

Supports for R-pots: R-pots need to be placed in a container with drainage holes because the R-pot bottoms need support. Four small R-pots fit in a 1-quart yogurt container with 5 drainage holes cut in the bottom. Eight fit in the tubs that baby lettuce comes in; any similar container will work. To hold drainage water and keep things tidy, cut drainage holes in one tub and place it inside another tub. Save the lids of recycled tubs because the tubs can be inverted and set up as miniature greenhouses for seed starting.

Supplemental propagation supplies you may want to make

Rodent protection screen: Mice or other rodents may eat your seeds and destroy your seedlings. One method for protecting them is to place your seed-starting cells in a 12" or taller tub that has a lid (see below for tub suggestions). Cut out the center of the lid leaving 2 – 3 inches all around so that the lid will still snap in place. Hot glue a piece of 1/4-inch hardware cloth or heavy screen (*right*) to cover the opening cut in the lid. For outdoor use, drill drainage holes in the bottom of the tub. For indoor use, see the tip below.

Rain garden shields:
If you're planting a rain garden, these DIY rain shields will help to protect young transplants. Cut a quart yogurt container in half. Stick it in the ground "upstream" from the plant. If used in the front yard, consider painting the shields brown or green.

rainwater flow

seedling

Propagation supplies you may have around the house or want to purchase

Watering can with a long nozzle

Hand-held sprayer with an adjustable gentle-spray nozzle for spraying fine seeds and emerging seedlings

Thermometer

Clear totes for holding small pots for mass propagation of seedlings. Under-the-bed storage totes are useful for holding pots. Two 28-quart totes (see photo on page 10.12) fit side-by-side on a 4-foot rack.

For stratifying seeds outdoors or **hardening off seedlings** (acclimating seedlings to the outdoors), taller clear 25-quart totes (16L x 12W x 12H inches; *right*) are handy because they're easy to carry and the lid can be put on for a chilly night.

Upcycled plastic milk jugs make handy stratification chambers for use outdoors. Simply cut off the top half leaving a small section intact to serve as hinge. Drill drainage holes in the bottom. Fill with seedling mix. After sowing the seed, replace the top and secure with tape. See page 10.17 for more information.

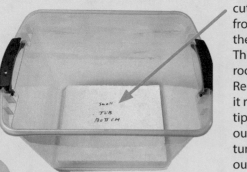

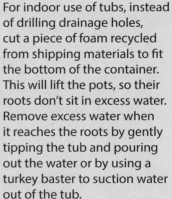

For indoor use of tubs, instead of drilling drainage holes, cut a piece of foam recycled from shipping materials to fit the bottom of the container. This will lift the pots, so their roots don't sit in excess water. Remove excess water when it reaches the roots by gently tipping the tub and pouring out the water or by using a turkey baster to suction water out of the tub.

Seedling heat mat: Heat encourages seed germination and root development on cuttings for many plant species. If the temperature of an indoor propagation location is below around 60°F, then a heating mat may speed up germination. Maintaining the temperature at around 70°F helps most cuttings to root.

Supplies needed on an ongoing basis

Soil, or to be precise, soilless potting media: If you plan to grow most of your own plants, it makes sense to purchase the components to make your own soilless media. For a detailed discussion about this, see page 10.13.

Plant propagules: *What the heck are plant propagules?* Plant propagules are any plant material used for propagation. It's handy to have a word for the many different plant parts that can be used for propagation: seeds, nuts, stem cuttings, root cuttings, leaf cuttings, bulbs, corms, tubers, stolons, rhizomes, spores, and more. But don't worry about any unfamiliar terms—here our focus will be on seeds, nuts, stems, and dividing the roots of plants.

Seeds: Purchase or collect your own.

Stems: Harvest from a parent plant OR bend stem down for layering.

Roots: Many plants are easily propagated by division when mature. Here, a shovel is used to divide an established clump of grass.

In a moment, we'll explain how to do each of these propagation methods.

Propagation set-up for the serious indoor plant propagator

If you want to do some serious indoor propagation, here is an efficient set up. Find a multi-tiered shelving unit with 4-foot (48 inches) long shelves—this length allows the lights, tubs, curtains, and heating mats to fit tidily.

Pole: Attach a pole, such as an old broom stick or PVC pipe, across the front.

Lights: Hang three 4-foot full spectrum LED or grow lights from the top three shelves.

Shower curtains or liners: Two plastic, repurposed shower curtains (clear, opaque, or patterned curtains work fine). One curtain wraps around the left side and the back of the shelving unit; the other wraps around the right side and, using curtain rings, slides onto the pole across the front creating an accessible, enclosed space.

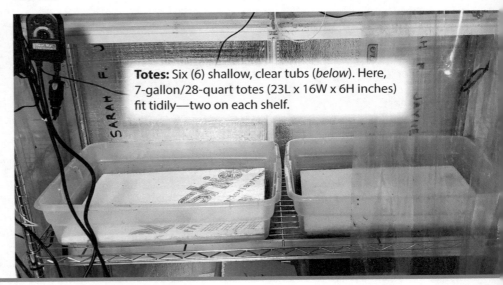

Totes: Six (6) shallow, clear tubs (*below*). Here, 7-gallon/28-quart totes (23L x 16W x 6H inches) fit tidily—two on each shelf.

Rack: 4-tier steel shelving unit (48L x 18W x 72H inches)

Mixing your own soilless potting media

If you plan to propagate a lot of your own plants, consider mixing your own soilless media. Not only is it more economical than buying ready-mixed bags, but it allows you to customize your mixtures to meet the needs of specific species. The guidelines shared here are starting points for your own experimentation.

Supplies needed:

Old totes, tubs, or other large containers to mix soil in such as upcycled drawers from old refrigerators

Soil sieve: A sieve to sift out larger materials in compost and leaf mold is easy to make. Either use the rodent protection screen described on page 10.11 if it was made with 1/4-inch hardware cloth OR cover the back of an old picture frame with 1/4-inch hardware cloth. Place the screen over a tub and you have a handy soil sieve.

Soilless media components

Since the 1950s, sphagnum peat moss has been the main ingredient in most potting mixtures sold in the United States. Unfortunately, the use of peat moss is particularly unsustainable. Peatlands store almost one-third of the earth's soil carbon—storing more carbon than all other types of vegetation combined! When harvested, harmful carbon dioxide is released representing a significant source of greenhouse gas emissions. Furthermore, the demand for peat is such that peatlands are harvested at a rate far faster than they can regrow considering it takes centuries for a peatland to develop to maturity.

coco peat

compost

rice hulls

perlite

vermiculite

Coco peat, also called coir peat, is a renewable peat substitute made from coconut husks. It's commonly shipped in small bricks that expand up to seven times in volume when water is added! With an almost neutral pH, coco peat works well as a base for all-purpose mixes.

Other peat alternatives include homemade fully rotted compost, **leaf mold** (decomposed leaves), or decomposed woody materials for acid-loving plants, such as blueberries and many woodland plants.

Rice hulls are useful in place of **perlite** and **vermiculite**, two popular potting soil ingredients used to improve drainage and retain moisture, respectively. Both perlite and vermiculite are naturally occurring minerals that are puffed up like popcorn. Neither material is sustainable as their mining and processing are energy intensive. A sustainable alternative, parboiled rice hulls (also called rice husk) increase the drainage of a potting mix, retain moisture, have a neutral pH, and add organic matter. Other materials to use in place of perlite and vermiculite include coco peat, horticultural grit, poultry grit, coarse sand, or wood chips. Experiment to find what works best for your mixes!

Purpose of Soilless Mix	Coco peat or other peat alternative	Rice hulls or other material	Coarse sand or grit
Potting mix – all-purpose	3 parts (this can be a mix of peat alternatives–see above)	1 part rice hulls OR coarse sand or grit	
Potting mix – acid-loving plants	Use the all-purpose potting ratio but include decomposed woody materials or pine needles, fine bark, or leaf mold as part of the peat substitute		
Seeding mix	Screen the all-purpose potting mix (avoid using compost in the seeding mix)	Sprinkle a thin layer of coarse sand or small gravel on top (optional)	
Rooting mix (for cuttings)	1 part (avoid adding compost)	1 part rice hulls or other material OR coarse sand	

NOTE: *Wear a face mask when working with dry soilless media, especially with perlite and vermiculite.*

How to COLLECT and STORE seeds and nuts

You can spot seeds that are ready for harvest by observing the seed capsules (or heads) that form after flowering. As the seeds mature, the seed heads typically dry up and turn brown and the seeds disperse.

Immature seed capsules

Seed capsules beginning to mature

Mature seed ready to disperse and ready to harvest!

Overripe seed capsules—most of the seed has dispersed already

Seeds come in many sizes and shapes. Seeds release in various ways, for example, some capsules split open, and the seed drops to the ground, whereas other seeds form **pappus** (fluffy tufts) that help the wind to scatter them.

Senna hebecarpa (wild senna)

Conoclinium coelestinum (wild ageratum, mistflower)

Echinacea purpurea (purple coneflower)

Chasmanthium latifolium (river oats)

Close monitoring of developing seed heads is required to ensure that you catch the magic window for harvest. You may want to tie paper bags over seed heads to capture the seed before it drops.

Gather seeds or nuts in an open container, paper bag, or envelope. Be sure to label each batch with the plant name and the location and date collected. Allow the seeds to dry* in a dark, cool, protected place. Once the seeds are fully dry, they can be stored as follows:

Store dry seeds that you have collected (or purchased) in a cool, dark, dry location. Place them in paper bags or airtight containers (if they are completely dry) in the refrigerator (33 to 44°F) to help maintain their viability until it is the right time to stratify or sow them.

*NOTE: Seeds of some plants should be kept slightly moist until sown to maintain their full vitality; for example, seeds of fleshy fruits (such as pawpaw) or nuts (such as acorns). These are called **recalcitrant** seeds.*

How to GERMINATE seeds and nuts

The trick to getting seeds to **germinate** (sprout) is determining what conditions the seeds or nuts require to germinate and then creating these conditions. After gathering or purchasing seed, store it under the proper conditions (see page 10.14). Do some research about the plant species to determine its germination code, ideal germination temperature, and what pre-treatment it requires (if any). Sometimes the results conflict, so just experiment!

 Different plant species have unique germination needs. A seed packet or your seed supplier's catalog may supply all the information you need. If not, search online for **germination requirements [genus species]**, or do a more focused search, such as **does [genus species] need light or darkness to germinate** or **germination temperature [genus species]**. One particularly handy resource is The **Lady Bird Johnson Wildflower Center** database (see page 10.24 for more details).

Germination codes

Most native plant seed suppliers include germination codes for each species in their catalog or on the seed package. Referring to the germination code will help ensure successful germination. Typically, the letter **A** represents easy germination, for example, the seed requires no pre-treatment and should germinate when sowed in a warm location. The letter **C** typically suggests that a period of stratification in damp, cool conditions is required, and a number may follow indicating the required number of days for stratification. Other letters may represent the need for scarification, light, or other requirements. Learn more about germination codes by searching online for **germination codes**. If the seed requires **scarification** (softening, rubbing off, or nicking a hard seed coat), this should be done before **stratification** (warm or cold moist treatment).

How to SCARIFY seeds and nuts

The seeds and nuts of some plants have a hard protective coating. To break dormancy, this hard coating must be softened, nicked, rubbed off, or heated in a process called **scarification** (not to be confused with **stratification**). Seed suppliers often indicate if the seed requires scarification, and if so, which method should be used.

Soften seed coats in boiling water—this is the easiest pre-treatment method.
1. Boil a small amount of water.
2. Allow it to cool for one minute.
3. Place the seeds in the water to soak overnight.

Rub seeds between two sheets of sandpaper (120 to 220-grit) or hold the seeds and sand them until you have rubbed off the seed coats in some areas but not the entire seed coat.

Nick seed coats with a sharp knife or nail clippers. Be sure not to damage the tender embryo inside the hard seed coat and avoid removing the entire seed coat.

There are other pre-treatment methods that seeds may require such as fire treatment for fire-response seeds. For example, the seeds of manzanita (*Arctostaphylos*) require fire scarification to break dormancy. Once seeds are scarified (if required), they are ready for stratification (if required).

NOTE: *When scarification is required, scarify seeds BEFORE starting the warm or cold stratification process.*

How to STRATIFY seeds and nuts

Most native plant species benefit from moist stratification to break seed dormancy and many species require it to germinate. This is the main difference between starting most traditional flower and vegetable seeds, but stratifying seeds is actually quite easy to do. Simply follow these steps:

- Determine if a species requires stratification and if so, for how long and at what temperature. Typically, warm stratification is done at room temperature (60 - 70°F) and cold stratification at about 35 - 40°F such as in a refrigerator.

Egg carton cells were filled with soilless seeding mix and topped with a mix of aquarium gravel and fine gravel. Seeds were sown and watered very gently.

 If your seed source doesn't supply this information, search online for **stratification days [genus species]**.

- Place seeds in a small amount of damp sand or on a paper towel. Place larger seeds, such as pawpaws or acorns in moist coco peat. Then, proceed to the next step. Or, if you have plenty of refrigerator space or a pest-free location outdoors, consider planting seeds directly in small potting cells such as upcycled egg cartons with drainage holes punched in them (*above*) or in milk jugs (see page 10.17). This will save you time later as the seeds are already planted. Individual egg carton cells are particularly helpful since the first division and repotting is already done.

- Place the moistened seed mixture (or planted containers) in a plastic bag.
- Label the bag or container with the current date and the date of the end of the stratification period.
- Leave the bag slightly open or poke a few holes for ventilation and place it in the refrigerator or in a safe location outdoors.
- When the stratification period ends, if not already done, plant seeds in containers. Place containers in the optimum temperature and lighting conditions; then, eagerly await their germination.

Timing the germination process

When planning your seed sowing, remember to allow time for any required pre-treatment, such as stratification. Once any required pre-treatment is complete, the seed is ready to be placed in the conditions it needs to germinate.

For example, if you want to start the germination process for seed that should germinate around February 15 to have young plants to plant outdoors in May, then a 60-day stratification period (C-60) should be started around December 18. This is less worrisome than it sounds since the timing is somewhat flexible, but waiting until May to sow the seeds would likely yield little success.

Desired date to start germination ↓

← Count back in time the number of days required for stratification

Or, say you are sowing partridge pea (*Chamaecrista fasciculata*) for young plants needed in May. This seed needs scarification and then 10 days of cold stratification (C-10). For seeds to start the germination process on February 15, stratification should be started on February 5.

Germination temperatures

Different species of seeds germinate at different temperatures; however, a temperature of around 60°F is sufficient for many native species. Adding heat to maintain temperatures of around 70°F will meet the needs of most species that need heat to germinate. Economize on your heated propagation space and seeding soil mix by sowing seed densely in small containers, such as egg cartons or shallow plastic food containers with holes punched in the bottom. For seeds that require light, a bright windowsill will do. If that's not available, additional lighting will be needed. Alternatively, sow seeds in recycled plastic containers such as milk jugs and place outdoors allowing Mother Nature to regulate the temperatures as she sees fit. For finicky species or species that need high humidity for germination or growing on, repurpose clear plastic containers and milk jugs to create microclimates.

What's the best location for germinating native seed?

Once you know the needs of the seeds you want to grow, it's just a matter of creating the conditions they need either outside in the ground or inside in containers. Which location is better? Native seeds are adapted to outdoor germination; however, to ensure success, seeds need to be protected. There are rodents and birds eager to dine on them; mice and squirrels who dig seeds up (sometimes just for fun I think!); slugs, rabbits, and other critters who will happily munch the young leaves; humans and pets who may unknowingly step on new seedlings; and pounding rains that may wash away any remaining survivors. For seeds and seedlings, it's a dangerous world out there!

Large areas outdoors

Still, if you have a large area of friable soil, seed is an economical option when purchased in bulk and sown generously at the right time of year. It's often a necessary approach for restoration projects and large landscapes. Once you start harvesting seed from your own plants, you'll have plenty of seed to experiment with outdoor sowing.

Containers outdoors—a safer bet

Since nature provides the right conditions for native plants, sowing seed in containers outdoors can save you the trouble of setting up an indoor propagation area. As mentioned, the big challenge outdoors is protecting your seed from all the hungry critters. For protection, seed can be sowed in screened tubs or milk jugs. Building a propagation frame with a hardware-cloth cover also works . . . but keep an eye out for slugs.

Cut off the top half of a milk jug leaving a small section under the handle intact to serve as hinge. Leave the cap off but screen it if slugs are present.

Poke holes in the bottom for drainage. Fill with moistened soilless seeding mix. Sow the seeds based on their germination requirements as explained in this action. Sprinkle a thin layer of coarse sand, aquarium gravel, or grit on the surface.

Replace the top half of the jug and secure with tape. Place jugs outside on an east facing wall. As seeds germinate and the weather warms up, open the jugs, and place them in a protected location until the seedlings are ready to grow on (see below).

Containers indoors—the safest bet

Sowing seed indoors makes sense for small properties and where growing conditions are less hospitable—it's much easier to protect seed, and microclimates can be set up to meet the specific germination requirements. See page 10.12 for a suggested propagation setup. Since sowing seed indoors requires the possible expense of setting up light, heat, and water, you may want to experiment with outdoor sowing first.

Growing on

Once the seeds germinate, they can be moved off the heating pad (if they've been on one). After seedlings develop their first true leaves (*below*), they can be gently separated and transplanted into deep, narrow cells such as the R-pots shown on page 10.10, using a soilless potting mix (see page 10.13).

true leaf

seed leaf
(cotyledon)

Keep the seedlings in protected conditions until they show active new growth. At which point, weather permitting, they can be moved to a sheltered location outdoors to grow into well-rooted plugs. The ease with which seed of native species germinates may surprise you. And even more surprising will be how fast your propagation space fills up!

Setting up your own nursery of plants provides a handy and economical source of plants.

How to propagate plants by DIVISION

Dividing plants is one of the most efficient ways of propagating quantities of plants and it yields larger-sized plants more quickly than by sowing seeds or taking cuttings. Keep in mind that division is a vegetative form of propagation, so this method doesn't contribute toward preserving the genetic diversity of a species. Still, it is a useful method for some species that are difficult to propagate from seed such as many sedges (*Carex*).

 Determine if and when a plant can be propagated by division by searching online for **propagation by division [genus species]**.

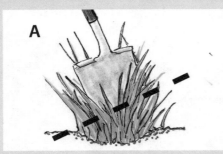 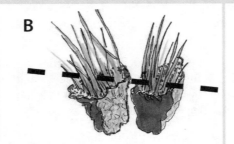 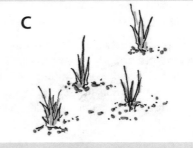

A—Grow or procure a "parent" plant. As new growth emerges in the spring, dig it up keeping as much soil intact as possible. If the parent plant is large, you can dig up just a portion of it.

B—Divide the clump into smaller clumps ensuring that each division has roots. Dividing clumps may require a sharp knife or hand pruners and considerable force.

C—Plant the divisions directly in the ground OR pot up the divisions adding moist potting soil to ensure that the freshly dug roots are in contact with soil and kept moist. Water thoroughly.

NOTE: *If the divisions have leafy growth, provide shade on sunny days by draping shade cloth or a sheet over stakes or placing lightweight plastic chairs or beach umbrellas over the newly planted divisions for a week or two.*

How to propagate plants by LAYERING

10 Propagate

For some native plant species, particularly shrubs, layering is a reliable propagation method that requires some patience but minimal effort. Like division, layering is a vegetative form of propagation, so the new plants will be clones of the parent plant. If you've grown blackberries, you've likely observed the tendency for the tips of their shoots to send out roots from which a new plant grows—this is an example of natural tip layering.

Determine if a plant can be propagated by layering by searching online for **propagation by layering [genus species]**. The range of plants that can be layered is limited; however, for some species, layering will work when propagation by seed, division, or cuttings is difficult.

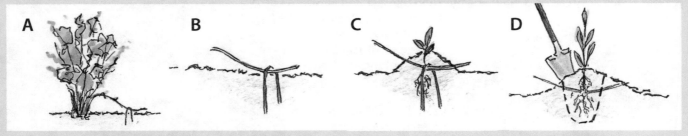

A—Select a new **shoot** (young stem) of a parent plant. Arch the shoot down until a section of it touches the soil in an open, sunny spot. Wound the part of the shoot that touches the ground by nicking it with a knife, scraping off some bark, or gently twisting the shoot until the bark cracks.

B—Pin the shoot to the ground with a U-shaped stake or mound soil over it to hold it in place. Water and weed, as necessary. C—When new shoots develop and reach about 3 inches tall, mound soil around them leaving the tips showing. Do this again when the shoots are about 6 inches tall.

D—Cut the new shoot from the parent plant keeping the soil intact around the newly formed roots. Pot up or transplant the rooted shoots and water. Another approach that takes a little more care is to pin the shoot directly in a pot (in Step B), then follow the same procedure.

How to propagate plants from CUTTINGS

softwood—new flexible shoots; leaves almost fully developed

semi-ripe—new developed shoots becoming firm

hardwood—mature stems

Like divisions and layering, taking cuttings is a type of vegetative propagation. Since the resulting plants lack the genetic diversity that seed-grown plants offer, it makes sense to limit vegetative propagation to species that are difficult or slow to grow from seed. For example, cuttings offer an easy, economical, and relatively quick way to propagate elderberry (*Sambucus*), willow (*Salix*), or dogwood (*Cornus*). Plants can also be propagated by root cuttings, parts of leaves, leaf buds, and other propagules, but we'll focus on taking cuttings from stems of shrubs and understory trees. There are three types of stem cuttings: **softwood, semi-ripe**, and **hardwood**. Propagation guidelines for a species usually recommend which growth stage and time of year to take cuttings.

Determine if a plant can be propagated by cuttings by searching online for **propagation by cuttings [genus species]**. If cuttings are an option, review the results of the search to determine the recommended growth stage and season.

If this is your first time taking cuttings, consider starting with hardwood cuttings of easy to root plants, such as red twig dogwood (*Cornus sericea*) or willow (*Salix*). In late winter, cut stems and place them in a bucket of water, drape a clear plastic bag over them making sure the plastic doesn't touch the cuttings. Place in a warm, protected area. Refresh the water weekly, and you'll likely start to notice roots within 2 to 6 weeks! When the roots are 1/2 to 1-inch long, pot up the cuttings and gradually move them to a sunny spot or plant out. Use the process described below with other easy to root native shrubs, such as elderberry (*Sambucus*), ninebark (*Physocarpus*), or snowberry (*Symphoricarpos*). Experiment!

rooting hormone

Identify the parent plant and determine the appropriate time(s) of year to take cuttings. Observe the plant to get familiar with the different growth stages of its stems. At the recommended growth stage, early in the morning, cut stems on a slant with a sharp knife or hand pruners just below a **node** (points on stem from which new leaves and branches sprout). Snip lower leaves.

Fill well-draining, clean pots with soilless cutting mix (see page 10.13) to a depth that will cover the lower 2/3 of the cutting. Make a hole with a pencil or stick that has a similar diameter to that of the cutting. Dip cutting in rooting hormone (optional). Stick each cutting in its own pre-made hole. Press the soil firmly around the cuttings which can be spaced densely (even bundled).

Drape plastic over the pots, staking it so that it doesn't touch the cuttings. Keep the soil moist but not soggy. Bottom heat (from a heating mat) may help some species to root. When leaves begin to develop, remove the cover a bit each day. Gently check for root development. Transplant rooted cuttings into larger individual pots filled with soilless potting mix. Plant out when roots begin to fill pots.

Rooting hormone: Rooting hormone can be purchased. Use a small amount at a time and dispose of leftovers. Alternatively, you may wish to experiment with **willow water,** an eco-friendly alternative. To make willow water, cut young, new growth of willow, remove the leaves, chop up the stems, and place them in boiling water (1 part willow stems to 2 parts water). Let stand overnight, then strain. Soak your cuttings in the willow water for several hours or overnight; then stick the cuttings in the pots and proceed as described above. Willow water can also be used to water cuttings. Some people dip cuttings in **honey**. Honey does not stimulate root growth, but it does have antiseptic and antifungal properties, so sticking the cuttings in honey may offer some benefit to your cuttings. Experiment to find out what works for you!

Advanced propagation techniques resource

If propagation fascinates you, check out the **Native Plant Network** *Propagation Protocol Database*. This database features detailed scientific reports describing propagation techniques used for numerous species of native plants, especially woody plants, grasses, and sedges. Not all the reports yield information helpful to the home propagator, so it takes a bit of sleuthing. To see the high-quality information available for many species, join us below as we explore common woodland sedge (*Carex blanda*).

Use the Native Plant Network *Propagation Protocol Database* **to delve into propagation**

Visit **npn.rngr.net/propagation**

or search online for **propagation protocol database** and navigate to the site.

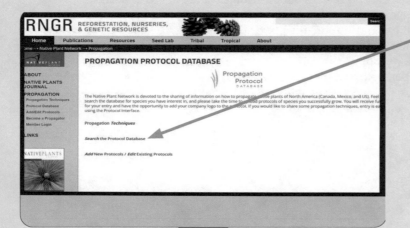

Click **Search the Protocol Database.**

In the **Text** field of the search form, type *Carex blanda* OR in the **Genus** field, enter *Carex* and scroll to *Carex blanda*.

In the **Search Results**, check the box to view or print the results for *Carex blanda*.

For many species, the protocol includes guidelines for pre-planting treatment (such as stratification), the establishment phase (germination), active growth (growing on after germination) and hardening off.

Center Manager
USDA NRCS - Appalachian Plant Materials Center
P. O. Box 390
Alderson, West Virginia 24910
304-445-3005
John.vandevender@wv.usda.gov
http://plant-materials.nrcs.usda.gov/wvpmc

USDA United States Department of Agriculture
Natural Resources Conservation Service

Family Scientific Name: **Cyperaceae**
Family Common Name: **sedges**
Scientific Name: ***Carex blanda* Dewey**
Common Name: **eastern woodland sedge**
Species Code: **CABL**
Ecotype: **Stones River**
Known Invasiveness: **none**
Propagation Goal: **plants**
Propagation Method: **seed**
ProductType: **Container (plug)**
Stock Type: **1+0 container plug**
Time To Grow: **6 Months**
Target Specifications: **A well developed plant suitable for mechanical transplanting that least 6 inches of top growth and a dense, fibrous root system.**
Propagule Collection: **Seed of Stones River source eastern woodland sedge was hand harvested from existing populations within the confines of Stones National Battlefield.**
Pre-Planting Treatments: **Seed is planted into round cell greenhouse flat liners with 38 cells flat that have been filled with coarse processed bark and compost pine bark growing medium. Seed is surface sown at a rate of 3-5 s**

The materials shown here are used with permission from: Reforestation, Nurseries, & Genetic Resources (RNGR), Propagation Protocol Database. Collaboration of United States Department of Agriculture Forest Service and Southern Regional Extension Forestry. Available online at https://npn.rngr.net/propagation.

10

Propagate

4 Review your landscape design plans to estimate your native plant requirements

Gather your plant list and landscape plans from previous actions along with seed and plant catalogs. Experiment with the propagation techniques explained in this action and decide on a planting area (preferably one that is not overly ambitious!). Depending upon the availability of specific seeds or plants, decide which plants you would like to plant this season. Make a rough estimate of how many plugs or pots of each plant you will need. A single packet of seed for each plant species usually yields enough plugs for a typical home landscape bed.

5 Decide whether you will propagate or purchase each plant species and locate sources for seeds and plants.

Locating sources for native plant seeds and plants is now relatively easy (see page 10.22). Use the internet and other resources to locate retail or online nurseries as local to your region as possible. Research a plant source prior to purchase to ensure the quality and provenance of the available plants. Hopefully, during planning, you designed your landscape beds around plants that you can easily buy or propagate as this will make procuring plants much easier.

When possible, buy local ecotypes of seeds and plants. Once you have confirmed that a specific species is native to your location, try to find seeds and plants with **local ecotypes** (the genetic makeup of the species is locally adapted). Local ecotype simply means that the seed or plant was propagated from locally grown sources. This will help the plant to thrive in your landscape. To find local ecotypes, ask your nursery person or seed supplier where their propagation material or seed was sourced. They may not have an answer for you, but the more people ask for this information, the more readily available it will become. Sources for local ecotypes can be hard to identify and find, so don't let this become an obstacle to planting native plants. Instead, focus on going ahead and planting as many native plants as you can, especially **straight species** (the original species not altered by humans; see page 5.2 for more botanical terms).

Focus on planting straight species native plants rather than nativars. When discussing native plants, a common question is often asked: *Are nativars okay to use in my landscape?* A wide variety of **nativars** (cultivars with native lineage; see page 5.2) are available in nurseries nationwide. Some of these offer attractive landscape features, such as colorful foliage, shorter heights for a tidier appearance, or resistance to diseases that plague the straight species. Some nativars fail to provide the same quality of ecological services as their straight species parents. For example, the nutritional content of nectar may be significantly lower, flowers may be sterile, and the leaves of nativars bred for red foliage may be unpalatable to the caterpillars that depend on this species for survival.

All these considerations aside, there is a far more important reason to choose straight species—ensuring genetic diversity. Most nativars must be propagated asexually, for example, by **tissue culture** (micro cuttings of the parent plant) resulting in genetically identical clones. A population of cloned plants lacks the genetic variation that provides resilience to help plant populations withstand challenges.

Despite the merits of individual nativar species, **when it comes to supporting biodiversity, we need to choose straight species grown from seed.**

nativars
propagated asexually

genetically IDENTICAL
(clones)

straight species
grown from seed

genetically UNIQUE

How to find sources of native plants for purchase

State and local native plant societies (see page 15.7) and Wild Ones chapters (see below) often provide lists of regional seed suppliers and plant nurseries. Here are some of the handy online resources for finding plants:

Homegrown National Park

Native Plant Resource Directory

Visit: **homegrownnationalpark.org**.
Click **Resources**.
Click **Find Native Plants & Services**.
Choose different categories to filter your search both for plants and services.

Regional plant suppliers of butterfly and moth host plants

See page 5.5 for directions to access the **National Wildlife Federation** lists of commercially available host plants for butterflies and moths which include lists of regional suppliers of these plants.

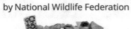

NWF Garden for Wildlife™

Visit: **gardenforwildlife.com**.
Scroll down and click **Shop Native by States.** Click your state to view native plants available through the **NWF** (*National Wildlife Federation*) *Garden for Wildlife™ program*. Plant collections include landscape bed designs.

Host plants for native pollen specialist bees in the Eastern U.S.

On his website, Jarrod Fowler provides a source list for host plants of pollen specialist bees of the Eastern U.S. (see page 6.9). The last column lists links for seed (S) and transplant (T) suppliers. The links go directly to the websites of suppliers. This is very helpful because it can be challenging to find sources for some of these plants.

Family; Subfamily; Tribe	Genus species	Authority	Common name	Duration	Habit	Habitat	Source
Apiaceae; Apioideae; Selineae	Zizia aptera	(A. Gray) Fernald	Meadow zizia	Perennial	Forb	FACU	S, T, T
	Zizia aurea	(L.) W.D.J. Koch	Golden zizia	Perennial	Forb	FAC	S, S, T, I, I, I, I, I, I
Aquifoliaceae	Ilex glabra	(L.) A. Gray	Inkberry	Perennial	Shrub	FACW	I, I, I, I, I, I, I
	Ilex montana	Torr. & A. Gray ex A. Gray	Mountain holly	Perennial	Shrub	FACU	S, S
	Ilex mucronata	(L.) Powell, Savolainen & Andrews	Catberry	Perennial	Shrub	OBL	S, S, T, I
	Ilex opaca	Aiton	American holly	Perennial	Tree	FACU	S, T, T, I, I, I, I, I
							S, S, T, I

Propagate 10

Wild Ones

FIND A NURSERY

Wild Ones chapters often hold plant sales, plant exchanges, or group plant purchases. To see if there is a chapter near you, visit **wildones.org.** In the top menu, click **Chapters.** Click **Find a Local Chapter.** Click on the map marker for contact information and social media links OR scroll down and on the right side of the page, click **Find a Nursery.** Select your state. Native plant nurseries are listed by states.

Profiles of native plant nurseries

Wood Thrush Natives (*woodthrushnatives.com*) in North Carolina is an example of a small native plant nursery. Nurseries such as this are outstanding sources for regional native plants that are hard to find and usually not available in retail chain stores. **Tree of Life Nursery** (*californianativeplants.com*) in Southern California offers over 500 species of regional native plants and workshops. A peaceful oasis on the edges of suburban sprawl, the nursery features Casa 'La Paz' (*left*), an authentic early-California adobe. Another example of a large native plant nursery is **Prairie Moon Nursery** (*prairiemoon.com*). It offers over 700 species of plants native to the Upper Midwest and beyond. Their website and the catalog with its accompanying cultural guide provide a wealth of information about growing and sowing native plants. Start exploring the native plant nurseries in your region!

Questions to ask when selecting native plants for purchase

Before purchasing seeds, nuts, or a plant, try to find the answers to these questions:

Is the plant native to your local ecoregion? Use the resources in this guide such as the **BONAP** maps to confirm that a specific species is native to where you live.

Were the seeds and plants produced from local ecotypes? Whenever possible, find out the original source of a plant. The **genotype** (genetic makeup of a plant) evolves slowly over time adapting to local conditions resulting in distinct populations within a species called **ecotypes**. For example, although two trees may appear identical and be the same genus and species, one from the southern United States may not survive in the brutal winters of northern states. Some native plant suppliers will be able to inform you of the local ecotypes of the seeds or plants they offer.

Is the plant the straight species, or is it a cultivar? Choose straight species plants whenever possible.

How was the plant propagated? If the plants were collected from the wild, don't purchase them. When possible, purchase plants propagated from seed (rather than from cuttings or division) because these offer the greatest genetic diversity.

Were the seeds or plants treated with neonicotinoids (neonics)? Still widely used, neonics are thousands of times more deadly to insects and other animals than DDT (which the U.S. banned in 1972). If seeds or plants have been treated with neonics, don't buy them!

What assorted sizes of plants are available? If your landscape plans and patience permit, buy the smallest plant size available. Besides being economical, younger plants establish faster and they typically will catch up with larger specimens planted at the same time.

Before purchasing seeds, nuts, or plants, try to find the answers to the questions above. Read plant labels, study the plant catalog (if available), and ask the nursery person.

Digging in deeper

Listed here are references and additional key resources for delving deeper into propagation (please refer to the Appendix for publication details).

Nature's Best Hope: A New Approach to Conservation That Starts in Your Yard: Although it is beyond the scope of *Nature's Best Hope* to discuss plant propagation, learning how to propagate plants supports the important action of generously filling your landscape with native plants.

Outstanding resources for learning about the propagation of native plants: William Cullina's trio of books feature how to select, propagate, and care for native trees, shrubs, vines, wildflowers, native ferns, mosses, and grasses. He generously shares his expertise with information that is hard to find elsewhere: ***Native Ferns, Moss, and Grasses***; ***Native Trees, Shrubs, and Vines: A Guide to Using, Growing, and Propagating North American Woody Plants*** and ***The New England Wild Flower Society Guide to Growing and Propagating Wildflowers of the United States and Canada.***

Growing Trees from Seed: A Practical Guide to Growing Native Trees, Vines, and Shrubs by Henry Kock, Paul Aird, John Ambrose, and Gerald Waldron. Although this book features propagation methods for woody species of the Great Lakes region, many of these species are widely grown elsewhere. Of special value are the hand drawn illustrations comparing the seeds and nuts of related species. Another must-have book for anyone aspiring to propagate woody plants.

The Gardener's Guide to Prairie Plants by Neil Diboll and Hilary Cox includes photos of the seedling stage of plants that alone make this book a propagator's best friend. Chapters on propagation by seed and vegetative propagation add to its value.

Propagating Plants: How to Create New Plants for Free by Alan Toogood is an extremely useful and comprehensive general guide to propagation. This show-rather-than-tell guide features over 1,800 illustrations and takes the mystery out of propagation. Although native plants are not the focus here, most native genera are covered. For propagation how-tos, this book is hard to beat.

Curious about botany? In ***The Nature of Plants: An Introduction to How Plants Work***, Craig Huegel explains botany in an easy-to-understand way using many native plant examples.

When it comes to propagating plants, the **Lady Bird Johnson Wildflower Center** database is a super handy resource covering many U.S. ecoregions. Simply visit *wildflower.org/plants*, search for the plant that you want to propagate, and scroll down to the **Propagation** section.

For West Coast landscapes, the **California Native Plant Society** *CalScape* (*calscape.org*) website is a must-visit. In addition to propagation methods for each species, you'll find distribution maps, wildlife supported by the species, growing requirements, companion plants, and much more. Search online for **calscape.**

If you live in an ecosystem where wildfire is an element, the seeds of local native plants may require fire scarification to germinate. Watch how to do this on the video ***How to Germinate Fire-Responsive Seeds*** offered by the **Theodore Payne Foundation** in Los Angeles, California.

The ***MGNV Illustrated Glossary*** offered by the **Master Gardeners of Northern Virginia**, described earlier on page 4.22, can come in handy when following propagation guidelines. Detailed high-quality photos take the mystery out of unfamiliar botanical terms.

Once you start propagating plants, you'll soon find your spaces overflowing with plants ready for transplant. In the next action, we'll fill your landscape with all the plants you have propagated or procured!

Action 11—CHECKLIST
Plant your landscape generously

Step:	✔	Action Needed:	Page:
1	☐	Review your landscape design plans to ensure they include keystone plants and the essential features needed to support wildlife	**11.4**
2	☐	Install hardscape features (or wait if these will be easier to install after prepping or planting the site)	**11.4**
3	☐	Prepare the ground for planting by removing lawn OR prepare sites within existing beds	**11.6**
4	☐	Time planting carefully and acclimate your plants to their growing site beforehand	**11.8**
5	☐	Plant your plants (preferably on an overcast day) and water them in	**11.8**
6	☐	Cover all ground with plants or ecoregion-appropriate mulch (except for areas left bare for ground-nesting bees)	**11.9**
7	☐	Water, weed, and protect your new plantings until established	**11.9**
8	☐	Plant areas that need to be visually lawn-like with native alternatives	**11.10**

A natural landscape in Southern California is generously planted from ground to sky.

11

Plant

How to make plant labels that last

Getting in the habit of labeling your plants at planting time will help you keep track of the plant species you plant. Plus, labels mark the location of plants to prevent their accidental removal when weeding. After experimentation with many types of labels, here's one that finally delivers in terms of legibility and longevity.

1

Gather supplies. Most of the supplies are common household items except for metal staples. Shown here is the 12-inch *Whonline*™ 11-gauge, heavy duty, garden staple (also called a stake). Staples with a square top work best.

2

Cut a sheet of aluminum from a recycled aluminum beverage can. Regular household scissors work fine for this. Wearing gloves is advisable.

3

Print the names of the plants. Put the aluminum sheet on a pad of paper. Use a cheap ballpoint pen and press hard to engrave the letters on the aluminum. Capital letters tend to be more legible than lower case letters. Leave a 1/2-inch margin blank (dotted red line) to allow for folding the label over the staple.

4

Cut out the labels and punch holes in them. It works best to cut out the individual labels *after* filling the aluminum sheet with different plant names. Fold the label over the staple. Use a large nail and hammer to punch two holes at the top of each label.

5

Round the lower edges of each label with scissors and wire the label to the garden staple. Cut a piece of wire about 3 inches long and secure the label to the staple.

6

Stick the tag in the ground next to the plant. To make it easier to locate plants when the landscape fills in, consider positioning labels in the same place for each plant, for example, to the left, in front, or to the right of the plant, as you prefer.

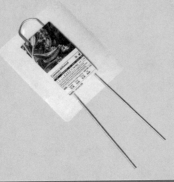

For the laminated tags (shown at left and on page 15.4), we used clear, 5 mil, UV laminating sheets to protect plant descriptions cut out of plant catalogs. Holes were punched in all-plastic areas of the label, and the label was mounted on a 12-inch heavy-duty, 11-gauge, galvanized, square-top or U-shaped garden staple (described in Step 1 above). These informative labels can be used repeatedly for native plant events, but they are less useful as permanent markers in the landscape as they tend to fade somewhat after a season outdoors.

Action 11—GUIDE
Plant your landscape generously

Planting day is finally here!

Now that you've propagated or purchased plants, it's time to get them in the ground! Planting may either be the culmination of a long planning process; or, if you have established gardens, an ongoing process of adding plants and hardscape features. In this action, we cover the basics of planting plugs, pots, and bareroot plants in the ground (or in large containers). We discuss procuring quality topsoil, **hardening off plants** (acclimating plants to outdoor conditions), planting, watering, and monitoring your new plantings.

It's a good idea to start thinking about how you will protect your plants *before* planting them. For example, if you live in an area heavily browsed by deer, protecting your plantings begins with choosing deer resistant plants. Or, if you have dogs or children, incorporating play areas into the landscape design will safeguard your plantings. Be sure to review *Action 2: Protect your wildlife habitat* before planting day.

As with all the other actions, planting is like a puzzle piece that is interdependent with all the other pieces to make a whole. At first, this may feel overwhelming, but quickly it becomes clear that this interdependence is a strength as taking one action supports another with the result ideally being a functioning ecosystem.

A patch of invasive plants was removed and temporarily covered with a 2-inch layer of wood chips. Homegrown native plants are now laid out and ready for planting.

11

Plant

1 Review your landscape design plans to ensure they include keystone plants and the essential features needed to support wildlife

Look over your property map and landscape bed design plans from earlier actions to ensure that they include keystone plants and the essential features needed to support wildlife. Once any needed adjustments to the plans are made, it's time to bring these plans to life!

Checklist of essential features to support wildlife

_____ Species from the keystone genera are featured, such as oaks and goldenrods

_____ Butterfly nectar and caterpillar host plants are included in the same area

_____ Pithy and hollow stem plants are included in the planting design

_____ Native grasses and sedges are included throughout the landscape

_____ Plants will be laid out in 3 x 3-foot or larger drifts (groups of plants)

_____ Caterpillar pupation sites are preserved or created

_____ Bare ground has been designated for ground-nesting bees

_____ Water features are included (with moving water, if possible)

_____ Spots for logs or large rocks are included

2 Install hardscape features (or wait if these will be easier to install after prepping or planting the site)

If you have hardscape features planned, you may wish to install these prior to prepping or planting the site. As we discussed in *Action 9: Design a layered landscape*, if your project requires grading, retaining walls, heavy-duty stormwater management, or other types of construction, you'll likely need to hire a landscape professional. See page 9.20 for tips about finding and working with landscape professionals. **Call 811 or visit call811.com before any digging** (see page 3.15)!

Placing hardscape features

Smaller hardscape features, such as birdbaths or well-placed rocks, may be easier to place after the landscape beds are prepped or sometimes even after the site has been planted. For example, when digging a hole for a shrub, you may hit nearby tree roots exactly where you were planning on placing the shrub. With the need to shift the placement of the shrub, a nice spot is created for a large rock or log.

Tackling a crumbled retaining wall such as this one may be more than you want to handle. It's likely a task best left to a landscape professional.

Plant your landscape bed in nine easy steps

1

Mark where utility lines run through the area. Before digging, call **811** to get your utility lines marked. See page 3.15 for more information. Know what's below. Call *before you dig!*

2

Define the shape and perimeter of the bed and make a plan. The plan can be a rough sketch or a detailed design. Be sure your plan includes the keystone plants and essential features needed by wildlife.

3

Prepare the site by removing lawn, invasive plants, and non-native plants. This step may take months or even a year. Don't add topsoil or fertilizer. Many native plants grow better in infertile soil.

4

Mark the spots for keystone trees shrubs, and accent plants. Plan to place trees first, then shrubs, keystone herbaceous plants, native grasses, and, finally, ground layer plants. Plant in drifts (masses) to make the plants more attractive to insects.

5

Install hardscape, logs, rocks, and water features. Or wait to install these if it will be easier to do later. If there are not ample water sources elsewhere, be sure to include a water feature.

6

Plant your plants. Time planting carefully to take advantage of the growth cycles of the plant species. Shade new plantings if sunny or hot weather is expected. Space plants as densely as possible to control invasives and protect the soil.

7

Fill in gaps with ground layer plants. Include plants from all the landscape layers from the ground to the sky including native grasses. Tuck in low-growing sedges (*Carex*), mosses, and other shade-loving native creepers.

8

Water the plants after planting. Limit water to 1-inch total water per week including rainfall. Six weeks of watering should be sufficient. Don't add fertilizer since fertilizer and continual irrigation tend to benefit invasive plants.

9

Remove weeds and invasive plants. Except where soil has been left bare for ground-nesting bees, replenish the leaf litter or other organic mulch, plant plugs, or allow volunteers to fill in gaps creating a living **"green mulch."**

③ Prepare the ground for planting by removing lawn OR prepare sites within existing beds

Healthy soil gradually forms an intricate structure that supports micro life which in turn nourishes plants. Soil disturbance, such as tilling, digging, and even hand weeding, destroys this fragile structure that took years to form. Always strive to avoid disturbing the soil; of course, when first establishing a landscape or a new garden bed, soil disturbance may be unavoidable.

Keep organic matter on your property!

Sometimes disturbing the soil is unavoidable, such as when installing fence posts, adding hardscape features, or installing a pond. At times like this, you may be able to salvage some byproducts from the soil disturbance for use elsewhere on your property, such as:

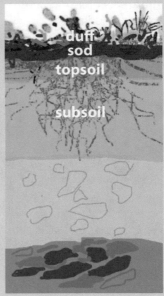

Duff (decaying leaf litter and other organic matter from the soil surface)— This can be raked into a pile prior to excavation for later use.

Sod (turf grass with its roots and soil attached)—This can be "sliced" off the top layer of soil when removing a lawn and piled up. Over time, it will decompose and turn into soil.

Topsoil—This upper layer of soil is usually higher in organic matter and nutrients that nourish plants. If you don't have an immediate need for topsoil, pile it somewhere out of view. It will no doubt come in handy for future projects.

Subsoil—This is the soil underneath the topsoil layer. Because it lacks organic matter and biological activity, subsoil on its own typically isn't optimal for growing plants. Subsoil can be used as fill dirt to stabilize pathways, fill holes, build up low areas, place at the base of fence posts and walls, or used for other construction projects in the landscape.

Make compost to supplement your topsoil

There is a science to making quality compost. A balance of **brown** (carbon-rich) materials and **green** (nitrogen-rich) materials must be kept moist and aerated. If the ratio of food scraps is too high or if the pile lacks oxygen, the composting process can produce methane gas. In this case, the compost pile contributes to the world's total greenhouse gas emissions. The good news is that by properly composting your food scraps and yard debris, you will be producing a nutrient-rich soil amendment while helping to reduce the volume of methane gas produced by waste in landfills.

Learn the ins and outs of making compost

The **EPA** offers *Backyard Composting: It's Only Natural*, a 2-page PDF summarizing the composting process. Find this handy resource by searching online for **epa pdf backyard composting**.

Explore the how-tos of making compost by searching online for **how to compost at home.** You'll find a multitude of articles, infographics, and videos that will help you take composting to a whole new level.

Ideas for procuring high quality topsoil

Native plants grow best in the local topsoil of their ecoregion. Sun-loving native plants generally perform better in low fertility soil. In contrast, shade-loving, moisture-preferring woodland plants tend to like a soil that is loose, loamy, and rich in organic matter. Home construction usually removes local topsoil and destroys soil structure. Here, we discuss how to procure the type of topsoil that naturally occurs in the different growing conditions of your ecoregion—not the "topsoil" generally available for purchase. Purchased "topsoil" may contain weed seeds, plant disease pathogens, and pesticide residues, or it may be of low quality. And, if you're on a tight budget, it may be cost prohibitive. Fortunately, with a little creativity, you can create most of the soil you need right on your property. Look for every opportunity to salvage topsoil. For example, if you are excavating a pond or digging holes for fence posts, store extra soil in a pile or in large pots with drainage holes for later use. Even surplus subsoil is worth saving since it can be mixed with compost for later use as topsoil. Consider these approaches to "creating" topsoil:

Get good at making compost. It's a great source of organic matter that adds volume to the existing topsoil and nourishes the soil micro life. Refer to the resources on the previous page for composting guidelines.

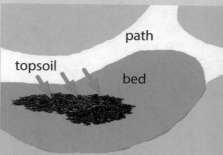

When installing paths, dig out any good topsoil for use in your garden beds. Refill the paths with a combination of logs, branches, removed sod, or **fill dirt** (subsoil or rocky soil). Top with gravel or wood chips.

"Borrow" soil from hidden areas of nice soil on your property. Move it to a woodland garden that needs topsoil or refill holes in beds after moving out a plant. Fill the hidden gap with fill dirt where it can build up organic matter over time.

If you use the *Dig It!* method to remove lawn, pile up the sod that you remove. Over time, the sod pile will decompose, after which it can be moved to a garden bed. Or place the fresh sod in an out-of-the-way place that you'd like to build up or over a patch of invasives or weeds that you would like to smother. To ensure that the weeds don't regrow, first lay down a thick layer of cardboard. Then, pile the sod at least 1 foot deep. The pile may need turning if the sod regrows.

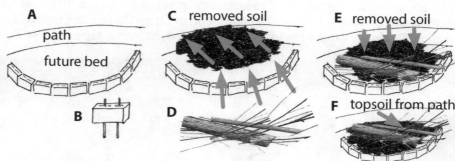

On a slope, create a terrace by digging out the topsoil above the bed and using it to fill the terrace bed.
A–Set out a crescent of concrete blocks (16L x 4W x 8H-inch standard 3-core blocks) on the downhill side of a slope digging in the higher ones as necessary to keep their bases level at a uniform elevation (kind of like a lower jaw of teeth).
B–Pound 18-inch rebar stakes inside the blocks to hold them upright.
C–Remove soil from the terrace interior, digging down about 10 inches.
D–Fill the dug area with logs and branches.
E–Replace the excavated soil (first removing any grass chunks).
F–Dig out the topsoil from a strip above the terrace bed to make a path. Use this topsoil to further fill the terrace bed, if needed.

Refill the path with a combination of logs, branches, removed sod, or fill dirt. Top the path with gravel or wood chips. Plant the terrace with tough native plants. Over time, the soil in the bed will develop a nice loamy structure.

11

Plant

4 Time planting carefully and acclimate your plants to their growing site beforehand

Timing your planting right will go a long way toward ensuring success. Your timing will vary depending upon your climate and whether you are sowing seeds or planting plugs, pots, or bareroot plants. Consult your seed supplier or plant nursery to determine the best time to plant specific plant species in your ecoregion.

Hardening off plants to prepare them for a change in growing conditions

When moving seedlings or plants from a warm environment to a colder or less protected location or from shade to sun, the transition must be made in stages—a process called **hardening off**. Hardening off plants gets them used to changes in temperature, sun exposure, precipitation, and wind.

Every day after germination: Brush your hand or set a fan to blow across seedlings to stimulate a thickening of their leaf **cuticle** (waxy coating) to help protect seedlings from dehydration and UV radiation.

A week or two before planting: Place the seedlings outdoors in partial sun for several hours in a draft-free place OR within a plastic tub with tall sides. Cover the seedlings at night or bring them in if the temperatures are expected to fall below 60°F.

Five or six days before planting: Begin leaving seedlings out overnight in a protected place unless there is severe weather. If seedlings are in a tub, take them out to expose them fully to the weather. For sun-loving species, gradually increase the length of time seedlings are exposed to sun.

5 Plant your plants (preferably on an overcast day) and water them in

When digging holes to plant your plugs, pots, or bareroot plants, minimize soil disturbance as much as possible. It can take years for soil to rebuild its natural structure. The newly developed roots of most plants are fragile, so handle your plants like you would a newborn baby. R-pots (see page 10.10) facilitate gentle planting because they open up, so no tapping is needed to loosen the plant from the pot. To protect plants from sunburn, plant on a cool, overcast day, cover plantings with shade cloth, or rig up shade using umbrellas, lawn chairs, or branches from pruning. Gradually expose the plants to more sunlight over a period of 1 to 2 weeks, depending on the weather.

Planting BAREROOT trees and shrubs

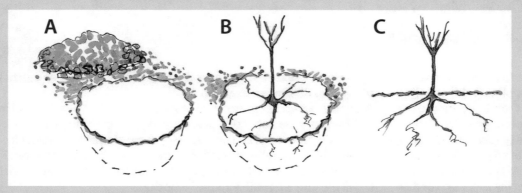

A—Soak the bareroot plant in a bucket of water. Dig a hole that is the size of the root ball of the bareroot plant. Piling the soil nearby on a tarp, in a wheelbarrow, or in an upcycled, large nursery pots makes clean-up easier.
B—Spread the roots out.
C—Gently fill the hole with the soil removed from the hole. Water the newly planted bareroot making sure that the place where the roots flare out is just under the surface and covered. Water until established, taking care to avoid overwatering (see page 11.9).

6   Cover all ground with plants or ecoregion-appropriate mulch (except for areas left bare for ground-nesting bees)

By now, it's probably clear that when we use the term "mulching" in this guide, we aren't referring to spreading plastic bag after bag of store-bought mulch; instead, we are using this term to describe covering the ground with a layer of mulching material appropriate to your ecoregion. Covering the ground with plants is called **green mulch** (as we discussed on page 7.9). For gaps in green mulch, the ideal mulching material depends on your ecoregion and the needs of the plants growing within it as well as what's readily available. Leaf litter in ecoregions where deciduous trees dominate the canopy and pine needles where pines are dominant make ideal organic mulches. In contrast, plants adapted to arid ecoregions benefit from inorganic mulches such as decomposed granite (DG), basalt gravel, or other crushed stones. Visit local public native plant gardens to get an idea of the ideal mulching material for your region.

Why, when, and how to mulch to benefit your plants

After planting, cover all bare ground with a regionally appropriate mulch leaving an area bare for ground-nesting bees. Avoid dyed or rubberized chips. Mulching newly planted beds will help to retain moisture, maintain more constant temperatures, provide habitat for the soil micro life, and suppress weeds. *How* mulch is applied matters; for example, building a **mulch volcano** (mounded mulch around a tree trunk) can kill a tree. Following a few simple mulching guidelines will ensure your mulching efforts will help your plants to thrive.

TREES	SHRUBS	FORBS
8 - 12 inches from trunk	5 - 8 inches from trunk	2 - 3 inches from stems

After planting trees, shrubs, and transplants, apply approximately 2 inches of organic mulch or 1 inch of crushed stone, as appropriate for your ecoregion. Apply this in a layer on the soil surface **without mixing it into the soil**. As it gets nearer to trunks or stems of plants, the mulch depth should be reduced so that it barely covers the soil in these areas and does NOT touch the trunks or stems of plants (refer to diagram at right).

For areas planted with seeds or nuts, adjust the mulch depth to the size of the seed or nut. Large seeds or nuts (such as those of pawpaws or oaks) can poke their way through 1 to 2 inches of mulch, but as the seed size gets smaller, you'll need to reduce both the depth of mulch and the size of the mulch particles. Very tiny seeds may not tolerate any mulching. Keep in mind that the less mulch that is applied, the greater the need to carefully monitor the planted area to remove invasive seedlings and ensure consistent moisture.

7   Water, weed, and protect your new plantings until established

Give your new plantings the equivalent of one inch of water weekly until established. Watering new plantings regularly for about 6 weeks is typically sufficient depending upon your climate. Avoid overwatering plants. Plants may wilt as a coping response to heat or drought (the leaf is likely to feel crisp), but plants may also wilt when overwatered (the leaf will likely be moist). If your plants are still wilted in the early morning, they probably need water, but first confirm that the soil is dry several inches down to avoid accidentally overwatering. Especially avoid overwatering tree and shrub seedlings after planting. Their micro roots take time to develop. Too much water creates an **anaerobic** (oxygen-lacking) environment which can kill these seedlings before their roots have a chance to get established.

In the upcoming action, we'll discuss how to manage your plantings without needing to resort to toxic chemicals. In the meantime, remove any invasive or unwanted plants and monitor your plants to ensure their well-being.

11

Plant

8 Plant areas that need to be visually lawn-like with native alternatives

Let's take a look at how to plant the lawn-like alternatives introduced earlier (see page 9.22):

- Plant a sedge (*Carex*) lawn
- Plant a pollinator-friendly bee lawn
- Plant mosses or encourage an existing mossy area
- Plant a native meadow or restore prairie garden

Invasive nutsedge vs. native sedges

If your main association with sedges is the noxious weed nutsedge (*left*) overtaking your garden, you may be tempted to skim over this section, but wait! Nutsedge (also called nutgrass, *Cyperus rotundus*) is an invasive plant and not native at all. It's even in a different genus than the native sedges we encourage you to plant which are all in the *Carex* genus. Native sedges are cool-season plants meaning that they grow actively during the spring and fall when soil temperatures are cool. They are important plants in wetland ecosystems worldwide and in our landscapes because their dense roots filter out pollutants and prevent erosion. They are valuable caterpillar host plants for skippers and some moths, and they provide seed for birds and other creatures.

Plant a sedge (*Carex*) lawn

Planting a mass of carefully selected low-growing native sedges can give the visual effect of a lawn and offer tranquil beauty. Despite their grass-like appearance, most *Carex* species require minimal mowing or no mowing at all, and they don't require fertilization or other chemical applications. Although most sedge lawns will not be durable like turf, stepping stones can be placed where people walk. The same techniques used for planting a sedge lawn that we explain here can be used to plant the ground layer of a landscape bed to fill your landscape with plants from ground to sky (see page 9.4).

Procuring enough plant material to plant a sedge (*Carex*) lawn

The biggest challenge in planting a sedge lawn is procuring enough plants to fill an area. Since many *Carex* species are hard to start from seed and slow growing, it's best to plant **plugs** (ready-to-plant seedlings that have been grown in individual cells in potting soil).

Purchasing plugs: Flats (or trays) of plugs are widely available in the wholesale market, but harder to find at the retail level. Some nurseries offer a limited selection of *Carex* species in multi-cell trays. In contrast, native seed suppliers often have a wide variety of *Carex* species available in seed packets, for example, for under $5 for a packet containing approximately 100 seeds.

Growing your own plugs from seed: Experiment with different species of Carex native to your region to find ones that are easy to grow from seed. For example, I find that Eastern star sedge (*Carex radiata*) readily germinates for me after a 60-day period of cold stratification. Most *Carex* seed requires 60 days of cold stratification (*see Action 10: Propagate or procure lots of keystone plants*). Prior to stratification, store seeds in an airtight container in the refrigerator.

Growing your own plugs from division: Learning how to propagate *Carex* by dividing clumps to make your own plugs is another economical DIY source of plants for a sedge lawn. See *Action 10: Propagate or procure lots of keystone plants* to learn this easy and reliable propagation method. Of course, this method requires having *Carex* parent plants to divide.

Plant a sedge (*Carex*) lawn, *continued*

Choosing a *Carex* species that will create the visual effect of lawn

In the genus *Carex*, there are almost 500 species native to the United States. Finding a *Carex* species that will give the visual effect of lawn and grow well in your ecoregion takes a bit of sleuthing. You'll need a *Carex* species that is:

- native to your ecoregion
- adapted to the growing conditions of the intended site (light, water, and soil)
- low-growing with a maximum height of 1 foot
- available for purchase or easily propagated in quantities sufficient to cover the intended planting area.

To get started with a sedge lawn, it's worthwhile getting to know the *Carex* species native to your ecoregion. Evaluate the *Carex* species available in your local nursery using the tools explained in *Action 5: Identify your keystone plants* such as the **BONAP** maps.

Planting and caring for your sedge lawn

After removing lawn and prepping the site, choose a cloudy day for planting. Lay your plugs out in a grid, spacing them approximately 6 to 10 inches apart. Plant the plugs. Water thoroughly. Mulch the spaces between the plugs, making sure that the mulch is not actually touching the plugs (see page 11.9). Mowing or trimming *Carex* once a month during its first growing season, leaving at least two-thirds of their height, may speed up **tillering** (the production of new shoots). Be sure to keep your *Carex* lawn weeded until the plants are large enough to block weeds from growing. Although not required, *Carex* plants may be trimmed by one-third, two to three times a year.

Sedges make attractive additions throughout the wildlife landscape

As you explore the *Carex* genus, take note of taller-growing *Carex* species, such as fox sedge (*left*). Taller sedges make attractive additions to the herbaceous layer while providing valuable ecoservices.

Fox sedge (*Carex vulpinoidea*) is widespread across the United States as this BONAP map (*above*) shows. Seed heads shaped like fox tails arise from clumps of narrow blades that arch gracefully. Where an eager grower is desired, this sedge is an ideal choice for sunny or partially shaded locations including rain gardens.

Plant a rush (*Juncus*) species for a "rush lawn"

It's easy to confuse sedges, rushes, and grasses. Here's a rhyme that may help you keep them straight:

Sedges have edges and rushes are round; grasses are hollow straight to the ground (and they have nodes!)

Path rush (*Juncus tenuis*) is a surprisingly tough little plant which, as its name suggests, often seeds itself on paths and other disturbed or abandoned sites. It prefers a sunny to partly shaded site that is moist to medium dry, and it even grows well in compacted soil. It's maintenance-free, deer-resistant, and tolerant of foot traffic and mowing (with a minimum cutting height of 4 inches or higher)! To create a rush lawn, follow the guidelines for planting and propagating sedge.

Plant a pollinator-friendly bee lawn

Creating a pollinator-friendly lawn or **bee lawn** requires the thoughtful selection of naturally low-growing native grasses and flowering plants that can tolerate well-timed mowing and light traffic. Researchers at the University of Minnesota (UMN) have popularized the concept of bee lawns. They developed a blend of fescue grasses and three flowering plants: Dutch white clover (*Trifolium repens*), self-heal (*Prunella vulgaris* ssp. *lanceolata*), and creeping thyme (*Thymus serpyllum*) that perform well in Minnesota and beyond. Most plants in this blend are not native; nevertheless, it attracts over 50 species of bees and requires less water and chemicals than a traditional lawn, and less frequent mowing (or no mowing for a more meadow-like look). Recently, some seed suppliers have developed bee lawn blends including mostly native plants.

Choosing plants for a bee lawn

You'll need to put on your scientist cap and experiment to come up with blends for bee lawns made up of plants native to your ecoregion. In fact, you may already have some semblance of a bee lawn if your lawn has patches of flowering plants. In this case, instead of removing your existing lawn, you may instead choose to encourage the native flowering plants and overseed or plant plugs into it. Ideally, plants for your bee lawn should be:

- perennials or self-seeding annuals native to your ecoregion
- adaptable to the growing conditions of the intended site (light, water, soil, climate)
- low-growing OR tolerant of occasional mowing to a height of 3 or 4 inches (depending on the maximum cutting height of your lawn mower)
- able to flower at low heights
- accessible sources of nectar and pollen to native insects
- easy to grow from seed that is readily available OR easy to propagate in large quantities
- vigorous and slightly aggressive so that different species can successfully compete with one another
- tolerant of light foot traffic. It's a challenge to find a blend of native plants that can replace lawn in heavily used areas such as where children or dogs play. Even where such a blend is possible, if the bee lawn is doing its job, there will be bloom periods when bees are active, and children should not be playing there. Stepping stones can be placed as a path through a bee lawn to reduce the impact of traffic.

As you transition an area to bee lawn, you may consider leaving plants considered by many to be weeds, such as native violets (*Viola*) or non-native clovers (*Trifolium*).

Finding sources of seed for a bee lawn

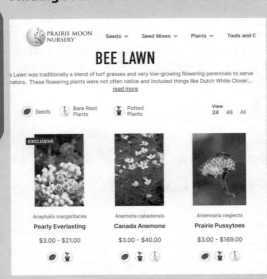

Anaphalis margaritacea
Pearly Everlasting
$3.00 - $21.00

Anemone canadensis
Canada Anemone
$3.00 - $40.00

Antennaria neglecta
Prairie Pussytoes
$3.00 - $169.00

Prairie Moon Nursery (*prairiemoon.com/bee-lawn*) has identified native plant options for planting a bee lawn in the Midwest and beyond. Included are low-growing plants and plants that can be mowed, such as pearly everlasting (*Anaphalis margaritacea*), pussytoes (*Antennaria*), several asters, black-eyed Susan (*Rudbeckia hirta*), and wild strawberry (*Fragaria virginiana*).

Other seed suppliers have developed mixes that are predominantly native for ecoregions in California and the Northwest. For example, **Northwest Meadowscapes** (*northwestmeadowscapes.com*) offers a *Nearly Native Bee Lawn Seed Mix*.

Plant a pollinator-friendly bee lawn, *continued*

Planting a bee lawn

A bee lawn is a low-growing meadow planting for which plants have been selected for their lawn-alternative potential and pollinator benefits. To plant a bee lawn, follow the steps for planting a meadow or reconstructing prairie (see page 11.18). Your choice of what to plant and how you manage the area is what will make it a bee lawn.

Caring for a bee lawn

Care for newly planted bee lawns as you would care for a new garden. Your bee lawn will require regular water until the plants get established. Fertilizer is not recommended. Before mowing, consider the life cycle of the plant species in your bee lawn. Refrain from mowing when a species is in full bloom as this is prime feeding time for the pollinators, and when possible, avoid cutting your bee lawn until the seed capsules of self-sowing plants have fully ripened. You can easily spot when seeds are ripe by monitoring your bee lawn plants and observing the seed capsules (or heads) that form after flowering. Typically, the capsules will dry up and turn brown. Some capsules split open to release their seeds, while other seeds will form pappus (fluffy tufts) and begin to scatter with the wind (see page 10.14).

When you mow, avoid mowing close to the ground. Set your mower at its maximum cutting height, ideally no less than 4 inches. Even better, use a string trimmer or handheld scythe to "mow" at a height of 8 inches or more.

 For detailed information about establishing and caring for a bee lawn, search online for **university of minnesota bee lawn**. Click the result: **Planting and maintaining a bee lawn | University of Minnesota.**

A plant to avoid in your bee lawn—creeping Charlie!

The ubiquitous weed creeping Charlie (*Glechoma hederacea*) may seem like a good plant to include in a bee lawn—but it isn't! Although it offers an early source of nectar, its production of nectar is limited, and its pollen is not readily available to native pollinators. Worse, creeping Charlie is a serious invasive that should be replaced with eco-beneficial natives. Sometimes after a good rain, a densely growing patch of creeping Charlie can be removed simply by lifting the edges of a patch and rolling it up as though it were a carpet while taking care to also remove any small roots that remain (see page 4.18). Be on the lookout for Charlie creeping into your garden!

11

Plant

Plant mosses or encourage an existing mossy area

Many thanks to Annie Martin who generously contributed to this discussion of mosses. Known as Mossin' Annie, she is the author of *The Magical World of Moss Gardening* (Timber Press, 2015) and the owner of Mountain Moss Enterprises in Brevard, North Carolina. ©Photographs courtesy of Annie Martin (www.mountainmoss.com).

A peaceful moss retreat created by Annie Martin offers a verdant landscape throughout all seasons.

A hallmark of mosses is their year-round green appeal, especially throughout winter months when many North American landscapes are drab. As a bonus, mosses provide jewel-tone accent colors when their reproductive **sporophytes** (their equivalent of flowers) occur, sometimes multiple times each year in different seasons.

Ceratodon purpureus (fire moss) sporophytes bring welcome color to landscapes, even in winter.

Mosses are native plants, too. Although commonly referred to as **"moss"** in a conglomerate, singular term (like "deer"), colonies are composed of thousands, perhaps millions, of individual moss plants. **Bryophyta** (commonly called **bryophytes**) is the scientific classification which includes mosses, liverworts, and hornworts. Often overlooked as an attractive and intentional choice for our landscapes, bryophytes are integral elements in healthy ecosystems. Mosses have a positive impact on our environment—they retain soil moisture, help prevent erosion, filter stormwater, and contribute to worldwide air purification.

Numerous beneficial relationships exist between bryophytes, animals, and other living organisms. Mosses provide homes for microorganisms, such as tardigrades and nitrogen-fixing blue-green bacteria, as well as invertebrates, such as insects, lizards, and salamanders. Mossy areas are ideal sites for the germination of vascular plant seeds, supporting the forest life cycle.

Working with the different growth habits of mosses

Upright-growing mound colonies will gain in dimension and size, but they won't spread (*bottom left*). Mound colonies can add depth and interest. When planting these upright growers, place colonies directly next to each other for a solid appearance.

Leucobryum glaucum (pincushion moss) is a mounding upright grower.

Only sideways growers will provide horizontal expansion. When planting, place plugs, hand-sized, or pancakes of mosses spaced like cookies on a baking pan. **Frags** (fragments of moss plants) can be used to fill in between the "cookies" to speed up the coverage process. Individual colonies of sideways growers can be interwoven by using an over-and-under process along the edges to blend into moss carpets.

Thuidium delicatulum (fern moss) is a sideways-growing species (*right*).

Plant mosses or encourage an existing mossy area, *continued*

Tips and growing requirements for a thriving mossy area

Choose species based upon their sun preference and the sun exposure of the intended site. A "right moss" exists for "every place" but not all moss species will thrive in all circumstances. Many moss species prefer shade; others are considered versatile, crossover species and will grow in shade or sun; and some desire sunny locations.

Mosses will grow in nutrient-poor soil where little else will grow because they don't derive their nutrients from the soil. In fact, mosses don't even have roots. Instead, they have tiny rhizoids that attach to various substrates including soil. Mosses get their nutrients through their leaves—unlike **vascular plants** (plants that have tubes through which minerals and water flow), such as flowers and trees.

Soil pH can be a factor in moss horticulture but it's not as critical as you might think. While many species prefer acidic soil (pH 4.5-5.5); others prefer calcareous soils (pH 6-8 or higher); and some just don't care—thriving in shady, acidic locations as well as sunny, alkaline surfaces.

Heat tolerance of different moss species is another important consideration. Hot temperatures are of more concern than cold. Plant hardiness zones are irrelevant since mosses are immune to the negative effects of sub-freezing temperatures. The verdant appeal of moss landscapes continues throughout all seasons. You can don your winter hat and plant moss colonies on frozen ground!

Climacium americanum (tree moss) is hardy to foot traffic.

Start small and create a moss focal feature rather than tackling an expansive grass lawn replacement. While mosses can grow in sunny locations, it is recommended to start in a shady location, especially where mosses are already growing.

Encourage existing mosses to grow in! If your lawn already has significant mosses growing as the understory in the grass, you'll have a better chance of converting it to a mossy area. Mow or string trim the grass down to nubbins to dislodge moss frags. Distribute them to vacant spots to spread the mosses around. Water the mosses thoroughly. Walk on the newly scattered frags wearing flat-soled shoes or boots.

Planting a new area of mosses

Step 1: Assess microclimates to find moisture niches and to predict the sun exposure throughout the day and during different seasons so that you can choose the right moss species.

Step 2: Plant at any time of the year. Cold temperatures are not detrimental. Scorching summer months and during droughts are the least desirable times. Planting prior to rain is ideal.

Step 3: Clear all debris and weeds from your target area. There's no need to add soil amendments to enrich soil—mosses prefer compacted soil. Slightly score (make irregular indentions) with a 3-prong digger tool or a pointy rock before placing mosses.

Step 4: Solid planting offers immediate gratification and erosion control. Planting individual moss colonies and frags, or frags alone, will take longer to fill in.

Step 5: If planting in a windy location or slope, use small twigs to hold colonies in place and cover frags with wildlife netting to keep them from blowing away.

Step 6: Water thoroughly and walk on your newly planted mosses to help rhizoids attach.

Trays of sun moss species are ready to plant.

Plant mosses or encourage an existing mossy area, *continued*

Maintaining your moss colonies for optimal growth

Supplement rainfall as needed. All mosses grow better (and look better) if you provide supplemental watering as needed. Provide brief watering sessions (lasting 2 to 4 minutes) several times each day, especially during droughts or when temperatures are above 90°F. The actual volume of water can be minimal. To facilitate regular watering, consider buying an outdoor battery-operated irrigation sprinkler system including a controller/timer, high-quality garden hoses, and gear-driven or oscillating sprinklers.

Keep mossy areas free of leaf litter and debris. If using a leaf blower, provide sweeping figure-8 motions rather than static, hard blowing. Avoid raking as a maintenance activity because this may dislodge colonies.

Be vigilant and carefully remove weed seedlings when you first spot them. Weeding will be necessary to prevent other plants from outcompeting the mosses.

Troubleshooting mossy areas. Mosses tolerate and even benefit from light foot traffic, but pets and other critters may disturb mossy areas with their digging. Gather loose colonies and frags to use for repairing vacant spots.

Mosses grow better with frequent, yet brief, supplemental watering sessions.

Here are a few ways mosses can be incorporated into your wildlife habitat

Mosses can be an ideal groundcover beneath flowers, shrubs, and trees as well as between stepping stones. Mosses and pathways go together like peanut butter and jelly!

Fill containers with bryophytes for a tiny wonderland. Easy to care for and charming are just two reasons mosses make ideal container plants.

Plant moss colonies on steep slopes to prevent erosion. Tack mosses in place with twigs to mitigate stormwater issues.

Further explore growing mosses with these resources

- *The Magical World of Moss Gardening* by Annie Martin (Timber Press, 2015)

- *Native Ferns, Moss, and Grasses* by William Cullina (Echo Point Books, 2020)

- *Bryophyte Ecology* by Dr. Janice Glime (digitalcommons.mtu.edu/bryophyte-ecology, 2017)

Making their appearance over 450 million years, bryophytes were Earth's first land plants. They grow everywhere from the mountains to the sea, deserts to tropical rain forests, and even in arctic regions.

Listen to the whispers of these ancient miniature plants and you, too, may be lured into the magical world of mosses!

11

Plant

Plant a meadow or prairie garden

Meadows and prairies recall sunny fields filled with a mix of tall grasses and flowering plants. In the Eastern United States, natural meadows are typically a temporary state of plant growth that occur, for example, when a tree falls and creates an opening bathed in sunlight. Within several years, tree seedlings grow tall and once again cast the area in shade and the meadow disappears. This natural process is called **succession**. In contrast, the shortgrass, transitional, and tallgrass prairies of the Midwest are naturally occurring ecosystems influenced by climate, rainfall, and the native vegetation of a region.

The idea of planting a meadow or prairie garden can be appealing and even nostalgic. Many people new to native plants begin with a meadow, but meadows can be a challenging landscape approach to establish and maintain. That said, they are an economical approach for large properties. Key to their success is the selection of plants adapted to the ecoregion and carefully timed mowing.

Meadows and prairies require ongoing human intervention, especially in the early years because of the pressure of natural plant succession. If not controlled, invasive plants and aggressive natives will overtake slower growing natives before they have a chance to establish, and shrub and tree seedlings will take root and thrive. Meadows and prairies are worthy undertakings that require thoughtful planning, site analysis, and land preparation to ensure success. In ecoregions where prairies are dominant, prairie plantings are an especially important part of restoring habitat to support biodiversity.

Picturesque native meadows, such as this one designed by LWLA, begin with careful planning, site analysis, and land preparation. They are managed with timed mowings and removal of invasives. The beauty of this orchestrated effort speaks for itself. *Photo courtesy of Larry Weaner.*

Pros and cons of planting meadows and prairie gardens

PROs	CONs
• The cost is minimal relative to other landscape design approaches, especially if the meadow or prairie garden is planted using seed rather than plugs.	• Neighbors may object to the more natural look.
• Once established, minimal labor is required (unless the surrounding invasive plant populations are high).	• Invasives are likely to volunteer and dominate the native growth requiring ongoing removal, especially in the early years.
• Large areas can be planted at a fraction of the cost of designed landscape beds making meadows and prairie gardens an ideal choice (and sometimes the only option) for large-scale, wildlife-friendly projects.	• Prairie gardens and meadows may not be an option in arid regions where fire risk is high. Elsewhere, to reduce the risk of fire, extra precautions should be considered, such as strips of tilled soil and mowed paths through the meadow or prairie garden.

For helpful information about growing meadows, search online for **how to create a meadow.** If you live in a prairie ecoregion, find resources to help you with prairie restoration by searching online for **prairie gardening.** Also, see page 11.20 for recommended reading about meadows and prairies.

Plant a meadow or prairie garden, *continued*

It may seem that we could simply stop mowing the lawn and a meadow or prairie will naturally occur. Unfortunately, conventional turf and its weedy companions are usually introduced species that, if not mowed, will grow into a weedy, invasive mess. Removing the lawn first makes it easier for native seed mixes to get established. Below are the basic steps for establishing meadows or planting prairie gardens.

Step 1: Identify the site and its growing conditions.

Step 2: Prepare the site by removing lawn, invasives, and introduced plants as described earlier. This step may take a year or more. Don't add topsoil or fertilizer. Native meadow and prairie species grow better in infertile soil!

Step 3: Choose a seed mix with species native to your ecoregion and suited to the site's growing conditions (refer to page 10.22 to find sources of seed). Be wary of wildflower and meadow mixes. Research and evaluate the individual species in a seed mix before buying it. Use the **BONAP** map tools explained in earlier actions to confirm that each of the species in a mix is native to your local area. Make sure there is a mix of flowers for continuous spring-to-fall bloom. If deer are present, make sure the mix is deer resistant.

Step 4: Sow your chosen seed mix according to the recommendations of your seed supplier. Time your planting carefully to take advantage of the growth cycles of the plant species.

Step 5: After sowing the site, keep the ground moist if precipitation isn't expected. Limit watering to a total of 1 inch per week including rainfall. Six weeks of watering should be sufficient. After this, water only if there is an extended dry spell. Watering and adding fertilizer help weeds—not native plants.

Step 6: Remove invasives and weeds.

Step 7: During the first summer, mow or string trim (weed whack) to a height of 4 to 8 inches whenever the growth reaches 8 inches or when weeds form seed heads. This helps to control weeds and keeps the faster growing native species from shading out the slower growing native species. Stop mowing in early fall.

Step 8: If you would like the planting to fill in faster, wait until after the first growing season of the seed mix, then plant some plugs. For example, if you sowed seed in spring, you could plant plugs in fall after the final mowing. You may wish to plant additional plugs in future years to add interest. Plugs need regular water until their roots grow into the soil *(see Step 5)*.

Step 9: Mow or string trim your meadow or prairie annually to control woody growth (shrub and tree seedlings). Time this trimming for early spring before new spring growth is 2 inches tall. Aim for a cutting height between 4 to 8 inches. Or you may choose not to mow annually to allow native shrubs or trees to grow and fill your landscape upwards.

Convert conventional turf to an eco-friendly grass that can tolerate some traffic

Most native grass species lend themselves better to meadows, prairies, and landscape beds than to traditional lawn. Native species tend to be more difficult to establish than conventional turf species and they lack the green carpet-like appearance of turf. If you have areas that are not heavily used that you are required to keep in lawn, you might consider an eco-friendly grass seed mix. Although these mixes are typically non-native grasses, they give a lawn-like appearance and don't require regular mowing other than a fall mowing and raking to reduce **thatch** (dead grass buildup). Such a mix offers advantages over energy-intensive conventional lawns including drought tolerance, significant reduction in mowing (and its pollution and injury to wildlife), lower costs overall, and natural beauty. The steps for planting an eco-friendly lawn are like those described for planting meadows or prairies.

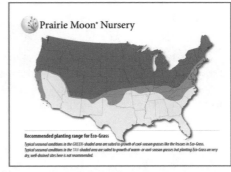

Some seed suppliers offer eco-friendly grass mixes such as Eco-Grass, a low maintenance lawn blend offered by Prairie Moon Nursery.

Include native grasses in your landscape beds

Native grasses are essential plants in a wildlife habitat providing shelter for creatures and seed for birds and mammals; plus, many are host plants for caterpillars. Fortunately, native grasses are easy to incorporate throughout the landscape in both natural and formal designs. When choosing native grass species, consider these five characteristics of a species:

- Is the species a warm-season or cool-season species?
- Is it clump-forming, or does it spread by runners?
- How tall does it grow?
- How much foot traffic, if any, can it tolerate?
- Does it tolerate occasional or regular mowing?

Let's take a look at the answers to these questions since they will help you plant the right native grass at the right time and place.

Little bluestem (*Schizachyrium scoparium*) is a reliable and lovely clumping grass that is native to all but the most western states.

Is the grass a warm-season or cool-season species?

To determine whether a grass is warm-season or cool-season, refer to your seed supplier's catalog, or search online for **[species] warm season or cool season**. Then, check out the table below for characteristics of warm-season versus cool-season native grasses. This information will help guide your grass choices and their planting time and placement in your landscape.

Characteristics of:	WARM-season native grasses	COOL-season native grasses
Soil temperature for germination	55°F	40°F (some require warmer temperatures)
Stratification (cool, moist storage to aid germination)	Usually not needed; except 14 - 60 days for Eastern gama grass (*Tripsacum dactyloides*)	60 days significantly improves germination
Planting time	Spring	Fall is ideal, but can be planted in spring
Growing temperatures	60 to 65°F	40 to 42°F
Optimum growing temperatures	85 to 95°F	65 to 75°F
Maximum growth period	Late summer to early fall	Spring and late fall
Dormancy (grass dies back to the root and blades turn brown)	Enter dormancy mid-fall to mid-spring	Enter dormancy when temperatures drop below 32°F; may go dormant in hottest summer months if not watered
Shade tolerance	Require full sun	Tolerate some shade (but require at least ½ to ¾ day of sun)
Native species examples	Purple love grass (*Eragrostis spectabilis*), sweet grass (*Hierochloe odorata*), little bluestem (*Schizachyrium scoparium*), Indian grass (*Sorghastrum nutans*), switchgrass (*Panicum virgatum*), prairie dropseed (*Sporobolus heterolepis*)	Big bluestem (*Andropogon gerardii*), side-oats grama (*Bouteloua curtipendula*), bottlebrush grass (*Elymus hystrix*), red fescue (*Festuca rubra*), June grass (*Koeleria macrantha*)

11

Plant

Digging in deeper

Listed here are references and additional key resources related to planting your landscape generously (please refer to the Appendix for publication details).

Nature's Best Hope: A New Approach to Conservation That Starts in Your Yard: Doug stresses the importance of being generous in our plantings (see page 107). He suggests that we consider the naturally occurring density of a forest and match that density in our plantings. He also suggests that we keep in mind the ecological benefit of planting shrubs and understory trees.

Books about meadows and prairies: The steps for planting a meadow or prairie that we shared in this action are just a starting point. Here are several books dedicated to these topics:

The Gardener's Guide to Prairie Plants by Neil Diboll and Hilary Cox. Packed with information explaining all the elements of designing, planting, and maintaining prairie gardens including an extensive table of prairie-seed mixes. The photographs of each stage of development of 148 prairie plants are a key feature of this must-have reference for aspiring prairie stewards.

Garden Revolution: How Our Landscapes Can Be a Source of Environmental Change by Larry Weaner and Thomas Christopher. This deep dive into establishing meadows provides a foundation for ecological landscaping.

Prairie Up: An Introduction to Natural Garden Design by Benjamin Vogt is an easy-to-read guide for including prairie plantings in your landscape. It includes many interesting lists, such as plant sociability, perennial forbs with ornamental winter seed heads or bracts, affordable flower seed, and much more.

The Tallgrass Prairie Center Guide to Prairie Restoration in the Upper Midwest by Daryl Smith, Dave Williams, Greg Houseal, and Kirk Henderson is a comprehensive manual that takes an in-depth look at prairie restoration.

A hidden gem of a resource, the **New York Botanical Garden** website hosts a list of all the native plants societies in the U.S. Not only is there information about each state's native plant society, but the pages also feature recommended reading about plants specific to each state. For example, the Wyoming page includes regional books about wildflowers and mushrooms. Find this super handy list by searching online for **native plant societies nybg**. In the top menu, click **Native Plant Societies of the U.S.A.**; click on your state.

Published plant trials for learning more about how different species of native plants perform in the landscape: For mid-Atlantic gardeners, the **Mt. Cuba Center** (*mtcubacenter.org*) in Delaware has published the results of their trials of *Carex, Echinacea, Hydrangea, Phlox*, and other native plant genera. The **Chicago Botanic Garden** (*chicagobotanicgarden.org*) trials include *Coreopsis, Geum, Vernonia*, and others. For trials near you, do an online search with the terms **trial gardens [region]**.

Hoffman Nursery (*hoffmannursery.com*)**,** a wholesale nursery in North Carolina, offers an informative *Carex Comparison Chart*. Visit their website or search online for **hoffman nursery carex comparison chart**. Although not all the species on the chart are native, you can learn a lot about *Carex*.

You've done the heavy lifting—your plants are in the ground! If needed, be sure to protect your new plantings from deer, rabbits, other rodents, pets, children, slugs, foot traffic, or other potential dangers. In ***Action 2: Protect your wildlife***, we covered strategies for protecting the plants, animals, and human residents of your wildlife habitat. In the next action, we'll go a step further by exploring methods to avoid using toxic chemicals in and around our homes.

Action 12—CHECKLIST
Use nontoxic home and yard products

Step:	✔	Action Needed:	Page:
1	☐	Make the decision to avoid using toxic chemicals in your home and landscape	12.4
2	☐	Embrace a wildlife-friendly attitude toward insects	12.5
3	☐	Design and manage your landscape in ways that discourage pests without the use of toxic chemicals	12.6
4	☐	When pest control measures are needed, use nontoxic pest control methods	12.7
5	☐	Remove invasive plants without using toxic herbicides	12.9
6	☐	Avoid adding fertilizer	12.10
7	☐	Use nontoxic household products	12.11
8	☐	Safely dispose of unused pesticides, herbicides, fertilizers, and household products	12.11

For many species of trees and shrubs, covering a stump with several layers of landscape fabric secured with string eliminates the need to treat the stump with toxic herbicides.

12

Nontoxic

What is Integrated Pest Management (IPM)?

In 1959, Vernon Stern introduced the "integrated control concept" which laid the foundation for an innovative approach to pest control that views conventional pesticides as a last resort. Now known as **integrated pest management (IPM)**, this approach is widely used in agriculture. IPM is also useful in guiding pest control in our home landscapes.

The five steps of IPM

1. Accurately identify the pest or invasive plant.
2. Monitor and assess the scope of the problem.
3. Set action thresholds. A small population of a pest may be tolerable. What level of population requires action?
4. Explore control options and apply the least toxic option.
5. Evaluate the results and repeat the cycle as needed.

Monitoring pest and beneficial insect populations is a key component of IPM (*left*).

Ladybug larvae are voracious consumers of aphids (*right*).

The pyramid of IPM approaches

Conventional pesticides
Chemical insecticides, fungicides, and herbicides

Biological controls
Diatomaceous earth, baking soda, vinegar, microbials, predators, beneficial nematodes

Physical and mechanical control
Traps, floating row covers, flaming, mulch

Cultural practices
Landscape management best practices, plant selection for resistance

most toxic

least toxic

The small scale of a residential landscape gives us more nontoxic pest control options. For example, in contrast to attempting to control several acres of an invasive plant blanketing a wildland, we can be vigilant and keep up on a small patch of an aggressive invasive. Similarly, the eradication of several acres of invasive trees is challenging; in contrast, when cutting down several invasive trees, avoiding the use of herbicides is easily accomplished by covering the stumps with landscape fabric and regularly snipping any regrowth. In almost all cases, because of the smaller scale of our home landscapes, we can entirely avoid the use of toxic insecticides, fungicides, and herbicides.

12

Nontoxic

Action 12—GUIDE
Use nontoxic home and yard products

Untreated lawns give pets a safe place to romp around.

The words pest**icide**, insect**icide**, herb**icide**, and fung**icide** all contain the root **"cide"** meaning "killer"—a role they perform all too well as it turns out. So well, in fact, that without widespread action to turn around the trend toward precipitous declines in the populations of insects and other creatures, many species will face extinction within 20 to 30 years.

In this action, we encourage a shift in attitudes toward insects. We discuss strategies for eliminating the use of toxic household and landscape chemicals along with landscape management practices that discourage pests without the use of toxic chemicals. For those instances where pest control is necessary, we share resources to identify nontoxic pest control methods. Finally, we discuss the safe disposal of unused pesticides, herbicides, fertilizer, household chemicals, and other toxic products.

Many toxic pesticides kill not only the intended pest, but also beneficial insects and plants that other creatures rely upon for survival.

Switching to nontoxic home and yard products contributes to the solution of the biodiversity crisis while simultaneously creating safer environments for our family, pets, and other living things.

Blue-winged wasps (*Scollia dubia*) lay their eggs on Japanese beetle grubs which are then eaten by the developing wasp larvae.

12

Nontoxic

① Make the decision to avoid using toxic chemicals in your home and landscape

Making the decision to stop using toxic chemicals in and around a home requires making a commitment to learning what works instead. Fortunately, there are lots of handy resources available to help you do exactly that.

The **Xerces Society's** *Reducing Pesticide Use & Impacts* program is a good starting place for learning why pesticides are such a threat to wildlife and what can be done about it. Visit *xerces.org*. Click on **Our Work**. Click on **Reducing Pesticide Use & Impacts**. Click on the images above any topic for in-depth information about it. For example, the resources for **Yards & Gardens** include downloadable articles such as *Western Monarchs Are in Trouble: This Is How You Can Help* and *Smarter Pest Management: Protecting Pollinators at Home.*

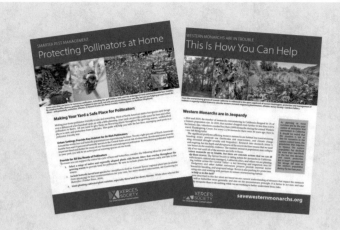

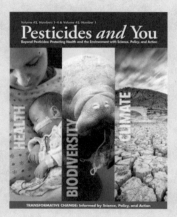

For the past 40 years, **Beyond Pesticides** (*beyondpesticides.org*) has worked with government agencies and nonprofits to identify the dangers of pesticide use and design safe pest management alternatives to share with the public. The 2022 - 2023 issue of their journal *Pesticides and You, Transformative Change* (Volume 42, Numbers 1-4 & Volume 43, Number 1) provides a thorough explanation of the magnitude of the threat that pesticide use poses to human health, biodiversity, and the climate. Find this free, 172-page publication by searching online for **pesticides and you 2022-23 transformative change pdf**. In a moment, we'll look at some additional resources that **Beyond Pesticides** offers for finding alternatives to pesticides.

A tribute to Rachel Carson (1907 - 1964)

In 1962, Rachel Carson launched the environmental movement with her book *Silent Spring*, issuing a stark warning about the careless and dangerous use of chemical pesticides. Unfortunately, in the over 60 years since its publication, toxic chemical products have infiltrated nearly every aspect of modern life, damaging our planet's ecosystems and burdening future generations. Carson was one person and she brought about the ban of DDT. What difference can each of us make?

Rachel Louise Carson (1907 - 1964)

"All the life of the planet is interrelated . . . . each species has its own ties to others, and . . . . all are related to the earth. This is . . . . the message of "Silent Spring."

~ Engraving on memorial plaque for Rachel Carson at the National Wildlife Refuge in Wells, Maine.

12

Nontoxic

② Embrace a wildlife-friendly attitude toward insects

By changing our attitude toward insects and other creatures traditionally thought of as pests, the use of toxic chemicals becomes less appealing. For example, when reaching for a chemical to kill aphids, it's hard not to think of the beneficial insects that will also inevitably be killed. It may take some time to adjust to co-existing with insects and creepy-crawly or slimy creatures. Looking at the problems from a different point of view and taking proactive precautions when necessary, may make the transition to a nontoxic approach easier.

Let native insects have their meals on mature plants. Typically, native insects will not kill their host plant. For example, the spicebush swallowtail caterpillar (*inset*) only requires three sassafras leaves (*above*) to reach adulthood. When your plants are young, it's a good idea to monitor them regularly in case overzealous diners threaten to defoliate the entire plant.

Use the 10-Step Rule: Landscape horticulturist Tammany Baumgarten recommends the 10-Step-Rule: *You may see signs of insects when you look closely at a plant but take ten steps back from the plant and all your insect problems go away.* Here, caterpillars have feasted on blackberry leaves (*above left*), but the signs of their dining disappear at just a few feet away from the plant (*above right*).

Find out the role that a "pest" plays in the ecosystem. Some of the bad guys are actually good guys; for example, slugs and snails are an important food source for firefly larvae (*above*), toads, and even foxes. You might tolerate a small slug population and control it only if the population gets out of hand. We'll discuss how to find alternatives to pesticides in a moment.

Plant extra edible plants, especially berries. A bountiful harvest makes it easy to share with wildlife! Take the pressure off from trying to protect the fruit you grow to eat by growing many different fruit-bearing plants to provide a plentiful buffet for fruit-loving birds, other creatures, AND you.

Recalibrate your sense of beauty. Holes in leaves means there is life in your landscape! Purple poop on the sidewalk is a sure sign that birds are enjoying the pokeweed (*Phytolacca*) you allowed to grow. Elderberry (*Sambucus*) panicles being stripped of their fruit indicate a population of fruit-eating birds, and pecked at strawberries may mean you have a resident turtle. This is what living with nature looks like!

③ Design and manage your landscape in ways that discourage pests without the use of toxic chemicals

Problematic pest populations tend to diminish as your wildlife habitat becomes more established and native populations of flora and fauna dominate the landscape. In the meantime, how you design and manage your landscape will help nudge this process in a positive direction. Here are a few suggestions:

Choose plants that are not preferred by pests. Depending upon the purpose of a planting, it's often possible to simply choose not to grow a plant that requires pesticides, fungicides, or fertilizers to thrive. For example, where Japanese beetles devour the native serviceberry (*Amelanchier, left*), it makes sense to choose a different native tree such as pawpaw (*Asimina triloba, middle*) which isn't attractive to these pests.

Choose plants that are native to your ecoregion. Native plants are adapted to the conditions where you live and typically won't require the use of pesticides and fertilizer that an introduced plant may demand.

Regularly monitor your landscape to catch potential pests in their early stages. Spotting a problem early makes it easier to control without toxic chemicals.

Place pest-prone plants in accessible locations. Placing a plant that is vulnerable to insect attack someplace that you often walk by not only makes it easier to spot pest problems right away, but it also makes eco-friendly control measures such as hand-picking easier to do. Pasture rose (*Rosa carolina*) is a Japanese beetle favorite.

Choose tough plants. Where the soil is poor, choose tough plants such as blue mistflower (*Conoclinium coelestinum*), goldenrods (*Solidago*), or native grasses. Not only are they likely to perform well, but they will do so without the help of toxic fertilizers and pesticides.

Sometimes pests will become problematic. It can take extra effort and patience to control a persistent pest without resorting to toxic chemicals; however, the reward is knowing that the well-being of your family and wildlife is better off for it! Next, we'll look at resources for finding nontoxic pest control methods and products for use around the landscape and in the home.

12

Nontoxic

4 When pest control measures are needed, use nontoxic pest control methods

Sometimes pest populations reach an unacceptable level. Perhaps there are no natural predators for an invasive insect, or a particularly aggressive invasive plant proves impossible to control. Fortunately, for times like these, there are valuable resources at our fingertips. An online search for **nontoxic control [pest]** may yield some methods of control although experimentation will be needed to prove their efficacy. A reliable source of control methods for many especially problematic pests is the non-profit **Beyond Pesticides** website.

Visit **beyondpesticides.org**

or search online for **beyond pesticides** and navigate to the site.

Click **Resources.**

In the drop-down menu, click **ManageSafe™.**

In the drop-down menu, click **Choose a Pest.**

Read through the ManageSafe™ introduction to understand the concept of "least-toxic pesticides."

Click the **Choose a Pest** image:

Depending on the pest's location, click on **Structural/Home** or **Lawns/ Landscapes/Gardens.**

Click on the pest to learn about the least-toxic control measures.

Shown here are the results for ground ivy (*Glechoma hederacea*) also known as creeping Charlie.

Check out the left menu for invaluable resources for adopting a pesticide-free lifestyle.

NOTE: *Some of the pests listed, such as poison ivy and ants, are actually beneficial native members of many regional ecosystems. Where possible, give them their space and allow them to exist.*

The Beyond Pesticides materials shown here and elsewhere in this book are used with permission from Beyond Pesticides (beyondpesticides.org).

12

Nontoxic

Control mosquitoes around your home and landscape

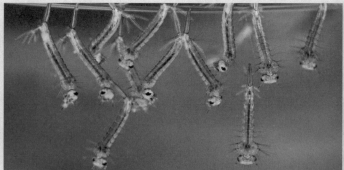

Close-up of mosquito larvae found in standing water in an Atlanta, Georgia residential area

Application of *Bacillus thuringiensis* (Bt) in granular form (Mosquito Bits®, *above*) and in floating donuts (Mosquito Dunks®, *below*).

Regularly scan your property for standing water to prevent mosquito breeding. Mosquitoes can breed in still water as little as 1/4-inch deep!

- Search your property high and low for places where water may be trapped: buckets, tarps over wood piles, gutters, flowerpot saucers, rims of tires or trash can lids, depressions in stones, BBQ pits, wheelbarrows, toys, and so forth.

- Refresh water in birdbaths and pet bowls every 2 to 3 days.

- Add movement to ponds and other water features.

Removing standing water from your property is the single most effective way to reduce mosquito populations.

Regularly scan standing bodies of water for mosquito larvae and treat with Bt if larvae are present. Where it's not practical to empty out water, use *Bacillus thuringiensis* (Bt) to kill mosquito larvae. At recommended dosages, Bt is safe for dragonfly larvae, frogs, and other wildlife. Use only in non-draining, closed systems, such as ponds.

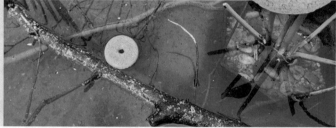

Oppose mosquito spraying!

Traditional mosquito control methods are touted as being safe for people, pets, and wildlife, but the problem is that along with mosquitoes, the chemicals used kill beneficial insects and get into the food chain. If you live in a community where spraying is conducted, urge your local policymakers to adopt ecologically safe methods of mosquito management. The **Xerces Society** guide, ***How to Help Your Community Create an Effective Mosquito Management Plan***, covers all aspects of how to effectively manage mosquitoes and oppose mosquito spraying.

HOW TO
Help Your Community Create an Effective Mosquito Management Plan

A Xerces Society Guide

12

Nontoxic

Organic, but deadly to foes and friends alike!

Derived from chrysanthemum flowers, pyrethrin is an organic pesticide that is widely used to kill mosquitoes, fleas, and other pests. The problem is that it is highly toxic to aquatic animals (such as fish, tadpoles, adult frogs, shrimp, and lobsters) and most insects (including bees, dragonflies, fireflies, and lady bugs). Natural though it may be, **keep pyrethrin out of your wildlife habitat!**

Pyrethrin is derived from the highly toxic Dalmatian chrysanthemum (*Tanacetum cinerariifolium*).

5 Remove invasive plants without using toxic herbicides

Removing invasives was explained in detail in *Action 4: Remove invasive species.* Below is a handy summary. These management practices will reduce the time needed to remove invasives.

How to remove and keep out invasive plants:

Garlic mustard *(Alliaria petiolata)* aggressively invades woodlands in many North American ecoregions.

- Learn to identify invasive plants, especially their seedling stages.

- Remove invasive plants when they first appear as soon as they are identified.

- Remove invasive plants BEFORE they go to seed!

- Remove small, isolated patches of invasive plants before tackling large patches.

- Tackle one invasive plant species at a time.

- Time your invasive plant removal with the weather conditions.

- Learn which method most effectively eliminates each invasive plant species on your property.

- Whenever possible, depending on the invasive plant species, leave the roots of the plants you are removing in the ground to avoid disturbing the soil.

- . . . BUT remove the roots when they are likely to regrow and reinfest an area.

- Deal with large patches of invasive plants using the *Block It!* method.

- Avoid using plastic or woven landscape weed-blocking fabric except for blocking stump regrowth.

- After removing invasive trees and shrubs, cover the stumps with landscape weed-blocking fabric to prevent regrowth.

- Plant densely.

- Plant aggressive native plants to outcompete and suppress the growth of invasive plants.

- Mulch new transplants with a 2-inch layer of mulch appropriate to your ecoregion.

- If invasive plants continue to reinfest an area, find the underlying parent source of each invasive plant and make eliminating that source a top priority.

- Reevaluate what is and isn't a weed.

⑥ Avoid adding fertilizer

The best fertilizer for a crop is the shadow of the farmer. The more frequently it's applied, the better the outcome."

⌘

Author unknown

Synthetic fertilizers contribute to ozone destruction and global warming and contaminate the watershed leading to **eutrophication** (excessive growth of microorganisms in oxygen depleted bodies of water). The use of fertilizer is easily avoided since many native plants perform better in soils with low fertility. For native plant species that require a rich soil such as many woodland plants, consider the following eco-friendly ways to build the fertility in your soil:

Leave the leaf litter. As it breaks down, leaf litter adds organic matter to the soil that the soil micro life depends upon for survival. Leaf litter is Mother Nature's way of doing the task of mulching and fertilizing for you!

Make compost and apply it to your soil. Earlier (see page 11.6), we discussed making and using compost. High quality compost not only adds organic matter to your soil, but it also helps ensure that your landscape is teeming with soil micro life.

Consider alternatives to fertilizer. Aggressive native plants can be allowed to grow, then chopped and left on the surface to slowly enrich the soil. Bacteria associated with **legumes** (bean family members, such as *Baptisia; above*) may help to add nitrogen to soil (see below).

Grow lush, green lawns without applying fertilizer

Seed clover into the lawn. Although clover is not native, it does offer pollen for generalist pollinators. Plus, in a process called **nitrogen fixation**, bacteria associated with clover, a legume, converts atmospheric nitrogen into a form that the clover plant uses to make protein. As new roots and leaves of clover form, the old ones die. Nitrogen is released and may become available to surrounding plants.

Use the mulch setting on your mower (*if your mower has this option*). The grass clippings will help to nourish your soil and its micro life.

Don't apply fertilizers to your lawn. Quick growth can lead to more maintenance; plus, excess nutrients contaminate the watershed.

Avoid applying mushroom compost. It contains high levels of nitrites and phosphorus that contaminate the watershed and cause excessive algae growth.

Grow plants adapted to your soil conditions. Instead of spending money and time amending soil to make it right for a plant, choose plants that will grow well in the soil you have (and avoid a lot of work!).

⑦ Use nontoxic household products

Many household products contain toxic chemicals that are harmful to humans and the environment. They contaminate the soil and watershed and pollute the air.

Use Environmental Working Group's *EWG Verified* database to find safe household products

Visit **ewg.org/ewgverified** or search online for **ewg verified** and navigate to the **ewg.org** site.

Click on a category: **Personal Care**, **Cleaning Products**, or **Baby and Diapers** to find products that EWG has verified as being safe for use.

To determine if products that you already have are safe, visit the *EWG's Guide to Healthy Cleaning*. To access, do an online search with the terms **ewg guide to healthy cleaning**. Enter a product brand name for a list of the brand's reviewed products. Products are given scores ranging from *EWG Verified* (meets strict standards for health and transparency), *A* (lowest concern) to *F* (highest concern), and their ingredients are scored individually.

Switch to phosphate-free, biodegradable soap, detergent, and car wash soap to prevent water pollution in your wildlife habitat and to protect your local watershed. Use the *EWG Verified* database to identify products that are safe for the environment (and your health!).

Of special concern . . . fabric softeners

Avoid using scented fabric softeners for your laundry. Fabric softener is the #1 cause of indoor air pollution. These toxins escape from your home and pollute the outdoor air as well. Many contain fragrances, preservatives, and petroleum-based phthalates which are known health hazards. Read the EWG article, *Skip the most toxic fabric softeners* (ewg.org/news-insights/news/skip-fabric-softeners) and you'll never want to use a toxic fabric softener again!

Use vinegar as a fabric softener. Instead of toxic fabric softener liquids and sheets, use 1/2 cup of white vinegar in the rinse cycle. The vinegar odor goes away, and your clothes will feel soft to the touch without fabric softener buildup.

⑧ Safely dispose of unused pesticides, herbicides, fertilizers, and household products

In addition to the obviously hazardous pesticides, many common household products are quite harmful. They contaminate the soil and waterways endangering terrestrial and aquatic life. It's important to carefully consider *how* we throw away what we throw away. Even products not typically stored with lawn care or cleaning supplies may be quite toxic, for example, some art supplies (and even beauty supplies!) contain extremely toxic heavy metals such as cadmium and lead.

Never pour household and yard care chemicals down the toilet, sink, sewer, or street drain. If these toxic chemicals enter the watershed, they can harm animals, plants, and other living things.

Read the labels. Follow the instructions for disposal on the product label. Some household products generally assumed to be safe are quite toxic.

To find a place to dispose of toxic things, search for **household hazardous waste collection [city]**. These authorities can answer questions about how to safely and legally dispose of pesticides, cleaning products, solvents, paint, and other toxic things.

12

Nontoxic

Digging in deeper

Here are references and additional resources to make it easier to adopt a nontoxic lifestyle (please refer to the Appendix for publication details).

Nature's Best Hope: A New Approach to Conservation That Starts in Your Yard: Doug explains the reasons to avoid pesticides and why it is also important to avoid fertilizer applications (see page 210). Not only do native plants not require fertilizer to thrive, but fertilizer also contaminates the watershed and causes **algal blooms** (excessive growth of algae in bodies of water) and other problems. He also discusses the ongoing problem of mosquito fogging (pages 210 and 224).

The Organic Gardener's Handbook of Natural Pest and Disease Control: A Complete Guide to Maintaining a Healthy Garden and Yard the Earth-Friendly Way by Fern Marshall Bradley, Barbara W. Ellis, and Deborah L. Martin. This updated classic is a rich resource for both identifying the insects you are likely to encounter in your garden and controlling the unwelcome ones. Keep in mind that although a recommended material may be organic, it may nevertheless be highly toxic to a broad range of animals.

Make your indoor space less toxic with the help of ***A Healthier Home: The Room-by-Room Guide to Make Any Space a Little Less Toxic*** by Shawna Holman. This book provides simple swaps and realistic steps toward making all your living spaces a lot safer.

Clear explanation of less toxic landscape products: In this online article ***Less Toxic Insecticides***, Karen Russ and Joey Williamson of the Clemson University Cooperative Extension Service Home & Garden Information Center provide a clear explanation of less toxic pesticides. Many of these are used by organic growers, such as insecticidal soaps and oils, *Bacillus thuringiensis* (Bt), **diatomaceous earth** (fossilized single cell algae), and **capsaicin** (active component of chili pepper extract). Remember that less toxic and organic alternatives to pest control may be harmful to more than the target pest—research these materials thoroughly beforehand and use judiciously, if at all.

Make your own DIY cleaners. Effective cleaning products can easily be made at home with inexpensive household ingredients, such as baking soda, vinegar, hydrogen peroxide, and phosphate-free biodegradable dish soap. Search online for ***DIY natural cleaners*** to find more DIY alternatives. For example, the University of Arkansas Cooperative Extension Service offers many DIY cleaner recipes. Find these recipes online by searching for **uaex clean and green homemade cleaners**. Making your own cleaning products will help you save money, your health, and the environment!

Now that your landscape is planted and you're armed with nontoxic approaches to pest and weed control, it's time to manage your wildlife habitat. Let's consider management strategies that will reduce the amount of monotonous yardwork and instead free up your time to enjoy your wildlife habitat.

Step:	✔	Action Needed:	Month:	Page:
1	☐	Mow and edge only as much as necessary for your lawn areas to meet neighborhood standards		**13.4**
2	☐	Edit your landscape design		**13.5**
3	☐	Groom your landscape only to the extent required for neighborhood acceptance		**13.6**
4	☐	Remove and keep out invasive plants		**13.7**
5	☐	Set up and maintain eco-friendly control measures for invasive insects and deer pressure (if present)		**13.7**
6	☐	Set up a calendar of management tasks		**13.8**
7	☐	Monitor your landscape on a regular basis	*year-round*	**13.8**
8	☐	Encourage landscape service providers to adopt wildlife-friendly approaches		**13.8**
9	☐	Minimize the need to water		**13.9**
10	☐	Maintain bird feeders, nesting boxes, birdbaths, and other water features		**13.9**

Calendar of Seasonal Tasks

JANUARY
_____
_____
_____
_____
_____
_____
_____
_____

FEBRUARY
_____
_____
_____
_____
_____
_____
_____
_____

MARCH
_____
_____
_____
_____
_____
_____
_____
_____

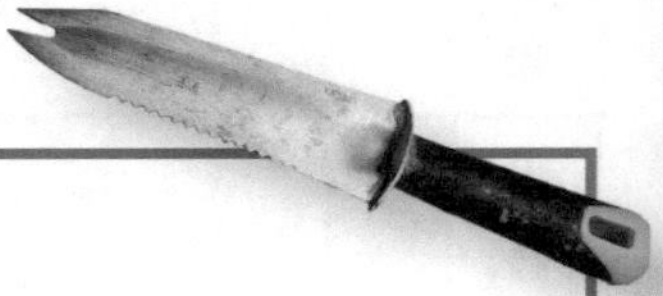

APRIL
_____
_____
_____
_____
_____
_____
_____
_____

MAY
_____
_____
_____
_____
_____
_____
_____
_____

JUNE
_____
_____
_____
_____
_____
_____
_____
_____

JULY
_____
_____
_____
_____
_____
_____
_____
_____

AUGUST
_____
_____
_____
_____
_____
_____
_____
_____

SEPTEMBER
_____
_____
_____
_____
_____
_____
_____
_____

OCTOBER
_____
_____
_____
_____
_____
_____
_____
_____

NOVEMBER
_____
_____
_____
_____
_____
_____
_____
_____

DECEMBER
_____
_____
_____
_____
_____
_____
_____
_____

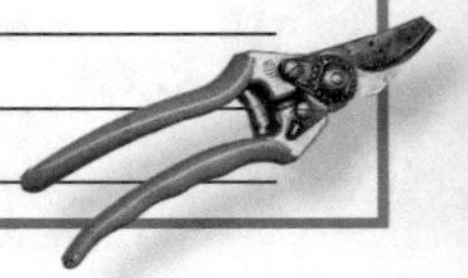

Action 13—GUIDE
Manage your wildlife habitat

A few tools take care of most management tasks on a small property—quality pruners, a garden knife, and gloves.

Enjoying regular walks around your property and observing what is going on will help you to identify needed management tasks. The maxim *"An ounce of prevention is worth a pound of cure"* holds true when it comes to managing a wildlife habitat. In the early years, caring for your landscape will be more demanding—new plantings will need protection, invasive plants will take advantage of the spaces between young plants and require removal, gaps created by plants that fail will need replanting, and so forth. The good news is that in later years, the workload decreases. Management becomes more of a process of editing: removing the occasional invasive, cutting back or replacing native plants that are too large for a space, and planting more native plants that offer ecological services or complement the design. Where invasives once took over, native plants will naturally fill in the established beds which are themselves expanding. The expanded beds reduce the lawn area and the need to mow.

In this action, we look at the typical routine tasks required to manage a wildlife landscape with a particular focus on strategies to reduce the need to mow, weed, plant annuals, water, stake, prune, edge, mulch and clean up each season. You'll get to spend more time examining a caterpillar or marveling over a new bird. In many ways, your wildlife habitat begins to manage itself!

As your wildlife habitat becomes established, caring for it becomes an experience of discovery and wonder. Shown here is the caterpillar of the brown-shaded gray moth (*Iridopsis defectaria*) on staghorn sumac (*Rhus typhina*).

Mow and edge only as much as necessary for your lawn areas to meet neighborhood standards

Some of the mowing we do is simply out of habit or because we haven't considered another approach to this area of our property. By reconsidering these habits or by coming up with different options to replace areas of lawn, it's possible to mow less often, saving time and money while reducing the hazard to wildlife. Following are some strategies that can help reduce the need to mow.

Strategies to reduce the need to mow

Shrink your lawn! This, of course, is the most effective strategy for reducing the need to mow. Shown at left is a prime opportunity to shrink the lawn!

Identify hard-to-mow areas of your lawn to convert to ecological plantings. When mowing, plan easy-to-mow routes. Identify the time-consuming, hard-to-mow areas of your lawn, and target these areas first for conversion to wildlife plantings (see page 3.5).

Mow only when the grass requires mowing rather than "every Saturday whether it needs it or not." As much as your schedule permits, adapt your mowing schedule to the growth patterns of the lawn.

Pause your mowing to allow flowering areas to bloom. If possible, pause long enough for the flowers to set seed. Self-seeding violets (*Viola*) have replaced lawn (*far right*).

Consider changing your aesthetics to allow flowering "weeds" to be a part of your lawn. Violets, clover, and other flowering plants (*far left*) naturally form a bee lawn (see pages 11.12 - 11.13).

Allow leaf litter to accumulate under deciduous trees. Eventually this will block out grass growth and provide a rich habitat for soil micro life and insect pupation (*left*).

Mow and edge only as much as necessary, *continued*

Strategies to reduce the need to edge landscape beds

In beds surrounded by grass, plant densely right up to the edge that meets the grass. Mowing right up to this edge creates a natural edge that reduces the need to edge with a string trimmer.

Edge beds with flat rocks that are flush to the ground. The mower can roll on the flat rocks while cutting the grass right to the edge reducing the need to edge.

Plant aggressive native plants that can encroach into the grass. A drift of plants contrasts with the low height of the lawn to form a legible edge that requires less care.

② Edit your landscape design

Keeping a planting looking good requires ongoing editing. Here your creativity is given free range as you:

- transplant native **volunteers** (seedlings self-sown by plants growing in the landscape)
- add new species to replant or reseed gaps where plants have died or failed to thrive
- add new native plant beds
- allow **succession** (the natural change in the composition of plant species in an area over time) to take place such as by allowing a tree seedling planted by a squirrel to grow
- prevent succession by trimming back or removing plants such as by removing volunteer tree seedlings from a meadow.

To prevent editing your landscape from becoming a burdensome chore, strive to intentionally reduce the need for annual planting and replanting.

Reduce the need for annual planting and replanting

Plant perennials instead of annuals. Many perennial natives are slower to establish and flower than splashy-colored annual bedding flowers, but with time and increased plant knowledge, your native blooms can provide lovely, artistic displays.

Welcome beneficial volunteer plants in your garden by not deadheading your native plants so that they can go to seed. Plus, you'll save yourself the task of deadheading! (Conversely, you may wish to deadhead eager native plants that threaten to take over a landscape bed.)

Transplant and replant missing plants at the ideal times for a plant species. Do an online search for **best time to [plant or transplant] [plant name]**. Your plant survival rates will be higher and their growth rate faster.

3 Groom your landscape only to the extent required for neighborhood acceptance

Grooming your landscape can be a relaxing activity that provides opportunities to interact with the landscape. In addition to caring for your lawn, which we discussed earlier, grooming a landscape involves the following activities:

- **staking** plants that flop onto pathways
- **deadheading** (removing flower heads) non-native plants that you want to keep in your landscape
- **pruning** broken branches that pose a danger
- **planning** the timing and limiting the extent of fall and spring cleanup of your landscape beds
- **mulching** only as needed for new plantings.

Stake plants that flop onto pathways. To prevent plants from flopping in the first place:

- Plant tall plants in the back of border beds and in the center of island beds.

- Plant tall and medium-sized plants away from walkways.

- Avoid fertilizing your native plantings. Many native plants are adapted to poor soil where they will develop into healthier, sturdier plants.
- Plant densely and intermingle plants so that they support one another.

- Use the "Chelsea chop" method of cutting back plants to prevent floppage and prolong bloom. Cut back 1/2 to 1/3 of a plant 4 to 6 weeks before bloom is expected.

The "Chelsea chop" pruning method (*right*) works well and gives a layered look to many native plant species, such as asters (*Symphyotrichum, Eurybia*), coneflowers (*Echinacea*), Joe-Pye weed (*Eutrochium*), mints (*Monarda, Pycnanthemum*), perennial sunflowers (*Helianthus*) and many other forbs.

Deadhead non-native plants that you want to keep in your landscape. To reduce the need for deadheading:

- Replace introduced plants that require deadheading with native plants that don't require deadheading.

- Leave dried flower stalks on native plants to reseed and nourish wildlife.

- For neighborhoods that require fall garden cleanup, leave pencil-width or larger stalks cut tidily to a minimum height of 8 inches (preferably 15- 24 inches). These stalks will provide future homes for stem-nesting bees.

Prune broken branches that pose a danger. To reduce the need for pruning:

- Site a plant carefully by considering its full-grown size. If a plant has enough room to spread out, you won't have to waste time in the future pruning it back to fit the space.
- Consider removing a plant whose pruning requirements become burdensome.

- Replace a rampant grower with a well-behaved plant.

- Leave dead branches and trees standing when they pose no danger.

leave full plant height

cut back 1/3 of plant height

cut back 1/2 of plant height

Limit the extent of fall and spring landscape cleanup

To allow nesting insects and other animals to complete their reproductive cycles, refrain from doing intensive landscape cleanup to the extent possible in your neighborhood. As tempting as undertaking an intensive garden cleanup may be, instead leave the stalks and canes of plants as explained in *Action 7: Preserve and create pupation and nesting sites*. Because there is such variation in insect reproductive cycles, there is no right time nor right temperature after which intensive cleanup can proceed without disrupting wildlife. Instead, relax, and enjoy the increased populations of butterflies, moths, pollinators, birds, and other welcome animals!

Groom your landscape only to the extent required for neighborhood acceptance, *continued*

Eliminate the need for annual mulching

oak seedling

Plant densely to create a "green mulch" instead of hauling in plastic bags of mulch. Plant perennials to temporarily fill in the area around newly planted shrubs and trees, reducing the need for mulch. Not only is a green mulch better for your plants, it's also better for the environment.

Mulch new plantings with regionally appropriate materials, such as homegrown leaf litter, pine needles, or crushed stone. Even dense plantings may need a layer of mulch at first as plants become established and fill in. Annual mulching is unnecessary except where there are gaps.

Allow landscape trimmings and leaf litter to remain in place. You'll save time and energy by leaving "chop 'n drop" organic matter and leaf litter in place to nourish the soil and its inhabitants. If the wind mounds leaves into piles, collect the surplus leaves and make leaf mold (see page 3.14).

Some plants cannot survive if covered with mulch. For example, in the wild, cardinal flower (*Lobelia cardinalis*) grows in wetlands or along stream edges where leaf litter tends not to collect. In our landscapes, it's important to remove leaf litter from the **basal rosettes** (circle of lower leaves that hug the ground) of plants like cardinal flower to prevent them from rotting, especially in the South. Mossy areas may also need the gentle removal of leaf litter. Monitor areas where seed germination is likely and remove leaf litter as seeds begin to germinate (see page 11.9 for more about mulching).

4 Remove and keep out invasive plants

Removing invasive plants was explained in detail in *Action 4: Remove invasive species* and summarized in *Action 12: Use nontoxic home and yard products.* See page 12.9 for a handy summary of methods to remove and keep out invasive plants.

5 Set up and maintain eco-friendly control measures for invasive insects and deer pressure *(if present)*

Protecting your wildlife habitat from invasive insects and overpopulation of aggressive native species such as deer is critical to ensure a self-sustaining ecosystem. Refer to *Action 2: Protect your wildlife habitat* and *Action 12: Use nontoxic home and yard products* for tips and techniques to manage these challenges.

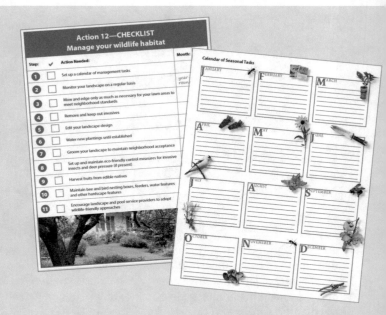

6 Set up a calendar of management tasks

It's helpful to set up an annual management plan that lays out the various tasks your wildlife landscape will require.

The checklist for this action (see page 13.1) is a good starting point for setting up an annual management plan. On it, you can note the month(s) each task should take place. If you want to take your planning a step further, consider making an annual plan for specific actions, such as propagation, planting, or invasive plant removal. By doing this, you won't miss the ideal window for collecting seed, planting a sought-after plant, or taking a cutting. For your convenience, there is also a reproducible *Calendar of Seasonal Tasks* on page 13.2 for this purpose.

To optimize your resources, consider the life cycles of both plants and the wildlife on your property when you set up your management systems. Removing invasive plants *before* they set seed, planting in time for the rainy season so that the rain will take care of watering, and limiting fall and spring cleanup to avoid disturbing pupating insects are just some of the ways you can support wildlife *and* reduce your workload.

7 Monitor your landscape on a regular basis

Regularly walking around your property and observing what is going on will help you to identify needed tasks. Slip on a comfortable pair of shoes, grab a tasty beverage, and stroll around your yard. Look closely into the branches of shrubs, behind rocks and logs, and all the way to the top of trees. Make mental or written notes about things needing attention or ideas for good additions to your wildlife habitat.

8 Encourage landscape service providers to adopt a wildlife-friendly approach

You may already have a team of landscapers who mow and maintain your landscape. As you transition your property into a richer wildlife habitat, you may need to explain any changes in care to the team. For example, you may need to ask them to raise their mower heights to at least 4 inches, leave leaf litter, not mow certain areas, or stop using toxic chemicals. Explain alternatives and provide the necessary equipment and materials to make the needed changes. You might consider sharing your landscape management calendar with them along with landscape plans with notes such as where not to mow.

Some services may offer wildlife-friendly approaches. For example, if you have a pool service, perhaps they could help you solve the problem of frogs drowning in the pool. See page 9.20 for more about hiring professional landscape services.

9 Minimize the need to water

Even drought-tolerant species need to be watered when they are first planted; however, once established, most native plants require little or no watering. In fact, overwatering can readily kill a plant. Of course, watering may be necessary at times depending upon your ecoregion, the growing requirements of the plant, and the weather. Here are some tips that will help reduce the need to water your landscape.

Reduce the need to water

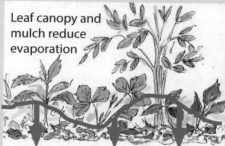
Leaf canopy and mulch reduce evaporation

Moisture is retained in the soil

4" or higher   mulch

Plant densely. The leaf canopy of a dense planting shades the ground and conserves moisture.

Mulch beds with an appropriate mulching material while new plantings are getting established. An appropriate mulch not only retains moisture, but also protects the soil and reduces evaporation. The ideal mulch depends on your ecoregion and the plants you are mulching (see page 11.9).

Mow your grass at the highest possible setting on your mower. Taller grass shades the soil reducing evaporation.

Set your mower to mulch the grass trimmings rather than collect them, if possible. The trimmings both reduce evaporation and nourish the soil.

Deadhead spent flowers to conserve moisture but allow at least half of native bloomers to reseed and nourish wildlife.

Water deeply and only when necessary. Water in the early morning. To avoid destroying fragile soil structure, use a gentle spray such as that from a rosette head of a watering can or spray option on a hose nozzle. Generally, it is best to avoid wetting the foliage, especially in arid regions.

Choose drought-tolerant plants. Keep in mind that newly planted drought-tolerant plants will need watering until established.

10 Maintain bird feeders, nesting boxes, birdbaths, and other water features

Maintain bird feeders and birdbaths. Clean out and disinfect bird feeders once every 2 weeks and more often in wet weather, heavy feeding seasons, and during bird health alerts. Birdbaths should be emptied, and the water should be refreshed daily or every other day. Hiding a scrub brush in the plants at the base of a birdbath makes it easy to do a quick scrub. Once a week, scrub the bath with 9 parts water to 1 part vinegar. Rinse well and refill.

Clean and disinfect nesting boxes annually. Remove nesting materials and scald with boiling water.

Prepare for a change in seasons. Cover small ponds with netting to prevent them from filling up with leaves. Where winters are freezing cold, store water features (such as bubblers or motion-activated sprinklers) that may be damaged from freezing temperatures. Place heaters in year-round water sources for wildlife. In the spring, set the water features back up.

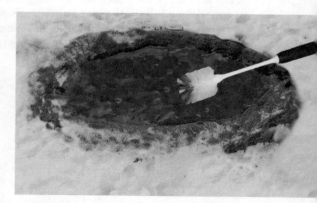
This ground-level *Farm Innovators 70-watt Four Seasons Heated Birdbath* is a popular wildlife destination, especially in winter.

Digging in deeper

Listed here are additional resources related to managing your wildlife habitat (please refer to the Appendix for publication details).

Nature's Best Hope: A New Approach to Conservation That Starts in Your Yard: Although managing a wildlife habitat is not directly addressed, there are key habitat management principles implicit throughout *Nature's Best Hope*. As Doug suggests, the importance of removing invasive plants, raising your mowing height, leaving pupation sites, waiting to perform spring cleanup, and leaving woody stems are all management approaches that are critical for ensuring a healthy local ecosystem.

We mentioned ***The Know Maintenance Perennial Garden*** by Roy Diblik in ***Action 9: Design a layered landscape filled with plants***. In addition to providing helpful strategies for designing a natural landscape, Roy stresses that ease of maintenance needs to be integral to the design. His kindly suggestion that we get to know our plants in the same way we get to know people whom we care about helps us to place plants in communities with one another where they are more likely to thrive. Healthy, happy plants make the tasks of maintenance much easier and much more enjoyable!

Many of the books mentioned elsewhere include discussions of management and maintenance related to the primary topic of the book, for example ***Planting in a Post-Wild World*** (see pages 9.28 and 14.2 of this guide) contains management methods for keeping natural plantings looking legible and attractive; ***Garden Revolution*** (see pages 10.9 and 11.20) covers management strategies for ecological plantings such as meadows; similarly ***Prairie Up*** (see page 11.20) explains managing prairie plantings; and ***The Magical World of Moss Gardening*** (see page 11.16) explains how to manage moss plantings. As with ***The Know Maintenance Perennial Garden***, all these books stress the need to keep in mind future management needs when initially designing a planting.

Pruning is a less demanding task in natural plantings, but when pruning is needed, it's helpful to have a good reference handy. Although there are numerous more current books about pruning, somehow, I always reach for the ***Sunset Pruning Handbook*** by John McClements. Although it doesn't focus on native plants, guidelines are included for pruning many native species. This slim, unassuming volume is filled with clear and concise diagrams that take the mystery out of pruning. It's out of print but available used for a few dollars.

By taking time to evaluate and streamline systems for managing your wildlife habitat, you can take the drudgery out of landscape maintenance and replace it with gratifying stewardship. Caring for your landscape will become an experience full of discovery and joy. Natural landscapes challenge the cultural aesthetics dominated by lawn, foundation plants, and mulched beds. We can help our landscapes become more attractive to our neighbors by employing effective strategies. This is the topic of the next action!

Action 14—CHECKLIST
Build acceptance for nature's natural look

Step:	✔	Action Needed:	Page:
1	☐	Give your wildlife landscape a cared-for appearance	14.4
2	☐	Design your wildlife landscape to give it a defined and organized look	14.5
3	☐	Surround wild, natural plantings with orderly frames	14.6
4	☐	Incorporate plants and features to enhance the beauty and visual experience of your wildlife landscape	14.7
5	☐	Incorporate plants and features that awaken the senses and create opportunities for discovery	14.8
6	☐	Build a welcoming feeling of familiarity into your wildlife landscape	14.9

Colorful seed heads and foliage add seasonal interest and beauty to the entrance of this stately home. *Photo courtesy of Roy Diblik.*

Delicious edible native plants—a tempting invitation for neighbors and friends!

One of the most satisfying rewards of a wildlife habitat is the potentially bountiful harvest of native fruits, nuts, and vegetables. If you're lucky, your wild visitors and residents will share a little of the bounty with you!

Blackberries *(Rubus)*

Blueberries *(Vaccinium)*

Pawpaw *(Asimina triloba)*

 Find lists of edible native plants by searching online for **edible native plants [your state]**. Plant choices vary by ecoregion, of course. Use the **BONAP** maps and other resources mentioned in this guide to determine which edible plants are native to your local ecoregion.

Many delicious edible plants are also highly valuable to wildlife

If you would like to add beneficial edible plants to your landscape, consider visiting the **Xerces Society** website for a list of edible plants that are valuable to pollinators. Some of these also support caterpillars!

Habitat Assessment Guides

Pacific Northwest Bumble Bee Habitat Assessment Form...

Habitat Assessment Guide for Pollinators in Yards,...

Pollinators: Farms and Agricultural Landscapes

Idaho Farms and Agricultural Landscapes

Pennsylvania Farms and Agricultural Landscapes

Beneficial Insects: Farms and Agricultural

To find this list, search online for **xerces habitat assessment guides**. Download the **Habitat Assessment Guide for Pollinators in Yards, Gardens, and Parks.** The table of edible plants is at the bottom of the last page. We'll take another look at this assessment later in this action guide (see page II).

TABLE 2: EDIBLE LANDSCAPING PLANTS WITH VALUE TO POLLINATORS		
Abelmoschus esculentus [okra]	*Cucumis* [cucumber, melon]	*Origanum vulgare** [o
Allium*† [chives, garlic, leek, onions, shallot]	*Cucurbita*† [pumpkin, squash]	*Passiflora*† [passionfru
Amelanchier† [juneberry, serviceberry]	*Diospyros virginiana*† [common persimmon]	*Persea americana* [avo
Asimina† [pawpaws]	*Fagopyrum esculentum** [buckwheat]	*Phaseolus*† [bean (cor
*Anethum graveolens** [dill]	*Foeniculum vulgare** [fennel]	*Prunus*† [almond, apri
*Brassica** [broccoli, cabbage, cauliflower, kale]	*Fragaria*† [strawberry]	*Pyrus* [pear]
Calendula [calendula]	*Helianthus annuus*† [sunflower]	*Ribes*† [currant (black
Capsicum† [peppers (bell/chili, habanero)]	*Lavandula* [lavender]	*Rosa*† [rose (dogrose,
Castanea† [chestnut, chinquapin]	*Malus*† [apple, crab apple]	*Rubus*† [blackberry, ra
Citrullus [pine melon, watermelon]	*Matricaria** [chamomile]	*Sambucus*† [elderber
Citrus [lemon, lime, tangerine]	*Mentha**† [mint]	*Solanum*† [eggplant,
*Coriandrum sativum** [coriander/cilantro]	*Ocimum** [basil]	*Vaccinium*† [blueberr
Corylus† [hazelnut]	*Opuntia*† [prickly pear]	*Vicia*† [fava bean, vet
NOTES: *Must be allowed to bolt/flower †Some or all members of the genus are NATIVE to North America		

Action 14—GUIDE
Build acceptance for nature's natural look

Flowering shrubs and large forbs help build acceptance because they are pretty to look at, easy to grow, and fill spaces quickly while also providing habitat for wildlife.

Creating an attractive landscape filled with wildlife helps to educate others about the feasibility of planting eco-friendly landscapes and may even encourage others to plant such a landscape of their own. Depending on the culture of your neighborhood, however, gaining neighborhood acceptance of your wildlife-based design may pose a significant challenge as you transition your yard to a wildlife habitat.

In this action, we look at how to manage and present your landscape so that it gains neighborhood acceptance for the natural look of nature even where strict HOAs are the law of the land. Specifically, we focus on:

- giving your wildlife landscape a cared-for appearance

- designing your wildlife landscape to have a defined and organized look

- surrounding wild, natural plantings with orderly frames

- incorporating plants and features to enhance the *visual* experience of your wildlife landscape

- incorporating plants and features that create a *sensual* experience and a sense of discovery

- building a welcoming feeling into your landscape.

With thoughtful planning, your native landscape can be an invitation for others to welcome nature into their yards.

BEFORE edging

AFTER edging

Tidy edges are one of the most effective ways to give a landscape a cared-for look.

① Give your wildlife landscape a cared-for appearance

In 1995, Joan Nassauer, a professor in the School for Environment and Sustainability at the University of Michigan, authored the impactful paper *Messy Ecosystems, Orderly Frames* in which she introduced the concepts of **cues to care** (signs that a landscape is being taken care of) and **orderly frames** (physical and conceptual "frames" that give order and definition to a landscape). Maintaining cues to care and orderly frames are efficient means to help a natural landscape be visually appealing and culturally acceptable. In this action, we discuss both concepts. Let's start with cues to care.

Include cues to care in your landscape

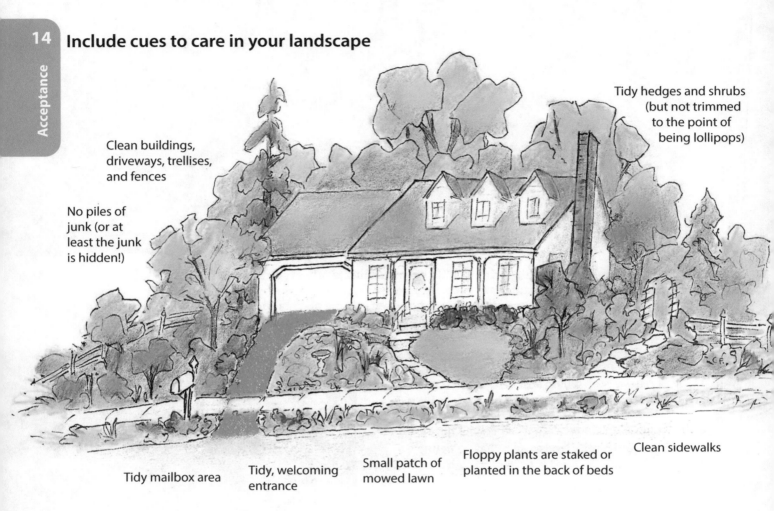

Clean buildings, driveways, trellises, and fences

No piles of junk (or at least the junk is hidden!)

Tidy hedges and shrubs (but not trimmed to the point of being lollipops)

Clean sidewalks

Tidy mailbox area

Tidy, welcoming entrance

Small patch of mowed lawn

Floppy plants are staked or planted in the back of beds

Life is busy, and it can be challenging to keep up with all the things that must be done. The cues-to-care shown above are some of the quickest, most visible actions to take when the pressure to gain neighborhood acceptance is high where you live.

Incorporating nature and beauty in our landscapes

In their book *Planting in a Post-Wild World: Designing Plant Communities for Resilient Landscapes*, Thomas Rainer and Claudia West highlight and explain Nassauer's concepts of cues to care and orderly frames and the important role they play in designing attractive natural landscapes. Through their compelling words and striking photographs, their message is clear: Our goal must be to keep it both wild *and* beautiful.

② Design your wildlife landscape to give it a defined and organized look

Nature can be messy, so it's our challenge to bring order while still enriching the wildlife ecosystem. If you're new to wildlife landscaping, consider starting with smaller plantings in the backyard, such as the **parent plant collection bed** or **starter bed** explained in *Action 9: Design a layered landscape.* Later, you can apply everything you learn in the backyard to landscaping the areas in public view. Now, let's look at some ways to get an attractive look right from the start.

Getting an attractive look right from the start

Make sure your landscape bed design is clear and orderly. Landscape designers refer to this as making the landscape **legible**. Using the design principles discussed in *Action 9: Design a layered landscape*, your landscape can provide wildlife benefits while ensuring that it has the added quality of being attractive.

Consider the height of plants when planning plant placement. Place low-growing plants in the front of planted areas. Place taller plants in the center of island beds and in the back of border beds. Not only will this be visually more pleasing, but it also will prevent plants from flopping onto walkways and needing staking.

Plant in drifts (groups of plants). Planting multiple plants of single species together gives the species presence and avoids the chaotic look of beds planted with individual specimens of many different species. Intermingle the drifts with each other at their edges (see page 9.9). Between the drifts, mass ground layer plants. Their lower height contrasts with the taller plants in the drifts creating easy to read garden patterns.

Select plants in keeping with the habitat a particular planting is intended to represent. For example, the jazzy colors of annual bedding plants would clash with a planting of coastal sage scrub. Similarly, the eastern prickly pear (*Opuntia humifusa*) would look odd growing among shade-loving woodland plants (and it would likely die in these growing conditions!).

Surround wild, natural plantings with orderly frames. Framing a planting is one of the most effective ways to give a landscape legibility—so much so that we dedicate the entire next step to the concept of frames and why frames matter.

3 Surround wild, natural plantings with orderly frames

Look at a framed picture on your wall and imagine it hanging on the wall without its frame. Likely it would look odd and less visually pleasing. Frames in a landscape are important because:

- frames provide crisp, clean edges that define the design of the landscape
- frames serve as a calming contrast, or foil, to the busyness of a planted bed
- frames invite viewers into the landscape and guide their eyes around it.

In the landscape, frames can be **physical**, such as a hedge, rock border, fence, or mowed path. Frames can also be **conceptual**, such as trees placed to frame a sunset view, or plants placed to guide—or "frame"—a visitor's experience of a space. To add definition and a sense of order to your wildlife landscape, consider incorporating frames into your landscape.

Incorporating frames to give definition and an organized look to your landscape

Mowing or trimming can give crisp, clean edges. For example, tidy, edged beds around caterpillar pupation sites under shrubs and trees show the neighborhood that your landscape is cared for.

Crisp, clean edges are made by the placement of pavers, stones, logs, bricks, or other materials. Hardscape borders help to organize a natural planting creating legibility for the viewer.

Walls and fences built of wood, stone, or other materials also create strong edges. They can define a space and give a sense of order.

Frames as a calming contrast

Frames as an invitation to experience the landscape

Hardscape provides a calming foil. Patios or decks can provide a calm contrast to wild or semi-wild plantings. A stone terrace can set off a planting. Lawn that remains can frame a planted bed or serve as a calm contrast to a meadow area.

Paths can define and organize a landscape. They're also an invitation to enter and explore the landscape. A formal garden will likely have defined, hardscape paths while a more natural landscape will likely have informal, unpaved, meandering paths.

4 Incorporate plants and features to enhance the beauty and visual experience of your wildlife landscape

Traditionally, color—that of flowers and foliage—has been foremost in designing an attractive landscape. Color will always be a draw; however, these days there is a trend toward appreciating other visual qualities of a planting. For example, the structure of plant arrangements enhances the overall visual experience while the individual structures of plants lend an intimate beauty. Noel Kingsbury, co-author with Piet Oudolf of *Planting: A New Perspective*, recommends taking black and white photographs of your landscape to analyze its structural strengths. With the factor of color removed, it is easier to evaluate the design and identify its weaknesses and strengths. Consider the following suggestions to increase the visual interest of your landscape.

Color of flowers, foliage, stems, branches, seed heads, and fruit

Colorful sequences of bloom

Contrasting color tones of foliage

Colorful branches—red-twig dogwood (*Cornus sericea*)

Colorful fruit or berries—American persimmon (*Diospyros virginiana*)

Contrasting and Interesting and plant structure

Contrasting structures—flower clumps, twisting trunks. A strong design of contrasting plant structures holds up even when viewed in black and white as shown above.

Multi-season interest

Spring ephemerals—brief but showy displays when little else is in bloom

Winter interest—variously shaped seed heads that last through the winter

Movement of wildlife, water, and wind

Wildlife activity around food and water sources

Fountains and waterfalls adding movement that draws attention

Architectural elements and decor

Terraces, gazebos, arches, stone walls, paths, pools

Garden art, statues, boulders that add interest

⑤ Incorporate plants and features that awaken the senses and create opportunities for discovery

In addition to designing gardens to be visually appealing, including plants that engage the senses of taste, touch, smell, and even sound will attract human visitors—especially children! Nancy Striniste, in her engaging book *Nature Play at Home: Creating Outdoor Spaces That Connect Children with the Natural World*, dedicates an entire chapter to "awakening the senses" with lists of mostly native plants that stimulate each sense. Here are some ideas for incorporating plants and features into your landscape to create a sensory experience and a sense of discovery.

Enhance the *sensory* interest of your landscape and create opportunities for discovery

Grow enchanting plants that seem to have a mind of their own. Some ripe seed heads will pop or explode when touched. The individual blooms of obedient plant (*Physostegia virginiana; above*) can be moved and they will stay in their new position (hence its name).

Grow plants that do curious things. Some plant species form **frost flowers** (miniature ice sculptures made from plant juices), such as *Verbesina* species or dittany (*Cunila origanoides; above*). The leaf stems of cup plant (*Silphium perfoliatum*) collect water and serve as drinking fountains for insects and birds.

Direct paths to interesting views or create secret hideaways that can only be discovered through exploration. Dense shrubs can form room-like spaces. Winding pathways among shrubbery or tall prairie plants and grasses can lead to unexpected clearings and secret gardens.

Grow fruiting plants along paths. Children and adults love to nibble on wild strawberries, black raspberries (*above*), lemonade berries, blueberries, and other tasty treats. Get to know your plants before snacking on them; raw elderberries are poisonous for example (see page 14.2 for more about edible plants).

Grow plants with different textures. Compare the surfaces of leaves and bark. Find smooth tree branches that can support your weight and use them like a gym bar to hang from. Plant trees with interesting bark, such as birches (*Betula*) whose bark peels off like thick sheets of paper.

Grow fragrant plants near seating. Since the sense of smell is closely linked with forming memories, their aroma may evoke happy recollections or form new memories to last a lifetime. Search online for **fragrant native plants [state]** or read native plant catalogs and plant labels.

Build a welcoming feeling of familiarity into your wildlife landscape

Removing lawn and replacing it with more natural plantings runs contrary to the prevailing landscape culture in the United States where foundation planting, pristine green lawns, and annual mulching is the norm. We humans are hardwired to perceive change as a threat. As we transition our landscapes to wildlife habitats, we can ease the worries of our less receptive family members and neighbors by making our landscape feel familiar and welcoming.

Ways to make your landscape feel familiar and welcoming

Create attractive entrances to your wildlife habitat that welcome visitors to enter and explore.

Guide people to destinations such as a bench from which to observe a birdbath, a scenic view, a fruit tree, or to a private outdoor "room" created by a planting of dense, leafy shrubs or conifers.

Set up benches or other seating areas in a prime pollinator or bird viewing area or beside a pond.

Grow plants that are familiar to people—for example, oak trees and daisy-like flowers, such as asters, coneflowers (*Echinacea*), black-eyed Susan or other *Rudbeckia* species.

Leave a small patch of lawn to appease reluctant neighbors. Lawn can be a calming offset to a natural native planting.

Put up signs that show your intentions. Signage helps educate people and build acceptance.

Finally, as Ian Caton, expert plantsperson and owner of the Wood Thrush Native Nursery in North Carolina, suggests:

> *You being out in your wildlife habitat enjoying your yard is one of the most effective ways to encourage neighborhood acceptance.*

Digging in deeper

Listed here are references and additional key resources related to building acceptance for nature's natural look (please refer to the Appendix for publication details).

Nature's Best Hope: A New Approach to Conservation That Starts in Your Yard: In *Action 9: Design a layered landscape filled with plants*, we referred to Doug's discussion about the challenges facing urban and suburban residents (see pages 185 - 201). This discussion is also relevant here. Doug gives examples of cues to care that show how native plants can fit well in managed landscapes.

In ***Planting in a Post-Wild World: Designing Plant Communities for Resilient Landscapes*** Thomas Rainer and Claudia West effectively popularized the concept of designing landscapes to be both ecologically functional and visually appealing. This impactful book contains a wealth of guidance for achieving balance between wild and beautiful.

In ***Planting: A New Perspective***, Piet Oudolf and Noel Kingsbury shed further insights into the role that thoughtful landscape design plays in building cultural acceptance for more natural landscapes. With structure being a key design element in bringing order and legibility to a planting, gaining an appreciation of the different structures of plants is essential. Oudolf and Kingsbury explain this well with clear diagrams (see pages 122 - 127 in their book) and go one step further by noting the structural type of each plant in their plant profiles (which include some plants native to the United States).

Creating appealing landscapes that also allow children to play and explore goes a long way toward building acceptance for nature's natural look. (When the kids are happy, everybody is happy!) In ***Nature Play at Home: Creating Outdoor Spaces That Connect Children with the Natural World***, Nancy Striniste provides page after page of inspiration for creating a rich wonderland that people from all ages will find engaging and, as a result, more acceptable.

Get a deeper understanding of the challenge of balancing ecological quality and our cultural concept of nature by reading Joan Nassauer's impactful article, ***Messy Ecosystems, Orderly Frames*** (1995). Get the thinking behind the concepts of ***cues to care*** and ***orderly frames***. Find the full article by searching online for the title. It is well worth the read!

The wilder your wildlife habitat and the more publicly visible it is, the more important it is to create legible landscape design that includes familiar elements in orderly frames and to maintain your landscape with cues to care in mind. Attractive native plantings serve as ambassadors that help to build acceptance for ecological landscapes among neighbors (and perhaps resistant spouses, too!). Your native landscape could be the inspiration for others to transform their yards into welcoming places for wildlife.

Action 15—CHECKLIST
Share, educate, and get involved

Step:	✔	Action Needed:	Page:
1	☐	Share your wildlife habitat experience to educate your family, friends, and neighbors	**15.4**
2	☐	Share your extra native plants—especially keystone species	**15.5**
3	☐	Network with your neighbors to create conservation corridors	**15.5**
4	☐	If your property is part of an HOA, become an active member and advocate to support insects and other wildlife	**15.6**
5	☐	Join local plant, nature, and conservation groups to take part in wildlife habitat protection and restoration efforts	**15.7**
6	☐	Participate in citizen science projects	**15.8**
7	☐	Engage children with nature	**15.9**

15

Share

15

Share

Action 15—GUIDE
Share, educate, and get involved

Large native gardens depend upon the help of volunteers. Here on the Golden West College campus in Huntington Beach, California, a convivial group of volunteers helps out weekly.

B y now, you may have planted every space you have available and taken every action you can to enhance your wildlife habitat, but you feel the urge to do more to support wildlife. This is an ideal time to reach out to people in your community who may be open to increasing the wildlife habitat on their properties. Sharing your knowledge and plants with neighbors, educating your community about the urgency of supporting wildlife, and getting involved at the local or national level can have profound positive effects on both the wildlife and human communities.

You may even wish to take it further and become an advocate or activist. Activism is usually associated with extroverts, but there are important behind-the-scenes roles for introverts as well. Public speaking or encouraging your neighbors to plant for wildlife may be too big a social stretch for you; fortunately, there are many ways to help wildlife and some of these are bound to be within your comfort zone.

In this action, we explore ways to share, educate, and get involved to help make supporting wildlife habitat a community priority.

Engaging people of all ages is essential to the success of restoring our local ecosystems.

Share your wildlife habitat experience to educate your family, friends, and neighbors

1

Sharing your experience with family, friends, and neighbors can go a long way toward educating the broader community about the urgency of supporting wildlife and the methods to do so. Casual interactions are an effective way of doing this. When a neighbor stops to chat, be ready to answer questions or share your goals. For example, a neighbor asking you about a certain plant is an opportunity to share that the plant is a host for a specific butterfly. Sharing your excitement about a pollinator garden you've just planted may inspire your friends to plant one. Family members may welcome your help in transforming an area of their property into wildlife habitat.

Signage helps to educate others by identifying the purpose of a planting.

Consider putting up signage that explains different aspects of your wildlife project. Such signage is likely to be a conversation starter. You may even want to put up small signs identifying plants. This not only helps visitors learn about plants, but it keeps track of the plant species you are growing. Laminating a catalog description of a plant makes a particularly informative label, and aluminum cans can be upcycled to make long-lasting plant labels.

Here we made plant labels by laminating plant catalog entries (*first and middle right*) to provide informative labels. Recycled aluminum cans are useful for making identification labels that last (*far right*). For directions to make these labels, see page 11.2.

As you gain expertise, you may offer to help a friend or neighbor identify invasive plants or even set a date to work together to begin removing them. If you are socially inclined, you might encourage people to visit your wildlife habitat so they can see what's working and get inspiration. Share things you've tried that didn't work along with your successes. As your yard fills with wildlife, you may want to share your experience on a more public scale by participating in a garden tour or helping with a native plant sale.

Local native plant nurseries sometimes team up with Wild Ones or native plant society chapters to hold special plant sales or bulk purchase events for members.

② Share your extra native plants—especially keystone species

With time, your plantings will expand allowing you to share plants and seeds with family, friends, and neighbors. Gather seeds, dig up a clump, or pot up volunteer seedlings especially keystone species! You might even consider intentionally sowing extra seed or taking extra cuttings to have some spare plants on hand to give away. If you have ambitious young helpers, perhaps they could set up a lemonade-style stand with extra plants. When sharing plants, it's helpful to include care sheets with the growing requirements for each plant.

Growing extra plants to share is a good way to help others establish their wildlife habitats.

③ Network with your neighbors to create conservation corridors

One of the most serious challenges facing wildlife survival is the lack of **conservation corridors** (connected wildlife habitats) due to urbanization and infrastructure such as roads. Ideally, these corridors (also called **biological, green, habitat,** or **wildlife corridors**) support wildlife populations in three primary ways:

- Corridors give animals access to the different types of habitats needed for their life cycle stages.
- Corridors allow nearby animal populations to interbreed resulting in genetic diversity.
- Corridors provide safe routes for migratory animals.

Conservation corridors should also be **dark corridors**. In urban settings where it may be challenging to create conservation corridors, a first step can be to turn out the lights at night to maintain dark corridors to allow nocturnal animals, such as bats and frogs, safe passage between the isolated habitats in which they may reside. The volunteer project **Pollinator Pathway** (*pollinator-pathway.org*) encourages communities to create **pollinator corridors** to provide pollinators with connected pollinator-friendly habitat and food sources.

Bringing communities together

Establishing conservation corridors by connecting wildlife habitats is one of the most effective actions a group of neighbors can take. A "neighboring property" might be the strip between the sidewalk and the road, the meridian in the center of a road, or the landscaped area of a local business. Even if these areas are not directly connected to your own wildlife habitat, the increase in the overall conservation mass will benefit some species.

With focused community advocacy, large projects can become a reality as well, such as restoring a local park to wildlife habitat, building bridges over busy roads, installing tunnels under new highway construction projects, growing native landscapes at libraries, churches, school yards, and so forth. Thoughtful analysis is needed to identify potential properties for corridors and advocate for their establishment. For invaluable information about wildlife corridors, visit **Conservation Corridor** (*conservationcorridor.org*).

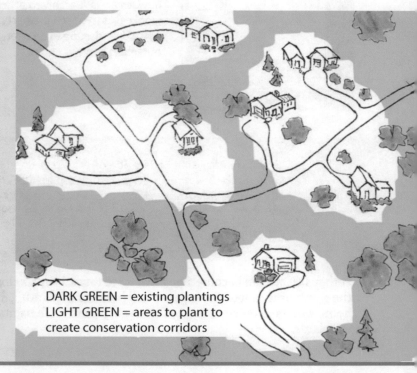

DARK GREEN = existing plantings
LIGHT GREEN = areas to plant to create conservation corridors

If your property is part of an HOA, become an active member and advocate to support insects and other wildlife

The urgency of creating space for wildlife to coexist in our human-dominated landscapes is immediate. As your wildlife habitat comes to life in your landscape, finding a way to share your experience will encourage others to welcome nature back into their lives. An effective way to make a difference is to participate in your homeowners association (HOA) if your property is subject to one. Many HOAs have a landscape committee which provides a vital opportunity to influence community landscape decisions and to encourage the planting of landscapes that support wildlife. Fortunately, some HOAs are becoming more receptive to the need for native plantings as awareness of the crisis of declining biodiversity grows; however, if you are facing a resistant HOA, consider reviewing some of the following resources.

HOAs often have the legal authority to enforce local ordinances which may include weed ordinances (also called **weed laws**) that may limit native plantings. If the "weed police" ever knock on your door, watch the **Wild Ones** *Weed Ordinances* video presented by Rosanne Plante, an attorney and **Wild Ones** *Wild Lawyer*. To view, do an online search for **wild ones weed ordinances webinar.**

Wild Ones *Wild Lawyer* Rosanne Plante also shares a *Sample Native Planting Ordinance*, a helpful starting point for incorporating native plant language into HOA rules or local ordinances. To watch the video *How to Make Friends with the "Weed Police"* and download the sample native planting ordinance, search online for **wild ones sample native planting ordinance.**

For a historic view of the legal battle to gain acceptance for natural plantings, search online for *Green Landscaping: Greenacres* in *The John Marshall Law Review,* an EPA-archived article from 1993. A fascinating read, it describes legal cases in which property owners fought to maintain their rights to a natural landscape in an even more restrictive time than the one we find ourselves in now.

The **National Wildlife Federation** offers the in-depth *Guide to Passing Wildlife-Friendly Property Maintenance Ordinances.* To read this 16-page PDF, do an online search for the title. This guide helps homeowners revise local ordinances and HOA policies to transform land into wildlife habitats. Sample model ordinances to guide natural landscaping (with links to a full ordinance) are included along with a model landscape master plan.

Perhaps HOAs can become a positive force toward supporting biodiversity and local abundance by educating the community about the urgency and benefits of planting for wildlife. They could encourage and guide homeowners to do what it takes to create rich wildlife habitat that meets the neighborhood landscape standards.

⑤ Join local plant, nature, and conservation groups to take part in wildlife habitat protection and restoration efforts

Becoming active in local and national groups provides opportunities to:

- connect and socialize with other people interested in supporting wildlife
- partake in community events, such as habitat restoration workdays or native plant sales
- attend presentations, workshops, and native garden and wildlife habitat tours
- advocate for regional or national conservation efforts.

Here, we focus on groups that have regional or state chapters or volunteer centers that organize events and meetings. If there is no group or chapter where you live, you might consider starting one.

Native plant societies

Many native plant societies host tours of members' native plant gardens.

Native plant societies provide a wealth of information. A native plant society chapter may not include the words "native plant society" in their name, such as the **Connecticut Botanical Society** founded in 1903. In addition to informative meetings and field trips, native plant societies have a wide variety of offerings, for example, the **Iowa Native Plant Society** offers restoration grant information and wildlife notecards. The **Georgia Native Plant Society** offers regional plant lists and educational events; the **Florida Native Plant Society** actively supports land acquisition for preservation, citizen science, restoration, and conservation of rare plants. Find the native plant society in your state by searching online for **native plant society [state or county].**

The **New York Botanical Garden** website hosts a list of all the native plant societies in the U.S. Find the list by searching online for **native plant societies nybg**. In the top menu, click **Native Plant Societies of the U.S.A**. A page for each state includes links to the state's native plant society, the society newsletter, region-specific recommended reading, and more.

Wild Ones: Native Plants, Natural Landscapes

The **Wild Ones** mission is to *"promote native landscapes through education, advocacy and collaborative action."* Members accomplish this mission through workshops, garden tours, meetings, a quarterly journal, and much more. Find the chapter nearest you by visiting **wildones.org/chapters** (see page 10.22). For information about the **Wild Ones** *Native Garden Plans*, see page 9.19. **Wild Ones** helps to provide practical approaches to building wildlife habitats.

The Nature Conservancy

Founded in 1951, the **Nature Conservancy** works on a global scale to conserve acres of land, river systems, lakes, wetlands, and oceans. To attend events, volunteer, or find educational resources, visit **nature.org**, click on the menu icon, click on **Get Involved**. Volunteer centers in 20 U.S. states need trail monitors, hike leaders, photographers and videographers, youth group leaders, social media ambassadors, and workday and event volunteers.

Join local plant, nature, and conservation groups to take part in wildlife habitat protection and restoration efforts, *continued*

The National Audubon Society

With over 450 local chapters nationwide and 41 centers, the **National Audubon Society** (NAS) offers countless events and opportunities to get involved. Join a birding group or learn from bird experts. Since birds require functioning global ecosystems to survive, the scope of the NAS is broad. Consider participating in their conservation projects. Visit **audubon.org**. In the top menu, click **Audubon Near You**. Click the interactive map or enter your state in the drop-down menu.

6 Participate in citizen science projects

Gathering data about the natural world and submitting the data to citizen science projects helps researchers find answers to real world problems. Here is a small sample of the many opportunities to participate in citizen science projects:

iNaturalist Projects

iNaturalist (*inaturalist.org/projects*). Start your own project or join ongoing projects taking place all over the world!

Night Sky

Measure Night-Sky Brightness Globe at Night (*globeatnight.org*). Learn to identify constellations and help document light pollution.

Invasive Species

EDDMapS (*eddmaps.org*). Track and report invasive plants and animals. Click *Training* to learn how to report data.

Bees

Bumble Bee Watch (*bumblebeewatch. org*). Participate in this collaborative effort to track and conserve North America's bumble bees.

Plants and Pollinators

Great Sunflower Project Program (*greatsunflower.org*). Help identify which plants best support pollinators. In the top menu, click *About,* click *How to Count.*

Plants

Budburst (*budburst.org*). Analyze plant life where you live and contribute data to help researchers identify the effects of climate change on plants and animals.

Butterflies

North American Butterfly Association Butterfly Count (*naba.org*). To participate in butterfly counts, from the *Get Involved* menu, click *Butterfly Monitoring.*

Monarch Watch (*monarchwatch. org*). Help track fall migration of the monarch butterfly. Scroll down and click *Research Projects* to view various monarch projects.

Butterflies and Birds

Journey North (*journeynorth.org*). Help track the migration of monarchs and birds and seasonal changes such as when trees leaf out.

Birds

eBird (*ebird.org*). Share your sightings. Between 2 and 3 million bird observations are recorded monthly.

Great Backyard Bird Count (*birdcount.org*) and the **National Audubon Society's Christmas Bird Count** (search online for **christmas bird count**). Help with global bird counts that assess global bird populations.

Nest Watch (*nestwatch.org*). Monitor nests to track status and trends in the reproductive biology of birds. Find nests. Record data. Directions are available for building nest boxes and structures for various bird species.

7 ## Engage children with nature

Children are one of the most compelling reasons for embarking on the journey to restore functional ecosystems where we live—not only to provide them with the rich experience of nature but also to ensure a legacy in which the rich biodiversity of our planet exists for them in the future.

In this action guide, we barely scratch the surface of the wealth of resources available to engage children with nature. An entire *Nature's Action Guide for Kids* would only begin to do justice to this important and expansive topic. Here, the best we can do is provide a tiny sample of these resources to spark further investigation. (Please refer to the Appendix for publication details.)

 For starters, ***Nature's Best Hope (Young Readers' Edition): How You Can Save the World in Your Own Yard*** by Doug Tallamy and adapted by Sarah L. Thomson is an exciting addition to the nonfiction genre for middle grades (ages 10 to 14). Also ideal for English-language learners and use in adult literacy programs, this small paperback is an easy-to-read adaptation of Tallamy's classic book. This resource helps to ensure that Doug's urgent call-to-action to support biodiversity and local abundance is accessible to all.

Creating a wildlife habitat is so ripe with opportunities to engage children with nature that an entire book could be written on the topic. Fortunately, Nancy Striniste has done exactly that in her book ***Nature Play at Home: Creating Outdoor Spaces that Connect Children with the Natural World***. It is chock-full of ideas that will inspire kids and grownup kids alike! Striniste considers all aspects of children's outdoor experience: arranging fascinating spaces, encouraging interaction with nature, building confidence, ensuring comfort and safety, and so much more. Helpful lists are relevant to wildlife habitats for people of all ages. This book is truly a work of art and well worth being in the personal library of every wildlife habitat steward.

Most nature and conservation organizations offer kids' activities, school kits, and other educational materials.

 An online search for **[organization's name] kids** usually yields enough educational materials and suggested activities to keep kids engaged for a long while. Or visit the website of your favorite nature group or your local native plant society chapter and search for **educational materials**. Here are two examples of what you might find:

The **Georgia Native Plant Society** (*gnps.org*) offers a list of K-12 materials listing over 20 state and national organizations, publications about gardening with children (including curriculum, activity books, and more), and a list of children's books about nature.

The **Xerces Society** *Xerces Kids (X Kids) Program* (*right*) offers an exciting package of free materials for children to embark upon an adventure to learn about invertebrates. Upon completion of the activity booklet, *X Kids* make a pledge and earn their *X Kids* badge. To join the adventure, search online for **xerces xkids**.

Join the adventure and become a Xerces Kid today!

What is the X Kids Program?

Many years ago, there was a butterfly called the Xerces blue. The Xerces blue lived in sand dunes on the edge of San Francisco in California and its caterpillars depended on specific plants growing there to eat. Over the years, the habitat got smaller as the city got bigger and eventually the butterflies no longer had the food and shelter they needed to survive. The Xerces blue butterfly was last seen alive in the early 1940s.

While this story is very sad, it sparked the idea to start an organization of people to help prevent this from happening to other butterflies and invertebrates. In 1971, the Xerces Society for Invertebrate Conservation was founded, named after the Xerces blue.

As an X Kid, you will use your superpowers to help the Xerces Society save incredible invertebrates!

Creating educational materials specific to your local ecoregion is a worthwhile project.

 Members of the **Native Plant Society of New Jersey** (npsnj.org) developed a 12-page **Native Plant School Guide** that introduces native plants and explains why they are important. The guide includes a garden design featuring eight readily available, reliable plants providing blooms from late Spring through Fall along with 50 nature activities across different subject areas. Find this guide by searching online for **npsnj native plant school guide**. You might find yourself inspired to create a similar booklet for your local ecoregion!

Once you start exploring all the resources available for children, you may be amazed by the quantity and quality of materials just waiting to engage the children in your life.

Digging in deeper

Listed here are additional resources related to sharing, educating, and getting involved in supporting wildlife biodiversity and abundance (please refer to the Appendix for publication details).

Nature's Best Hope: A New Approach to Conservation That Starts in Your Yard: Teaming up with neighbors and like-minded community members increases the likelihood of success (see pages 207 - 208). Doug urges people to join civic organizations such as HOAs and educate their fellow members while keeping an open mind and a willingness to compromise (see page 211).

Wildlife and conservation organizations

There are numerous worthwhile organizations dedicated to wildlife and conservation, some of which have been mentioned elsewhere in this guide. Although they may not offer local activities, your participation or membership in these organizations helps to support their important efforts. Here are just a few that you may wish to explore:

American Bird Conservancy

American Conservation Experience

American Forests

Bat Conservation International

Butterflies and Moths of North America

Center for Biological Diversity

Conservation Corridor

Conservation International

Cornell Lab of Ornithology

DarkSky International

Defenders of Wildlife

Ducks Unlimited, Inc.

Earthwatch

Firefly Atlas

Firefly Conservation & Research

Friends of the Earth

Green America

Greenpeace

The Grey Water Project

Homegrown National Park

iNaturalist

Land Trust Alliance

Master Gardener programs (Cooperative Extension Service)

Master Naturalist programs (Cooperative Extension Service)

National Audubon Society

National Park Foundation

National Wildlife Federation

Native plant societies

Natural Resources Defense Council

The Nature Conservancy

North American Butterfly Association

Oceana

Pollinator Pathway

Pollinator Partnership

Quiet Communities

River Network

Sierra Club

Student Conservation Association

Trout Unlimited

Trust for Public Land

Wild Ones

Wildlife Conservation Society

Wildlife Habitat Council

Wildlife Society

Wilderness Society

Wildlife Conservation Society

WWF—World Wildlife Fund

Xerces Society

And many other specialized groups

To learn more about these organizations and get involved, do an online search for the name of the organization.

In this action, we explored ways to share, educate, and get involved in supporting biodiversity and abundance. You can help make supporting wildlife habitat a community priority and an attainable goal.

CONCLUSION
Enjoy your wildlife habitat!

A magnolia warbler (*Setophaga magnolia*) pauses in its hunt for caterpillars on bald cypress (*Taxodium distichum*). *Photo courtesy of Sharon Sorenson.*

As you take the actions outlined in this guide, know that you are part of a broad community working to welcome nature back into our yards. Every action you take matters as we give it our all to preserve and create the habitats required to sustain wildlife. In this final chapter, we share several tools for assessing your wildlife habitat. We also show just a few of the telltale signs that your landscape is brimming with life and doing its job of providing essential ecological services. As your own wildlife habitat unfolds, we wish you many happy wildlife surprises.

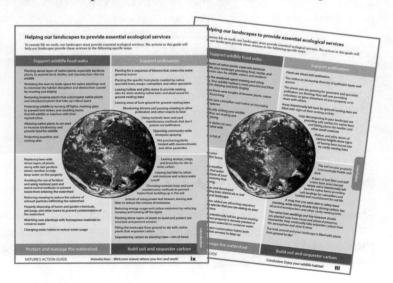

We began this journey by discussing the ways we can help our landscapes to provide essential ecological services (see page ix). Now, we can appreciate all the essential ecological services our landscape is providing (see page III)!

Assess your wildlife habitat

Spending time in your landscape has no doubt given you a pretty good idea about how well your wildlife ecosystem is functioning. Observing and documenting what you see can provide helpful records for spotting trends, such as the date of the first sighting of a butterfly species each year, the annual arrival of a migrating bird, the bloom peaks of different plants, or the dates of an oak **mast year** (a year in which the harvest is greater than normal).

Use the D.A.F.O.R. scale to record fluctuating wildlife populations

D.A.F.O.R scale:

D - Species observed is **Dominant** in a given area.

A - Species observed is **Abundant** in a given area.

F - Species observed is **Frequent** in a given area.

O - Species observed is **Occasional** in a given area.

R - Species observed is **Rare** in a given area.

Documenting the fluctuating populations of the flora and fauna on your property is a useful measure of biodiversity and local abundance. Along with keeping a tally of sightings, the D.A.F.O.R. scale is a handy, informal tool for recording bird, pollinator, and Lepidoptera populations. These are naturally occurring populations, in contrast to the populations of plants that are heavily influenced by our planting choices. Although this scale gives only a rough estimate of species abundance, it can provide insight into the population fluctuations of a wildlife ecosystem when recorded at regular intervals.

Pollinator habitat assessment guides from the Xerces Society

The **Xerces Society** *Habitat Assessment Guide for Pollinators in Yards, Gardens, and Parks* is an informative tool that guides readers through the habitat assessment process using photos that clearly illustrate assessment criteria. For example, a chart tracking the movement of pollinators through a neighborhood is shown to explain how important neighborhood efforts can be for pollinator survival. Another graphic shows three landscapes representing less than 10% native flowers, approximately 50%, and greater than 80% native flowers, and elsewhere, front and back yard before-and-after photos are shown. A score can be assigned for each item; then, all the scores can be tallied for an overall habitat assessment score. After making habitat improvements, the Xerces Society recommends doing the assessment again.

The Xerces Society offers equally impressive pollinator habitat guides for farms, agricultural landscapes, natural areas, rangelands, and more. Visit *xerces.org/habitat-assessment-guides*.

Recording "life lists" of birds and other animals

Along with the excitement of spotting a new bird or other animal, adding the sighting to a **life list** is another form of wildlife habitat assessment. A life list might be something as simple as checking off and recording the date and location of a new sighting in a bird or caterpillar identification book or adding a sighting to a life list maintained on a birding app such as Merlin.

Helping our landscapes to provide essential ecological services

All your efforts have come to fruition! If you are just starting out, your landscape is poised to come to life; or it may already be teeming with movement and birdsong as it provides these essential ecological services.

Support wildlife food webs

Dense layers of native plants, especially keystone plants, fill your landscape providing food, shelter, and reproduction sites for wildlife visitors and residents.

Gone are the weekends spent mowing and string trimming. Your wildlife habitat is more peaceful and filled with insects chirping and birds singing.

Where once there were tangles of invasive plants, native plants are flourishing.

You regularly spot caterpillars and notice an increasing diversity of species.

Birds are not only visiting your wildlife habitat, but they are staying and raising their young.

The nights are darker on your property and alive with insects.

Your property is full of movement.

Support pollinators

Plants are abuzz with pollinators.

You notice an increasing diversity of pollinator types and species.

The plants you are growing for generalist and specialist pollinators are thriving; they self-sow providing volunteers to grow elsewhere on your property or to share with others.

Areas intentionally left bare for ground-nesting bees are filled with signs of their nesting activity.

Logs decomposing in your landscape are providing safe cavities for native bees and hiding places for beetles and other small creatures.

Pithy and hollow stems of various heights show signs of having been bored into by cavity-nesting bees.

Protect and manage the watershed

Water soaks into your property without leaving, even after heavy rainfall.

During an intense weather event, you notice that water flowing across sections of your property is clear, meaning that erosion isn't occurring.

You have found ways and developed systems to avoid using toxic chemicals in and around your home and landscape.

The water features you added are attracting migratory birds including some species that you are seeing on your property for the first time

Except for bare spots intentionally left for ground-nesting bees, your property is densely planted or mulched with homegrown materials to conserve water.

You have developed water conservation habits both indoors and outdoors.

Build soil and sequester carbon

The soil on your property is increasingly friable and dark.

A layer of leaf litter and duff covers bare areas (except where soil is intentionally left bare for native bees) providing habitat and nourishment for soil life and soft landings for caterpillars.

A snag that you were able to safely leave standing has attracted woodpeckers and other cavity-nesting birds while doing double duty storing carbon.

The native tree seedlings and tiny bareroot shrubs you planted now have a visual and physical presence; plus, they continually sequester carbon from the atmosphere and store it away.

You look around and your landscape is filled with plants from ground to sky!

Conclusion

Signs that your wildlife habitat is brimming with life

Small treasures, such as feathers, nests, and hatched eggshells start showing up.

Birds that need spacious habitat are at home and reproducing in your landscape.

A baby confirms that a pair of birds you rarely see is nesting in your wildlife habitat.

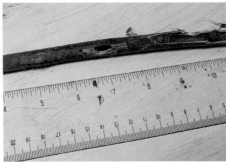

You spot holes in the stems that you left standing for insects to pupate and nest in.

You notice shavings that have dropped from stems that you left for stem-nesting bees.

You happen to snap a photo just as a small stem-nesting bee is entering a stem.

You discover a pupa in the leaf litter that you left beneath an oak tree.

Throughout your landscape, you find rolled and bundled up leaves housing pupating caterpillars.

You chance upon a pair of butterflies mating.

You build and they come (within minutes and before it's even done!).

Where once there were none, now there are five!

Be it ever so humble, there's no place like home.

Onward and upward!

Although we have come to the end of this action guide, whether you are just starting out or leagues beyond, an exciting journey lies ahead as we work together to build functioning ecosystems that support biodiversity and local abundance. I hope we meet someday along the way!

Let's show the world it can be done!

APPENDIX
References & Recommended Resources

Listed here are the books, articles, videos, and other media used as references and recommended for further exploration of the topics in *Nature's Action Guide*. The page numbers in brackets at the end of each entry indicate the location where the entry was used as a reference or mentioned in *Nature's Action Guide*.

Alexander, Rosemary, and Rachel Myers. (2017). *The Essential Garden Design Workbook: Completely Revised and Expanded* [Book]. Portland, OR: Timber Press. [see p. 9.28]

All About Birds. (n.d.). Why birds hit windows: And how you can prevent it [Article]. *Cornell Lab of Ornithology*. https://www.allaboutbirds.org/news/why-birds-hit-windows-and-how-you-can-help-prevent-. [see p. 2.6]

Allen, Thomas J., James P. Brock, and Jeffrey Glassberg. (2005). *Caterpillars in the Field and Garden: A Field Guide to the Butterfly Caterpillars of North America* [Book]. Cary, NC: Oxford University Press. [see p. 5.24]

American Bird Conservancy [Website]. abcbirds.org. [see pp. 2.6, 2.10]

Beaury, E. M., Patrick, M., & Bradley, B. A. (2021). Invaders for sale: the ongoing spread of invasive species by the plant trade industry [Article]. *Frontiers in Ecology and the Environment*, 19(10), 550–556. doi.org/10.1002/fee.2392. [see p. 4.6]

Beck, Travis (2013). *Principles of Ecological Design* [Book]. Washington, DC: Island Press. [see p. 9.28]

Bee and Pollinator Books by Heather Holm [Website]. pollinatorsnativeplants.com. [see pp. 6.12, 7.16]

Bee City USA [Website]. Xerces Society Initiative. beecity.usa. [see p. 3.16]

Bee Machine [Website]. beemachine.ai. [see page 6.11]

Bennie, J., Thomas, D. W., Cruse, D., & Gaston, K. J. (2016). *Ecological effects of artificial light at night on wild plants* [Article]. Journal of Ecology. 104, 611-620. https://besjournals.onlinelibrary.wiley.com/doi/pdf/10.1111/1365-2745.12551. [see p. 1.11]

Benyus, Janine M. (1989). *The Field Guide to Wildlife Habitats of the Eastern United States* [Book]. New York, NY: Fireside. [see pp. xiii, 5.24]

Benyus, Janine M. (1989). *The Field Guide to Wildlife Habitats of the Western United States* [Book]. New York, NY: Fireside. [see pp. xiii, 5.24]

Beyond Pesticides [Website]. beyondpesticides.org. [see pp. 10.23, 12.4, 12.7]

Beyond Pesticides. (2022-23). *Transformative Change 2022-23. Pesticides and You* [PDF Book]. 42(1-4) and 43(1). https://www.beyondpesticides.org/assets/media/documents/journal/BP-TransformativeChange.2022.23.pdf. [see p. 12.4]

Biota of North America Project (BONAP) [Website]. bonap.org. Kartesz, J.T., 2015. North American Plant Atlas (http://bonap.net/napa). Chapel Hill, N.C. [maps generated from Kartesz, J.T. 2015. Floristic Synthesis of North America, Version 1.0. Biota of North America Program (BONAP). (in press)]. [see pp. 5.4, 5.12-5.17, 6.8, 11.11]

Birdcast [Website]. Cornell Lab of Ornithology, Colorado State University, & University of Massachusetts Amherst. birdcast.info. [see p. 1.5]

Bradley, Fern Marshall, Barbara W. Ellis, and Deborah L. Martin. (2010). *The Organic Gardener's Handbook of Natural Pest and Disease Control: A Complete Guide to Maintaining a Healthy Garden and Yard the Earth-Friendly Way* [Book]. Emmaus, PA: Rodale Books. [see p. 12.12]

Brenner, Kelly. (2023). *The Naturalist at Home: Projects for Discovering the Hidden World Around Us* [Book]. Seattle, WA: Mountaineers Books. [see p. 15.9]

Bryce, S. A., Woods, A. J., Morefield, J. D., Omernik, J. M., McKay, T. R., Brackley, G. K., Hall, R. K., Higgins, D. K., McMorran, D. C., Vargas, K. E., Petersen, E. B., Zamudio, D. C., and Comstock, J. A. (2003). *Ecoregions of Nevada* [Color poster with map, descriptive text, summary tables, and photographs]. Reston, Virginia, U.S. Geological Survey (map scale 1:1,350,000). [see p. 5.19]

Budburst [Website]. budburst.org. [see p. 15.8]

Bumble Bee Atlas [Website]. Xerces Society Project. bumblebeeatlas.org. [see p. 6.11]

Bumble Bee Watch [Website]. bumblebeewatch.org. [see p. 15.8]

Burrell, C. Colston. (2011). *Native Alternatives to Invasive Plants* [Book]. Brooklyn, NY: Brooklyn Botanic Gardens. [see p. 4.22]

Burris, Judy, and Wayne Richards. (2011). *The Secret Lives of Backyard Bugs: Discover Amazing Butterflies, Moths, Spiders, Dragonflies, and Other Insects* [Book]. North Adams, MA: Storey Publishing. [see p. 7.4]

Butterflies and Moths of North America (BAMONA) [Website]. butterfliesandmoths.org. Lotts, Kelly and Naberhaus, Thomas, coordinators, 2021. [see p. 7.5]

California Invasive Pest Council--Don't Plant a Pest! [Website]. cnps.org. [see p. 4.22]

Call 811 [Website]. Common Ground Alliance. call811.com. [see p. 3.15]

Calscape [Website]. California Native Plant Society. calscape.org. [see p. 10.24]

Carson, Rachel L. (1962). *Silent Spring* [Book]. New York, NY: Houghton Mifflin Company. [see p. 12.4]

Cary Memorial Library. (2022, May 11). *Kill your lawn with Dan Jaffe Wilder* [Video]. YouTube. youtube.com/watch?v=TF3elkOcqr8. [see p. 3.16]

Center for Disease Control and Prevention (CDC) [Website]. cdc.gov. [see pp. 2.10, 2.14]

Chapman, Karen. (2019). *Deer-Resistant Design: Fence-free Gardens That Thrive Despite the Deer* [Book]. Portland, OR: Timber Press. [see p. 2.16].

ChipDrop [Website]. getchipdrop.com. [see p. 3.16]

Chisholm, Linda A. (2018). *The History of Landscape Design in 100 Gardens* [Book]. Portland, OR: Timber Press. [see p. 9.28].

Clausen, Ruth Rogers, and Gregory D. Tepper. (2021). *Deer-Resistant Native Plants for the Northeast* [Book]. Portland, OR: Timber Press. [see p. 2.16]

Colla, Sheila, Leif Richardson, and Paul Williams. (2011). *Bumble Bees of the Eastern United States* [Book]. Washington, DC: USDA. Forest Service & Pollinator Partnership. [see p. 6.11].

Conservation Corridor [Website]. conservationcorridor.org. [see p. 15.5]

The Conservation Foundation. (2021, March 17). *It starts with a raindrop: Planning your rain garden* [Video]. YouTube. youtube.com/watch?v=IpzSfyfP9lg. [see p. 8.6]

Cornell Lab All About Birds [Website]. allaboutbirds.org. [see p. 2.6]

Cubie, Jim. (2020, Nov 12). *Consumer Guide to Bird Window Strike and Collision Prevention* [PDF Guide]. ornithologycenter.com/protectbirds. [see p. 2.16]

Cullina, William. (2000). *The New England Wild Flower Society Guide to Growing and Propagating Wildflowers of the United States and Canada* [Book]. New York, NY: Houghton Mifflin Company. [see p. 10.24]

Cullina, William. (2008). *Native Ferns, Moss & Grasses* [Book]. New York, NY: Houghton Mifflin Company. [see p. 10.24]

Cullina, William. (2019). *Native Trees, Shrubs, and Vines: A Guide to Using, Growing, and Propagating North American Woody Plants* [Book]. Brattleboro, VT: Echo Point Books. [see p. 10.24]

Cullina, William. (2020). *Native Ferns, Moss & Grasses (Reprint Edition)* [Book]. Brattleboro, VT: Echo Point Books. [see pp. 10.24, 11.16]

Czarapata, Elizabeth J. (2005). *Invasive Plants of the Upper Midwest: An Illustrated Guide to Their Identification and Control* [Book]. Madison, DE: University of Wisconsin Press. [see p. 4.22]

Darke, Rick, and Douglas W. Tallamy. (2014). *The Living Landscape: Designing for Beauty and Biodiversity in the Home Garden* [Book]. Portland, OR: Timber Press. [see p. 9.28]

DarkSky International [Website]. darksky.org. [see pp. 1.2, 1.6-1.7]

dBird. A project of NYC Audubon [Website]. dbird.org. [see p. 2.7]

Department of Climate Change, Energy, the Environment and Water, Australian Government. (n.d.). Light pollution undermines ecological communities [Article]. dcceew.gov.au/environment/biodiversity/publications/national-light-pollution-guidelines-wildlife. [see p. 1.12]

Diblik, Roy. (2014). *The Know Maintenance Perennial Garden* [Book]. Portland, OR: Timber Press. [see pp. 9.5, 9.18, 9.28, 13.10]

Diboll, Neil, and Hilary Cox. (2023). *The Gardener's Guide to Prairie Plants* [Book]. Chicago, IL: University of Chicago Press. [see pp. 5.24, 10.2, 11.2]

Discover Life [Website]. Sam Houston State University, Texas. discoverlife.org. [see p. 5.24]

Early Detection & Distribution Mapping System (EDDMapS) [Website]. eddmaps.org. The University of Georgia–Center for Invasive Species and Ecosystem Health. [see pp. 4.12-4.13, 15.8]

eBird [Website]. ebird.org. [see p. 9.20]

Eisenbeis, G. & Hänel, A. (2009). Chapter 15. Light pollution and the impact of artificial night lighting on insects [Chapter]. In McDonnell, M. J., Hahs, A. H., Breuste, J. H. *Ecology of Cities and Towns* (pp. 243-263). New York, NY: Cambridge University Press. [see p. 1.4]

ELA Ecological Landscaping Alliance [Website]. ecolandscaping.org. [see p. 15.8]

Environmental Working Group (EWG) [Website]. ewg.org. [see p. 12.11]

Falchi, F., Cinzano, P., Duriscoe, D., Kyba, C. C. M., Elvidge, C. D., Baugh, K., Portnov, B. A., Rybnikova, N. A., & Furgoni, R. (2016). The new world atlas of artificial night sky brightness [Article]. *Science Advances*, 2(6), doi.org/10.1126/sciadv.1600377. [see p. 1.4]

Fallon, Candace, Sarah Hoyle, Sara Lewis, Avalon Owens, Eric Lee-Mäder, Scott Hoffman Black, and Sarina Jepsen. (2019). *Conserving the Jewels of the Night: Guidelines for Protecting Fireflies in the United States and Canada* [PDF Book]. Portland, OR: Xerces Society for Invertebrate Conservation. [see p. 1.9]

Firefly [Website], firefly.org. [see p. 1.12]

Firefly Atlas [Website], fireflyatlas.org. [see p. 1.12]

Fowler, J. (2020). Host Plants for Pollen Specialist Bees of the Eastern United States [Website]. jarrodfowler.com/host_plants.htm. [see pp. 6.9, 10.22]

Fowler, J. (2020). Pollen Specialist Bees of the Central United States [Website]. jarrodfowler.com/bees_pollen.html. [see pp. 6.7, 6.9]

Fowler, J. (2020). Pollen Specialist Bees of the Western United States [Website]. jarrodfowler.com/pollen_specialist.html. [see pp. 6.7, 6.9]

Fowler, J. (2022), Bumble Bee Flower Finder [Website]. bumblebeeflowerfinder.info. [see p. 6.10]

Fowler, J., & Droege, S. (2020). Pollen Specialist Bees of the Eastern United States [Website]. jarrodfowler.com/specialist_bees.html. [see pp. 6.7, 6.9]

Garden for Wildlife [Website]. National Wildlife Federation. https://gardenforwildlife.com. [see p. 10.22]

Gènissel, A., Aupinel, P., Bressac, C., Tasei, J.-N., & Chevrier, C. (2002). Influence of pollen origin on performance of Bombus terrestris micro-colonies [Article]. Entomologia Experimentalis et Applicata, 104(2-3), 329-336,. https://doi.org/10.1046/j.1570-7458.2002.01019.x. [see p. 4.20]

Ghazoul, Jaboury. (2020). *Ecology: A Very Short Introduction* [Book]. New York, NY: Oxford University Press. [see p. xiv]

Glime, Janice M. (2017). *Bryophyte Ecology* [eBook]. Houghton, MI: Michigan Technological University. digitalcommons.mtu.edu/bryophyte-ecology. [see p. 11.16].

Globe at Night [Website]. globeatnight.org. [see p. 15.8]

Great Backyard Bird Count [Website]. birdcount.org. [see p. 15.8]

Great Sunflower Project [Website]. greatsunflower.org. [see p. 15.8]

Griffith, G. E., Omernik, J. M., Comstock, J. A., Schafale, M. P., McNab, W. H., Lenat, D. R., MacPherson, T. F., Glover, J. B., and Shelburne, V. B. (2002). *Ecoregions of North Carolina and South Carolina* [Color poster with map, descriptive text, summary tables, and photographs]. Reston, Virginia, U.S. Geological Survey (map scale 1:1,500,000). [see p. 5.21]

Griffith, G.E., Omernik, J.M., Smith, D.W., Cook, T.D., Tallyn, E., Moseley, K., and Johnson, C.B. (2016) *Ecoregions of California* [Poster: U.S. Geological Survey Open-File Report 2016–1021, with map, scale 1:1,100,000]. http://dx.doi.org/10.3133/ofr20161021. [see p. 5.21]

Hallmann, C. A., Sorg, M., Jongejans, E., Siepel, H., Hofland, N., Schwan, H., Stenmans, W., Müller, A., Sumser, H., Hörren, T., Goulson, D., & de Kroon, H. (2017). More than 75 percent decline over 27 years in total flying insect biomass in protected areas [Article]. *PloS One,* 12(10). https://doi.org/10.1371/journal.pone.0185809. [see p. 1.4]

Hoffman Nursery [Website]. hoffmannursery.com. [see p. 11.20]

Hoffman, Shawna. (2023). *A Healthier Home: The Room-by-Room Guide to Make Any Space a Little Less Toxic* [Book]. Beverly, MA: Fair Winds Press. [see p. 12.12]

Holm, Heather N. (2014). *Pollinators of Native Plants: Attract, Observe and Identify Pollinators and Beneficial Insects with Native Plants* [Book]. Minnetonka, MN: Pollinator Press LLC. [see p. 6.12]

Holm, Heather N. (2017). *Bees: An Identification and Native Plant Forage Guide* [Book]. Minnetonka, MN: Pollinator Press LLC. [see p. 6.12]

Holm, Heather N. (2021). *Wasps: Their Biology, Diversity, and Role as Beneficial Insects and Pollinators of Native Plants* [Book]. Minnetonka, MN: Pollinator Press LLC. [see p. 6.12]

Homegrown National Park (HNP) [Website]. homegrownnationalpark.org. [see pp. xi, 5.11, 9.20, 9.26-9.27, 10.22]

Horton, K. G., Nilsson, C., Van Doren, B. M., La Sorte, F. A., Dokter, A. M., & Farnsworth, A. (2019). Bright lights in the big cities: migratory birds' exposure to artificial light [Article]. *Frontiers in Ecology and the Environment,* 17(4), 209–214. doi.org/10.1002/fee.2029. [see p. 1.5]

Huegel, Craig N. (2019). *The Nature of Plants: An Introduction to How Plants Work* [Book]. Gainesville, FL: University Press of Florida. [see p. 11.24]

The Humane Society of the United States. (n.d.) Pool safety for wild animals: Simple ways to save the lives of your wild neighbors [Article]. https://www.humanesociety.org/resources/pool-safety-wild-animals. [see p. 2.5]

iNaturalist [Website]. inaturalist.org. [see p. 15.8]

Invasive Plant Atlas [Website]. invasive.org. [see pp. 4.14-4.15]

Johnson, Catherine. J., and Susan McDiarmid. (2004). *Welcoming Wildlife to the Garden: Creating Backyard and Balcony Habitats for Wildlife* [Book]. Vancouver, BC: Hartley and Marks Publishers. [see p. 7.16]

Journey North [Website]. journeynorth.org. [see pp. 7.14, 15.8]

Justice, M. J., & Justice, T. C. (2016). Attraction of insects to incandescent, compact fluorescent, halogen, and LED lamps in a light trap: Implications for light pollution and urban ecologies [Article]. *Entomological News,* 125(5), 315–326. doi.org/10.3157/021.125.0502. [see p. 1.8]

Kaufman, Syl Ramsey, and Wallace Kaufman. (2013). *Invasive Plants: Guide to Identification and the Impacts and Control of Common North American Species* [Book]. Mechanicsburg, PA: Stackpole Books. [see p. 4.22]

Klem, Daniel, Jr. (2021). *Solid Air. Invisible Killer: Saving Billions of Birds from Windows* [Book]. Blaine, WA: Hancock House Publishers. [see p. 2.16]

Koch, Jonathan, James Strange, and Paul Williams. (2012). *Bumble Bees of the Western United States* [PDF Book]. Publication No. FS-972. Washington, DC: USDA Forest Service Research Notes. [see p. 6.11]

Kock, Henry, Paul Aird, John Ambrose, and Gerald Waldron. (2008). *Growing Trees from Seed: A Practical Guide to Growing Native Trees, Vines and Shrubs* [Book]. Buffalo, NY: Firefly Books. [see p. 10.24]

Lady Bird Johnson and Xerces Society Plant Database for Pollinators [Website]. wildflower.org/project/pollinator-conservation. [see p. 7.13]

Lady Bird Johnson Wildflower Center: Native Plants of North America [Website]. wildflower.org/plants-main. [see pp. 9.5, 10.24]

Lavelle, C. and M. Lavelle. (2017). *The Illustrated Practical Guide to Wildlife Gardening: How to Make Wildflower Meadows, Ponds, Hedges, Flower Borders, Bird Feeders, Wildlife Shelters, Nesting Boxes, and Hibernation Sites* [Book]. London, UK: Hermes House. [see p. xiv]

Lawson, Nancy. (2017). *The Humane Gardener: Nurturing a Backyard Habitat for Wildlife (How to Create a Sustainable and Ethical Garden That Promotes Native Wildlife, Plants, and Biodiversity)* [Book]. New York, NY: Princeton Architectural Press. [see p. 2.16]

Leopold, Donald J. (2005). *Native Plants of the Northeast: A Guide for Gardening and Conservation* [Book]. Portland, OR: Timber Press. [see p. 5.24]

Loss S. R., Will, T., & Marra, P. P. (2013). The impact of free-ranging domestic cats on wildlife of the United States [Article]. *Nature Communications.* 4:1396. doi: 10.1038/ncomms2380. [see p. 2.10]

Loss, S. R., Will, T., Loss, S. S., & Marra, P. P. (2014). Bird–building collisions in the United States: Estimates of annual mortality and species vulnerability [Article]. *The Condor* (Los Angeles, CA.).116(1), 8–23. [see p. 1.5]

Loughnan, D., Thomson, J. D. Ogilvie, J. E., & Gilbert, B. (2014). Taraxacum officinale pollen depresses seed set of montane wildflowers through pollen allelopathy. *Journal of Pollination Ecology,* 13, 146-150. https://doi.org/10.26786/1920-7603)2014)13. (see p. 4.20].

Martin, Annie. (2015). *The Magical World of Moss Gardening* [Book]. Portland, OR: Timber Press. [see pp. 11.14, 11.16, 13.10]

Master Gardeners of Northern Virginia (MGVN) Illustrated Glossary [Website]. mgnv.org/plants/glossary. [see pp. 4.22, 5.24, 10.24]

APPENDIX
References & Recommended Resources

Master Gardeners of Northern Virginia. (2023, May 9). *Browsers of the garden buffet: Strategies for living with deer* [Video]. YouTube. youtube.com/watch?v=BJ1DIFGRza8. [see p. 2.16]

McClements, John K. (1990). *Pruning Handbook* [Book]. Menlo Park, CA: Sunset Publishing Company. [see p. 13.10]

Mellichamp, Larry. (2014). *Native Plants of the Southeast: A Comprehensive Guide to the Best 460 Species for the Garden* [Book]. Portland, OR: Timber Press. [see p. 5.24]

Merlin Bird ID [Website]. Cornell Lab of Ornithology. merlin.allaboutbirds.org. [see p. 7.16]

Missouri Botanical Garden: Plant Finder [Website]. missouribotanicalgarden.org/plantfinder/plantfindersearch.aspx. [see p. 9.5]

Møller, A. P. (2019). Parallel declines in abundance of insects and insectivorous birds in Denmark over 22 years [Article]. *Ecology and Evolution*, 9(11), 6581–6587. doi.org/10.1002/ece3.5236. [see p. 1.4]

Monarch Watch [Website]. monarchwatch.org. [see p. 15.8]

Morris, Peter. (1995). *Methods of Environmental Impact Assessment* [Book]. Vancouver, BC: University of British Columbia Press. [see p. II]

Mountain Moss [Website]. mountainmoss.com. [see pp. 11.14-11.16]

Mt. Cuba Center: Trial Garden [Website]. mtcubacenter.org/research/trial-garden. [see p. 11.20]

Narango, D. L. (2018). *The effects of nonnative plants on food webs in residential landscapes* [Dissertation]. University of Delaware. [see p. 5.1]

Narango, D. L., Tallamy, D. W., & Shropshire, K. J. (2020). Few keystone plant genera support the majority of Lepidoptera species [Article]. *Nature Communications*, 11(1). doi.org/10.1038/s41467-020-19565-4. [see p. 5.3]

Narem, D. M., & Meyer, M. H. (2020). Native grasses benefit butterflies and moths [Article]. University of Minnesota Extension. [see p. 11.19]

Nassauer, J. I. (1995). Messy ecosystems, orderly frames [Article]. *Landscape Journal*, 14(2), 161–170. http://www.jstor.org/stable/43324192. [see p. 14.4]

National Audubon Society [Website]. audubon.org. [see pp. 1.5, 6.6, 15.8]

National Audubon Society. (2022, May 4). *Lights out: Philadelphia darkens its skyline to protect migrating birds* [Video]. YouTube. youtube.com/watch?v=EfhuU5Ceo_w. [see p. 1.5]

National Invasive Species Information Center (NISIC) [Website]. U.S. Department of Agriculture. invasivespeciesinfo.gov. [see pp. 4.10-4.11, 4.21]

National Wildlife Federation [Website]. Host Plants by Ecoregion. nwf.org/garden-for-wildlife/about/native-plants/find-available-natives. [see p. 5.5]

National Wildlife Federation [Website]. Keystone Plants by Ecoregion. nwf.org/keystoneplants. [see p. 5.5]

National Wildlife Federation [Website]. Native Plant Finder [BETA]. nativeplantfinder.nwf.org. [see pp. 5.4, 5.8-5.9, 5.22-5.23]

Native Plant Society of New Jersey. (2023). NPSNJ Native plant school guide [Booklet]. npsnj.org/native-plants/schoolguide. [see p. 15.9]

The Nature Conservancy [Website]. nature.org. [see p. 15.7]

Navarrete-Tindall, N. (2010). Native cool-season grasses in Missouri [Article]. *Missouri Prairie Journal*. 31 (2), 20-25. https://www.nrs.fs.usda.gov/pubs/jrnl/2010/nrs_2010_navarrete-tindall_002.pdf. [see p. 11.19]

Nest Watch [Website]. nestwatch.org. [see p. 15.8]

New York Botanical Garden [Website]. libguides.nybg.org/c.php?g=680688. [see p. 11.20]

North American Butterfly Association (NABA) [Website]. naba.org. [see p. 15.8]

Northwest Meadowscapes [Website]. northwestmeadowscapes.com. [see p. 11.12]

Omernik, J. M. (1987). Ecoregions of the Conterminous United States. [Map (Scale 1:7,500,000)]. *Annals of the Association of American Geographers*, 77(1):118-125. [see p. 5.4]

Oudolf, Piet, and Noel Kingsbury. (2013). *Planting: A New Perspective* [Book]. Portland, OR: Timber Press. [see pp. 9.28, 14.7] Owens, A. C. S., Van den Broeck, M., De Cock, R., & Lewis, S. M. (2022). Behavioral responses of bioluminescent fireflies to artificial light at night [Article]. *Frontiers in Ecology and Evolution*, 10. doi.org/10.3389/fevo.2022.946640. [see p. 1.8, 1.9]

Pasztor, Zsofia, Keri DeTore, and Jill Nunemaker. (2017). *Rain Gardens for the Pacific Northwest: Design and Build Your Own* [Book]. Seattle, WA: Skipstone. [see p. 8.12]

Pavlis, Robert. (2017). *Building Natural Ponds: Create a Clean, Algae-free Pond without Pumps, Filters, or Chemicals* [Book]. Gabriola Island, BC, Canada: New Society Publishers. [see pp. 8.7, 8.12]

Penn State Extension. (2022). Grass spiders [Article]. https://extension.psu.edu/grass-spiders. [see p. 3.10]

Pennsylvania Association of Wildlife Rehabilitators. (n.d.). *Introduction to wildlife rehabilitation: Part I* [Video]. YouTube. pawr.com/becoming-a-wildlife-rehabilitator-in-pennsylvania-is-it-for-you/part-1/. [see p. 2.16]

Pollinator Partnership [Website]. pollinator.org. [see pp. 1.12, 6.12, 15.9]

Pollinator Partnership. (n.d.). Quick reference guide: Light pollution [Article]. pollinator.org/pollinator.org/assets/generalFiles/Light-Pollution-Quick-Reference-Guide.pdf. [see p. 1.12]

Pollinator Pathway of Addison County. (2023, April 30). *Managing invasive plants by Mike Bald* [Video]. YouTube. youtube.com/watch?v=HQAxjQHkgg0. [see p. 4.22]

Pollinator Pathways [Website]. pollinator-pathway.org. [see pp. 6.12, 15.5]

Pope, K. (2024). Researchers show how light pollution can harm imperiled bats [Article]. *Bat Conservation International*. batcon.org/new-paper-suggests-light-pollution-limits-bat-habitat [see p. 1.9]

Prairie Moon Nursery [Website]. prairiemoon.com. [see pp. 9.18, 10.8, 10-.21, 10.22, 11.12, 11.18]

Prairie Moon Nursery. (2024). *Cultural Guide* [Book]. Winona, MN: Prairie Moon Nursery. [see p. 9.18]

Rainer, Thomas, and Claudia West. (2015). *Planting in a Post-Wild World: Designing Plant Communities for Resilient Landscapes* [Book]. Portland, OR: Timber Press. [see p. 9.28, 13.10, 14. 2]

Reforestation, Nurseries, & Genetic Resources (RNGR) [Website]. Propagation Protocol Database. Collaboration of United States Department of Agriculture Forest Service and Southern Regional Extension Forestry. npn.rngr.net/propagation. [see p. 10.20]

Rubin, Greg and Lucy Warren. (2013). *The California Native Landscape: The Homeowner's Design Guide to Restoring Its Beauty and Balance* [Book]. Portland, OR: Timber Press. [see p. 9.28]

Rubin, Greg, and Lucy Warren. (2016). *The Drought-Defying California Garden: 230 Native Plants for a Lush, Low-Water Landscape* [Book]. Portland, OR: Timber Press. [see p. 5.24]

Russ, K., & Williamson, J. (2023, August 27). Less toxic insecticides [Article]. *Clemson University Cooperative Extension Service Home & Garden Information Center.* hgic.clemson.edu/factsheet/less-toxic-insecticide. [see p. 12.12]

Sarver, Matthew, Amanda Treher, Lenny Willson, Robert Naczi, and Faith B. Kuehn. (2008). *Mistaken Identity?: Invasive Plants and Their Native Look-alikes: An Identification Guide for the Mid-Atlantic* [PDF Book]. Dover, DE: Delaware Department of Agriculture. [see p. 4.22]

Seed Savers Exchange. (2016). An inexpensive but effective deer fence [Blogpost]. https://blog.seedsavers.org/blog/deerfence. [see p. 2.12]

Shmukler, I., & Harr, G. (2021). *Protect the East Branch Waterway (PEBW)* [Report]. https://www.wrc.udel.edu/wp-content/uploads/2021/06/PEBW-Report-2021.pdf. [see p. 12.10]

Signify. (2018, June 5). Going bats: Dutch town is first in world to install bat-friendly LED street lights [Press Release]. https://www.signify.com/global/our-company/news/press-releases/2018/20180605-going-bats-dutch-town-is-first-in-world-to-install-bat-friendly-led-street-lights. [see p. 1.9]

Smith, Daryl, Dave Williams, Greg Houseal, and Kirk Henderson. (2010). *The Tallgrass Prairie Center Guide to Prairie Restoration in the Upper Midwest* [Book]. Iowa City, IA: University of Iowa Press. [see p. 11.2]

Sorenson, Sharon. (2018). *Planting Native to Attract Birds to Your Yard* [Book]. Mechanicsburg, Pennsylvania: Stackpole Books. [see p. 7.16]

Steiner, Lynn M. (2012). *Rain Gardens: Sustainable Landscaping for a Beautiful Yard and a Healthy World* [Book]. Minneapolis. MN: Voyageur Press. [see p. 8.12]

Stern, Vernon. (1959). *The Integration of Chemical and Biological Control of the Spotted Alfalfa Aphid* [Book]. Berkeley, CA: University of California Berkeley. [see p. 12.2]

Striniste, Nancy. (2019). *Nature Play at Home: Creating Outdoor Spaces That Connect Children with the Natural World* [Book]. Portland, OR: Timber Press. [see pp. 14.8, 14.9, 15.9]

Swearingen, Jil, Britt Slattery, Kathryn Reshetiloff, and Susan Zwicker. (2010). *Plant invaders of Mid-Atlantic Natural Areas (6th ed.)* [Book]. Washington, D.C.: National Park Service and U.S. Fish and Wildlife Service. [see pp. 4.17, 4.22]

Tallamy, D., Klem, D., & Cubie, Jim, J.D. (2023, March 8). 5 surprising things that could be preventing your backyard from serving as a wildlife sanctuary [Article]. *Nation of Change.* nationofchange.org/2023/03/08/5-surprising-things-that-could-be-preventing-your-backyard-from-serving-as-a-wildlife-sanctuary. [see p. 2.16]

Tallamy, Douglas W. (2020). *Nature's Best Hope: A New Approach to Conservation That Starts in Your Yard* [Book]. Portland, OR: Timber Press. [see pp. vii, xii, and the last page of every action]

Tallamy, Douglas W. (2021). *The Nature of Oaks: The Rich Ecology of Our Most Essential Native Trees* [Book]. Portland, OR: Timber Press. [see pp. vii, xiv, 5.24]

Tallamy, Douglas W. (Author), and Sarah L. Thomson (Adapter). (2023). *Nature's Best Hope (Young Readers' Edition): How You Can Save the World in Your Own Yard* [Book]. Portland, OR: Timber Press. [see pp. xiv, 15.9]

Tallamy, Douglas W., and Ricke Darke. (2009). *Bringing Nature Home: How You Can Sustain Wildlife with Native Plants, Updated and Expanded* [Book]. Portland, OR: Timber Press. [see p. vii, xiv, 9.28]

Temkin, A. M., Geller, S. L., Swanson, S. A., Leiba, N. S., Naidenko, O. V., & Andrews, D. Q. (2023). Volatile organic compounds emitted by conventional and "green" cleaning products in the U.S. market [Article]. *Chemosphere.* Vol. 341. https://www.sciencedirect.com/science/article/pii/S0045653523018374. [see p. 12.11]

Theodore Payne Foundation. (2022, June 30). *How to germinate fire-responsive seeds* [Video]. YouTube. youtube.com/watch?v=G9xm-NJTOFA. [see p. 10.24]

Three Rivers Rain Garden Alliance [Website]. http://raingardenalliance.org/. [see pp. 8.6, 8.12]

Toogood, Alan. (2019). *Propagating Plants: How to Create New Plants for Free* [Book]. New York, NY: DK. [see p. 10.24]

Tree of Life Nursery [Website]. californianativeplants.com. [see p. 10.22]

U.S Environmental Protection Agency. How's my waterway? [Website]. mywaterway.epa.gov. [see p. 8.9]

U.S. Environmental Protection Agency: Archive. (1993). Green landscaping: Greenacres [Article]. *The John Marshall Law Review.* 26(4). archive.epa.gov/greenacres/web/html/jmlr.html#Little%20Rock. [see p. 15.6]

U.S. Environmental Protection Agency. (2006). *Level I - II Ecological regions of North America.* gaftp.epa.gov/EPADataCommons/ORD/Ecoregions/cec_na/NA_LEVEL_II.pdf. [see p. 5.19]

U.S. Environmental Protection Agency. (2009). *Backyard composting: It's only natural* [Pamphlet]. www3.epa.gov/recyclecity/pdf/compost-guide.pdf. [see p. 11.6]

U.S. Environmental Protection Agency. (2013). *Level III ecoregions of the continental United States.* Corvallis, Oregon, U.S. EPA – National Health and Environmental Effects Research Laboratory [Map; map scale 1:7,500,000]. epa.gov/eco-research/level-iii-and-iv-ecoregions-continental-united-states. [see pp. 5.19, 12.6]

Appendix

U.S. Environmental Protection Agency. (n.d.). *Level I Ecological regions of North America* [Map]. gaftp.epa.gov/EPADataCommons/ORD/Ecoregions/cec_na/NA_LEVEL_I.pdf. [see p. 5.19]

Uncapher, Apryl, and Cleo Woelfle-Erskine. (2012). *Creating Rain Gardens: Capturing the Rain for Your Own Water-Efficient Garden* [Book]. Portland, OR: Timber Press. [see p. 8.12]

University of Arkansas, Cooperative Extension Service. (n.d.). Clean and green homemade cleaners [Article]. uaex.uada.edu/environment-nature/water/quality/clean-green-homemade-cleaners.aspx. [see p. 12.12]

University of Georgia–Center for Invasive Species and Ecosystem Health. [see Early Detection & Distribution Mapping System: EDDMapS, and Invasive Plant Atlas.]

University of Minnesota Extension [Website]. Planting and maintaining a bee lawn. extension.umn.edu/landscape-design/planting-and-maintaining-bee-lawn. [see pp. 11.12-11.13]

USDA Plant Database [Website]. plants.usda.gov. [see p. 9.5]

USDA Plant Hardiness Zone Map [Map]. (2023). planthardiness.ars.usda.gov. [see p. 5.18]

USDA-NRCS, Maryland. (2004). Comparing warm-season and cool-season grasses for erosion control, water quality, and wildlife habitat [Article]. efotg.sc.egov.usda.gov/references/public/va/NWSG_CSG_comparison.pdf. [see p. 11.19]

van Dyke, Maria, Kristine Boys, Rosemarie Parker, Robert Wesley, and Bryan Danforth. (2021). *Creating a Pollinator Garden for Native Specialist Bees of New York and the Northeast* [PDF Book]. Ithaca, NY: Cornell University. [see p. 6.12]

Vogt, Benjamin. (2023). *Prairie Up: An Introduction to Natural Garden Design* [Book]. Champaign, IL: 3 Fields Press, University of Illinois. [see pp. 9.28, 11.2, 13.10]

Wagner, David. (2005). *Caterpillars of Eastern North America: A Guide to Identification and Natural History* [Book]. Princeton, NJ: Princeton University Press. [see p. 5.24]

Wakefield, A., Broyles, M., Stone, E. L., Jones, G., & Harris, S. (2016). Experimentally comparing the attractiveness of domestic lights to insects: Do LEDs attract fewer insects than conventional light types? [Article]. *Ecology and Evolution*, 6(22), 8028–8036. doi.org/10.1002/ece3.2527. [see p. 1.8]

Watershed-Friendly PA [Website]. Collaboration between Penn State Extension Master Watershed Steward Program and Nurture Nature Center in Easton, PA. watershedfriendlypa.org/. [see pp. 8.12, 15. 4]

Weaner, Larry, and Thomas Christopher. (2016). *Garden Revolution: How Our Landscapes Can Be a Source of Environmental Change* [Book]. Portland, OR: Timber Press. [see pp. 10.9, 11.20, 13.10]

White, A. (2016). From nursery to nature: Evaluating native herbaceous flowering plants versus native cultivars for pollinator habitat restoration [Article]. *University of Vermont Burlington VT, Graduate College Dissertations and Theses*. 626. https://scholarworks.uvm.edu/graddis/626. [see p. 10.21]

Wild Ones [Website]. wildones.org. [see pp. 9.19, 10.22, 15.6, 15.7]

Wild Seed Project [Website]. wildseedproject.net. [see p. 7.8]

Wildlife Informer. (2024). Deer population by state (estimates and info) [Blogpost]. https://wildlifeinformer.com/deer-population-by-state. [see p. 2.12]

Wilson, E. O. (2016, Mar 12). Opinion: The global solution to extinction [Article]. *The New York Times*. https://www.nytimes.com/2016/03/13/opinion/sunday/the-global-solution-to-extinction.html. [see p. viii]

Woldemeskel, M., & Styer, E. L. (2010). Feeding behavior-related toxicity due to Nandina domestica in cedar waxwings (Bombycilla cedrorum) [Article]. *Veterinary Medicine International*, 818159–4. doi.org/10.4061/2010/818159. [see p. 4.1]

Wood Thrush Natives [Website]. woodthrushnatives.com. [see pp. 10.22, 14.9]

Woods, A. J., Omernik, J. M., Butler, D. R., Ford, J. G., Henley, J. E., Hoagland, B. W., Arndt, D. S., and Moran, B. C. (2005). *Ecoregions of Oklahoma*. [Color poster with map (map scale 1:1,250,000), descriptive text, summary tables, and photographs]. Reston, Virginia, U.S. Geological Survey. [see pp. 5.19, 5.20]

Wormser, Owen. (2022). *Lawns into Meadows, 2nd Edition: Growing a Regenerative Landscape* [Book]. San Francisco, CA: Stone Pier Press. [see p. 3.16]

Xerces Society for Invertebrate Conservation [Website]. xerces.org. [see pp. x, 1.9, 6.4-6.5, 6.11, 6.12, 7.4, 7.10, 9.21, 12.4, 12.8, 14.2, 15.9, II]

Xerces Society. (2011). *Attracting Native Pollinators: Protecting North America's Bees and Butterflies: The Xerces Society Guide* [Book]. North Adams, MA: Storey Publishing. [see p. 6.12]

Xerces Society. (2020). *Nesting & Overwintering Habitat for Pollinators & Other Beneficial Insects* [PDF Guide]. xerces.org/sites/default/files/publications/18-014.pdf. [see p. 7.4]

Xerces Society. (2023, May 12). *Turn the lights out for fireflies and other insects* [Video]. YouTube. youtube.com/watch?v=ahwnDeWzF0E. [see p. 1.12]

Xerces Society. (2024). *Habitat Assessment Guide for Pollinators in Yards, Gardens, and Parks* [PDF Guide]. https://www.xerces.org/sites/default/files/publications/19-038_02_HAG_Yard-Park-Garden_web.pdf . [see pp

. 14.2, II]

Xerces Society. (n.d.) Bumble bees: Nesting and overwintering [Article]. xerces.org/bumblebeenests. [see p. 7.4]

Zona, S. (2022). Fruits of Nandina domestica are (sometimes) cyanogenic and (sometimes) hazardous to birds. *Poisonous Plant Research* (PPR): Vol. 5, p. 1-12. doi.org/10.26077/hv81-8t11. [see p. 4.1]

APPENDIX
Photo Credits

Images are key to conveying the message of *Nature's Action Guide*. To give a realistic idea of the suggested DIY actions, I've taken most of the photos and drawn most of the diagrams. Yet in some cases, my own property lacked the subject matter to capture needed photos. The following people generously came forth with photographs that perfectly filled the missing spots. I sincerely appreciate these valuable contributions to this book.

There were other gaps in subject matter that my own property could not fill. It is with sincere respect and admiration that I recognize the contributions of photographs from people who over the years have selflessly shared their prized photographs on sites such as Wikimedia Commons (WC), Pixabay, Morguefile, and elsewhere. Photo credits are organized by the page number in *Nature's Action Guide* on which the photo is found (t = top; m = middle; b = bottom; l = left; r = right).

p. 4.2 br, field of *Lythrum salicaria*: Liz West, CC BY 2.0 via WC

p. 4.6 (flipped), *Rhamnus cathartica*: Krzysztof Ziarnek, Kenraiz, CC BY 4.0 via WC

p. 4.8 (cropped, flipped), using-iNaturalist: Srloarie2, CC BY-SA 4.0 via WC

p. 4.9 mr (cropped), porcelain berry: Oliver Vanpé, CC BY-SA 3.0 via WC

p. 4.10 bm, common teasel: Steve Dewey, Utah State University

p. 4.10 br, brown tree snake: Gordon Rodda, DOi, US Geological Society

p. 4.11 tr, yellow toadflax: Wendy VanDyk Evans, invasive.org

p. 4.12 t, *Ailanthus altissima*: Karduelis, Public domain via WC

p. 4.14 (trimmed), *Fallopia japonica*: Famartin, CC BY-SA 4.0 via WC

p. 5.2 tml (cropped), *Quercus agrifolia*: Peter O'Malley, CC BY-SA 3.0 via WC

p. 5.2 bl, *Prunella vulgaris lanceolata*: Peganum from Henfield, England, CC BY-SA 2.0 via WC

p. 5.2 bmr (cropped), *Echinacea purpurea* 'Razzmatazz': David J. Stang, CC BY-SA 4.0 via WC

p. 5.2 br, *Prunella laciniata* × *vulgaris*: Stefan. lefnaer, CC BY-SA 4.0 via WC

p. 5.12 tr, *Lonicera involucrata*: Peter Pearsall, U.S. Fish and Wildlife Service

p. 5.21 tm (cropped), stream, NC: Brian Stansberry, CC BY-SA 3.0 via WC

p. 5.21 tr (cropped), meadow: Greyfiveys, CC BY-SA 4.0 via WC

p. 5.21 bm (cropped), Upper Newport Bay: Nandaro, CC BY-SA 3.0 via WC

p. 5.21 br (cropped), coastal sage scrub: Z3lvs, CC0 via WC

p. 6.1 bl (cropped), *Habropoda laboriosa*: Jerry A. Payne, CC BY 3.0 via WC

p. 6.3 t (cropped), *Andrena clarkella*: S. Rae from Scotland, UK, CC BY 2.0 via WC

p. 6.4 t (reversed), *Salix discolor*: Silk666, CC BY-SA 3.0 via WC

p. 6.4 m, *Melissodes druriellus* female: Jacy Lucier, CC BY-SA 4.0 via WC

p. 7.4 ml (cropped), *Papilio polyxenes* larva: Jacy Lucier, CC BY-SA 4.0 via WC

p. 7.4 mm (cropped), *Papilio polyxenes* caterpillar, fifth instar: Galukalock (talk) (Uploads), CC BY-SA 3.0 via WC

p. 7.4 mr, *Papilio polyxenes* adult: Kaldari, CC0 via WC

p. 7.7 bl (cropped), tree lit by streetlamp: Stiller Beobachter from Ansbach, Germany, CC BY 2.0 via WC

p. 7.11 mb (cropped), *Andrena clarkella* in ground nest: Aiwok, CC BY-SA 3.0 via WC

p. 8.6 tl, rain garden: U.S. EPA-Environmental Protection Agency, Public domain via WC

p. 8.6 b, rain garden: Arlington County, CC BY-SA 2.0 via WC

p. 8.8 tl, watershed: Internet Archive Book Images, No restrictions via WC

p. 8.8 tr, Mississippi watershed: Long, Stephen Harriman; Young & Delleker, Public domain via WC

p. 8.8 br, Colorado River basin: Shannon1, CC BY-SA 4.0 via WC

p. 8.10 mml (cropped), rain barrel-rustic: Benoit Rochon, CC BY-3.0 via WC

p. 8.10 mmr (cropped), rain barrel-vase: Phoebe, CC BY-SA 4.0 via WC

p. 8.10 mr (cropped), car wash: CurranH (talk) (Uploads), Public domain via WC

p. 8.10 b, postage stamp:, water conservation, Bureau of Engraving and Printing, Public domain via WC

p. 8.11 tl, riparian buffer: USDA Natural Resources Conservation Service, Public domain

pp. 8.11 tm and 12.2 m, lawn chemicals: Cohdra, Morguefile.com

pp. 9.6 and 9.7 bl (cropped), formal design: Christopher Figge, CC BY-SA 3.0 via WC

p. 9.8 t (cropped), *Echinacea* 'PowWow White®': cultivar413, CC BY-SA 2.0 via WC

p. 9.22 bl, moss: Rolling Roscoe, Morguefile.com

p. 10.1 br, flat of plants: Forest Service Northern Region from Missoula, MT, Public domain via WC

pp. 10.7 and 10.23, greenhouse: David-Avila, via Pixabay.com

p. 11.4, retaining wall (cropped): Joe Mabel, CC BY-SA 4.0 via WC

p. 11.11 bl, *Carex vulpinoidea* botanical print: Prof. Dr. Otto Wilhelm Thomé, Public domain via WC

p. 12.2 tl, nontoxic ipm monitoring: Tim McCabe, USDA Natural Resources Conservation Service

p. 12.2 m, ladybug: Marienkäfe, Public domain via WC

p. 12.2 m, floating row cover: Keith Evans, CC BY 2.0 via WC

p. 12.2 b, nursery: Hoo House Nursery by Jonathan Billinger, CC BY 2.0 via WC

P. 12.3 bl (trimmed), swallowtail caterpillar; Didier Descouens, CC BY-SA 4.0 via WC

p. 12.4 br, Rachel Carson plaque: Captain-tucker, Public domain via WC

p. 12.4 bl, Rachel Carson: Smithsonian Institution from U.S., No restrictions, via WC

p. 12.5 tl-inset, swallowtail caterpillar: NCBioTeache, CC0 via WC

p. 12.5 bl (cropped), firefly feeding on snail: Dr. Raju Kasambe, CC BY-SA 4.0 via WC

p. 12.5 bm (cropped), *Fragaria virginiana*: Laval University, CC BY-SA 4.0 via WC

p. 12.6 tl (cropped; flipped), *Amelanchier* sp.: Laval University, CC BY-SA 4.0 via WC

p. 12.6 bl (cropped), Carolina rose: D. Gordon E. Robertson, CC BY-SA 3.0 via WC

p. 12.8 tl, mosquito larvae: CDC/James Gathany, Public domain via WC

p. 14.7 tr, persimmon: Katja Schulz from Washington, DC, CC BY 2.0 via WC

p. 14.7 bml (cropped), waterfall in NYBG: Rohdodentrites, CC BY 4.0 via WC

p. 14.8 tl (cropped), black raspberries: Karen Hine, CC BY-SA 2.0 via WC

p. 14.8 tl, The Secret Garden: Frances Hodgson Burnett, Public domain via WC

p. 14.8 tr, ice flower, Ozarks: Josiah Johnston, CC BY 3.0 via WC

p. 14.8 bm (cropped), Carolina rose: Aarongunnar, CC BY 4.0 via WC

p. 14.9 tr, garden bench: Acabashi, CC BY 4.0 via WC

p. 15.3 b, photo of youth, written permission for its use graciously provided by subject and her parents

p. V, (modified), children in nature, MaggieJuo, Morguefile.com

APPENDIX
Index of Topics

The index below includes the topics discussed in *Nature's Action Guide*. For organizations, websites, books, articles, videos, and other media, please see pages VI - XI. Please note that although many plants have been used as examples in this guide, only a select few are included here since regional plant palettes vary significantly,

Appendix

APPENDIX
Index of Topics

Appendix

Made in United States
Cleveland, OH
12 December 2024

11691893R00151